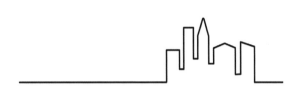

Also by William B. Patrick

Metrofix

THE COMBATIVE COMEBACK OF A COMPANY TOWN

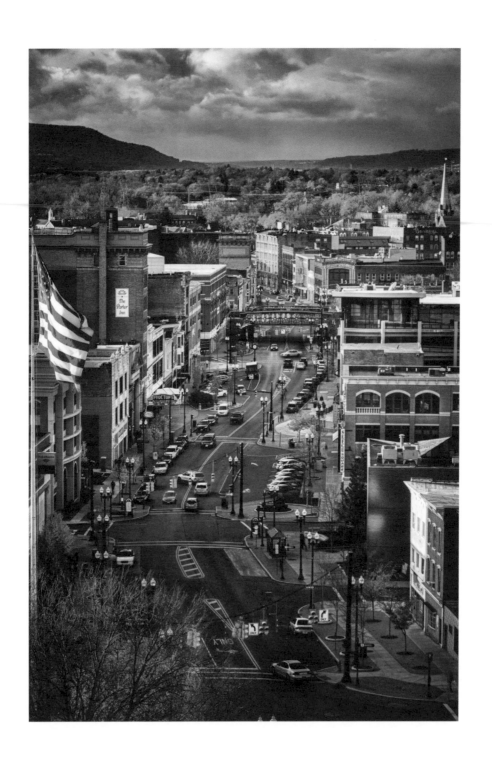

Metrofix

THE COMBATIVE COMEBACK OF A COMPANY TOWN

WILLIAM B. PATRICK

DOWNTOWN PUBLISHING

To order bulk copies, please contact metrofixbook.com for rates.

Downtown Publishing
461 Nott Street
Schenectady, NY 12308-1812

www.metrofixbook.com

First Edition: December 2021.

Photo credits: p. 390

Book print interior design by Lisa N. Comstock.

ISBN (hardcover): 979-8-9850947-0-1

Printed in the U.S. by Benchemark Printing, Schenectady, NY.
10 9 8 7 6 5 4 3 2 1

Praise for *Metrofix*

"Generations from now, the citizens of Schenectady will thank William B. Patrick for his commitment and skill in putting down onto the page the glory and heartache of their city like no other writer has ever done. In *Metrofix*, Patrick has produced the one indispensable volume on this authentic American city. Patrick lives in Schenectady, and he has an affinity for the place, but this is no gauzy love letter like so many nostalgic reminiscences that came before it. This is a deeply reported urban history in the vein of Jane Jacobs and Lewis Mumford, but it never becomes academic or pedantic. In lively prose, Patrick deconstructs "the city that lights and hauls the world" from its heyday as a manufacturing titan for the General Electric Co. and the American Locomotive Company to its long spiral into urban blight and decay. He documents the recent rebirth of downtown, fueled by large investments from Metroplex; the allure of Broadway shows and the performing arts at Proctors; aided by assorted visionaries and civic leaders. Patrick is at once clear-eyed, critical, and generous in his assessment. Patrick has published poetry, fiction, screenplays and dramas and he brings to bear his multitudinous talents in this potent narrative."

Paul Grondahl
Director of the NYS Writers Institute at the
University at Albany, journalist and author

"In *Metrofix*, William B. Patrick performs an extraordinary feat of literary alchemy, transforming material that seems like dull base metal – the history of Schenectady, an industrial city in upstate New York – into pure gold. In Patrick's hands, the elements meld into a brilliant amalgam of urban history, politics, dizzying turns of fortune, and cautionary tales. The book chronicles the stories of hundreds of fascinating people. Here, you'll meet Schenectadians – famous, infamous, and unheralded – all essential to the life of the city. There is a vast cast of fully-realized characters here: social workers, teachers, engineers, artists, a terrorist, librarians, police officers, impresarios, drug dealers, politicians, immigrants, developers, charlatans, restaurant owners, college students, architects, high school kids, and many more. The penultimate chapter is a stunning presentation of dramatic monologues based on interviews with people who served the city, in a variety of ways, during the Covid-19 crisis. To create work this comprehensive and humane, a writer has to be not only a meticulous researcher, tireless interviewer, and obsessive collector of facts, but also a poet and damn fine storyteller. William B. Patrick is all of these things and more. In *Metrofix*, he takes the history of one small city and enlivens it, creating an entertaining, exhilarating, and enlightening reading experience."

Hollis Seamon
author of *Somebody Up There Hates You* and *Corporeality*

"Communities are made of stories, and the heart of every story is the people. Bill Patrick understands storytelling, and he understands Schenectady. *Metrofix: The Combative Comeback of a Company Town* is a meticulously-researched, compelling story of urban decline, renewal, and rebirth. An essential book for anyone interested in the lifecycle of city centers and how urban planning can succeed."

Dinty W. Moore
author of *Between Panic & Desire*

"Henry David Thoreau wrote, in Walden, about the existence of an imagined instrument called the realometer, capable of measuring the extent of reality inherent in one's perceptions. William B. Patrick possesses such an instrument, and in *Metrofix: The Combative Comeback of a Company Town*, he plumbs the economic, political, and historic realities of Schenectady, New York. But Patrick offers not only the panoramic story of the rise and fall and resurrection of a representative American city, but also a rich and diverse gallery of characters drawn from life, each of them dreaming, planning, scheming, working, helping to shape the future of the city they love. Nobody knows the Capital Region of New York better than its native son, William B. Patrick, author of *Saving Troy*. Now, in *Metrofix*, Patrick has given us a portrait of a great American city, and honored the struggles of the people who made it so."

Richard Hoffman
author of *Half the House*

for the Golubs – Neil, Jane, and Mona –
who inspired this story and wanted all of it told

Contents

This is a book about cities as they are, not as they might be. It is also about cities' evolution, for I'm convinced our undistinguished record of the last fifty years in building cities and towns stems at least in part from a willful ignorance of our urban past. In order to understand where we're going, it's necessary to know where we've been.

– *City Life*
Witold Rybczynski

Preface

Clearly, William B. Patrick talked to many people and read many books in order to write this one, *Metrofix: The Combative Comeback of a Company Town*. One marvel of the book is how straightforward the narrative manages to be, as Patrick spans the better part of two centuries to show how Schenectady evolved, devolved and got back on its feet. Yet he also shows how the world-at-large influenced what happened in one city: particularly the coming of suburbia and the emptying out of cities, a process repeated all over the United States as car culture took hold and presented each family with the possibility of a personal, lawn-to-be-mowed fiefdom.

Cities are about living with other people; suburbs are about isolate happiness. Cities wake us up; suburbs drowse as the houses wait for the cars to return and the weekend to begin. Cities, as they encourage density of population, offer possibilities that speak to commerce, cuisine, education, communication, and art. Cities offer the possibility of that much-bruited word, "community." Patrick gets all this in these pages, so we have the story of numerous insights and confusions as Schenectady tries to get its urban act together (to use a Patrick-like phrase), but we also get the story of citizens, often immigrants, who have believed in cities and wanted their city to thrive. They have, typically, deserved better than they have received, but Schenectady has kept trying and has succeeded, particularly as more people decide they want to live in a viable urban environment.

The author of this book about the trials, tribulations and successes of urban planning in Schenectady, New York, is a poet, writer, and citizen rather than a professional historian, sociologist, or urban designer. His approach is refreshingly direct as his characters are often identified as this or that "guy." His ear for how people talk is perfect. His grasp of local and broader history is all to the point. The pizzazz in his language makes the reader feel what the various characters – all very real people – are doing and not doing. His willingness to call the shots as he sees them is bracing because many shots in the course of decades went awry. All of which makes this an eminently readable book, very far from a tome but rather a vibrant testimonial to many lives, hopes, and vicissitudes.

Patrick has done Schenectady and the world-at-large a particular favor in writing this book. Here is a real story about a real city. Read and ponder the difficulties – economic, political, and individual – that go with democracy and the rewards, all the energy that goes with a downtown that means something to people.

– Baron Wormser, author of *The Road Washes Out*
in Spring: A Poet's Memoir of Living Off the Grid

1

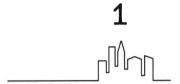

Canal Square Is Burning

The smallest of cities have major investments in their downtowns, in the structures themselves as well as in the infrastructure … The importance of downtowns, however, goes well beyond economics. Downtown holds together the most varied mix of economic, civic, and social functions. It is the place where everyone can meet and interact, where monuments are located, where speeches are made, where parades are held and crowds are entertained. More than anyplace else, downtown gives a community its collective identity and thus its pride. It is the keystone that keeps the other pieces of the city in place. Downtown is the heart and soul of the metropolis.

– Changing Places: Rebuilding
Community in the Age of Sprawl
Richard Moe and Carter Wilkie

At first, nobody could find the fire. When Angelo Mazzone got to Peggy's Canal Side Restaurant a little after 6 a.m. on Thursday, July 23, 1987, to supervise the breakfast prep, he was already sweating. A heat wave had edged into the Northeast overnight and it was already above 90 degrees in Schenectady. Baltimore had reached 104 the evening before, and Angelo had hoped the worst of it would stay south, but no such luck. His day manager, Cathy Kearney, met him at the door to State Street, not smiling, and said, "Good morning. Come here,

okay? Can you smell that, like toast burning? I can't find where it's coming from."
There was a faint odor, but it didn't smell like toast to Angelo.

Peggy's was Angelo's first restaurant, and he had made it one of the few profitable businesses in Canal Square, the urban mall that was supposed to save downtown Schenectady during the 1980s. He had finally paid off the mortgage his friend, Le Grande Serras, had offered to hold and, over the last couple of months, Angelo had dropped the better part of a hundred grand into renovating the place. So even the thought of a fire got his stomach churning.

As he hurried along the central counter, Angelo spun a glistening stool and peered over the countertop at the open kitchen, but he couldn't see anything burning in there. Then he crossed quickly through the lines of new tables, adjusting chairs out of habit, and checked the orange and brown booths along both walls. Nothing around them either, so Angelo worked his way toward the bar in back. Okay, there the smell cranked up. That wasn't a food smell. Too metallic, or chemical, he couldn't tell which.

He searched all behind the bar and finally stepped out the back door, glancing away from the empty terrace that used to be one of the two large pools for the filled-in canal, scanning up and down the sidewalk behind the other stores in the urban mall, until he finally spotted something. A little light smoke was snaking from the basement of Merle Norman, the cosmetics shop next door. Angelo turned back toward Cathy. "Okay, I found it, it's over here," he told her. "It's not us, and I hope it's not that big a deal. They'll probably get it cleaned up and we can open for lunch. Call the fire department, okay? And let's be safe – better get everybody outside, fast."

Standing out front on State Street with his employees, Angelo surveyed the neighboring businesses: Collins Footwear, on the other side of Merle Norman's, was dark on all three floors. The Squire Shop, an upscale men's store, looked okay, too. The Carl Co. didn't open until 10, so there was no action there yet. Suddenly, though, the sirens began to blast and everybody jumped. Schenectady's main fire station was close by, and it had an arsenal of equipment to respond not only to city fires but also to act as a back-up for General Electric's smaller fire company on its main campus. The first blasts echoed up and down State Street, and more, even louder, screeched toward them from over on Erie Boulevard, making it feel like the whole downtown was primed to explode. Then Angelo heard a sharp crack and he looked up. A flicker-

ing light appeared on the empty second floor above the cosmetics shop, brightened, and then blew the window glass into the street beside him.

CANAL SQUARE IS BURNING: that news spread faster than the fire itself, and people swarmed in to see if the remaining retail heart of Schenectady – the 400 block of State Street – would survive. Police had cordoned off the area, so people parked blocks away and ran over to watch. All the firefighters on the Thursday shift rushed to fight the fire, of course, but even a bunch of guys who had worked their full, 24-hour Wednesday shift stayed on to help. Jeff Wilkin from the *Daily Gazette* was covering the story, and he had to press through the swelling crowd of onlookers to monitor the action. He couldn't help but wonder, *Where are all these people on a normal day, when the stores aren't burning, when the merchants need them to stay in business?* But he already knew the answer. Downtown Schenectady had been rotting slowly for years, many of its former patrons migrating to safer suburbs like Niskayuna or Glenville or Rotterdam, leaving their parents' duplexes behind and becoming absentee landlords, enrolling their kids in the better suburban schools. The burning of Canal Square would soon be just another reason to find someplace newer, someplace greener.

As much as any other post-industrial city, Schenectady, New York had become a poster child for the era's worsening urban dilemma. The largest urban renewal program in the city, touted as the Town of Tomorrow plan, had been envisioned in 1948 and then promoted heavily to the citizens for several years. Implemented with mostly federal funds from 1955 through the early 1970s, its centerpiece was the razing of twenty-two acres surrounding City Hall and the forced removal of hundreds of homes that had been deemed substandard housing units to make way for a stronger, commercial tax base. The city fathers had promised "a hometown which will be the envy of thousands of other communities and the pride of every Schenectadian … the metropolis of the Mohawk Valley, the distribution center for upstate New York and the transportation hub of the northeastern states."

However, even once the houses were gone and many of the misplaced people exiled to low-income housing in other neighborhoods, the city still couldn't attract an interested developer. What it had done quite successfully was reduce the downtown population by thousands – mostly Italian and Greek and Polish families who shopped in the nearby 400 block of State Street – as it bulldozed the residential area into a scarred wasteland. In his thesis about Schenectady's downtown, *Shovel Ready: Razing Hopes, History, and a Sense of Place,* Chris Spencer said, "Overall, the site appears underdeveloped, with large parking lots occupying important intersections, a few nondescript buildings, minimal landscaping, and almost no pedestrian activity or street life. Despite the futuristic visions, lofty proclamations, and millions in taxpayer dollars spent, the Town of Tomorrow was a thing of the past before its time ever came." And he wrote that in the late 1990s, thirty years after all the homes had been demolished and their inhabitants scattered.

The two major industries in the city, General Electric and American Locomotive Company (ALCO), had employed between fifty-five and sixty thousand people during World War II, and maintained those levels throughout much of the 1960s. However, ALCO had steadily laid off its twelve thousand workers until it finally closed in 1969. GE, under the lash of Jack Welch – or Neutron Jack as residents dubbed him – had slashed GE's work-force in Schenectady, shifted thousands of jobs to non-union states like South Carolina, and moved the company's headquarters away from its origins and down to Fairfield, Connecticut.

In the summer of 1987, as Angelo Mazzone stood watching his restaurant burn, only four thousand or so employees were clocking in to work in General Electric's sprawling main plant. Throughout most of the '80s, though, GE had continued to send three or four shuttle buses every midday to downtown Schenectady, and many of their employees had eaten at Peggy's or at the lunch counter at The Carl Co., so Peggy's was probably the most successful business in Canal Square before the fire. Recently, however, GE had cut that lunch hour from an hour to half an hour, and that simply wouldn't afford enough time for lunch or for midday shopping. More and more, Angelo had begun to rely on the crowded, Friday-night beer parties at Peggy's to make ends meet.

Schenectady was by no means alone in its plight. Most of the mid-sized American downtowns in the 1960s and '70s struggled not just to retain retail stores and restaurants but also to save their signature buildings. Twenty-five years of federally-funded interstate highway and ring-road expansions, suburban mall openings, factory closings, scorched-earth urban renewal projects, federally-subsidized sub-urban home ownership programs with the white flight they encouraged, as well as increasing inner-city crime, had decimated city tax revenues. Once-thriving down-town department stores – as well as scores of mom-and-pop specialty shops – either gave up completely or relocated to one of the new suburban malls.

After all, living and shopping in the burgeoning suburbs outside Schenectady or Albany or Troy seemed to offer the space and protection that people felt they couldn't find in cities anymore. Whatever felt dangerous or unpleasant could be left behind, and shiny new suburban malls offered the illusion of a whole new start. Colonie Center, for example, situated on a recently-converted, nine-hole golf course – what had been the Colonie Country Club – featured two enclosed floors of stores that were anchored by a Macy's at one end and a Sears at the other. Compared by the local media to "the sidewalk cafes of Paris," but even better because enclosed stores "would make window shopping a reborn pleasure," Colonie Center was an instant sensation. Macy's had been the first store in the mall to open its doors, on March 24, 1966, and 100,000 people showed up on that first day for a new shopping adventure. And to underscore the demographic shift, population in the town of Colonie grew by almost 40,000 people – from 29,500 in 1950 to 69,250 in 1970 – while Albany's population dropped from 135,000 to 116,000 during those same twenty years.

Schenectady was next in line for a suburban makeover. The developers of Mohawk Mall spent twenty-five million dollars to turn the fifty-acre, Stanford golf course into an enclosed, 750,000-square-foot shopping extravaganza that featured shiny, giant department stores like Montgomery Ward, the Boston Store, J.M. Fields, and Woolworth's, plus seventy smaller stores, three courtyards, numerous foun-tains, comfortable seating areas, an indoor temperature that was set at a constant 72 degrees, and a parking lot that could hold 4000 cars. On opening day – October 5, 1970 – Native American dancers greeted the horde of shoppers with 10,000 free toys and balloons.

Mohawk Mall turned into a slow-motion disaster, though, its anchor stores either filing for Chapter 11 or fleeing one by one to busier locations, with the small-er stores toppling like dominoes after them. Sections of the mall were sold to dif-ferent realty investment companies. Strip malls had popped up nearby to ride the mall's coattails but had only si-phoned off potential customers. After about fifteen years, when 25% of the mall was vacant and revenue had slipped consider-ably, the mall's primary owners, Wilmorite, opened another mall called Rotterdam Square just west of Schenectady, near GE's main campus, and even more Mo-hawk Mall businesses migrated there. And to add insult to injury, just after Thanksgiving in 1986, the snake-bit mall's Santa Claus had a heart attack and died in front of a line of expectant chil-dren. By 2001, most of the build-ings had been torn down.

Despite the suburban mall's failure, the city of Schenectady continued to shrink. Before the Edison Machine Works moved to Schenectady in 1886, about 13,000 people had lived in the quiet town along the Mohawk River. By 1900, eight years after General Electric had been created and lured a flood of immigrant factory workers to it, the city's population almost tripled. GE sent employment scouts to recruit workers in Italy and Poland, and by 1910, more than 70,000 people lived and worked in the place that people proudly called "The City that Lights and Hauls the World," honoring Schenectady's electrical and railroad industries.

The head count kept increasing through the 1950s and remained over 90,000 until the 1960 census, when the population dropped off by almost 12%. In the 1970 census, another recorded drop of 3.8%. By 1980, 12.8% more, mostly laid-off factory workers. Between 1960 and 2000, 30,000 people lost their jobs and left town – one out of every three residents – and most of them never came back.

But not everyone had given up on the city. Jim Duggan, a local architect, had returned in 1963 and stayed. He had been raised on upper Union Street, where his grandfather had run a grocery store, before spending his teenage years in nearby Watervliet. He studied architecture at Rensselaer Polytechnic Institute and, after he graduated, served in the Air Force in Dayton, Ohio. Duggan stayed on to work in an architectural firm there for a year, watching a Midwestern city grapple with its own urban changes, but felt a constant pull to go back and help out his hometown.

From the mid-'60s on, he had written concerned letters to the *Schenectady Gazette*, the city's family-owned, hometown newspaper, complaining about "a lack of leadership and public awareness of the needs and opportunities for planning in Schenectady." He railed against hiring outside housing consultants, called for visionary planning to help Schenectady's failing neighborhoods, and told the local NAACP that, "Our new planning efforts should be rooted as deeply as possible in community needs." Most of his concerns weren't shared by Frank Duci, the mayor throughout most of the '70s, or the City Council members – the majority of whom, as it turned out, were conservative, upstate Republicans.

Duggan also lectured to mostly-empty university auditoriums in the area, telling the few like-minded professors and students who showed up that, "America is copping out by sprawling away from its cities. Human activity can happen if we get the cars out, and cities should be the center of human activity." Moreover, he was among the prescient architects and city planners of that era who foreshadowed the arguments that James Howard Kunstler so cogently presented more than twenty years later in his influential book, *The Geography of Nowhere: The Rise and Fall of America's Man-Made Landscape*.

But not enough movers and shakers in local governments were listening. For example, as Executive Director of FOCUS – the acronym for Future Opportunities Created by a Unified Schenectady, a citizen-run redevelopment corporation – Duggan offered more than just his ideas about revitalizing Schenectady's downtown to the City Council. In letters between August and November in 1975, he wrote and said:

> *Through the community emphasis and make-up of FOCUS, the City Council*
> *has the unique opportunity to coordinate prospective projects, gain broad*

support, and strengthen their chances for successful implementation. Yet the City Council is deliberately avoiding this kind of operating relationship between community interests, local government, and private redevelopment concerns, a type of relationship which has proven to be the way in which cities of all sizes are re-activating their downtowns and strengthening their property tax base.

Successful downtown revitalization in many other American cities depends heavily on close working relationships between city councils, administrations, and their business community. In our nineteen months, FOCUS has tried desperately to do that.

Schenectady has many things going for it: location, a major industry operating at high capacity, talented people, fine local services, etc. With all these, why hasn't the community been successful in redeveloping its Downtown Core area? Why are one-upsmanship, suspicions, and foot-dragging allowed to continue – hindering a unified community effort to redevelop in the total community's best interest? Our taxpayers deserve a sincere answer.

It's no great surprise, then, that again and again after City Council meetings throughout the mid-1970s, its elected members routinely walked away, muttering, "We've heard this all before. How much more garbage are we expected to buy?"

However, when Jim Duggan floated the idea for a Canal Square in Schenectady about that same time, touting it as not only a way to recapture the city's former retail glory but also as an unexpected, 11th-hour savior of downtown Schenectady, he captured Mayor Frank Duci's ear. A well-designed urban mall could offer a more accessible antidote to the toxic spread of suburban malls, he argued and, at first, Duci jumped on board. This was a project that would conserve historic buildings and echo the city's once-crucial location along the Erie Canal. It didn't hurt that, if it worked, Duci would be a shoe-in for the next mayoral term. And to sweeten the deal, Duggan recruited a big gun from Washington, D.C. to sell it.

Arthur Cotton Moore rose to prominence in the preservation field pretty quickly. Although he had founded his own architectural firm in 1965, "on a wing, a prayer, and a small residential commission which died the day I finished the preliminary drawings," as he explained in his 1998 book, *The Powers of Preservation: New Life for Urban Historic Places*, Arthur Cotton Moore/Associates actually completed a headline-grabbing urban project within a few years of its founding. For the original Canal Square, finished in 1970, Moore converted a rundown, 19th-century industrial warehouse district located beside the Chesapeake and Ohio Canal in Georgetown into a thriving commercial and retail center, and for only 2.5 million dollars. The warehouse that anchored the new development had once contained the predecessor of IBM, the Tabulating Machine Company of Dayton, Ohio and Endicott, New York, where the 1890 census had been compiled with the use of a revolutionary card-collating machine. "Through a process that came to be known as adaptive reuse, Canal Square showed how preservation could yield both aesthetic and financial rewards exceeding those of replacement," Moore wrote. And in this initial undertaking, Moore succeeded in envisioning and completing a project that, even fifty years later, still serves as a model for helping to renew urban waterfront districts.

All that was music to Jim Duggan's weary ears. This guy Moore was definitely preaching to the converted. After all, Schenectady had historic buildings that could certainly benefit from adaptive reuse. *Check*. The city stretched out along the Mohawk River, and its Erie Boulevard had been, literally, a significant part of the Erie Canal, so water was a key element. Check. The city was cash-poor and bleeding people, so a relatively inexpensive, aesthetically-pleasing downtown mall might just revitalize the retail district and help to renew the City Council's faith in FOCUS, Duggan's grassroots development corporation. *Check*, and *check*.

Duggan approached GE's Herman Hill first. He was Vice President and General Manager of the Steam Turbine Generator Department – still a powerful and lucrative part of General Electric in 1974 – and Hill had supported FOCUS and Duggan's conservation efforts throughout the development organization's first, difficult year and a half. GE also sponsored Moore's initial visit to the city, for a presentation and lecture on revitalizing downtowns. That visit led to a preliminary adaptive reuse plan for the empty building on lower State Street where Barney's, one of the city's four major department stores, had thrived for decades. Moore produced a plan and worked with Duggan for a couple of years, but the City Council wouldn't climb on board and the job went to a local developer who had different ideas for the site.

After that defeat, Duggan sidestepped local government and enlisted the primary downtown merchants and bankers for a much grander, private-investor development project – their own version of Canal Square – and they all visited Georgetown to see what Moore had accomplished there. Le Grande Serras, whose family had owned and managed Peggy's Restaurant since 1945, hosted their planning meetings after that trip, and they agreed that somebody had better do something big before there was nothing left to save.

Another major department store, Wallace's, had followed Barney's into bankruptcy. Proctor's Theater, a famous vaudeville theater and once the pride of Schenectady, had been presenting only porno flicks for more than a year, and the city had recently arranged for its demolition. It was hard to deny that the fringes of the city were being eaten away, block by block, and even the 400 block of State Street – for decades the retail heart of the city – was crumbling from the inside out. Sketchy characters roamed the streets, day and night. Finally, Le Grande's wife and mother were assaulted while shopping near the restaurant, and that pushed him over the edge. "This is my hometown," he said. "We're going to stay here and fight it out with these guys."

Chuck Carl of the one remaining department store in town, The Carl Co., Jim Cushing of Cushing Stone Co., and Joe Flora from Schenectady Savings Bank became the first and largest investors, each of them ponying up $15,000 toward Moore's asking price of $50,000 for the schematics, the preliminary drawings for the project. Not for blueprints – just for schematics, speculative renderings. Le Grande called them "the pretty pictures – fifty grand for pretty pictures," but he was definitely attracted by Moore's design: "Tying these properties all together, running hallways through the second floors to take people from one store to another, constructing a recreational canal system around all of it, was a compelling concept. Being the young, enthusiastic guy that I was, I was impressed by all his pictures and by what his plan was." So with some other storeowners – Paul Isenberg of The Squire Shop, Jack and Cathy Sheehan of The Costumer, Angelo Dellario, who owned Lafayette Men's Store – Le Grande helped to raise the rest of Moore's fee.

Right about that time, Jim Duggan was fighting City Hall to keep his development corporation operating. In July of 1976, he voluntarily reduced his salary from $25,000 to $20,000, arguing that over the preceding thirty months, his citizen-advisory agency, FOCUS, had achieved a free off-street parking system for downtown, offered other numerous plans that had been ignored by the City Council, and had initiated an almost-complete architectural study which would revitalize the retail heart of Schenectady. He would work for less, and FOCUS, he promised them, would soon achieve far more. No dice. The individual members of the FOCUS board could remain intact as advisors to the city's planning commission, if they wanted, but that was all the Council offered by way of support. Jim Duggan was out.

That year, Le Grande Serras was only twenty-eight years old. He had majored in Music at the University of Michigan, and had planned on following his passion for voice and piano, but when he graduated in 1969, his father coaxed him to take over his Schenectady business, Peggy's Restaurant, saying he was ready to retire. "Why don't you come back? Make $12,000 a year and steal a thousand, you'll be on top of the world," his father assured Le Grande. It wasn't a bad offer – twelve grand a year was a lot of money in 1969, especially for a kid right out of college. So Le Grande had come back, gotten married, had a daughter, and had taken over as manager of Peggy's. With his long hair, ebullient moustache, and commanding voice, he quickly became a prominent figure in downtown Schenectady, so he was a natural pitch man for the newly-formed 400 Block Development Corporation. That may have been why the merchants selected him to be president of their organization, or perhaps, as Le Grande considered, because he'd be the front guy if or when the whole thing went down the drain.

In the late 1970s, the United States Department of Housing and Development (HUD), was well aware of the country's deteriorating cities and offered two main avenues of financial aid. Community Development Block Grants were a bottom-up approach to help communities alleviate poverty and combat urban blight, and they were complemented by Urban Action Development Grants (UDAG), a more top-down government program to assist cities and urban counties that were experiencing economic distress. Both of them promised sizeable grants, quickly delivered, to communities and local governments, and even to private investment groups who could demonstrate substantial need and viable plans for revitalization projects. That sounded made to order for the fledgling, 400 Block Development Corporation.

Le Grande took Moore's pretty pictures and hopped on a train to Washington, where he met with Samuel Pierce Jr. at HUD. "In order to get this thing rolling," he began, "we'll need $500,000." Pierce, who would become Ronald Reagan's HUD Secretary during both his terms as president, looked bored. He fielded these pitches day in and day out. Then Le Grande outlined his organization's unique management idea: "It's a grassroots concept. Essentially, the owners of all these business properties will donate their buildings to this entity – this 400 Block Development Corporation – and get shares of stock back after their mortgages are paid off. The entity will own everything, not the business owners."

Suddenly, Pierce looked more interested.

"Say my restaurant is worth 50,000 and I owe 10,000 on my mortgage," Le Grande continued. "Grants and loans get made, my mortgage gets paid off, and I receive 40,000 worth of stock in the corporation, the entity. No individuals will get any money. Plus, we've convinced the city to turn over all the buildings on Smith Street, as well as our theater, Proctor's, that's in poor shape and slated to be torn down. All the buildings on that block are now part of our corporation, and Arthur Cotton Moore is our architect."

"I don't believe 500,000 will do it," Pierce said. "You'll need more than that to get started. How about I give you a million?"

What did Le Grande know? He was a twenty-eight-year-old kid, pumped up and proud as any conquering hero, with government money as good as in his pocket, but later on he kicked himself: "I should have asked for ten million," he said. "And I probably would have gotten it." No matter. The UDAG had conferred validation on the corporation's plan, and the merchants quickly raised another $200,000 for Moore's "design development" stage, which produced the blueprints they needed to begin construction – as well as an overall cost estimate of twelve million dollars. They sent Le Grande out to drum up interest.

Albany, Troy, Schenectady, Saratoga, Utica, Syracuse, Glens Falls, Hudson – Le Grande must have trotted out his dog-and-pony show in twenty or twenty-five cities, but one by one, their banks refused. Eventually, though, Robert Keith, who had replaced Joe Flora as president of Schenectady Savings Bank, called Le Grande in and revealed he had engineered a consortium of local banks to help. "You're asking for eleven million dollars," Keith said, and paused too long for comfort. "I'm going to give you the money, but I want you to do two things."

"Mr. Keith, what are those?" Le Grande asked.

"First, you're going to sell your restaurant, because as president of the corporation and general manager of Canal Square, you'll be running this whole shebang. I don't want any conflict of interest here. And second, you'll get a fucking haircut." He did both, and then strutted around town until, as he explains, his friends responded:

> *This will tell you where my head was at. Here I was, thrust into this massive 400 Block entity at twenty-eight years old. The businessmen in the project had made me its president and, at the time, my head was so big. I was in the paper every day, and I was on TV all the time, doing interviews. Plus, I was out every night of the week, telling people about it. I was thinking I was the smartest guy who ever existed. And then I got a letter from* Time Magazine *and it said,*

> *Dear Mr. Serras,*

> *We've been following your career with great interest, and we'd love to do a story on what is happening in downtown Schenectady. Specifically, we are anxious to do an interview with you. Enclosed, please accept a one-way ticket to fly you down here, and rest assured that our private plane will fly you back. Mr. Jerome Smith will be discussing your project with you. Would you please come into our offices so we can conduct an interview?*

> *And I thought,* Yeah, of course, they want to talk to me, I'm a big shot. *So I flew down to New York City. It was October 17th, and I was supposed to show up at* Time Magazine *at 2 o'clock but I got there early – about quarter to two – and I had my pretty pictures from Arthur Cotton Moore with me, and I went upstairs and walked in and I said, "I'm Le Grande Serras and I'm here for my interview with Mr. Smith." And they said, "Who?"*

"Jerome Smith. I'm going to be interviewed about my 400 Block Project in Schenectady."

And they said, "We don't know what you're talking about."

Then I realized – Son of a B! Well, it turned out that my friends – Angelo Mazzone and Paul Isenberg and Jack Sheehan and a couple of others were involved – somehow got Time Magazine *letterhead from down in New York City, typed the invitation out and made it look all official. They chipped in ten bucks apiece for the one-way plane ticket, which was nothing in those years, maybe $40 total. And my wife at the time was involved in it, too. Now usually back then I carried a lot of cash in my wallet, but that day I only had twenty-four dollars. I figured* Time Magazine *was taking care of me, so I had never looked. There I was with only the twenty-four bucks, and the Greyhound bus back to Schenectady cost twenty-two. And to make it even worse, they were all waiting down at the bus station for me to come back, saying, "You just got too big for your britches." Those bastards.*

By 1978, with the architectural plans complete and the financial package in place, the 400 Block Development Corporation was more than optimistic. What their members envisioned was something like Boston's Quincy Marketplace or the Galleria in Philadelphia. Those were successful urban malls that had become not only extremely viable retail and social centers for their cities but also actual tourist destinations. Why couldn't Schenectady's Canal Square emulate them? Market studies the corporation had commissioned suggested that a similar, local impact was possible. They would have an accessible, 200,000-square-foot specialty shopping center with a unique feature – a canal suitable for paddle boats in the summer and ice skating in the winter – and eighty-five retail establishments, sixty-five of which would be totally new to the area. With completed plans and the funds they needed to build, the corporation was raring to go, but they couldn't find a builder.

For months, every developer they approached turned them down. And when a company called Universal Concept, Inc. finally accepted the job, they quickly discovered that all the buildings weren't safe. Next to Lafayette Men's Store, the building that housed the Vendome Restaurant collapsed almost immediately, so they had to clear away the rubble and designate that empty space as one of the Canal Square entrances. For two years, the developer worked to guarantee the structures were structurally sound, to connect all the buildings via second-floor, glassed-in hallways, to construct an attractive pedestrian arcade that made the mall feel unified, and to build the signature canal. The narrow waterway, which ran from one square pool on Franklin St. to a much larger pool behind Peggy's Restaurant at Broadway, featured several pedestrian bridges and full lighting for nighttime events.

The Moore plan also called for Canal Square's building facades to be uniform, to present a unified appearance, so they were all painted a dark brown with mustard-colored trim. However, the Cushing building, at the corner of State and Broadway, had a severe pigeon problem. Every day at 4 P.M., the pigeons would roost there, and their droppings coated the front with white streaks. Another problem for Le Grande to solve. So first he had electric wires strung along the eaves where the pigeons sat, but the pigeons just moved lower, to the window ledges. He tried playing recorded shotgun sounds every fifteen seconds, but the pigeons got used to the blasts, and

seemed to crap more in response. After an article about it appeared in the *Gazette*, a guy telephoned Le Grande and assured him, "I'll get rid of that mess for you."

Le Grande enlisted Jack Sheehan to go along, and they met the guy on the third floor of the building, where broken windows allowed the pigeons easy access. "Well, how do you expect to get rid of them?" Le Grande said. The guy had heavy boots on, and he walked over to one of the pigeons, which was hurrying away from him, and stepped hard on its head. "That's how I'll get rid of them." Seeing that, Le Grande turned to Jack and said, "Oh, my God, if they ever find out about this, we'll be crucified." One demonstration was enough for him. "I don't want to know anything about it," he said, and left. But every month for three months, the guy called him and said, "You owe me fifty bucks." Like so many other inhabitants of the city, the pigeons never returned.

Le Grande did indeed sell Peggy's Canal Side Restaurant to Angelo Mazzone, who had previously managed the food and beverage operations for nearby Union College, and the restaurant thrived. Angelo didn't have the money to buy it at the time, so Le Grande held the paper on the loan for him. From 1981 on, crowds poured in for Peggy's all-weekend beer parties from late spring to mid-autumn, draining kegs and dancing to local bands by the canal pool, and Angelo had Le Grande paid off in a couple of years. So even amid the never-ending construction, with strange disruptions occurring, businesses continued to operate.

A day after one of those beer blasts, September 23, 1981, a bomb exploded outside the second-floor offices of the Eastern Rugby Association above the Nuts 'n Sweet Store and damaged a suite of offices. Even State Police investigators couldn't find the bomber. And swarms of kids from neighboring Hamilton Hill claimed the Franklin Street canal pool as their own personal swimming hole, defying paddle-boaters to enter. No matter how many times Le Grande or Jack Sheehan chased them off, they always came back, laid out their towels on the pedestrian walkway, and splashed back in. Plus, the swimming hole dried up pretty fast – the canal had leaked

To Le Grande Serras
With best wishes,

Ronald Reagan

into the buildings' basements from the moment it was filled, and had to be drained and covered over within its first two years.

Despite all the setbacks, through four years of construction and two million dollars over budget, Canal Square officially opened the day after Thanksgiving in 1982. Le Grande had resigned as its general manager the previous July, but two weeks past the opening, on Thursday, December 9, he and Mayor Duci accepted HUD's Award of National Excellence for Community Development from President Reagan for the Canal Square downtown development project. Out of 500 cities that had submitted projects, only eleven were chosen for awards, and Schenectady was placed at the top.

"Canal Square was chosen from many applicants nationwide as Urban Development of the Year, the number one project in the country to best represent public and private sector financial participation in launching an urban development project," Reagan read. "You have demonstrated that there is no such thing as, 'It can't be done." Then, looking at Le Grande, he added, "That's a very handsome moustache." What Le Grande didn't reveal to the president was that the 400 Block Development Corporation – the entity that was held up as the government's current model of strategic urban planning and excellence – had been unable to make its mortgage payments since June of 1981, and that Northeast Savings, the current lienholder, had already started foreclosure proceedings. No need to ruin a fancy awards ceremony.

400 Block Fire Cause Probed; Five Firefighters Are Injured

Some Merchants Temporarily Out of Business

Friday Morning, July 24, 1987

JEFF WILKIN
Gazette Reporter

Schenectady firefighters are still trying to determine the cause of the early-morning fire that gutted one Canal Square store yesterday and heavily damaged two others.

The hot, smoky fire at Merle Norman Cosmetics Store at 424 State St. destroyed the interior of the small shop and forced nine other merchants to close their doors in the city's downtown shopping block. Five firefighters were hurt fighting the blaze.

Damage was estimated at several hundred thousand dollars.

Peggy's Canal Side Restaurant and Collins Footwear, on either side of Merle Norman, were the next hardest hit. For Peggy's owner Angelo Mazzone, the fire wiped out a $100,000 renovation project that was completed only two months ago. He estimated damages at $250,000.

"We're totaled, we're out, we're history," he said. "Fire, smoke, water (damage), you name it, we've got it."

The front windows of the cosmetics store were blown out by the intense heat. About 30 firefighters, some of them from the previous work shift, fought the fire in rotating teams.

Firefighters believe flames may have been smoldering for up to four hours before the blaze broke out. A team of firefighters and police checked for any signs of arson, although Fire Chief Thomas A. Varno does not think the cause of the fire is suspicious.

"We want to definitely rule it out if it wasn't," he said.

The fire began in the rear of the store. Smoke traveled to the back of the building and entered a common hallway that runs from the Carl Co. department store through other stores on the block. The smoke then seeped into those stores.

"So it looked like a much bigger fire than it actually was," said Assistant Fire Chief Carl Derwig.

Deputy Chief Skip Johnson said firefighters are fortunate that a large explosion didn't occur when air rushed into the store after the windows shattered. "People would have been hurt," he said.

Firefighters are also fortunate the fire was discovered when it was.

"If Peggy's didn't open at 6 o'clock, this thing would have been a lot worse," Johnson said.

Deputy Chief Michael Santor said the Merle Norman store was not equipped with a sprinkler system but added that because the building is not designed for resident occupancy, such a system is not required.

*   *   *

The Carl Co. closed for the day, as did the Something Special Home Shop, Time Center Jewelers, Arnow Shoes, the Squire Shop and Lafayette clothing stores and the Peter Pam Children's Shop.

Mazzone, like other merchants on the block, is looking at a long shutdown period for repairs and cleanup. "Everything is gone," he said. "We still owe a ton of money on the renovation."

Other problems lie ahead. Mazzone said people in business count on handling a certain amount of business each day. "When you stop doing it, you still have the bills you have to pay and you don't have the money," he said.

At the Squire Shop, thin clouds of smoke were still visible in the rear of the store at noon. "It's pretty bad smoke damage," said Jeff Isenberg, store vice president. "There's water in the basement and I would say 100 percent smoke damage throughout the store." He said some of the items may be salvaged but had no estimate of monetary loss. "Right now, it's really hard to assess," he said.

At the Pizazz Store, co-owners Steven Menaged and Ruth Saloff were selling smoke-damaged clothing at reduced prices. When Menaged opened up the store, he found thick smoke inside. "I couldn't even see this over here," he said, pointing to a nearby table full of clothes.

The Lafayette store fared no better. "We've got extensive smoke damage and some water damage," said co-owner Rocco Peluso.

"Part of the ceiling is down," added bookkeeper Beverly Amorosi.

Peluso said smoke damaged a Lafayette store in Mohawk Mall several years ago, so he knew what to expect. "We expected a lot of smoke odor in the clothes, which there is," he said. Like the others, Peluso said his store will re-open as soon as possible.

But while clothing damaged by smoke can be sold and perhaps salvaged, contaminated food must be thrown out. "We lost all our ice cream, we lost all our chocolate," said Michele Joyce, one of the owners of the Candy Nut store.

Joyce eventually opened and sold roasted nuts and ice cream that had been stored in sealed cases. She said several regular customers made visits. "I really want to thank them," she said. "It means a lot to me that they cared enough to patronize me at a time when I'm suffering a loss like this."

G. Jack Parisi, the city's environmental health director, said city personnel and members of the state Agriculture and Markets Department inspected food at the Candy Nut, Mr. Meyer's Bakery, and Papa Cicco's pizzeria. "All the food that was exposed to smoke had to be destroyed," Parisi said, "paper products, anything that would absorb smoke – dough from Papa Cicco's, salt and pepper on the table."

Parisi also said that walls and windows in the establishments had to be washed down before they were permitted to open.

Firefighters remained at the scene during the late evening hours to check for flare-ups.

By 8 A.M. the day of the fire in 1987, water from the ladder truck's hoses that were trained on the second and third floors was cascading through Peggy's ceiling and spilling out into the street. Here and there, through the clouds of steam roiling inside the restaurant, Angelo Mazzone could see that a patch of ceiling above the bar, as well as a longer stretch above what used to be the wall that Peggy's shared with Merle Norman, was bright orange. *Matches the color my booths were,* he thought, and the stench of burning vinyl upholstery briefly overwhelmed him.

Firefighters with pikes were tearing away what was left of that wall, rooting out the tendrils of flame that had spiraled up from the adjoining basement and spread out so fast. *At least Le Grande's paid off, and the insurance should cover the remodel.*

But neither of those thoughts was comforting either. *At least nobody got hurt. That's the only important thing. I'll be fine. I can make something better here, something bigger. Three months, maybe four, we'll be back again, and so will the crowds, every weekend, thousands of people, drinking here, eating my food, having a ball.* And as he remembered, and began to plan, he could see straight through his restaurant to the wide, terraced space behind, waiting to be filled up again.

Although Angelo didn't throw in the towel right away, within a year he would sell off Peggy's, buy a down-at-the-heels colonial mansion on the other side of the river, in Scotia, and start to build what would become a catering empire. Part of him loved the day-to-day, face-to-face business of running a restaurant – he wasn't about to give that up – but downtown Schenectady was dead for him. The fire at Canal Square was just the smoldering cherry on a shit sundae, as far as he was concerned. Some new bank would take the project over, foreclose on it or not, force the city to swallow the back taxes, run the urban mall until the old buildings crumbled, and then sell what was left to an out-of-town developer. For the money boys, it was just developing real estate and monitoring economic cycles. But for many of the local merchants, Angelo's friends, this was the death knell for their dreams and livelihoods. All they had now were what they could salvage from their soaked and smoke-damaged merchandise, their worthless shares in a bankrupt, downtown corporation, and a drastically-reduced local workforce at the world-famous company that had sustained the city for close to a hundred years. Somebody else would have to find something new to save Schenectady. How the hell had they ended up in this mess?

2

The Town and Its Company

*The great liquid highway – the Erie Canal – would be built
farther north by New Yorkers, and it would connect the
Hudson River to the Great Lakes. New York's victory
reflected both its geographical advantages and the
willingness of its government to bet vast sums of public
money on a canal. They were right to bet. The canal turned
a profit almost immediately because of the huge demand
for east-west transport.*

*– Triumph of the City: How Our Greatest Invention Makes Us
Richer, Smarter, Greener, Healthier, and Happier*

Edward Glaeser

The Gilded Age was glistening, just out of reach, and the merchants of Schenectady wanted more. They weren't necessarily interested in transforming their city into a planned, industrial company town like Lowell, Massachusetts, or imitating George Pullman's eponymous community on Lake Calumet, fourteen miles outside Chicago, where the vast fortune he had earned from his ornate railroad cars had allowed him to create a 4000-acre, utopian factory town for his workers. The merchants weren't advocating for wholesale change. After all, they loved their city and honored its rich history, but it simply wasn't living up to its potential.

Schenectady had been the important, eastern terminus for the Erie Canal from 1822 through the late 1840s, and had relished its reputation as the Gateway to the West before the railroads changed America. However, all that was ancient history for the town's prominent citizens in 1886. The last census in 1880 had recorded 13,665 people in the city, up a couple of thousand from the decade before, but that was decidedly slow growth at best. The pastoral "land beyond the pines," as the Mohawks had once called it, still felt to its merchants like an old dorp, the Dutch slur for a sleepy village. A backwater. There were various, small manufacturers in town, of course: broom-making companies like C. Whitmyer, or Flinn's; George Weller's sarsaparilla bottling plant on North College Street; the Westinghouse Agricultural Works that turned out farm machinery on the vast meadow alongside the canal; Cantine's foundry that fashioned ornamental fencing; John Weiderhold's Mill that made hoopskirts and ladies' muslin underwear; to say nothing of the several brickyards and stone quarries, among many other going concerns that had fueled Schenectady's economy for most of the 19th Century. These were the anchors that shored up the drowsy town along the Mohawk River, and Schenectady's merchants were thankful to have them all. But in the grand scheme of America during the prime of its Industrial Revolution, with robber barons amassing scandalous fortunes, assuaging their guilt by endowing ornate libraries, museums, opera houses and hospitals in other, more well-to-do cities, and throwing newsworthy parties at mansions in exotic enclaves decidedly unlike Schenectady, it was hard for the merchants to deny that their own small, local manufacturing companies remained just that – small, and regional.

While Schenectady could legitimately brag about its one major industry – the Schenectady Locomotive Works, which had become the largest employer in the city after the Civil War ended – that company's fortunes rose and fell too regularly to make it a reliable economic engine. In 1868, for example, the Works produced a banner year, assembling 100 coal-and-wood-burning locomotives with their 800 employees. Its most famous locomotive, the *Jupiter*, was shipped around Cape Horn to California for the Central Pacific Railroad, and carried Leland Stanford from Sacramento to Promotory, Utah. There, the Central Pacific and Union Pacific joined their rails, creating the first transcontinental railroad line with the Golden Spike Ceremony on May 10, 1869. Stanford made sure that world-class event was chronicled, and the iconic photographs of the symbolic ceremony sparked a flurry of orders for the *Jupiter's* maker.

Unfortunately, the Schenectady Locomotive Works had lost so much from two earlier disasters – a fire that consumed half its buildings and most of its uninsured, unfinished locomotives in 1866, as well as a massive, Mohawk River ice-jam that flooded their entire site the following year – that the profits they made from the new orders were literally just keeping the company's head above water. Its next twenty years proved to be even more haphazard. The economic Panic of 1873 slid into a long depression, and the Works completed only nine locomotives in 1874. Two years after that, the company was actually forced to shut down completely for several months. By 1882, though, the company had rebounded once again, hired over 1,000 men, and was regarded as one of the major locomotive builders in the country. That boom-and-bust cycle lasted well into the 1880s, until a feud between the company's founding Ellis family and its Chief Engineer and Vice President, Walter McQueen, offered Schenectady the unlikely chance its merchants had been hoping for.

McQueen agreed to start a rival company, egotistically dubbed the McQueen Locomotive Works, and partnered with Senator Charles Stanford, who bought ten acres of land on the south side of Schenectady near the Mohawk River. Stanford paid $80,000.00 to purchase the property and to erect two large shop buildings there. But before their roofs were even finished, the venture failed: first McQueen got cold feet, settled his rift with the Ellis family, and rejoined the original Works; then Stanford died suddenly. Soon after that, the ten acres and two uncovered buildings fell into receivership.

Around the same time, and in spite of his worldwide fame for creating the first long-lasting lightbulb, many of Thomas Edison's start-up lighting companies and municipal licensees were barely surviving. The Edison Electric Illuminating Company of Jackson, Mississippi reported profits of only $139 for the first four months of 1886, for instance, and the electric company in New Bedford, Massachusetts did even worse: $155 for its first *eight* months. On top of that, Edison's workers on Goerck Street in lower Manhattan at the Edison Machine Works, which manufactured incandescent lamps, generators, and engines, among other things – everything needed to power these new lighting companies – were on strike, in spite of the fact that he had recently given them a 25-cents-an-hour raise above the prevailing rate of wages, attributing his generosity to "a socialistic strain in him."

But even back then, no good deed would go unpunished. As soon as the men received that raise, they struck to get even more, not realizing that the company was so short on cash that it couldn't even meet the following week's payroll. After Edison and his managers failed to appear at their offices for the following two weeks, however, the strikers returned to their jobs, relieved to find them still there. But the strike gave Edison a good excuse to move. The shop on Goerck Street was so small that machine lathes had to sit outside on the sidewalk, run by leather belts that passed through the windows, after all. Moreover, his workers' ingratitude infuriated Edison, and worried him enough that in the spring of 1886 he sent three agents off, in different directions, to locate a new home for the Edison Machine Works.

Harry Livor was the Edison agent who traveled to upstate New York, scouting the cities with access to railroads, but he was disappointed with every site he visited. On his way back south, though, watching the scenery flow past, one possible site startled him. Here is John Winthrop Hammond's description of that moment, in his exhaustive history of the first thirty years of General Electric, *Men and Volts:* "So it was that Destiny called to the Mohawk Valley one day in the spring of 1886 a man who felt an immediate interest in such a spectacle as met his eye from the car-window of a train puffing across the 'big flat,' past the two lonely factory buildings on the outskirts of Schenectady." Hidden inside Hammond's turgid prose lies Livor's instinctive recognition that the still-warm body of the McQueen Locomotive Works was a solution to Edison's problem: two brand new buildings on a substantial tract of land, and all of that sitting beside operational railroad tracks. Throw in proximity to the Erie Canal, and the Mohawk River within spitting distance, and Harry Livor couldn't wait to get back to Menlo Park and tell his boss what he had discovered.

An appraisal set the price for the ten acres and two unfinished buildings at a steal – $45,000 – but Edison would offer only $37,500, not a penny more, and he gave the town a deadline of June 2, 1886 to respond. N.I. Schermerhorn, who

owned the land, along with Charles Stanford's family, wouldn't accept one penny less than their asking price, and the stalemate dragged on for weeks. Robert Furman, a prosperous dry-goods merchant in Schenectady, stepped into the fray. He was the first to recognize the future when it banged on the door. This was Thomas Edison, the most famous inventor of the century, offering to move his Edison Machine Works to their little city, for God's sake. Maybe a thousand new workers for Schenectady, or more. Who couldn't see what that might mean? Furman threw in the first $250, and solicited similar contributions from his fellow State Street merchants. In the end, eighty-two citizens and businesses raised the $7,500 balance that Edison refused to pay. That was the first time a group of Schenectady's farsighted residents would band together to help shape the economic future of the city, and it wouldn't be the last. Whether any of them understood what they had wrought is another question, but almost immediately, they got what they believed they wanted.

Once the deal was done, Edison did in fact visit Schenectady, on August 20, 1886, and described for a *Schenectady Gazette* reporter the plans he envisioned for the new Edison Machine Works site, joking with the town's civic leaders that he had come to "look over my new ranch." The next day he was gone, hurrying back to the workaholic comforts of his laboratory in Menlo Park, assured by his chief assistant, Charles Batchelor, that Schenectady was a place where, "We will have no more trouble from strikes." If Batchelor could have known the future, he might not have been so cavalier in his assessment. But his assurance sounded true enough to Edison, who ceded responsibility for the project to his twenty-seven-year-old assistant and former private secretary, Samuel Insull.

Young and ambitious, Insull hit the ground running: he directed Pop Turner, an experienced Edison millwright, to finish the two buildings and manage the set-up of all the machinery shipped up from the now-shuttered Goerck Street site. He also enlisted Batchelor, who had acted as shop superintendent at the machine works in Manhattan, to supervise the opening of the new plant. Within six weeks, Insull had hired 200 men and, by the middle of December, he had incorporated the Edison Tube Company and the Edison Shafting Works into the Schenectady operation, quickly exceeding the highest expectations of the Schenectady merchants who had contributed to the venture.

For the next six years, the Edison Machine Works expanded at an exponential rate. In 1889, Drexel, Morgan & Co. financed a merger of Edison's companies into one corporation – the Edison General Electric Company – and quickly acquired the Sprague Electric Railway & "Motor Company. As word-of-mouth reports of this new powerhouse electric company reached not only adjoining states in America but also Italy and other European countries saddled with high rates of poverty and unemployment, workers poured through the newly-opened reception center at Ellis Island and headed upstate for the steady jobs and higher wages Schenectady offered.

All the new arrivals needed places to live, of course. Hotels sprang up near the bustling worksite, and many city residents happily took in boarders. Local entrepreneurs cooked hot lunches for throngs of hungry workers, hauled them to the main gate in horse-drawn wagons, and sold them for 25 cents apiece. New houses mushroomed, the city's businesses thrived, and its population swelled beyond 20,000. Most significantly, Insull increased his workforce from 200 to 8,000 employees between 1886 and 1892, and his management expertise powered an income dynamo. Although Edison regarded the Schenectady works as an easy funding source and siphoned off as much as he could by overcharging the factory for his lab services, Insull retained enough control to ensure steady profits, telling a reporter years later, "We never made a dollar until we got the factory 180 miles away from Mr. Edison."

Then, for Schenectady, economic lightning struck. While Edison had been obsessed with winning the war of the currents – sponsoring the electrocution of hundreds of dogs, cats, sheep, and horses with alternating current to discredit rival George Westinghouse and prove Edison's use of direct current was far safer than Nicola Tesla's alternating model – Samuel Insull had patiently been negotiating with a larger electric company, Thomson-Houston of Lynn, Massachusetts, to consider a consolida-

tion. With the backing of the financier J.P. Morgan, the deal went through in early 1892. Samuel Insull was rewarded with the job of second vice-president, the only Edison executive offered a key position in the new company. Afterwards, Edison fumed that he had been the victim of a hostile takeover, but he ended up receiving five million dollars in cash, or 10% of the final fifty million once Morgan had capitalized the merger of these two leading electric companies.

Facing reporters the day after the deal was closed, Edison told them he was thrilled – he had been the first person to propose the merger, after all. Besides, he had scores of new inventions in the works. He was simply too busy to waste any more of his time on electricity.

The Edison name was dropped from the new company, which was simply shortened to General Electric, although the company would continuously trumpet its early relationship with Edison and exploit his name throughout its lifetime to enhance its own origins and brand. And even though Edison may have moved on, selling all of his shares in the company by 1894, the merchants and leaders of Schenectady were ecstatic: their quiet city was poised to become the center of the new electric world.

3

So Big, So Fast

*No discussion of ideal company towns would be
complete if it failed to include a singular type –
the domicile of the high-tech company.
Such places include Schenectady, New York,
long associated with General Electric.*

– *The Company Town: The Industrial Edens and
Satanic Mills That Shaped the American Economy*

Hardy Green

What did this new corporation, General Electric, want at the start? The reductionist response – vast profits – is what all companies hope for, of course. But that may be too simple an answer. If it's possible to combine the separate parts – executives, managers, workers, an elite board of directors, celebrated investors, as well as all the shareholders – into one corporate identity with a common aspiration, you could safely say the new General Electric as an industrial-era manufacturing corporation wanted to make money by inventing and producing useful and innovative goods for people, for other companies, and for municipalities, at the very least. But it soon became apparent that GE wanted more than business success: like other leading industries of the day, it craved the kind of market dominance that would translate into unlimited growth and power.

That all businesses, legitimate or otherwise, want to be productive and successful is a given, no matter when they are founded. However, massive corporations like GE that become successful rapidly often exceed their initial goals and morph into entities that can exert control over, first, the people who work for them and, more often than not, the communities that grow up in and around them. If they become multi-national companies, they may even wield outsize influence on their country and perhaps even on the world. In time, General Electric would certainly get that big, and then some, but its various leaders remained consistently clever enough to mask the giant company's motives and misdeeds for more than half a century.

From its earliest days in Schenectady, GE was able to convince most of its citizens that the town and the company were one happy, symbiotic family. Just consider the evolving taglines that the men who headed the company used in their different eras and you'll understand how they manipulated the public to regard General Electric as a benevolent patriarch – slogans like, *Initials of a Friend – GE*, and, *You Can Put Your Confidence in General Electric*. They were smart marketers, that's for sure, and boy, did all their plans work in Schenectady, through several generations of prosperity and achievement and, ultimately, severe downsizing, until no one in upstate New York could deny the corporation had systematically undermined its workers and eventually betrayed the city where it was born.

At the beginning, though, an economic tornado rampaged through America: a procession of major railroad companies failed, causing a financial panic in 1893, and that led to a five-year, country-wide depression that saw 500 banks go under and 16,000 businesses declare bankruptcy. General Electric was forced to lay off half its workforce at the Schenectady plant just a year after it was formed. But in spite of that, and in the midst of the downturn, the corporation was already important enough to join American Sugar, Chicago Gas, U.S. Leather, United States Rubber, and seven other large companies that comprised the twelve original members of the Dow Jones Industrial Average in 1896. And by 1900, GE had shaken off the decade's economic downturns and was ready to anchor the country's burgeoning Progressive Era. The Gilded Age may have screeched to an inglorious stop for most of America at the end of the 19th century, but for Schenectady the good times were just beginning.

PROGRESS REPORT: 1895

Schenectady GE Employees:	3,880
Schenectady Population:	25,900
GE Net Earnings:	$877,645.00
GE Tagline of the Time:	*The guarantee of excellence in goods electrical*

How did General Electric get so big, so fast? For one thing, it epitomized and marketed the cutting-edge technology of electricity – the 600-hour incandescent light bulb, along with all the mysterious dynamos and hardware that made lighting systems possible – and electricity had lifted Americans out of the darkness with the flick of a switch. More importantly for its public image, GE harnessed that same expertise with electricity to power revolutionary, afford-able home appliances that everyone wanted all at once: the electric toaster in 1905; the electric range, the Hotpoint, in 1910; the electric, sealed home refrigerator in 1917; home radios, filled with words and music by the Radio Corporation of America, RCA, in 1919; and the electric

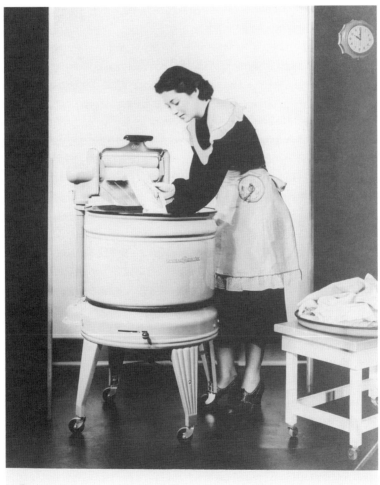

557178   G-E CLOTHES WASHER IN USE.

FILING NO.9932   728.3   E357.23   6-7-37

clothes washer in 1930. Every home could sample the future right *NOW*, and all these life-changing inventions bore General Electric's famous stamp.

As Elizabeth Rosner describes it in her novel, *Electric City*, "Picture the logo – you can still see it anywhere. A monogram of curling letters meant to look like someone's handwriting, adorning some appliance or other, your fridge or your stove, maybe a washing machine, or your dryer … In a company town, everything wore the Company insignia. 'Live better electrically!' the slogan said. Everyone believed it." And like the Sears catalogue or groceries from A&P, a new tagline, *Initials of a Friend – GE,* signified enviable progress in homes throughout America.

However, the lighting systems and home appliance lines were merely the most identifiable face of GE – the everyday products that served as mechanical companions to make life easier and subtly coax Americans into believing they were not just beneficiaries of the modern era but perhaps even necessary partners in a massive, family-centered enterprise. At the same time, General Electric also produced inventions and products that made it indispensable to any number of industries. GE manufactured underground electric conduits for street railway companies; 100-horsepower motors for locomotive passenger cars; electric motors and controls for gun turrets on Navy cruisers; electrical equipment for producing X-rays and stereoscopic "roentgen" pictures to diagnose bone fractures and locate foreign objects in the body; a battery-run electric carriage, the "Wagonette," one of the first cars ever sold; and electric mining locomotives, among many other less-visible products. And for a finale, GE constructed the largest hydroelectric plant in America, located at Niagara Falls. Once the corporation had accomplished that, and all of it before 1900, immediate and constant expansion became an obsession.

The Edison Machine Works in Schenectady had begun with two buildings, about ten acres of land, 200 employees, and 70,406 square feet of shop space in 1886. By 1909, General Electric had grown to 178 buildings on 330 acres, employed 11,000 people, and featured 3,758,679 square feet of shop space. Seventeen years later, in 1926, just three years before the stock market crash of 1929, GE's main works consisted of 645 acres in Schenectady and neighboring Rotterdam, with 357 buildings, 19,393 employees, and 6,579,684 square feet of usable work space. Plus, GE didn't just build factory and office space: the corporation installed an internal railroad system; relied on autonomous power plants; placed chemical and utility transmission lines underground throughout its vast property; and contained its own firehouse, printing plant, photography studio, and infirmary, as well as various restaurants and athletic facilities. It operated a separate city within a city.

From 1886 to 1926, the population of Schenectady, General Electric's headquarters, had increased from 13,655 to almost 95,000. The city was bursting at its seams. Housing developments and small retail shops had sprung up in new suburbs called Bellevue, Mont Pleasant, and Woodlawn, and trolley lines ferried workers from them to GE's main plant and home again. Jobs were plentiful. Fathers and sons, and even a smattering of mothers and daughters, worked side by side. Life was more than good: for the vast majority of immigrants in Schenectady, General Electric had offered them the living embodiment of the American Dream they had been promised when they left their native countries.

PROGRESS REPORT: 1929

Schenectady GE Employees:	24,384
Schenectady Population:	95,540
GE Net Earnings:	$60,525,463.00
GE Tagline of the Time:	*Initials of a friend …GE*

Under E.W. Rice, Jr., General Electric's chief officer in Schenectady from the 1890s through the 1920s and its President from 1913-1922, the company created a technical corporate culture that revered engineering, scientific invention, technical innovation, masculinity, moral fitness, physical fitness through outdoor recreation, and strong support for family life. Between 1880 and 1920, an age when engineering was a respected and lucrative career dominated almost completely by men, technical schools and colleges helped to increase the number of engineers in America from 7,000 to 130,000. GE hired the cream of that engineering crop right out of school, and established an elite training program for them in Schenectady. However, the corporation was also relentless in demanding that all their male employees subscribe to the ideals they promoted to enhance its corporate identity within the community.

While the new company did hire "G-E girls" mostly as office workers, for light factory jobs like coil-winding and polishing ceramic lamp sockets, and for service jobs like cleaners or restroom matrons, company management unashamedly treated them as second-class citizens. General Electric, for example, offered home mortgages to men but not to women, and garden plots on company property were reserved for male employees. That women were paid less for their work at GE is reprehensible, though hardly surprising for that era, but during the corporation's first twenty years, its women employees were also denied the medical and retirement benefits offered to all men who worked for them. General Electric mandated separate lunch rooms, athletic teams, and rest areas for women, essentially segregating them. As GE's publicists framed the situation for its admiring public, "G-E girls work and play and enjoy it under the protective wing of the Company," and for an up-and-coming town dependent on its main employer in the first quarter of the 20th century, why rock the boat for people who couldn't even vote yet? That brand of benevolent, corporate reassurance seemed worth believing.

Although General Electric primarily built its culture around men, class segregation also existed in its ranks by design: executives at the top, then scientists and engineers of all stripes below them, and finally the less-privileged factory and service workers on the lowest rung of the ladder. The top brass respected GE's scientists and their essential discoveries, but they all made sure to curry favor with the engineers. Scientists and researchers contributed breakthrough discoveries, sure, but engineers were the ones, after all, who were essential in creating signature electrical devices for the marketplace, and the corporation's profitability rested squarely on their shoulders.

For almost seventy years, General Electric sought out talented engineering students and shaped them strictly in the company mold through its two-year Student Engineers' Training Course (TEST), which was a hands-on, work-apprenticeship program that provided practical experience and an inside track into GE's labyrinth of complex manufacturing operations. TEST began in 1892 with forty engineering recruits, grew to 500 by 1907, and levelled off at about 400 trainees a year through the 1920s. According to Julia Kirk Blackwelder in *Electric City: General Electric in Schenectady,* "The GE training program stood somewhere between basic training and fraternity pledging. The TEST course 'sought not to educate, but to initiate, indoctrinate, and select.' It permitted GE to match young engineers with the jobs they thought best suited them."

Investing in the careers of these student engineers and compensating them well ensured not just that they would acquire the appropriate skills and expertise to be optimally productive for General Electric, but it also built a deeply loyal base of well-paid, top employees who would willingly subscribe to the expected corporate identity. Perhaps more importantly, these human GE products would maintain the company's secrets and side with management in any possible

UNWOUND LARGE STATIONARY ARMATURE (WITH FINGER FLANGES) FOR G-E
MOTOR, BEING PREPARED TO RECEIVE WINDINGS.

FILING NO.8313   E312.5 E310.1 E320

labor disputes. What GE didn't foresee, however, was that within the TEST program's continuing success, it had planted the seeds of income inequality and sown a profound disaffection within its ranks of factory workers that would eventually result in strikes that were not only inevitable, but ultimately quite costly to GE's bottom line.

E. W. Rice, Jr. was clever enough during his tenure, though, to convince most of his employees that the company had their best interests in mind. Again, Julia Kirk Blackwelder explains, "Through its corporate benefits programs and publicity, Schenectady General Electric sought to discourage the organizational impulses of its manufacturing workers. Class divisions among employees proved an important tool for GE management in initially discouraging production workers from forming effective unions." Rice may have offered workers good wages and life-enhancing benefits on the surface, but at the same time he exploited language barriers between ethnic groups from different countries to discourage broad-based camaraderie, for instance, and sponsored separate recreational activities that solidified exclusionary activities, like providing bocce courts for the Italian workers.

 464276   AMERICANIZATION ACTIVITY. BOCCIE BOWLING AT NOON RECESS
BESIDE BUILDING 49.
E320   8-21-29

Occasionally, some of GE's programs also provided benefits to its workers that weren't just self-serving or manipulative. In 1919, for example, Charles A. Coffin, who had been heading the company since 1892 when he was hand-picked by J. P. Morgan, asked E. W. Rice to begin an Americanization program for their foreign-born employees. While his underlying purpose was ideological – "To inculcate the spirit of Americanism and to combat the fallacies and false-hoods which are being taught in Bolshevik and I.W.W. propagandas," Coffin had written – the ironic result was a workforce which did learn English and subsequently helped their own families to assimilate more easily into their new country. Hearing over and over about "the freedoms and opportunities that citizens of no other nation enjoyed" may or may not have convinced the workers that GE had their best interests in mind, but it is true that unions couldn't establish a viable foothold inside General Electric for many years.

At the same time, Rice was making sure that a constant stream of favorable propaganda was pumped into the local press. He also encouraged company executives to become involved in the city's social and business organizations, like the Mohawk Club or the Schenectady Chamber of Commerce or the First Unitarian Church, to underscore GE's commitment to Schenectady and to support the company's well-publicized philanthropic efforts in the community. Most of those company executives were usually dedicated and sincere in their volunteer efforts, and Schenectady would never have developed into the thriving city it became without their input and expertise. In addition, Rice offered his male employees at all levels a generous helping of benefits and activities, including a dining hall with a moving cafeteria line which could serve 800 men every thirty minutes, as well as a bowling alley and a gymnasium.

Rice's seemingly altruistic strategies fundamentally paid off. There were a couple of small strikes by armature winders, and in the sixty-five hour "folded arms" strike of 1904, renowned as the first sit-down strike in America, those workers did win some minor concessions from the company. Two years after that, though, GE fired a man who was caught trying to organize the draftsmen in the plant, and the International Workers of the World (I.W.W.) called for all the factory workers in Schenectady to walk out. 3000 answered that call and left for three weeks, but the vast majority, who were associated with the American Federation of Labor (AFL) unions, stayed on the job. The strike failed and the I.W.W. was eventually broken.

A 1913 job action supported strongly by Dr. George Lunn, Schenectady's only socialist mayor, looked promising at first. All 15,000 factory workers, led by 2000 women from Wire and Cable Shops 69 and 77, demanded the reinstatement of two fired shop stewards. In a grand anti-climax, E.W. Rice, Jr. simply gave those shop stewards new assignments and everyone was back at work within the week. In stoppage after stoppage, General Electric's leaders found timely methods of mollifying the workers to keep production humming and avert any substantial loss of income from its largest facility. It was smart business and, if we had been in charge back then, would we have acted differently? In fact, labor organizers had such an uphill battle gaining a foothold in Schenectady that, by 1926, all craft unions had been eliminated at GE's headquarters. For the most part, the company succeeded in avoiding the larger, occasionally crippling strikes that plagued the steel, railroad, mining, automobile, and other major industries until after WWII.

Were the citizens of Schenectady happy with GE and its tactics? Except for the strikers, it's probable that most people wouldn't have spoken too harshly about the biggest employer in town. If you didn't already work there, it's a fair bet someone in your family did, or that you may want a job there sometime in the future. The merchants in town certainly couldn't have been happier: all their businesses were booming, so they weren't squawking. Local government was lining its pockets, in part from company largesse, and that corruption went largely unchecked until Lunn the socialist mayor took office. He won elections in 1911, 1919, and 1921, so that clearly indicated a substantial level of continuing, community discontent with the status quo, but there is little indication that GE was affected much by it.

However, General Electric's Realty Plot became a glaring example that class divisions were widening, and it's hard to know what Schenectady's tens of thousands of new immigrant workers and their families felt if and when they saw the mansions start to appear. General Electric paid $57,000 for the seventy-five-acre College Woods to Union College, which could not pay its debt of $30,000 in 1899, and created the Schenectady Realty Company to develop the large property. Buyers had to agree to four main elements in the contract: the new house built in the plot had to be constructed within two years; the value of each house must be at least twice the mean value of a typical house in the city; each house must be a single-family home; and any wall or fence could stand no higher than three feet, six inches. The developers didn't have to worry. The only people who could afford the giant houses that mushroomed there were General Electric bigwigs like E.W. Rice, Jr., successful merchants, and rich politicians. Schenectady's cream of the crop inhabited the Realty Plot, and GE used it as a recruiting tool for prominent executives, scientists and engineers they wanted to lure away from other companies.

469141   BUILDINGS 5 AND 37, VIEWED FROM CORNER OF BUILDING 23.
                                SCHENECTADY WORKS.

                         E320   3-24-30

Like most industries, General Electric was hit hard by the Great Depression, and they reduced their work force in Schenectady from 29,000 in 1930 to 13,000 in 1933 – 2,500 of whom were salaried workers – and none who lost their jobs had contracts or unions for recourse. With a growing pool of unemployed, skilled workers available, GE took advantage of the situation and cut wages twice over two years, 10% in 1931 and another 10% in 1932. If the workers got upset, too bad – there were plenty of hungry people out there to replace them, and no mother-hen union to protect their rights. In 1934, the company discontinued the vacation pay that workers had always received, and began to subtract eight hours of pay for every legal holiday when the plant was closed. Finally, they eliminated all overtime pay, and expected workers to work their forty-eight-hour, six-day week without interruptions or complaints.

Eventually, the company's abuses were flagrant enough throughout that time to solidify opposition and spark a systemic change: in 1936, the United Electrical, Radio and Machine Workers – Local 301 of the UE (AFL-CIO) – was formed as the bargaining agent for hourly factory employees at General Electric in Schenectady. Although only 650 members joined the UE local at first, the union's elected leaders worked hard enough over the following four years to recruit the vast majority of GE's labor force and turn Schenectady into a union town. However, while almost all the production employees at the main plant were now organized into a single industrial union, everyone had to be more concerned with rebounding from the economic paralysis of the 1930s than forcing wage hikes or improved working conditions out of the company. The longed-for reckoning would have to wait for quieter times.

When the war department came calling in 1941, over 50,000 GE employees signed up to fight, and the company switched over to wartime production. Under those circumstances, union ranks were naturally depleted and any work stoppages would have appeared clearly unpatriotic. The CIO, Congress of Industrial Organizations, pledged not to strike during the war years, and Schenectady's UE Local 301 honored that commitment. Lucrative defense contracts rolled in, and GE churned out tens of thousands of radar sets; giant, precisely-machined gears for warships; turbine-electric drives for propulsion on escort tankers; breech mechanisms for the Army's 75-mm howitzers; radio transmitters for the Navy; remote-controlled two-gun aircraft turrets, as well as the first automatic pilot system for the Air Force; projectiles for P-47 rocket launchers; 60-inch anti-aircraft searchlights; portable smoke generators for the Chemical Warfare Service; and, of course, massive land turbine-generators to power the entire war effort. With so many of its men headed overseas to fight, GE hired thousands more women to do their jobs, and its employee population in Schenectady surged to an all-time high – 45,000 workers – and the company stayed safe from internal disruptions until after the war was won.

PROGRESS REPORT: 1943

Schenectady GE Employees:	45,000
Schenectady Population:	88,750
GE Net Earnings:	$48,200,000.00
GE Tagline of the Time:	*You can put your confidence in General Electric*

War Service Record of the Schenectady Works. Note Service Flags, Liberty Bond purchases and donations.

In 1945, Helen Quirini was twenty-five years old, and was surprised she had worked through the war years at General Electric in Schenectady. Growing up, hearing the stories about "job selling" during the Depression, she had vowed to avoid ever working there. "If you had the money and made the right contact," she wrote in her memoir, "you could purchase a job for about $300, which was a lot of money in those days." It turned out to be true. General Electric's employment office manager was the man selling the jobs in 1936, and the newly-formed Local 301 had cooperated with the police and the district attorney in getting him arrested, found guilty, and sent to prison. Only after his conviction had the company discharged him, and Helen wondered why GE had allowed the practice to exist in the first place. Apart from that, she had learned the company was hiring only boys, males under twenty-one, and girls, because they could pay both groups less than they paid older men. Plus, everybody in town knew about the widespread discrimination at the plant, not only the usual kind against women and blacks and Italians and Chinese and Polish and Jewish workers, but the kind that included where you worked, what your job was, or where you lived. Helen wouldn't put up with anybody who acted like that.

Right out of high school, she and her brother had opened a "Brother and Sister Cash Market," and did well for a few years until "the war clouds over Europe" disrupted the supply chain and forced them to close the business. Unable to find work elsewhere, and desperately wanting money to eventually pay for college, Helen applied to one of the few places looking for help in Schenectady. Hired on April Fool's Day in 1941, and wondering what kind of omen that might portend, she chose a factory job doing piece work instead of daily wages. Helen proved so fast at "forming wires on top of fixtures" that she made as much as her sister, who had worked in one of GE's offices for five years. But as she recounted, that better rate of pay came with an emotional charge:

> *I slowly learned the ropes about piece work. Piece work rates were established by the timing of the job. I watched while such a time study took place. The rate setter used a special watch that recorded hundreds of a minute. He would keep track of the operations and write down the time for each operation. After a certain number of the operations was recorded, and if there was no protest, the union and the company would negotiate the results. Protests by the company might include accusations of workers intentionally stalling, working too slowly, or failing to follow instructions. Union objections were based on the worker being nervous or so concerned about making a good impression that he/she worked faster than normal. Some workers could not work at a normal pace while being timed because they got too nervous. It isn't easy to work while someone is timing you because you know your time study will be used for all future prices on this particular job.*

In spite of Local 301 UE looking out for Helen's welfare, she refused to join after her first month on the job. Her father had told her unions were "communistic." She had read all the derogatory criticisms of the union in the local press, and still believed that GE would "treat a worker right if the person was a good worker and gave a good day's effort." Helen knew she was a good worker. Even when the local union membership swelled to 19,280 late in 1941, and even after she learned that Pope Leo XIII backed unions, and although she could clearly see that the union at GE was fighting against the discrimination she witnessed, Helen kept saying, "No way."

"Don't believe everything you read in the local press," a friend at work finally told her.

"Get involved. If you find things you don't like, work to change them. First make sure that your facts are accurate. Then work for change." By that time, Helen had seen enough to reject her father's prejudices: 1945 wages were no better for women than 1941 wages, and some women had given up their children because they couldn't take care of them while they were working, plus there were no options for child care provided at the plant, of course. It was a man's world there. In addition, the War Labor Board had investigated working conditions at General Electric in Schenectady and "stated that women were being exploited by the Company."

Then, after Helen learned that GE, along with other giant corporations in America, had been guaranteed their costs plus a certain profit by the government – and that these corporations had amassed 117 billion dollars in wartime profits while wages for GE workers had been frozen by government order during the previous three and a half years of the war – that was too much. The cost of living had increased 45% during the war years, while many GE workers earned half of what they had three years earlier. She realized at that point the situation was beyond corporate greed: GE would never correct its discriminatory practices without constant pressure from a powerful union, so she not only joined up but was elected to serve as a shop steward.

To make up for workers' losses during the war, UE Local 301 asked the company for a twenty-five cents an hour wage hike in 1945 – two dollars a day more. GE's CEO, Charles Wilson, refused at first to even consider an increase. Then he suggested one half of one cent per hour. After the union threatened to strike, he countered with a conciliatory offer of ten cents an hour, eighty cents a day – take it or leave it. Major national corporations like General Motors and U.S. Steel and General Electric, flush with their wartime profits, were confident they could ride out any temporary work stoppages, so even when President Truman intervened to help avoid a strike, advocating for an eighteen and a half cents an hour compromise figure, Wilson and GE wouldn't budge.

The union's newspaper revealed that a typical machine operator in the plant had earned a weekly pay check of $48.55 in 1943, but that his weekly pay dropped to $23.73 in 1945. He was married, had four children, and paid $35 a month rent. How could GE's factory workers make ends meet if they weren't paid a fair wage by the company, especially when the corporation was sitting on a war chest? The response from General Electric? It would continue its policy of paying miserly wages because the rest of the corporate community did likewise, and asserted that nothing could be gained through a strike. During the negotiations, the union learned, GE had been secretly meeting with other large corporations in New York City to explore ways to force down wages even more and destroy their unions. Schenectady's UE Local 301 approved a vote to join a national strike against General Electric on January 15, 1946.

200,000 workers for General Electric and Westinghouse walked off their jobs all over the country on that freezing January day in the Northeast. The following week, they were joined by 800,000 steelworkers. It was the first and only time in history that America's largest industries were shuttered by unified union actions. Only a decade past its founding, the United Electrical,

Radio and Machine Workers had declared war on the largest electrical manufacturing companies in the world.

In Schenectady, which contained the biggest UE local of all, the union's executive board installed strike committees right away – picketing, publicity, kitchens, community relations, fund-raising, entertainment, and others – and Helen served on several. The union ensured a mass of strikers at every gate and no one was allowed to pass in or out of the plant. Picket rosters were established, and members received picket cards which were punched whenever they reported for picket-line duty. But they faced record-breaking cold during their two-hour shifts every day. Steel barrels at each gate held constant fires. A trolley car was parked at the front gate to provide temporary respite from the weather. Families and friends brought coffee and soup and hot food, and the union's welfare committee made sure their members' families had financial support for rent and heat. Helen pretty much lived at the union hall during the strike. She showed up to picket when it was her turn, but a separate need occurred to her:

> *I got permission to drive a beat-up car which one of the union members had donated. This car had loudspeakers mounted on the roof, with a record player and microphone inside. My friend Bert and I took over this car. We drove from gate to gate, playing music and announcing news. Sometimes we would bring other women and we would get the strikers to join in and dance. We passed out song sheets and led the strikers in singing as they marched. Before the strike was over, the strikers had learned some famous union songs:*

Solidarity Forever, We Will Overcome, We Shall Not Be Moved, Joe Hill, Roll the Union On, and others. Of course, we also sang The Star-Spangled Banner, God Bless America, *and other well-known songs. This helped relieve the monotony of just walking the line and helped to keep morale high.*

One month after the strike began, on February 16, GE's attorneys won an injunction against the strike. But that judgment only strengthened the union's resolve. 20,000 members joined the picket lines and, for the next five weeks, not one person entered General Electric's main plant. Finally, a full nine weeks in, the company cried uncle, and agreed to President Truman's original compromise offer of eighteen and a half cents an hour – one dollar and forty-eight cents a day more. CEO Wilson had tried to keep women employees of all ages, whom he called "bobbysoxers," fixed at a fifteen-cents-an-hour jump, but the union had refused his offer and continued the strike until women received the same wage raise as men. And in May of that year, Local 301 also forced another three-cent–an-hour pay hike for women workers to help correct GE's prior discriminatory practices. While the raises seem miniscule by today's standards, they were substantial in 1946. Moreover, the union had accomplished what no one thought possible. It had defeated one of the most powerful corporations in America.

Helen's father, however, couldn't forgive her for joining the union, for acting like a Communist, and for her ingratitude toward the company that he believed had built Schenectady.

Unapologetic, Helen said, "Neither one of us is going to change. Maybe I should move out. Just tell me when you want this to happen and I will leave." He answered, "The devil has got you." Her father suffered an aneurysm shortly after that, and underwent an operation in a New York City hospital. Helen used her vacation time to stay with him for that operation, and visited him every weekend for a month until he died in September of 1946. After his death, Helen gave up her dream of going to college. She had spent all her savings on transportation, lodging and food attending to her father. So she stayed on at GE until she retired, being elected an officer in UE Local 301, being red-baited like all the officers were, and becoming "a leader in the fight for equal rights for women."

But most Americans were tired of thinking about wars – military or labor or any other kind in 1946. They had lost more than 400,000 people to WWII, defeated "Roberto" – the Axis powers of fascism – and survived four years of strict rationing. Wasn't it high time for marriages and babies, building their families in new, modern houses, getting back to work, and thanking their lucky stars they could enjoy the conveniences and diversions of peacetime? General Electric, expanding enormously to meet pent-up postwar demand for consumer products, turned back to its reliable domestic appliance lines as well as niche-market industrial products. And the country was in a spending mood, poised to believe again in GE's tagline of the era, *You can put your*

confidence in General Electric.

People snapped up two-door, refrigerator-freezer combinations, and new washing machines that had been supercharged with methods GE had developed building bazookas during the war. Fast-food pioneers grabbed custom-matched cooking equipment and electronic ovens that thawed and cooked meals in a couple of minutes. Railroad companies wanted the first gas-turbine electric locomotives produced in America through a GE/ALCO partnership. Aircraft companies needed improved jet engines for their Stratojet bombers. And everybody bought GE's better-than-ever, black-and-white televisions with their two-to-one brightness enhancement so they could relax with "Queen for a Day," "You Bet Your Life," or "The Ed Sullivan Show."

Even as it ramped up to satisfy consumer desires, though, General Electric couldn't escape its costly fights with UE. The company was stung by two more strikes, in 1947 and 1948, that won an additional two-dollars-a-day pay hike for all factory workers and not only forced GE to pay for vacations again but also made it compensate employees for six holidays when they weren't even working. That finally broke the camel's back. Firstly, the company helped to engineer the Taft-Hartley anti-labor law, written by the National Association of Manufacturers and the U. S. Chamber of Commerce. Passed in 1947, the national legislation contained numerous labor-weakening provisions, among them the demand that all labor leaders sign a non-communist affidavit. In unison, GE's CEO, Charles Wilson declared, "The problems of the United States can be summed up in two words: *Russia* abroad and *Labor* at home." With a new Cold War mentality gripping America, the Congress of Industrial Organizations expelled eleven "Left Wing" unions, Schenectady's Local 301 among them, for being "Communist-dominated." The tide of public sentiment was turning.

Secondly, Charles Wilson appointed his Vice President for Industrial Relations, Lemuel Boulware, to initiate a comprehensive public relations campaign to influence the general public and to turn union members against each other. Boulware found a charismatic, out-of-work actor named Ronald Reagan to deliver conservative, pro-GE speeches all across America, and to host a national television series called "GE Theater," which ran from 1954 through 1961. At the same time, Boulware completely revamped the company's bargaining policy, introducing the slogan, "Do the right thing voluntarily, but nothing under duress." That translated pragmatically to no real negotiations on GE's part. Make an initial offer, meet and listen for months at the bargaining table, and then present a "first and final" contract offer – unchanged from the company's original offer. With its propaganda working to shift attitudes and this new non-negotiating strategy, General Electric didn't care if the union walked out for ten years at a time: they had done the right thing voluntarily, and would do no more under the duress of a strike. Boulware's campaign worked so effectively that many members quit the union, and strikes basically failed for almost twenty years.

However, General Electric in Schenectady did far more than merely support the public face of Boulwarism to break up the unions. In fact, the corporation began to implement a far-reaching master plan – decentralization. In 1955, 85% of GE employees worked in seven major plants, and the strongest unions existed in those places. A new president, Ralph Cordiner, proposed "a plant in every cornfield," dispersing the company's operations into 100 separate departments, each run by a powerful unit manager.

Chris Hunter, Vice President of Collections and Exhibitions at the Museum of Innovation and Science in Schenectady, is in charge of the extensive General Electric archives there. Chris contends that while General Electric was primarily a company based in the Northeast for its first sixty years, that model wouldn't fly in the second half of the 20th century. "In response to getting its butt kicked by the unions, the executive committee of the board of directors came up with a plan to decentralize the company," Chris explained. "On the one hand, it was getting so big that no one person could manage it all. But on the other hand, the company needed to decentralize not just organizationally but geographically."

Several dozen GE satellites were formed over the next fifteen years: Syracuse, New York for Electronics Park; Louisville, Kentucky for Appliance Park; Rome, Georgia; Columbia, South Carolina; Roanoke and Waynesboro in central Virginia; Small Motor Business in Springfield, Missouri; Atomic Products in San Jose, California, and so many more. Within a year or two, in the mid-50s, GE had amassed 117 plants in twenty-four states. Only a few years later, though, by 1961, it had increased to 170 plants in 134 locations spread throughout America. As many of Schenectady's departments were shipped off to their own faraway cornfields, employee ranks at the original company headquarters had plummeted by close to 20,000 workers in only fifteen years.

PROGRESS REPORT: 1961

Schenectady GE Employees:	25,200
Schenectady Population:	79,700
GE Net Earnings:	$242,100,000.00
GE Tagline of the Time:	*Progress for people*

Decentralization brightened the future for General Electric, but it pretty much ruined Schenectady. Over the next forty years, GE would become a prototypical global corporation and demonstrate its dominance in myriad ways. By 1997, the global corporation contained a number of the most profitable companies in the country, if not the world, leading *Business Week's* list of Top 100 Companies in Market Value for the second year in a row. The corporation's $240 billion market value was fifty billion dollars more than its closest competitor, Royal Dutch/ Shell, and almost 100 billion more than Microsoft that year. With its 270,000 employees world-

wide, General Electric could boast annual revenues greater than all but forty-eight of the 185 countries that comprised the United Nations. However, in Schenectady, GE had chipped away at its employee population, downsizing from a high of 45,000 during WWII to less than 5,000 in the late 90s, with the most precipitous drop occurring after 1985. What happened?

Jack Welch, that's what happened. Neutron Jack, they dubbed him: nuke the people, leave the buildings. Although, to be honest, plenty of GE's buildings at the main plant in Schenectady were demolished as well, primarily to get them off the city's tax rolls, when Jack grabbed the reins of power.

4

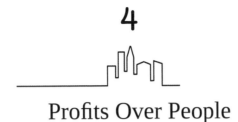

Profits Over People

*A proper balance between shareholders, employees,
and communities is what we all try to achieve.
But it is a tough balancing act because, in the end,
if you don't satisfy shareholders, you don't have the flexibility
to do the things you have to do to take care of employees
or communities. In our society, like it or not,
we have to satisfy shareholders.*

*— Jack Welch Speaks: Wisdom from the
World's Greatest Business Leader*

Operations at Schenectady's main plant were sometimes antiquated, to say the least, before Jack Welch took over as Chairman of General Electric in 1981 and, to use the kindest word possible, *streamlined* everything. For instance, after Bill Leader completed his three-year, Financial Management Program training course, he was given a series of managerial assignments across GE businesses in Schenectady. As Manager of General Accounting, he kept the books for all of the energy business field there:

When I first took that job, and this would be late '70s, I walked into that office and there was a pile of paper five-foot high on the floor of letters and complaints from people who hadn't been paid, and they had just migrated to a new accounts-payable system. So in my infinite wisdom, I threw all the letters away and I said, "If you haven't been paid yet, you're going to write to me again. We'll start fresh." Sure enough, they did. At times I would take a check that we had generated in the system and I would meet a vendor at Albany Airport to pay them, hand them a check. This was before we had electronic transfers and things like that. They didn't want it in the mail. They'd come and pick it up in person. I'm talking millions of dollars. All the vendors who supplied castings and equipment and things like that to GE – all the raw materials that the energy business needed to produce their steam turbines and generators. Millions of dollars.

In the Jack Welch era, inefficiencies were rooted out along with anyone who couldn't produce what he demanded. Jack touted his "vitality curve:" identify the top 20% of employees and nurture them but, at the same time, find the bottom 10% who aren't producing and get rid of them. Again, Bill Leader:

It was part of making GE lean and mean and productive. GE is always about the bottom line. Always about cost-cutting. Always about productivity. Always working hard. Everybody was worried about whether or not they were going to be let go. Probably one of the toughest things I had to do as a manager every year in GE was to evaluate my employees, and we had to identify the bottom 10% of our employees, in terms of performance. And we either had to develop a plan to fix those employees or get rid of them. Pretty soon you're down to some damned good people that you have to deal with. Unpleasant, but that was the Jack Welch approach, you know. If you didn't make your commitments with Jack Welch, you were history. It wasn't what you did for me before. What did you do for me today?

By his own admission, Jack Welch was all about WINNING, by cultivating the strong and culling the weak. That's even the title of one of his ghost-written books, and his own life reads like an obsessive playbook in squashing the competition. In his "distinctive, no b.s." management manual, *Winning*, Jack lays out his rationalizations for pursuing business dominance right near the beginning:

- Winning in business is great because when companies win, people thrive and grow.

- There will be more jobs and more opportunities everywhere and for everyone.

- People will feel upbeat about the future. They'll have the resources to send their kids to college, get better health care, buy vacation homes, and secure a comfortable retirement.

- Winning gives them the opportunity to give back to society in hugely important ways beyond just paying more taxes.

- Winning companies and the people who work for them are the engine of a healthy economy. In providing the revenues for government, they are the foundation of a free and democratic society.

- Winning lifts everyone it touches – it just makes the world a better place.

In his autobiography, *Jack: Straight from the Gut*, Welch traces his competitive streak to being co-captain and lead scorer on his high school hockey team in Salem, Massachusetts, where his mother stormed into the locker room after the final loss of his senior season and admonished him, "If you don't know how to lose, you'll never know how to win!" And as a boy, Jack stuttered badly, but his mother reassured him, "It's because you're so smart. No one's tongue could keep up with a brain like yours." Fully armed then with a potent brand of myopic self-confidence by his mother, Jack pursued a quest throughout his career at GE to differentiate himself – "getting out of the pile," as he called it.

At only forty-four years old, he elbowed his way past rivals until he landed on top, succeeding Reg Jones as CEO. And once there, he needed to win every encounter with every business rival during General Electric's *We bring good things to life* era, claiming his Darwinian methods actually stemmed from his demanding nature and the sensitivity he needed to display in his "stewardship" role as GE Chairman. And by the capitalist standards of business in America, Jack did pretty damned well: when he retired in 2001, relinquishing his $2,500,000 package of perks that included courtside seats at Knicks games, the U.S. Open, and Wimbledon, as well as box seats at all Yankees and Red Sox home games, Jack's walk-away retirement package totaled $417,361,902. That's right, almost 420 million dollars. However, GE's shareholders, whose stock increased exponentially during Welch's tenure, may not resent that retirement figure quite as much as the thousands of employees who lost their jobs in Schenectady because of him.

Karen Johnson, who was the city's first female mayor during the initial decade of Jack Welch's reign, served two terms from 1983 to 1991. As she relates here, dealing with the constant layoffs and their consequences fell directly to her:

> *Now remember that many of the workers at General Electric had come back from fighting in World War II and they were nearing their regular retirement age, and people were retiring like mad. Neutron Jack Welch certainly wanted to get rid of a lot of workers, but there was a lot of natural attrition that occurred, too, so that by the time I was mayor, it finally hit and people really did notice what was happening.*
>
> *GE didn't make their decisions with any input from me, of course, and they had a regular routine on Fridays. Friday was a slow-news day at City Hall – they just didn't cover us then as much as on the other days – so on Fridays, GE higher-ups would go to the unions, and then to the managers, and then they would come to me and tell me what was going on. I guess, when it did hit the papers, they wanted me to be a little bit prepared. They*

communicated with me, but I certainly didn't have any belief that I could affect the downsizing decisions at the company.

When I finally decided not to run for re-election, aside from the GE decisions, I was spending all my time laying off people who worked for the City. I was near the end of my term, and the person who was supposed to do our personnel work wasn't being too effective, so I was working with the union and firing people myself. Our union at the time was American Federation of State and Local Employees – AFSLE. But we would be sitting there at the table and I would give the union the list and we would go through and decide who we should go to in the first instance, because it isn't necessarily the one you name who gets laid off. There was seniority.

That was one of the most depressing times of my life, because peoples' livelihoods, their pensions – everything about them – was under threat. And the City had all these really good jobs with excellent benefits, and some people in town may or may not have realized it, but I think a lot of the people who worked for the City did. But we had nothing we could do, and no spare money. We were looking for any idea we could come up with. And there was a certain amount of drag on the budget because you still had to pave the streets, keep the streetlights paid for, and on and on, so there were just a lot of expenses. And when your tax base isn't going up, you're really under a lot of pressure. So we did a few projects, things where we could get grants. But all together, it was a very hard time.

Mary Kuykendall, in her tell-all book about her years at General Electric, *Rebuilding the GE House That Jack Blew Down*, ascribes Welch's 180-degree turn-around from the program of increasing productivity by investing in modern equipment and processes favored by Reg Jones to one that transformed GE into a financial company. "Welch would sell off product businesses and advanced technology," she writes, "to the point where 85% of GE revenues came from financial services and just 15% from what was left of products." Welch himself extolled the major shift away from GE's traditional, industrial concerns – making useful products – to a reliance on GE Capital, the financial arm of the corporation: "From that small base in 1977, a business earning 67 million with fewer than 7,000 employees, GE Capital has grown explosively. In 2000, the business had $5.2 billion in earnings, with more than 89,000 employees," he boasted.

Jack's message to all his managers when he took over in 1981 was, "Become Number One or Two in your business. Fix, sell, or close!" as Kuykendall reports it.

Jack Welch wouldn't argue with that assessment. In his first speech to Wall Street analysts about his vision for the new GE, he said that the "winners of the future would be companies that search out and participate in the real growth industries and insist upon being either number one or two in every business they are in – the number one or number two leanest, lowest-cost, world-wide producers of quality goods and services." He assured them that managements and companies in the 1980s who hang on to losers wouldn't last until 1990. And then he got to work selling and closing the marginal performers.

In his first two years as CEO, Jack sold seventy-one businesses and product lines and made a little over 500 million dollars from them. That was peanuts, so he looked for more lucrative businesses to liquidate. GE's central air-conditioning business went to Trane Co. for 135 million. Utah International, which sold metallurgical coal to the Japanese and contained a small U.S. oil and gas company, went for

2.4 billion to Australia-based Broken Hill Proprietary. GE Housewares – which included steam irons, toasters, hair dryers, and blenders – landed on the chopping block after that. Jack Welch did a quick survey to see how much the corporation benefited from having its famous logo on all these smaller products, and concluded that nobody much cared or noticed anymore. Dismissing small appliances as not so valuable to GE – and therefore outside his three essential circles of core manufacturing, high technology, and services – he peddled what he called this "low-tech, tin-bending housewares business" to Black and Decker for 300 million.

Within Jack's first five years on the job, one of every four people on GE's payroll – 118,000 employees – would lose their jobs. 37,000 of them held jobs in the businesses that were sold. By 1990, nine years after he took over as head of the company, he had dispensed with more than 200 businesses in the United States and freed up eleven billion dollars of capital. As Mary Kuykendall notes, "His major drive now was to turn GE into a financial company to make huge profits fast by buying, harvesting, and selling businesses here as well as offshore, in addition to providing financial services. Thus, he began touting the company as a global player." The soaring profits insulated Jack Welch. After all, he always met his earnings predictions, didn't he? No matter what went away or who got hurt, the Board of Directors hardly ever complained. Managers who followed his lead saw their stock options balloon from six million in 1981 to fifty-two million in 1985. And GE's stock price just kept rising so, after the stock had split several times, GE's shareholders couldn't have been happier.

However, there were those pesky labor problems to be handled. Decade after decade, union demands and costly strikes had remained a tedious fact of life for General Electric executives. From GE's perspective, the pattern usually demanded heated negotiations, early refusals to concede, advertising campaigns to sway public opinion, eventual surrender to some union demands followed by modest financial losses, which were, eventually and incrementally, answered with retaliatory repercussions. Pressure would diminish for a while, then start building year by year until, as Yogi Berra opined, it was déjà vu all over again.

But the strike that began in October of 1969 – the first countrywide action against GE since the national strike in 1946 – was a whole different ballgame. 150,000 workers walked off the job, and picketed for 102 days. The U.S Second Court of Appeals had sided with the unions, ruling that General Electric had once more reverted to Boulwarism – employing "sham discussions instead of genuine arguments –" and had refused to engage in good-faith bargaining. Apart from the fact that GE lost seventy-nine million dollars in that strike – earnings plunged 88% in the fourth quarter of 1969 and overall profits fell by 22% for the entire year – what really hurt the company was the unity built on those picket lines between its various unions. The new contract that resulted allowed them to wrest significant improvements from GE for years, without having their members struggle to survive during painful strikes. And none of these developments were lost on a young and determined Jack Welch as he rose through the ranks. Enough was enough. When he took over, he found simpler ways to combat the unions: sell businesses, lay off employees, and move operations

to non-union states. The gas turbine unit of GE Power was relocated to Greenville, South Carolina, and that left only the faltering steam turbine unit in Schenectady.

Bob Farley, currently Senior Counsel with the New York State Senate, worked briefly in the legal department at General Electric in Schenectady during the Welch reign. Bob was in his third year of law school in 1986, and there were thirty-six lawyers in that department when Bob became a legal intern. The company liked his work so much that they offered him a job. Bob refused, not only because the department had dwindled to three lawyers by the time he graduated twelve months later, in 1987, but because everything at the main plant was tanking:

> *I did that because I knew GE was in a power dive. I saw people who were fifty years old, with kids in college, weeping as they cleaned out their offices and went home. Gas turbine was lost, and that left the company with large steam turbine for their primary operation in Schenectady, which constructed power plants for two types of power generators. One was coal, and another was nuclear power. And after the Three Mile Island meltdown, you didn't build another nuclear power plant in the United States. And for the coal-generating power plants, GE's only steam turbine business with them was providing spare parts, because everybody was going to gas and they had moved gas turbine out of town. And even in the '80s, steam turbines cost four billion dollars, so a spare parts business was significant.*
>
> *But the only orders for new turbines that the company was doing were overseas. They were selling to India, and they were selling to China, but those contracts would be outbid by literally a billion dollars by the Germans and the French and other electrical power companies that were subsidized by their national governments. So GE simply couldn't compete on the product line that they were selling from Schenectady. And at that time, Jack Welch basically said, "If you don't make money, I don't really want to have much to do with you." Plus, Jack hated manufacturing, he wanted to divest out of manufacturing, which turned out to be insane. That's why GE today is having problems. The one thing he did was dump a lot of money into the R&D facility here in Niska-*

yuna, because his dear friend, Walt Robb, worked there, and Walt
was the one who had hired Jack in the first place.

It's important to note, then, a couple of things: firstly, worldwide competition was bludgeoning one of GE's last basic businesses in Schenectady, so any CEO at that time would have been up against the prevailing global and political realities. If you don't have sufficient demand, you have to make cuts – otherwise you'll be out of business. And number two, not everyone hated Jack Welch. Plenty of people who worked with him and for him expressed unqualified admiration. Walt Robb, who was in charge of the Chemical Engineering group at the General Electric Research and Development Center when Jack became Chairman, praised his methods:

> *When Jack Welch took over, he started moving businesses to Atlanta, and to places that did not have unions. The labor union not giving in to Jack, that was too much. The world had a different reality, and the Schenectady union wasn't willing to work with him. The union's inability to change, to accept the new global environment, that was the true problem, not Jack. And the work rules, God, he took some tours through the Schenectady steam turbine plant and he couldn't believe the number of workers standing all the time. He put in new managers who saw this was the case. He needed to increase efficiency and lower salaries, because of the competition. Siemens and other companies were being much more aggressive. For years, GE and Westinghouse sort of had the game to themselves.*

Jan Smith, who was a Human Resources manager and who took over GE's Communications Department after Len Doviak died, was an ardent supporter:

> *Jack was a driver, he was quite a man, and he wanted more activity, he wanted more focus, he wanted those kinds of things. And he wanted to be able to expand the business, and that's what they*

were here to do. He got people who were more focused on getting the future in order, as opposed to perhaps spending a little less time on the past. Sometimes there was hiring and sometimes there were layoffs that needed to happen. I remember that at various sundry times, we had them, and I remember defending the position. Although I have to say, and I'll give GE a compliment on this one, I really will. There was a lot of climate setting, people knew ahead of time, unlike some companies where you get up one morning and somebody gives you a pink slip. And GE was working with him to help a lot of those people who were laid off start other businesses.

But the truth, in the long history of America, is the history of company towns where the companies have either left or closed or changed. That's the history of America. You can look at Lowell, you can look at the Midwest, all these manufacturing towns, Schenectady was just another manufacturing town where the business changed. That's the problem with company towns. GE had no desire to crush the city at all. I mean, it wasn't that; it was how do we do it together so that we can all continue to move forward.

CNBC, owned by General Electric in the '90s, called Jack Welch a business genius. *Fortune* dubbed him "Manager of the Century." Add to those endorsements the fact that investors in General Electric stock certainly appreciated what Welch's ten-billion-dollar buyback strategy in 1989 did for their portfolios. As Thomas F. O'Boyle points out in *At Any Cost: Jack Welch, General Electric, and the Pursuit of Profit*, "After fifty-one consecutive quarters of earnings gains, after increasing the value of GE's stock from twelve billion in 1981 to ninety billion early in 1994 and making the company the most valuable and arguably the most powerful in the United States, Jack Welch at fifty-eight had earned, by most measures, the right to universal acclaim."

Increasing shareholder value, making tons of money, and building the company's stock price for its shareholders were Jack's signature missions, as he often said. Therein lay the dilemma for so many people in Schenectady who had worked for General Electric: they had good pensions from the company, they had bought a lot of GE stock over the years, and many of their retirements rested on the value of that stock. They didn't see the virtue in bad-mouthing a company whose profitable future would guarantee their own. Moreover, as Bob Farley explains, "GE executives sat on every community board. They were very active in every not-for-profit and every civic organization, and they brought their culture to those organizations and into the community. GE dominated local society in Schenectady. So for people here, when they started to disappear – the only thing I can ever compare that to is like being a child of divorced parents. You can go back through the letters to the editor in the *Daily Gazette*, or the statements by our politicians. They saw GE leaving and they all said the same thing: 'What can we do? How do we get GE to come back?'"

Slowly, though, shock turned to resentment, as it often will in broken families. Maybe if GE's stock price had not tanked in the 2008 recession – so that a share today is worth, conservatively, eighty percent less than its value twenty years ago – and if the corporation were not struggling to recover from many of Jack's short-term decisions that proved so damaging to it in the long run, perhaps more people in Schenectady could revert to prior loyalties and feel some gratitude for what Welch accomplished. But even people who worked their whole careers there have pretty much soured on the guy now. As Bernie Witkowski, who worked as a GE electrician for thirty-one years, succinctly characterizes Jack, "After he took over, there was nothing but layoffs."

PROGRESS REPORT: 2000

Schenectady GE Employees:	4,700
Schenectady Population:	61,821
GE Net Earnings:	$12,735,000,000.00
GE Tagline of the Time:	*Imagination at work*

Cities often begin with dreams. Explorers, generals, politicians, business leaders, developers, company presidents, and other movers and shakers often get to manifest their urban visions in the real world and ordinary citizens inherit the actual conse-quences – utopian or dystopian or somewhere in between – and regular workers in their engineered cities almost inevitably end up fighting for their fair share. One company, General Electric, transformed life in Schenectady for over a century, offering a small, nondescript town the chance not only to grow exponentially but also to be an early home for one of the world's most productive and powerful corporations.

Its huge corporate logo – 150 feet long, 70 feet tall, and lit by 1,400 incandescent lamps when it first appeared atop Building 37 in October of 1932 – still glows every night, its watchful "meatball" assuring Schenectady of its continuing, tangible presence, of course, but perhaps also as a reminder to the citizens that they owe an intangible but massive debt to the company that built their city. Maybe you can't blame the past generations of workers and the retired beneficiaries of General Electric for once believing that life would always be better with GE. Even today, when you search for information on this multi-national corporation that seems ever ready to recast its history and underscore its many achievements, leaving out the inconve-

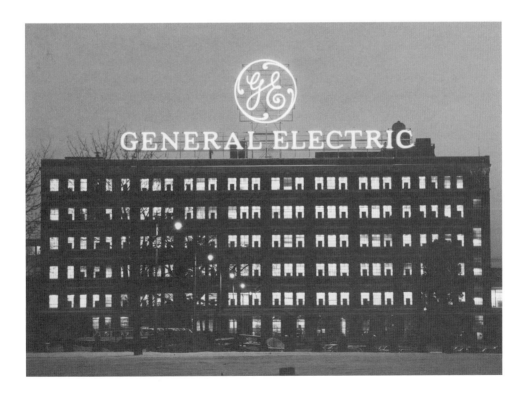

nient bits about what has been jettisoned, you can almost be forgiven if you swallow its origin story:

Do you know GE?

Admittedly, it's not easy. We create things that build, move, power, and cure our world, and we do this in over 180 countries. You probably know our founder, Thomas Edison, developed the light bulb, but he also took this idea further by building our first electrical grid. This powerful network brought electricity into our homes, workplaces, and everywhere in between. Edison also established a mindset, and a brand that stands for making our world work better. His own words, "I find out what the world needs and then proceed to invent it," are a promise to live in the present, keep an eye on the future, anticipate what the world needs, and make it happen. As brand builders, we ask ourselves, how do we express our ideas more effectively? How do we use brand to signal who we are, what we are doing, and where we are headed?

Without question, though, to be fair, General Electric has to be counted among the greatest American corporations of the last 125 years. The company of *"We bring good things to life"* and *"Imagination at work"* can boast a staggering string of first accomplishments: the X-ray machine; the electric locomotive; the original air-tight refrigerator; the trans-oceanic radio system that helped the Allies win WWII; the first electric range, the Hotpoint; a supercharger jet engine; fluorescent lighting; the initial television network; a cloud-seeding process that unleashed rain; autopilot systems; a toaster oven; synthetic diamonds; the first licensed nuclear power plant; LED lights; silicone chemistry, which produced the boots worn by Neil Armstrong when he walked on the moon; solid-state lasers; magnets that allowed the invention of the MRI; self-cleaning ovens; and technological contributions that created industrial plastics, early electronics, innovative power generation, and literally thousands of other inventions that have facilitated and defined human progress since the late 19th Century. Although the corporation has struggled during the last twenty years to recover from many of Jack Welch's decisions and actions, GE has been, and remains, an estimable force in the global business landscape.

However, things do change: In June of 2018, GE was thrown off the Dow Jones Industrial Average, and replaced by Walgreen Boots Alliance (WBA), so the last of the original twelve members of the Dow index has finally been kicked to the curb. Jack Welch died at 84 on March 1, 2020, and his good pal, Walt Robb, succumbed to Covid-19 – the first person in Schenectady County to die of that disease – three weeks later, on March 23. General Electric's charitable foundation recently announced it will no longer match contributions made by its retirees, and that will have a serious impact on Schenectady's non-profit sector. And now, despite its continued boasting about Edison and "electrifying the world," General Electric opted most recently to sell its lighting division to Savant Systems, Inc. of Massachusetts. The people who "build, power, move, and cure the world" will no longer illuminate it.

At the same time, some things, inevitably, stay the same: the week GE revealed the lighting division divestment, it announced it would slash 13,000 jobs from its jet-engine operation. One month after that, the company said it has plans to eliminate 120 jobs in Schenectady County – almost half of those at its turbine and generator business in the city – and send some of those jobs to Poland and Switzerland. Maybe it was misguided and parochial for people in Schenectady to take General Electric's business decisions now or during the 1980s and '90s so personally – it has always been a corporation founded and managed to make as much profit as possible, right? – or to portray its corporate strategies of consistent downsizing and business relocations as any kind of a betrayal. Business, after all, is business. But those things did happen then, causing untold pain and suffering, and the corporation's usual obfuscation might lead one to believe it isn't so terribly different now.

Even though GE is still a major employer and an essential presence in Schenectady, most residents no longer consider the company a guiding light for the local economy. Hard-won self-reliance over the past twenty-five years has produced a much-envied economic revitalization that has been forged by a diverse group of philanthropists, merchants, community leaders, civic volunteers, educators, archi-

tects, non-profit organizations, developers, artists, and politicians, to say nothing of Metroplex, its unique and highly-effective economic development authority.

However, thirty years ago, that unusual consortium for change didn't exist. Anyone who was able to read the writing on the wall back then realized that rebuilding their city would take far more than General Electric hiring back some of its furloughed employees. By 1990, Schenectady had become a violent dump, no two ways about it. In the middle of that long-lived crisis, it may have been hard to divine the future, but a couple of things were abundantly clear: one, the city was critically wounded and someone with vision had to step in and stop the bleeding; and two, if residents wanted their city to survive, they would have to rely on themselves.

5

Who Makes the Future?

Whose responsibility is it to make our cities?
While the forms they take are usually unintentional,
cities are not mere accidents … Good city-making
requires myriad acts of persistence and courage
that need to be aligned like a good piece of music.
There is not just one conductor, which is why leader-
ship in its fullest sense is so important – seemingly
disparate parts have to be melded into a whole.

– The Art of City Making
Charles Landry

Billy Crystal plays a Borscht-belt comedian named Buddy Young in *Mr. Saturday Night*, and in the voice-over interview that accompanies the title sequence, he jokes about starving family members who emigrated to America from Russia: "In my family, my uncle Schmooklik, when he came here and saw a supermarket for the first time, he proposed to a brisket … although there was talk he had to." That movie was released in 1992, the same year that Bill Golub was in and out of Ellis Hospital and Sunnyview Rehabilitation Center, fighting for his life, so chances are he never saw the movie. If he had, he would have loved it, not only because it started off with a line that included a supermarket and a brisket, but because he loved entertaining dinner companions with jokes himself.

Throughout his career, Bill always carried a small notebook in his pocket that was filled with one-liners, observations, and ironic adages, in tiny print, all of which he labeled "Words of Wisdom:"

– *Statistics are the human beings with tears wiped off.*

– *To carry a grudge is like being stung to death by one bee.*

– *Short order cook: a frequent fryer.*

– *A prayer for atheists – they call and no one answers.*

– *I can pinpoint the exact time our marriage fell apart.*
  After we bought a waterbed, my wife and I kind of drifted apart.

– *We work to become, not to acquire.*

– *On getting old: I'd rather be over the hill than under it.*

Even after he was diagnosed with a chronic and debilitating condition, Bill Golub added humorous entries to that notebook and hauled them out at all kinds of events as he pursued ways to lead a purposeful life and to dream up schemes to revitalize his failing hometown. He had retired in 1982 from the supermarket chain he and his brother, Ben, had built – called Central Market at first, Price Chopper later on, and now Market 32 – but beginning in the mid-1980s, he gradually found it harder and harder to maintain his morning exercise regimen. Finally, his doctor diagnosed him with polymyositis, an inflammatory disease that depletes your muscles because your immune system is attacking its own healthy body tissues, and told him there was no cure for it. What Bill knew was that his legs ached more and more during his daily, hour-long workouts, and that he felt weaker with every new year. In spite of that, his autoimmune disorder didn't keep him from trying to help others.

During one stay in Sunnyview, for example, he saw that wheelchair-bound patients had trouble getting into the pool for hydrotherapy, so Bill commissioned the Watervliet Arsenal to make two massive, cannon-like pistons that could raise and lower the entire pool floor for easier access: the new pool came up to let them enter, and then went down to immerse them in the water. And in one of his last stays at the rehabilitation center, he established a humor clinic. He knew first-hand the healing power of humor. He had spent most of his life trying to make people laugh, after all, and who needs humor more than sick people? So he stocked a reading room with funny books and magazines to lift patients' spirits and brighten their days at the center.

Philanthropy, volunteering, and organizing civic initiatives had always been an important part of Bill's life and faith, expressed as *tikkun olam* – literally, repairing the world through human actions – and he honored that responsibility during his career and throughout his retirement. He financed a major renovation of his synagogue, Temple Gates of Heaven, and donated the Family Park at Schenectady's Jewish Community Center. Bill was dubbed "Mr. Kids Day" for standing on downtown street corners and selling newspapers to benefit the Kiwanis program to benefit children. However, the lifelong cornerstone of his commitment was his pioneering work in developing the original, modern food markets that have evolved now into the Price Chopper, Market 32 and Market Bistro stores spread throughout the Northeast. Providing the highest-quality food for people and communities was an essential service that Bill Golub and his family always took seriously, even if many people consider the supermarket business just another potentially-lucrative, commercial enterprise.

However, success and money were hard-won and came late for Bill Golub. In the mid-1920s, Bill and Ben had graduated from college and joined their father in his wholesale grocery business. In those days, people had to visit separate shops to buy their eggs and poultry, meat, fish, canned and packaged goods, produce, and dairy products. No one-stop shopping in the good old days, not until August of 1930 when Mike Cullen opened King Kullen Grocery Company in Jamaica, New York – the first supermarket in America. Soon after that, Mike Cullen visited his friends, the Golubs, in Schenectady and told them, "You're driving a hearse. Go retail." So they did. But when Bill's father died later that same year, he left not only a struggling new business but also an unwelcome partnership with Joe Grosberg, whose autocratic style plagued the Golub brothers until they bought out his interest in 1940.

Starting with the Public Service Market in Green Island, the Golubs quickly opened another supermarket in Schenectady on Eastern Parkway, switched the name to Central Market, and kept going from there. There were no how-to manuals for novel grocery enterprises in the 1930s, and the brothers built everything from scratch. Early on, there were no cash registers, no shopping carts, no metal-shelving displays, no sophisticated refrigeration to keep perishables from spoiling inside the stores, no stocked warehouses, and no delivery trucks. The big national retailers like A&P could use loss leaders and hot specials to offer discounts impossible to match and pressure the small, family-owned market chains into unprofitable promotions just to stay competitive. To counteract that pressure, sixteen small, non-competing food retailers, including Central Market, created an association named the Super Market Institute.

Through the decades of the Great Depression and World War II, the Golub brothers were often forced to run a hands-on, hand-to-mouth operation, inventing and creating as they went. Bill's son, Neil Golub, who is currently chairman of Price Chopper and Market 32, remembers his father taking him along on delivery trips in his car when he was nine or ten:

> In the old days, I would occasionally travel with my dad to the markets. I can remember sitting in the back seat as he was driving some hind-quarters of beef, or fore-quarters, to different stores. I remember specifically going once to Mechanicville. He had a hind-quarter, and every once in a while he'd throw a crate of chickens in the back with me. That was not good, because blood would mix with melted ice and spill all over the floor and stink. The chickens were killed and then packed in ice, and they weren't even eviscerated. They used to do that in the stores. And they weren't in cardboard boxes. They were packed in wooden crates.

Bill Golub provided the creative spark for the burgeoning supermarket business, and he operated under a simple theory: "If you try something that makes sense without blowing your brains out, you may learn something worthwhile." Plus, he respected everyone who worked for him – grocery clerks, delivery drivers, company executives, warehouse selectors, produce managers, or shelf stockers – encouraged all of them to offer their own ideas, and imparted that crucial lesson to Neil as well. If the new ideas worked, great, and if they didn't, get out fast and move on to the next one. That's how Central Market latched on to S&H Green Stamps in the 1950s. Spend a dollar, get a stamp. Spend ten bucks, get ten stamps, paste them into a little book, fill up some books and redeem them for products at your S&H Rewards Store – from everyday cutlery to sterling silver, bath towels, sheets, pillows, small appliances, whatever strikes your fancy. The key was discovering the new ideas that would work, and Bill was especially good at that.

Bill also established agreements with local farmers during the 1950s to be exclusive suppliers for locally-grown summer items, long before farm-to-table became a marketing trend in restaurants. He engineered a program with Cornell University that bolstered the local egg industry and became the Red Label Egg Program, and sponsored a 4-H seed program that not only spurred farmers' children to grow and sell products directly through the Golub supermarkets but also taught them food economics.

Another innovative notion was delegated to Neil when he was a district manager in charge of eight stores. The market in Oneonta, New York was part of a Jamesway department store, and it was under-performing. In February of 1969, Neil was charged with figuring out how to fix the problem and build the business. It was close to George Washington's birthday, and Neil's advertising vice-president suggested, "Why not name the store for the guy who chopped down the cherry tree and wouldn't tell a lie about it?" The Price Chopper brand was born in that moment and it stuck, to say the least, becoming the company brand for the following fifty years.

By the time he retired in 1982, the company had grown to fifty-eight stores with 8,000 employees, and Bill Golub had finally realized some financial security from his company stock, so he could devote more time to his volunteer concerns and retirement. The family started the Golub Foundation, and that has grown into a philanthropic operation which supports more than 1,500 organizations.

Near the end of the decade, though, Bill could no longer ignore the reality that Schenectady was in desperate need of repair. After the 1987 fire, Canal Square had never truly recovered, and almost all the downtown department stores had closed or re-located, one by one, until the last holdout, The Carl Co., finally shut its doors. It was no secret that General Electric had transferred much of its manufacturing operations to other states and gutted its local workforce, or that a third of Schenectady's population had abandoned the city during the last twenty years, but Bill wasn't about to give up on his hometown just because his body was failing him.

Bill convinced his pal from the Jewish Community Center, Ernie Kahn, to work with him, and enlisted Al Lawrence, a prominent local insurance broker to come on board, too. The mayor, Karen Johnson, pledged her support as well, even though they all realized she was struggling to balance the city's budget every single year. But if Robert Furman could get merchants to donate in 1886 and convince Thomas Edison to locate a new manufacturing venture in Schenectady, why couldn't they, together, make lightning strike for their city a hundred years later?

Nobody would visit a dying place unless they had a good reason to, Bill argued, and they just had to figure out what that compelling reason might be. So what if they could create one unique attraction that would lure tourists off Route 90, the nearby Thruway, and lead them to an exciting destination in a revitalized, up-and-coming city? What magic catalyst could they envision that would spur economic development in the area? They could build a hands-on museum of invention, maybe, to highlight GE's century of scientific innovation or – crazy as it sounded – perhaps situate a floating casino on a giant tour boat docked in the Mohawk River, the way Mayor Duci had once suggested, although Bill thought Duci's ideas were nuts most of the time. What about a semi-professional sports stadium, even though Bill wasn't much of a sports fan? For a couple of years, Bill threw idea after idea at the wall, but nothing seemed to stick. And then he just got too sick to keep going.

After he was released from Sunnyview Rehabilitation Center in June of 1990, Celebrating Schenectady 300, marking the 300th anniversary of the city, honored Bill Golub as Citizen of the Century, saying, "Through his personal contributions to many of Schenectady County's organizations, plus the works of the

Golub Foundation and Price Chopper, he has demonstrated his commitment to helping others and to strengthening the community, as well as working tirelessly on behalf of the people of Schenectady." Citizen of the Century, a remarkable achievement. "I can't possibly accept," Bill joked. "I'm not a century old yet. I'm only 88."

However, two months later, Bill's wife of sixty years, Estelle, passed away. His polymyositis worsened, and finally forced him back into Ellis Hospital. A little before he died in October of 1992, Bill said to Neil, "I was born here, but the city's become a piece of junk. Please continue my efforts. Let's do something for Schenectady. I'm willing to give a million dollars." At that moment, perhaps Bill remembered a story his parents had told him, the one about him as a baby in the house where Veeder Avenue met Broadway at the foot of Pleasant Valley, the house where the trolley ran out front, and where kids would place torpedo caps on the tracks to

Remembering Mr. Bill

Mr. William Golub, Chairman Emeritus, Golub Corporation
1904 - 1992

celebrate holidays, how loud the explosions were when the trolley wheels hit them, loud enough to scare people on the streets, loud enough to wake the midwife who was there to watch the infant Bill Golub, who was choking, turning blue in his crib, and how she revived him just in time. And now, maybe just in time for Schenectady, his money might help revive his city.

Almost thirty years ago, while a million dollars was no small pledge, especially for a man who had struggled for years to become financially secure, Bill's gift could only function as seed money when the ultimate goal was rebuilding a failing city. However, no one else had earmarked a bequest to address such a huge problem and, as it turned out, that million dollars achieved exactly what Bill Golub hoped it might, but not in a way that anyone could have predicted.

REVERSE SCHENECTADY'S DECLINE

Downtown Schenectady was once all hustle and bustle. It was the place to be, for businesses and people. Now the sidewalks are uncrowded at midday, and nearly empty at night. Vacant storefronts are visible everywhere. For anyone who remembers the old Schenectady, it is a poignant, discouraging sight.

With the growth of the suburbs and their shopping malls, downtown's decline may have been predictable, perhaps even inevitable. But it is not irreversible. Downtown will never again be the only place to shop or eat or conduct business, but it can thrive again. This isn't going to just happen, though; Schenectady residents must make it happen by getting involved in developing a plan for the city and seeing it through.

Schenectady 2000 is a good start, if for no other reason than that it has the support of some of the city's heaviest hitters. Their prestige, and some of their money, is at stake. Since the plan's introduction

this summer, they and George Robertson, the city's economic development chief, have worked hard to enlist volunteers and win community support.

The plan is right to focus, initially, on improving the looks of downtown. Perception is half the battle, and despite many beautiful buildings, much of downtown looks ugly and uninviting. Trees, uniform lighting, tasteful signs, flowers, and clean streets are no replacement for businesses and people but, as Saratoga Springs has shown, they create a pleasing environment that can attract them. We also like the fact that the plan doesn't pretend to be "the plan." While it offers some ideas and a process, it is designed to get citizens involved in developing their own plan.

– Excerpt from an October 31, 1993
editorial in *The Sunday Gazette*

In late 1993, the writing that spelled the demise of Schenectady was clearly on the wall, but many city residents refused to accept the words. Even with its relentless downsizing, a decimated General Electric remained the biggest corporate employer in town, and thousands of its local stockholders especially, confident in their steady stock returns, still harbored the notion that the company would halt its layoffs and help sponsor a return to the glory days before Jack Welch sold off so many of its company assets. Hardly anyone wanted to admit that a miraculous recovery was all but impossible. The realization that it was up to them if they wanted to save their city – that, simply, their illustrious, corporate parent had pretty much abandoned them for a new and distant family and they were now saddled with a do-it-yourself project – had not fully sunk in.

Moreover, as older residents died or unemployment forced more and more laid-off workers to sell or rent their family duplexes in Schenectady, a steady stream of downstate residents poured north and away from the tag team of Mayor Rudy Giuliani and Police Commissioner Bill Bratton during the early days of their broken-windows, stop-and-frisk war on lower-echelon criminals in the five boroughs of New York City. Posters in the subway system there even announced that welfare benefits were easier to obtain in Schenectady, specifically. It only made sense that people who were struggling to make ends meet in New York City would move up-state to seek a better quality of life. However, as it turned out, within the arriving waves of displaced renters, a smattering of experienced, more violent criminals from downstate altered the balance of power in some of Schenectady's neighborhoods for years to come.

But Neil Golub wasn't overly concerned about any of that. He was a man on a mission. To honor his father's dying wish, Neil wanted to develop a plan by 2000 that would redevelop Schenectady and contain a viable funding source. He enlisted several of his friends to help engineer what became Schenectady 2000, including Roger Hull, the president of Union College, George Robertson of the Schenectady Economic Development Corporation, and Wally Graham, head of Schenectady International, a chemical company that was founded and still headquartered in Schenectady County.

"This is the first official meeting of Schenectady 2000, and for many of us, it's going to be the first opportunity to kind of get a feeling of how some of the committees are working – a little about what's going on, where they're going, and when they hope to be there." That's how Neil Golub began the presentation about the extensive volunteer effort on January 20, 1994 in a meeting room donated for the evening by General Electric.

"I would just like to point out that we wanted to electrify the podium," Neil continued, "but we couldn't find anybody here who could do that. We do want to thank our friends at General Electric for providing this venue for our meeting, and I asked my friend here from GE what he could do and he said, 'I can't hook it up.'" Len Doviak, GE's public affairs manager in Schenectady, stood up and explained, "I'll say this again. I don't understand electricity. I'm serious. You may be like this, too. When I flip a switch and something goes on, I think it's a miracle."

This may have represented Schenectady 2000's opening rollout, but Neil and Roger Hull had been working on the project since Neil's father had died. During 1993, they had already hosted eighty-three private presentations around the city for

3,400 attendees, had organized thirty functioning committees inside fourteen task forces, and recruited 800 volunteers. The project's Communications Committee had broadcast its message through radio and television stations, and local newspapers had provided decent coverage of its progress. The purpose of the locally-televised, January 20th forum was to introduce spokespeople for those task forces and committees, to hear what their plans entailed, and to whip up greater enthusiasm for their shared endeavor in a broader audience. 800 volunteers might seem like a good start, but the city's plight posed a daunting challenge.

In 1993, none of us had smartphones in our pockets to offer the security of

instant communications or a vicarious escape route from our moment-to-moment lives. The World Wide Web was in its virtual infancy, so a dial-up Internet search to provide possible solutions for almost any dilemma would have just dangled out there in the virtual ether. Kickstarter, GoFundMe, and other online fundraising platforms weren't even fever dreams back then, and though Neil and Roger had utilized do-it-yourself crowdsourcing techniques to build their volunteer coalition, that buzz-word, "crowdsourcing," hadn't been invented yet either. Like most Rust Belt cities in America in the early 1990s, Schenectady was declining fast, and the modern tools of the Information Age didn't exist to provide at-your-fingertips revitalization mod-els from other cities. An ebbing financial tide had lowered most urban boats, and a slow slide toward bankruptcy seemed more than plausible. Schenectady's best bet at that time came down to the philanthropy, networking, and volunteer efforts of Neil Golub, Roger Hull, and some other concerned citizens.

"Foremost, I think," Neil continued, "what's most exciting is the willingness of the people in our community to take on what seems like a massive mountain to climb, and to have committed themselves to participating in a process that we know is difficult, that we know is going to take time, but is something for which we all have some feeling in our guts, if you will, that it is something that we can accomplish."

Then Roger took hold of the baton: "This project will work. There's absolutely no doubt in my mind that it will work. There is some question in some peoples' minds as to whether it goes *far* enough. There are many projects that we can un-dertake, but so long as we keep focused on the primary thing which is, in my mind, to change the attitudes and feelings of people in this community *towards* the com-munity, we will achieve a positive result in the final analysis. The point I would like to emphasize again is that this project will work, and it will work because it will be a combination of public and private, for profit and not for profit, people throughout this community who believe in it and who realize there are challenges to be faced and who are willing to face them. You know, I have a two-year-old at home and his favorite book for me to read to him is *The Little Engine that Could* – 'I think I can. I think I can. I think I can.'"

In the long pause that followed, Neil leaned toward Roger, and Roger finished his point for the audience. "I think we can. I think we can. I think we can." Neil smiled, put his arm around Roger and said, "That's it, huh?"

"Well, the book ends there, so maybe we're being a bit premature."

"I'm laughing, too," Neil explained, "because our advertising people came to us a couple of months ago and Roger introduced this same theme to them … It didn't get very far."

Although Bill Golub, Neil, and Roger had initiated Schenectady 2000 together, it wasn't Roger's first bout with revitalization. Before he moved to Schenectady in 1990 to become president of Union College, Roger had been president of Beloit College in Wisconsin. With the help of an accomplished landscape architecture professor named Philip Lewis, he had initiated a program that had reinvigorated Beloit's downtown. And in Roger's opinion, Schenectady had far more attributes than that Midwestern city half its size: its location beside the Mohawk River; Central Park, with its extensive rose gardens; a truly impressive City Hall; Proctor's Theater; the GE Realty Plot; its historic Stockade district; two colleges; tremendous diversity among its people; a vibrant arts scene; and proximity to what he labeled the "ABCs" (Adirondacks, Berkshires, and Catskills) – and he cited those as key aspects of the area in an editorial published by *The Daily Gazette*.

Years later, well-known urban planning author Richard Florida, in *The Rise of the Creative Class*, would trumpet some of those very elements as essential for attracting a "creative class" – artists, engineers, scientists, media types, professors, etc. – to settle in post-industrial cities like Schenectady. Philip Lewis had a sense of that cultural geometry many years before, and as Roger explained in his editorial, he wanted to hire him to develop a realistic plan for Schenectady's revival:

> *Schenectady 2000 was based on Beloit 2000, an organization I spearheaded in 1987 to turn around a rust-belt city eerily similar to Schenectady. In 1990, I came here to a city economically dying and attitudinally near death, to lead a college with 65 fewer freshmen than had been budgeted, 150 empty beds, a $2 million hole in a $53 million budget, and the Union Board of Trustees seeking funding to demolish the iconic Nott Memorial. When Bill Golub asked me to join a meeting with then-mayor Karen Johnson*

and Neil Golub to discuss a plan for Schenectady, I proposed we hire Phil Lewis. We did, and his ideas became the blueprint for what was to take place downtown. Phil Lewis was the architect for Schenectady's downtown revival, but his blueprint lacked one important thing – funding.

However, there was enough money to get rolling at the start. Apart from the million dollars in seed money that Bill Golub had bequeathed, in June of 1993, the Schenectady City Council shifted a little over $273,000 that had been set aside for a previous downtown improvement to help fund Schenectady 2000, and they authorized an additional $30,000 to pay a share of the first-year administrative costs, including hiring a coordinator. Then the Golub Corporation and Trustco Bank chipped in twenty-five grand apiece around the same time, so more than $1.3 million in startup money was available when Neil and Roger presented their plan to the public in early 1994.

George Robertson, president of the Schenectady Economic Development Corporation, was the other key player at the table during that meeting. If Neil was professionally efficient and Roger was confidently sincere, George's persona was ebullient pitchman. He underscored the group's commitment and excitement by noting that, in January alone, they had conducted "two to four meetings every single day for a committee or a task force of Schenectady 2000." He outlined the phases of the project:

1. *What can we do in the next year – what are the short-term goals? And to define short-term, what is visible, what is affordable, and what is do-able right away?*

2. *Past the short-term, what are the projects that we can't do within the first year, projects that would take multiple years to achieve?*

*3. What are the challenges without solutions at the
   moment?*

Then George worked the crowd, offering details of what the plan's leaders had worried about. They had asked each other, "What will get our community excited? Would our citizens feel this city has a future, and will they help us make that future better?" And while George claimed he believed the people of Schenectady would help, he had wondered privately if enough people would actually show up to help make their program work. But the 800 volunteers, the fourteen operating task forces, and the sixty-eight people who had already assumed leadership positions on committees had allayed his fears.

There was a lighting task force, chaired by Brian Merriam, that would try to establish uniform lighting standards throughout the city. Wally Graham of SI Group would head the Vale Park task force and attempt to clean up one of the largest and most historic parks in Schenectady. Alan Holmes and Judy Broder from Power Technologies would co-chair the landscape task force and determine, with hired landscape

architects, how to plant trees and shrubs and beautify various city blocks and parks. Roger Hull had committed the 500 incoming freshmen at Union College to not only help with the landscape work but also to paint the rusting Conrail overpasses that lined Erie Boulevard. And there were task forces for the larger projects as well: build a long-desired museum of invention; purchase vacant buildings and start to establish an arts and entertainment district; assess and improve the State Street corridor; launch a feasibility study for a Mohawk River marina; and develop a plan to build a walkway linking Union College with Nott Terrace and the Science Museum.

"As you look around this room," George said, "I think you will be as amazed as we are at the depth, breadth, and the diversity of the people who have stepped forward to lead this community into the future. We thank everyone here because you're a part of that group, and with people like you helping us lead, there is no doubt that the little train will say, 'We did it. Yes, we did. We all did it.'" George had studied at a seminary, and he could whip up a crowd like a Bible-belt preacher.

He had come to upstate New York in early 1985 from South Dakota, where he had served as director of economic development for the governor there. His primary job was to poach businesses from other states. Once satellites had been launched

and allowed telecommunications options for private companies, for instance, George had been able to lure Citibank's credit card operations and its 2,500 jobs away from New York City – "a high-rent area for a sensitive-cost operation" – and out to South Dakota. In Schenectady, the head hunter who recruited George asked him, "Would you be as good at keeping jobs in New York as you've been at stealing them?" George thought that was a provocative question, so he went straight into challenge mode. "Look," he answered, "you're in the highest-taxed state in the country, with the worst regulatory climate. You're going to have to develop with what you've got, and that means business retention and expansion. That means a strong entrepreneurial start-up program – don't waste your money on trying to recruit companies." What did he have to lose? Confrontation would pay off or it wouldn't. When Schenectady quickly extended a job offer, George immediately negotiated a higher salary, citing the cost-of-living difference between South Dakota and New York. And he got it. If they had been Eskimos, he could have sold them ice cubes.

However, a decaying city whose citizens had lost civic self-esteem wasn't the only problem. According to George Robertson, if you had listened to Schenectady's mayor in early 1994, Frank Duci, you would have lost any hope for economic revitalization. One of Duci's brilliant ideas for a fiscal bailout had once been winning the lottery, literally. A few days after a State of the City address, he had gathered local reporters at an area newsstand, bought three lottery tickets and announced, "I will do this with every lottery, and when I win, I'm donating the money to the city. That will solve our budget problems!" Later on, after months of not winning, he offered a second plan: set up a toll booth on every road leading into Schenectady and make all out-of-towners – those visiting the Rose Garden in Central Park or people coming to see a show at Proctor's, for example – pay a tax to enter the city. Luckily, George and a few others were able to talk him out of that idea.

In his closing comments during that January presentation, and echoing beliefs he had learned from his dad, Neil Golub reminded the attendees, "We're all part of the solution, but we're going to make some mistakes. Part of the teamwork when we make mistakes is in helping team members get over the wall, or around it, or under it, or through it – or whatever it takes to get to the other side. All of us have got to start with somebody near us to change this attitude from "We can't do it" to "We can do it, and we will do it."

In its manual of conceptual design options for the city, the steering committee for Schenectady 2000 laid out its strategies to stimulate economic development and revitalization for the full seven-year period before the decade's end. Citing the marketing concept of a "new direction," their plan claimed it "will begin to instill renewed spirit in citizens, corporations, and government officials within the community as well as encourage businesses to consider Schenectady as a progressive city for investment." A fluid framework for discussion, along with a series of do-able steps, one after another, each step building momentum for another step over a period of years, was what they wanted – not a "single, one-giant-step project that will quickly solve all problems." Through community-wide involvement and a public-private partnership, and by leveraging limited federal, state, and local dollars against private-sector investment, the project hoped to create an environment in Schenectady by the 21st century that would give its citizens renewed pride in their community, highlight the city's assets, and attract new residents and businesses to locate there. As Roger Hull succinctly put it, they wanted to change pessimism to optimism. However, as Mike Tyson once said, "Everyone has a plan until they get punched in the mouth."

GE PLAN CAUSES DISMAY
IN SCHENECTADY COUNTY

February 4, 1994
Marv Cermak

County, city and town government leaders expressed dismay about General Electric Co. layoffs coinciding with the launch of Schenectady 2000. "GE is one of the Schenectady 2000 rejuvenation leaders. So this is like talking out of both sides of their mouth," Michael Iacobucci, a city businessman and brand-new county legislator, said. "GE has done it to Schenectady one more time, but residents here are survivors, so we have to pull ourselves up by the bootstraps again."

**Some of the elected officials said they were dis-
turbed that one of the world's most prosperous firms
would jettison about 500 workers at once rather than
trying to gradually reduce the work force.**

**Mayor Frank J. Duci said he was stunned by the
news because GE stock has been rocketing to new
highs for many months. "I notice the stock is now
$109 a share. The company could have attritioned out
these jobs. Today one job is precious. We're working
on bringing in new jobs, but you can't replace 500
overnight."**

So General Electric swung at the city first, only two weeks after hosting the
Schenectady 2000 public presentation. Then, two months later in April of 1994,
Mayor Duci landed a harder punch, re-appropriating $100,000 of the funds already
allocated for the downtown revitalization initiative, saying he wanted to support
people who had come to him in tears for public-service aid, like a Hamilton Hill
health agency that ran a teen pregnancy prevention program. "I felt people-oriented
programs should have priority over downtown," Duci told reporters.

Being responsive to the needs of city residents wasn't out of character for Frank
Duci. He had been the first Italian-American mayor in the city, elected in 1972 and
serving three successive terms, and he knew just about everybody in town. Caring
about his fellow citizens had won him the title of Schenectady's longest-serving
mayor – sixteen years, with his one final term going from 1992 to 1995 – essentially
bookending Karen Johnson's two terms between 1983 and 1991. And even then,
Frank Duci had proved to be a thorn in her side as a Republican member of the City
Council for seven of her eight years in office.

When he took charge again, Duci happily battled the then Democratic-majority
City Council during his last term. He had been a skilled sketch artist since high
school, with a collection of accomplished portraits that included Jimmy Carter and
Pope John Paul II, each of them signed by the subjects and hanging in Frank's home.
To annoy the members, he would often dash off caricatures of them rather than pay

attention to their ideas during City Council meetings.

"There are a lot of little projects under way to better the community," Neil Golub shot back at Mayor Duci after he took back that 100 grand. "Let's open our eyes and see what's happening." Everyone knew the city was on fiscal life-support, and a major downtown improvement plan like Schenectady 2000 needed city and community support as it was just getting started. It couldn't be self-sustaining forever, and a sincere commitment from City Hall would help. It needed not only continuing money from the city, but also its sponsorship to access state and federal funds.

If the sitting mayor and General Electric, both major players who claimed to care about revitalizing the city, wouldn't be reliable allies, who would? And could better boulevard lighting, cleaner sidewalks, rows of new saplings on the boulevards and re-painted train bridges in downtown slow the crack epidemic and gang violence in the neighborhoods, as well as counter the simultaneous corruption in the police department? As it would turn out, fixing an entire city was a tall order for a do-it-yourself, downtown improvement project, especially when Schenectady's Hamilton Hill and Mont Pleasant neighborhoods were boiling.

Jim Horton, who ran the Major Crimes division of the New York State Police during the 1990s, spent way too much time in Schenectady. "We were there more than anywhere else," he said, "because there was a culture of crack cocaine. Schenectady was being infiltrated, from downstate drug dealers coming up. It was kind of an open market, and nobody was taking control of it. They had way more homicides than Albany or Troy back then, and 90% of them were drug-related. On top of that, they had an issue with trusting each other, the uniforms and the detectives. We had a good relationship with the D.A., Bob Carney, and he would call us in all the time."

"We got crack cocaine here around 1990. We found it in the pockets of a man murdered in Vale Cemetery, and we hadn't seen it before," Bob Carney remembered. "Well, then, like every other place in the country, we had an explosion of violence. We went from a town where we had a murder every other year, maybe one every two years, to steadily six or seven a year, and drug-related in a sense of every permutation you can imagine: Dealers killed users for non-payment of drug debt. Users killed dealers for desperately wanting the product. Then we had the robberies where a drug dealer was being robbed. That was probably the most counted one because they got money, they got drugs, and they weren't likely to go to the police. And then there were retaliatory murders for prior robberies."

Jamel Muhammad grew up in Albany, but he had extended family throughout the Capital Region. When he left home at fifteen, he entered Schenectady's drug culture:

> When I came in the '80s, you really had to have relationships and connections to get a gun. If you had one in the '80s, it was rare. Even from the street guys, if you had guns, then you were a very high-level player. Your typical street guy on the corner, we had no interest in it. And that's the other thing, they're cheap now. To purchase a gun back then, you had to spend, easy, $800, $1000, $1500. Hustling in the '80s, and pardon the bluntness of the language, but our attitude was party and bullshit. It was all about fun. We made money. We had fun. We partied. We had the cars, the girls, the champagne and that's all it was about.
>
> When we had conflicts back then, the conflicts were pretty much you manned it up. Sometimes it was man-to-man, sometimes it was crew-to-crew, but it was never with a gun. It was never with a knife. Sometimes it may have been one of the little slugger baseball bats involved or whatever, but that was a rarity. And on top of that, once that conflict was over, we shook hands, we walked away as gentlemen. We went and we were at the club that night, we sat down, we drank together. We were in basketball leagues, we'd go to the centers and we'd play basketball against each other and it was no big thing.
>
> What was also different then was that we had plans. We looked at the idea of opening businesses, buying property, real estate, and things like that, and developing it for our families, and putting our families that worked hard but still didn't have much in a better situation. Not trying to moralize it and make it right but just saying where the mindset was then versus now. The idea was we needed money to make our circumstances better.

That all changed when crack, and the criminals who controlled it, targeted upstate New York. Jamel explained:

You're talking about an era when you had the five mob families of New York that controlled a lot of things. And people didn't know it, but this was one of their biggest seats of – hiding, if you will. They were very saturated up in the Capital District. The younger, rogue guys got into drugs, touching areas the older guys never would. And Schenectady was always riddled with corruption. You had those who were your honest cops that just wanted to keep the city safe and go home after their job and hug their families. Then you had those who were vulnerable because of their own struggles, whether it was drug addiction or financial desperation or whatever the case may be, who just felt like they were untouchable. They were given that kind of latitude without a lot of accountability on them, and they were doing a lot of shake-downs.

Where the heavy shift came is when the Feds came in to the region and did those sweeps. It took all of the individuals that were involved with the structure of the streets and took us out of the picture. Then you have the influx of people migrating from down in New York City coming up. And that was it. That left the market open for three things: it left those new people able to come in who didn't know, therefore didn't care; then you had the young people who were our children or our nieces and nephews that were attracted and then lured to the things that they saw us having and everything, so they were easy recruits; and finally you bring the Bloods into the East and this is the recipe for hell. And from that point on you had people demoralized, who don't feel today's even gonna be worth anything, not even thinking about tomorrow. Then the economic environment is nothing. There's hopelessness.

In the end, convicted of selling cocaine, Jamel spent seventeen years and seven months in nineteen different prisons, from Auburn and Attica in-state to federal lock-ups in Ohio, Georgia, Oklahoma, and Kentucky. Under federal guidelines at the time of his conviction, Jamel could have received anywhere from Probation to Twenty Years, but the judge opted to make an example and send a message to the street. During the last ten years, since his release, Jamel has led the Youth L.I.F.E. Support Network, which partners with local law enforcement and provides community outreach, violence intervention, education support, and recreation throughout the Capital Region.

Will Rivas, who runs Save Our Streets, among several other non-profit organizations that serve and support neighborhood communities in Schenectady, echoes Jamel:

> Place Beyond the Pines – *that movie got it right. I was here then. Around that time, the doors were open for drugs, and I can speak to what I saw, what I experienced. What I saw was police officers pulling people over and evidence disappearing and being resold. Everybody knows now that was exactly what was happening then. They'd let the people go, they wouldn't hold them. Unfortunately, that was part of the arrangement – sanctioned robbery. I was a kid just coming up then, witnessing all this. But everybody had to pay their taxes, basically, so they could operate. We had a heavy influx of gang members from New York City because of the RICO law statute. That destabilized our community because we had people coming here who weren't from here.*
>
> *The first thing they did was attack our community. People were getting cut, stabbed, shot. They started having gang initiations, where kids who were fourteen, fifteen, sixteen – they had to cut somebody, they had to shoot somebody – and they did what they did out of fear. Again, a lot of the adult men in our community were in prison or on their way home from prison so they weren't in the community, and there was nothing but kids here. You had Crips and Bloods and all these different gangs coming up here from NYC, bringing with them their friends and their families. They were coming in large groups and they were settling in among us – how do you protect yourself from something like that? The thing is, these were adults, grown men, thirty years old, and battle-hardened from banging downstate. But as far as positive male role models to engage with us, there were none left. We were young boys trying to teach each other how to be men. When you mixed money, drugs, and gang culture, it just led to a disastrous few years.*

Jim Bradshaw is currently a judge in Rotterdam, but he was a patrol officer when Jamel was working the streets. "I was a Zone Three car operator. That's Hamilton Hill. It was busy, busy, busy all the time. There was never a dull moment. I worked in that car for fifteen years, from 1985 to 2000, and I locked up a lot of people. I worked through that whole time when the officers got arrested."

According to Bradshaw, Schenectady was infamous in the early '90s for its porno shops and prostitutes. Street-walkers paraded up and down Albany Street, monitored by a handful of stereotypical pimps – "I'm talking big Cadillacs with the wide, whitewall tires," Bradshaw said. "It was like in the movies. I couldn't believe it. They had their girls, and they beat them up. The girls would come back with black eyes, and we'd see if they wanted to press charges, but no way, there was never a chance they wanted to get these guys locked up. But then came crack cocaine, and that whole scene. *Wow, this is crazy*, I thought. I never knew Schenectady was like that."

Dealing paid better than pimping, so the pimps became dealers. The hookers were always jonesing for more crack, and they'd get their johns to party with them. Pretty soon, the johns got addicted, and the parties moved to their houses in the better parts of town. "After that, they're taking the guy's car, they're going through his bank accounts. I can show you countless cases, and they would never want the girl arrested because they needed the drugs, and the girls were their connections." From there, Bradshaw said, some of the cops took advantage, and other cops threw them under the bus:

> Nobody is doing anything for nothing. If you're giving informa-
> tion, you're getting something back. The prostitutes were giving
> our guys information and whether they were turning a blind eye
> and letting them work the street or something, you know what I
> mean? I used to ride with a lot of these guys and I'd tell them,
> 'Man, you can't go across that line. These girls, they'll use you
> just like you're using them.' They were all good cops, but they
> tried to do – how should I put it? – too good a job.
>   They wanted the collars, the great arrests. If somebody tells
> you the house down there on the corner is selling drugs, as a

patrolman, what I would do with that information is pass it on to the vice squad. That's the normal protocol, what you're supposed to do. But when some of these guys passed the information to the vice squad, they thought it was falling on deaf ears. For investigators, building a case takes time, and the patrol guys wanted to act quicker. They wanted the great collars. So they made the vice squad look bad. The vice guys were getting pissed because these officers were either locking somebody up or shutting down the house, and rumor has it that one investigator was talking with the FBI.

To his credit, Jim Bradshaw is being loyal and generous, even though the whole affair blew up in spectacular fashion. Several officers went to prison, and one committed suicide. "Instead of airing their dirty laundry in the paper and having this big long investigation which, personally, I thought it was unwarranted … I'm not saying the guys shouldn't have been reprimanded in some way if they were doing some of the things people said they were doing, but there's no way anybody should have gone to frigging prison over that nonsense, when the bottom line was they were out there risking their asses to get the drugs off the street."

In any case, anyone who read the papers in the Capital Region during the '90s could follow Schenectady's troubles – not only with crime and corruption, but with educational scandals, constant political squabbles, and business closings – and conclude it wasn't a community where they might want to live. For Neil Golub and Roger Hull and the volunteers of Schenectady 2000, lifting the morale of the city's residents and countering the constant stream of bad press was becoming a Herculean task. So what did they actually get done?

Even with parts of the city in turmoil, Schenectady 2000 delivered on its promises, at least most of the short-term ones – the visible, affordable, do-able ones George Robertson had outlined. In April of 1994, George hired Kim Perone to serve as its program director, and she was its only paid staff member until Debbie DeLuke came on two years later to run galas for the organization. That meant Kim wore all the hats – public relations person, liaison to landscape architects, organizer of task force committee meetings, equipment purchaser, volunteer coordinator – and was responsible for managing every aspect of an organization that was 99.99% volunteer.

So early on, when Roger Hull created Union College's Freshman Day, Kim had to facilitate it. Roger actually stipulated two days of mandatory volunteerism as part of the orientation for the entire incoming freshman class as a way of helping his students, first, to see what was there in the community, warts and all, but secondly to make them recognize and appreciate the fact that they were going to be spending their four years behind the cloistered gates of the college. For the initial two work days, when Roger tasked them with assisting the landscape task force and with painting the seven train bridges, Kim had to make sure they were equipped to work:

> *There I was, a twenty-seven-year-old pregnant woman, running around town and buying equipment to outfit 500 kids. Buying all that took quite a bit of energy. The supplies included shrubs, flowers, topsoil, mulch, and all that was needed for that effort – shovels, garden tools, gloves – and we're talking hundreds of items. Plus, there was the paint, wire brushes, rollers, scaffolding, and other stuff for the bridges. I was very nervous that their parents had just sent them to college with brand new sneakers and that they were going to have green, railroad-overpass paint on them in the first week and that we would have angry parents.*

And to complicate the matter, the students had to paint quickly. For two months, Amtrak and Conrail had repeatedly responded to George Robertson, "Hell, no!" as he had tried to get permission to dig out the weeds, scrape off the rust, erase the graffiti that covered the trestles and the long concrete wall that ran alongside the train station, and apply two coats of rust-resistant paint to everything. "Do it anyway," Roger and Neil Golub told George. "What are they going to do?"

So they went ahead, tackling the bridge where Union Street met Erie Boulevard first. That one sat above the route that Union students and their parents most often used to reach the college, and Roger, rightly so, wanted their first impression of Schenectady to be a positive one. He had already put himself in hot water by claiming approaches to Schenectady "presently are so depressing that the college has a defined route for all visitors to Union, and General Electric tries to bring visitors into Schenectady at night" in Union's alumni magazine. When Mayor Duci complained to the *Daily Gazette* he was disappointed with those remarks and admonished Roger to speak favorably about the city, Roger replied, "When we get through with Schenectady 2000, we won't have to worry about it. Impressions are always important."

But there were so many aspects of downtown that needed fixing up to create those good impressions. Brian Merriam, who ran one of the most successful insurance companies in the city, co-chaired the lighting task force and explained how they replaced the hodge-podge of old streetlights with new, uniform light poles:

> *We were responsible for categorizing and recommending a standard light system. We had something like sixteen different kinds of lights, so the city felt broken up. We needed to unify, to give the*

city the feel that no matter where you were, you were part of the same city, and one of the goals was to have lights that were somewhat consistent. We recommended the Edgewater, like the lights at Union College, and the other one was a Columbine, which was more of a rounded feel, which is on Union Street now. So we really only had the two types of lights.

Wally Graham of SI Industries led the Vale Park task force, and sponsored more than ten years of activities there.

Vale Park, in those days, was very rundown, and some parts of it were being used as a trash heap: people would dump building materials and various other materials into the park and it was kind of a dark place for Schenectady. No citizen would want to spend any time in that park. We would call various companies

to come in and haul those materials out of there. There were old cars buried in the mucky ponds there, so we had to get wrecking crew companies to come in with cables and winch them out of the marshy areas. They were just rusting hulks.

We also had a committee that built a flower garden in the front there by the gates. We cleaned up the park, planted flowers, and put in a playground as well on the Nott Terrace side. Anyway, we devoted energy to doing that, and we tried to revitalize the ponds because they had a lot of scum on them. We aerated the water so it wouldn't get stagnant. SI Group was financially responsible for all of that. We volunteered to do it, but it was a lot. So we cleaned it up, we installed infrastructure, did a Vale Park run once a year, and then we would have other activities, like concerts and a car show, too. The idea was to provide facilities that would make it a more inhabitable place. The costs were extensive, of course.

Even as the volunteers of Schenectady 2000 pitched in to improve the way downtown looked, Kim Perone's friends, as well as a few family members would say to her, "Downtown? Just burn it. With all the political in-fighting, you can't get anything done there." But for her and for Neil and Roger and countless others, there wasn't a choice. It was the middle of Schenectady County, after all, with a rich history and, in their minds, great potential, in spite of all the store closings and foreclosures.

However, myriad expenses began to whittle down the organization's limited resources within the first year. Volunteer labor was free, of course, but everything those volunteers needed to complete their tasks took real money: Kim's salary; office supplies and operating costs; the sets of various plans generated by the landscape architects; all the planting and gardening and painting materials; cleanup and disposal tools for beautifying the city's parks; as well as larger-ticket items like the two, new standards of street lighting that ended up costing $195,000, and the large-capacity water truck to maintain the fresh landscaping and the flower baskets that hung from all the new and improved light poles. The City Council could only squeeze so much from the mayor's budget, and Schenectady 2000 needed to generate more revenue.

They turned to lavish galas, held at Union College, which were black-tie-and-evening-gown affairs, held inside and in a tent beside the historic Nott Memorial. $125 per person in the tent, and $500 a couple to be listed in the program on the honorary committee and attend the reception inside the building. In 1996, that wasn't chump change, but the galas were packed. Debbie DeLuke, along with the women in town who could identify all the influential people – Marie Gorman, Gert Purcell, Janet Crystal – definitely knew how to throw a bash. There were silent auctions under the elaborate tent to raise more money, beautifully-catered food by restaurateur Angelo Mazzone, floral arrangements by the interior decorators at Experience & Creative Design, an open bar, and dancing to up-tempo music by the New York Players. And to close out the memorable evenings, breathtaking fireworks above the Nott Memorial.

The funds Schenectady 2000 raised at these galas kept them going a few more years, but the sustainable cosmetic improvements to downtown weren't ever going to be enough to rejuvenate business in Schenectady, or to lure new, tax-paying home-owners to town. However, that had never been the only goal for Schenectady 2000. "Cleaning up the city was never the end-all and be-all," Kim Perone said. The volunteers had produced visible changes, and they definitely helped to raise the morale of many city residents. Their work restored the belief for many that the downtown was worth the substantial time and effort it took to improve it. Their accomplishments, at the very least, demonstrated that. As Neil Golub said, "What we did do, though, was start doing a number of things to revitalize the emotional spirit of the community."

Some people were energized by the attractive changes in their city. Some people stopped blaming themselves for General Electric's disloyal and crippling downsizing. Some people noted a perceptible shift in momentum that underscored commitment, as if to say: *We care about our downtown. We care about how it looks. It might be dirty, and it might be crumbling, and we might have some empty buildings, but we want to make it better. We can work together to do that, and we're working toward bigger things.*

The galas promised those bigger things, and not simply because of the funds they raised. They also brought people together, the people who could spark substantive change in the city, and involved people who gathered and brainstormed at those events.

One of those people was Bob Farley, a junior Republican legislator of Schenectady County. Bob was part of a business and government alliance group that brought in prominent business and academic leaders to speak – like Neil Golub and Roger Hull – and they met regularly at Union College in the late '90s. Fixing Schenectady was always a main subject for them, and they knew that if they wanted to improve public safety, and the culture of the city, it wasn't simply a matter of, "Bring back GE and all things will be solved." They were past the point of no return on General Electric. They would have to find a means of improving all aspects of the city, raising everybody's boat somehow with a rising economic tide of revitalization.

After one of their meetings, Neil asked Bob, "What do we have, and what can we do?" "Neil, I've got an idea," Bob answered. "What would you think about doing a funded public authority? You know, it's way out in left field, but that's the vehicle we need in Schenectady County to bring business here. The trouble is, we've got to find a funding stream for it, and that will be controversial."

Then Bob smiled and added, "It'll be a bitch, and I don't know if it will work."

6

A Battle for Metroplex

Smart thinking today recognizes one incontrovertible fact:
The way we have been developing for the past fifty years
just does not work. Innovation, creativity, a willingness
to try something different are key to setting a new direction.
In fact, dense, unpredictable, and complex urban districts
that developed over time are the future, wherever a
downtown is fortunate enough to have them left to build on.
Predictions were wrong that cities no longer
offer appeal as living sites.

– Cities, Back from the Edge: New Life for Downtown
Roberta Brandes Gratz

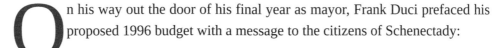

n his way out the door of his final year as mayor, Frank Duci prefaced his proposed 1996 budget with a message to the citizens of Schenectady:

> *Initially, let me say that on January 1, 1992, I placed a sign on my door that reads,* ***"People Working Together"*** *–* ***"My Office is Your Office."*** *Thereafter, I continued to stress the importance of promoting the three "Cs" on a daily basis – COOPERATION, COORDINATION, AND COMMUNICATION. I'm happy to say*

that as a result, this administration is very proud of our overall accomplishments, which includes the fact that for four years – we controlled spending and were able to retain all essential services between 1992 and 1995. However, the past four years was not a picnic. To begin, in 1992 we inherited a 2.7 million-dollar deficit.

The lame-duck Mayor Duci went on from there to boast that, by employing the above-mentioned three "Cs," he had established a sound fiscal management process that was able to absorb that large deficit, and he referred readers to his "Brief Re-cap of Accomplishments, 1992-1995," which followed the budget message. Perhaps he was hoping people would jump to the end of the document – what he saw as his noteworthy achievements – because the rest of the budget message was decidedly bleak and contradictory. That 2.7 million-dollar deficit he claimed to have absorbed had actually grown into a 3.7 million-dollar deficit for his newly-elected successor, Al Jurczynski. Duci railed against the Full-Value Assessment Program, the reduction in property tax assessments for General Electric (because of the unstated demolition of many older buildings), and the construction of a parking garage, not only to explain the revenue shortfalls but also to justify the thirty-eight permanent city positions he was eliminating.

"The task was most heartbreaking for me," Duci revealed, "especially since I was able in the past to overcome the deficits of 1980 and 1992 without eliminating jobs." No such luck this time around: among those slated for the chopping block were life guards and pool monitors for the Central Park Pool, the crack-sealing and storm-sewer-cleaning programs from the Bureau of Services, the Deputy Mayor position, the Assistant Building Inspector, a Dispatch Trainer, and a Bingo Inspector. And to supplement the savings from all of those eliminated positions, Duci proposed that the thirteen jobs on the city payroll from which people would be retiring in 1996 – administrators, secretaries, firefighters, as well as the five current police vacancies – simply remain unfilled.

Heartbroken or not, Duci was characteristically unrepentant: "The revenue shortfalls so identified on page 6 can in no way, shape, or manner be attributed to me, and/or my administration," he emphasized at the bottom of the first page. Then he waited until page four for the kicker: "I truly expected after controlling spending for four years that a tax increase for 1996 would be minimal. However, the uncontrollable 2.7 million-dollar revenue shortfall that I inherited has dampened that hope. Currently, the proposed 1996 budget has a projected property tax increase of 15.35%." Blame-shifting couldn't provide adequate cover, and no excuses could ease the pain of a 15.35% property tax raise for homeowners in Schenectady.

Finally, Duci promised he would fight on against difficult economic challenges, claiming that 35% of properties in the city – including all hospitals, churches, colleges, museums, and most of the non-profit organizations – were in the tax-free category. He was quick to remind his readers that many of those properties serviced residents of the entire county, and Schenectady County wasn't giving Schenectady City its fair share of sales tax revenue. That year, the city had generated sixteen million dollars in sales taxes, but the county had only sent back eleven million of that. Duci was upset over the inequity, and he had already written to Robert McEvoy, the Schenectady County Manager, about renegotiating the revenue-sharing agreement.

As a final alternative, if that failed, the mayor dangled the possibility of proposing a sales tax increase in Schenectady County, raising it from 7% to 8%. But Duci was on his way out, after all, and he wasn't the only one with his eye on that sales tax revenue. Bob Farley knew a piece of that county sales tax could be the skeleton key that might open a profitable door to enhanced economic development in Schenectady, and he had a hunch about how he could forge that key. However, given the political hurdles in county and state government, getting all the right people to sign on wouldn't be so easy.

He had already prepared Neil Golub for an uphill battle – the "bitch" he had mentioned at the business and government alliance meeting at Union College – and he had told Neil, "You're going to have to carry the ball for a lot of this." If Neil had let that moment pass, if he had not understood that this plan could actually be a monumental turning point for Schenectady, the future would have been entirely different. But Neil was smart enough to get on board. And Bob also knew, absolutely, that if he could count Neil and Roger and Schenectady 2000 as supporters, his chances of getting part of a planned sales tax increase to underwrite his public authority would be a whole lot better.

But if anybody was born to legislative maneuvering, it was Bob Farley. He had earned his law degree from Hofstra in 1987 and was the first associate trial lawyer ever hired right out of law school by the prestigious Albany firm of Mcnamee and Lochner. In just seven years, at 32, Bob had become the youngest Deputy Attorney General for the State of New York.

However, after only two years in that job, concerned that it was keeping him away from his wife and two young daughters, he left to join the Counsel's office in the New York State Senate in 1996. That same year, Bob was re-elected to the Schenectady County Legislature for a second term. So, clearly, he knew all the influential players. Moreover, his father was Hugh Farley – a powerful, senior state senator who represented Schenectady County. And not to put too fine a point on it, but Bob was a staunch Republican, like the majority of his colleagues on the County Legislature, although he might have been the most conservative one of all:

> *My dad and I have a different way that we view things because we're thirty years apart. He's a Republican, but he started his career as a Kennedy Democrat, and I started mine as a Reagan Republican. As a matter of fact, I was a very odd child. Did you ever see the show, "Family Ties?" – the one with Alex Keaton? It was a show about a conservative young man who grew up in a house with two hippies for parents. I won't say that I was that extreme when I was growing up, but I used to call my father a limousine liberal, which he wasn't. But I used to subscribe to* The Wilson Quarterly *when I was a kid. My father would just look at me like,* Where did you come from?

Bob's idea of a new direction – something innovative, creative, and different – was a public authority for Schenectady, although that seemed like a crazy and impossible solution at a small-city level. Public authorities had originated in London in 1899, when its port was old, grimy, and too small to accommodate the new luxury passenger liners like the R.M.S. *Titanic*. To provide a remedy, the British Parliament decided to create an entity that would be able to bond and expend monies to build and operate a new port for England's capital. In 1921, when New York City faced a similar problem, they proposed the British concept to the Congress of the United States. Congress decreed that the two states which shared and owned the port – New York and New Jersey – could form their own public authority by state legislation. If they passed it together, they could rehabilitate the port, and the first public authority in America became The Port of New York Authority, which got shortened colloquially to Port Authority.

Now the general purpose of an authority is to build or rehabilitate things, to operate and manage them, and to get money back through fees or tolls, the way the Thruway Authority does throughout New York State. The money the authority collects is used to repay bonds and support maintenance. That made sense to Bob Farley: in Schenectady, they needed to find suitable sites they could invest in, demolish the decaying buildings on those sites, clean up the industrial brownfields, build new structures and businesses and, hopefully, kick-start the city's sluggish economy. An authority seemed like a no-brainer to him, but his colleagues on the county board thought he was nuts. Even Roger Hull was initially somewhat skeptical because he knew an authority would have to be approved by the State Legislature, which seemed unlikely. George Robertson, who had tirelessly promoted Schenectady 2000, bailed on Bob's idea because he wanted to use Schenectady's lightly-funded IDA, its Industrial Development Agency, which he managed as part of the Schenectady Economic Development Corporation (SEDC). But Farley knew what George was really up to there:

> *IDAs are under Article 18 of the General Municipal Law, whereby they can issue debt for a private business at not-for-profit rates. That's basically what an industrial development agency does. So if, let's say a business in Schenectady, a small business, wants to open a new office building, they don't have the financing to do it, the IDA can issue the debt for that, and they pay it back at that low-interest loan. And George was able to run that and get a fee*

every year to run the IDA. But the IDA, because it didn't do any of the finances for the big organizations like GE, didn't have a lot of income. It just didn't have the money we needed.

In Farley's estimation, though, the most significant hurdle was Frank Potter, the chairman of the County Legislature. Don Ackerman and some other Democrats on the legislative board had seemed sympathetic to his idea, which surprised Farley. The first time he had run for a seat there, he had defeated a powerful Democrat, Chris Gardner, and he had assumed Gardner's fellow Dems had not forgiven him for that. But Bob knew getting all his Republicans colleagues on board was crucial. He couldn't afford to lose any of them, but if Frank Potter was against it, forget about getting the rest. The idea would be dead on arrival with the other Republicans – Majority Leader Peter Guidarelli, John DeGeorgio, Nicola DiLeva, Frank Ranucci and the others. Hell, the County Legislature didn't even have an economic development committee when Bob was first elected in 1993 – the only upstate county that didn't contain one at that time – and all his colleagues stalled when he had proposed one.

"Schenectady needs to help itself," Bob told them.

"We already have SEDC, and things are going pretty well. Why would we need one?" came the response.

"Because SEDC doesn't have enough money to make much happen," Bob explained.

"Well, you're chair of the Education Committee. Just add the name, Economic Development, to that one."

As far as the county board was concerned, economic development could fit snugly and quietly right alongside Schenectady County Community College, so Bob Farley could see the end in sight at the beginning: the legislators would fall in line with Frank Potter's assessment of his vision for a new authority, and they'd all echo whatever knee-jerk arguments he espoused.

Plus, Potter was a tough cookie – unlike Farley, he had grown up dirt-poor on Albany Street in Schenectady – and his father was no state senator. His dad had worked in a textile mill in Cohoes to provide for Frank and his seven other kids. As a local, small-business owner, Frank ran a floor covering store on Broadway, and he was opposed to anything that would favor fat cats and large enterprises. On top of that, Frank had ridden motorcycles since he was a teenager, and sponsored a motorcycle rally – the Harley Rendezvous – every June on his 177 acres out in Mariahville, near Duanesburg. Frank Potter wasn't likely to back down from a fight.

In spite of all that, Bob was optimistic. When he had been elected to the county legislature, both times, he became the deciding vote – his election assured the Republicans of a majority – so he thought, just maybe, that might give him some leverage with Potter. Moreover, they did agree on a number of things, including the fact that McEvoy, the County Manager, was a control freak and a penny-pincher, even if it was mostly to help poor people throughout the county. McEvoy would be wildly opposed to any fraction of the sales tax being allocated to anything but his favored social services. They were sacred, according to Farley. Moreover, with some sales tax money allocated to fund this new authority plan, McEvoy wouldn't be able to draft the county budget the way he wanted to, the way he always had.

"McEvoy was a daily communicant and a good human being, but he couldn't find his way out of the room on politics," Bob explained. "And he was a remarkable manager, but he wanted to control anything related to the county. He kept whispering into Frank Potter's ear, constantly telling him, 'You've got to kill this, Frank. You can't allow this to happen.'" And Frank had been listening to him.

"Look, you're a young guy, and you're brand new here," Potter told Farley. "We've never done things like this before. It's going to cost a lot of money, and we have other ideas. You'll have to raise taxes again, and that won't fly. This will never work. No way in hell are we going to do this."

"Frank, it's only a proposal right now – a work-in-progress," Bob countered.

Then McEvoy stepped in: "I know for a fact, because I called Pataki," he said. "The governor won't sign this bill. I talked with him myself."

For a minute, Farley didn't say a word. Maybe McEvoy had talked with Pataki. That could be true. As counsel to the Senate, Bob Farley worked for Joe Bruno, the majority leader, and he spoke with Governor Pataki all the time. Hell, he had volunteered for Pataki during his campaign, and he knew that the governor would never commit to anything until it looked like a sure thing. George wouldn't commit to Bob Farley, and he certainly wouldn't commit to County Manager McEvoy. And Bob was also pretty sure that the governor didn't want to oppose something that Neil Golub wanted. Alienate one of the most powerful businessmen in upstate New York, with thousands of voting employees? Hardly a wise political move.

Farley could tell a brick wall when he ran into one, but he knew the sales tax argument was a smoke screen. He knew the real reason Potter was against his idea was control: who would be in charge of this thing? If Farley wrote the bill and somehow got an authority approved by the State Legislature, he'd be the expert on it – the go-to guy – not Potter, and Potter wasn't about to let that happen. Public opinion had to be managed. Pressure needed to be applied. Minds had to be changed.

Bob decided to hold his cards close to his vest for the moment: "It's awful hard for the governor to say what he would do on a bill until he sees it, and we don't even have a bill yet," he said. "Let me do this: let me draft something, okay, and then we can conference that. I'll be doing all the work, and it won't cost you a thing. Everybody on the board can go through it then and tell me where I'm full of bananas, say what you don't like and what you do. If you hate it, you can tell me to go jump in the lake." Bob was thinking, *Once it's in front of them, more real than just an idea, it might be harder for them to say no. As an opening gambit, it could work, and that would buy me some time for a stronger move.*

Neil Golub was the only one who had been immediately enthusiastic, the only one he thought he could really count on, but Bob had to present what he envisioned the right way. Night after night, he ran over the argument inside his head: *We'll never get GE back, so we've got to attract other businesses. How can we do that, with such high taxes in New York State? And we're already crushed with real property taxes, so we can't ask people to pay more there. What's the one tax that relates to business – where if you create more business, you produce more revenue?* **Sales Tax!** *We should raise the sales tax rate in the county and guarantee a portion of that to this new authority. More economic activity will mean more businesses and homes, and more assessed value on those new businesses and homes raises the overall tax base, so maybe property taxes could be lowered, or at least slowed. Neil Golub, one of the most powerful businessmen in the Capital Region, is on board, and my boss* *at the Senate is the majority leader – I know I can get this thing passed.*

When he was ready, he asked Neil to set up a meeting with the editors at the *Daily Gazette*. Now in his entire career, Neil had never leaned on the press for special privileges. That was a significant point of pride for him. He had co-anchored the Jerry Lewis Telethon on CBS-6 TV for thirty years and had, along with his wife Jane, hosted countless fundraisers for charitable organizations. However, Price Chopper, Neil Golub's company, was one of the paper's major advertisers – maybe the biggest – and that was a simple but apparent fact. Jack Hume, its publisher, was aware of it. So were Bob Conner and Art Clayman, the editors who attended the meeting with Neil and Bob Farley. Neil didn't have to apply any pressure: he was famous for championing worthwhile causes and generously supporting Schenectady, so they were more than ready to listen when Bob delivered the pitch he had honed in his head for so long. "Metroplex: that's what we want to call it," Neil told them. "Nobody ever has an original idea, right? The community around Dallas, Texas is called Metroplex because it's a multi-jurisdictional community, working together for one single purpose."

"Our entity," Bob chimed in, "our proposed authority, is going to be a multi-jurisdictional authority because it will benefit all the communities in Schenectady County not just the City of Schenectady, but the small villages of Delanson and Scotia, as well as the towns of Duanesburg, Glenville, Niskayuna, Princetown, and Rotterdam. They'll all share in it, so let's borrow the name from Dallas and call ours the Metroplex Economic Development Authority."

"Not only do we love your idea," Art Clayman said immediately, "we think it's what could bring Schenectady back. And we're going to run an article every single day in our paper, on this issue, to see how it's progressing."

Oh, my God, Bob thought, *this is huge, and important for the public to know about, but politically it will touch off a firestorm. My colleagues will hand me my head. They want to stop this authority, and this coverage will expose them to everyone who reads the* Daily Gazette. *A freight train of public opinion could be heading their way.*

Authority would oversee
Schenectady redevelopment

Daily Gazette excerpt – February 10, 1998

By Matthew Roy

SCHENECTADY – A state authority run by 17 political appointees would oversee massive redevelopment efforts in the heart of downtown Schenectady, under a proposal being discussed by some local officials.

Neil M. Golub, the chairman of Schenectady 2000, a coalition of public and private interests combating the decline of the Electric City, said Monday the formation of a public authority could bring funds crucial to the effort. The cash otherwise available for investment would "no way, no how" be enough to turn the city's fate around, he said.

But some county officials on Monday were already questioning the proposal's requirement to hike the local sales tax from 7 percent to 8 percent – the rate in Albany and Rensselaer counties – in order to raise an additional $15 million annually to pay for projects like a convention center. That cash would finance the proposed Schenectady Metroplex Authority.

Emerging details of the plan were sketchy, and some officials believe the actual hike in sales tax sought would be just one half of 1 percentage point. Golub was reluctant to answer all questions put to him late Monday afternoon, saying he didn't want to undermine the "delicate" proposal for the authority. "Schenectady has had so many false starts," he said.

To establish some background, Art Clayman made his first call to Senator Hugh Farley. "What do you think of this new Metroplex that your son is pitching?" he asked him.

"What are you talking about?" Senator Farley wanted to know, although his son, Bob, had already told his dad the Republican legislators on the county board were firmly against his idea.

Art ignored his feint and barreled ahead: "Will you be able to pass this in the State Legislature?"

Senator Farley played dumb again: "Pass what?"

"What do you mean, pass what? This new public authority."

"Well, the last public authority we did in New York State was the MTA in 1969, so I don't know." Finally, the senator gave Art something: "Bob is a good and talented lawyer, but we haven't discussed this much. I know he's working with Neil Golub on this, and we are supportive of whatever direction Neil wants to go in."

As soon as Art hung up, he called Bob. "Do you not talk with your father?" he asked him.

"Every day. Multiple times a day," Bob answered, though he was thinking, *I love my dad. He's my hero, one of my favorite people in the world. I'll do anything for him, and he'll do anything for me, usually, but I can't tell him what to do. I can't presume to try that. He's got five counties to represent, and he's got state issues to deal with. This is my mess, not his.*

"I made you a promise I'd run a story in the paper every day," Art reminded him, "but I can't quote what he said."

Bob had only given his father tangential information, and he was sure the senator had demurred. A wishy-washy response from Senator Farley wouldn't bolster Bob's case at all. "Please don't," he told Art.

The meeting in his dad's office didn't go so well after that. Bob, tail firmly tucked between his legs, closed the door and said, "Look, I'm sorry. I should have told you more, but you can't say to Art Clayman, 'What the hell are you talking about?'"

"You do realize what you're biting off here?" the senator asked his son.

"Yeah, I'm trying to save Schenectady."

"Save Schenectady? Talk about trying to push a boulder uphill."

In the week after that, someone leaked Schenectady 2000's plan, the downtown projects of Bob Farley's Metroplex idea, to the *Daily Gazette* and they, of course, published the ambitious details – a 100,000-square-foot convention center; a luxury convention hotel; an intermodal transportation facility to accommodate high-speed rail and buses; a multiplex theater; a multi-story government and business office complex; a major expansion for Proctor's Theater and upgrades to city parks, recreational facilities, and historic preservation districts like the Stockade; as well as the reconstruction of many retail and commercial businesses – a pie-in-the-sky wish-list if there ever was one. However, the editors at the *Daily Gazette* had surrounded the plan's details with a ringing endorsement of the whole enterprise, saying,

> *Schenectady is truly at a precipice. If it turns in one direction, it could decay beyond repair, becoming a modern industrial ghost town survived only by decay, decline and despair. If, however, it turns in the other direction, and reinvents itself to be poised for the economic realities of the future, it could well prove to be a state and national success story on how to uplift and rebuild a community from an economic basket case into a thriving and prosperous economic engine for the entire Capital Region.*

Almost immediately, the *Gazette*'s articles and opinion pieces engaged readers better than Bob and Neil could have hoped: impassioned letters to the editor, for and against the Metroplex idea, flooded the paper. Clearly, the weary residents of Schenectady had weathered so many urban development schemes that had fizzled out over the preceding four decades that they certainly weren't shy about airing their opinions.

Dennis Quinn wrote, "Count me as one taxpayer unwilling to fork over more sales tax to support the proposed Metroplex ... the city desperately needs development and job creation, but multi-million-dollar monuments to self-aggrandizing public officials is not the answer."

Charles Kubly pointed out that, "Huge cost overruns are associated with government projects of this nature … the prospects of higher sales taxes and costs of urban development failure do not a business climate make."

Wayne Wagner, the Glenville supervisor, compared Metroplex with efforts to save a terminally-ill patient: "When someone's dying, everyone is eager to pursue whatever options a doctor offers, fully aware that in the end they will be fruitless."

But the staunchest critic was a self-described "31-year-old housewife with lots of free time and disposable income," Catherine Ross Wajda, who declared that she "lives in the suburbs, goes downtown at least twice a week for church and the library's story time," and often shops on Jay Street. In this brief excerpt from a long, vitriolic editorial that appeared in the *Daily Gazette*, Catherine presented her argument that Metroplex was not what the city needed:

> *I am fighting the Metroplex because I want more people like me to come downtown, and I don't think this is the way to do it. Metroplex looks to me like a project designed by 50-year-old men, for 50-year-old men. The only 50-year-old men I ever see downtown are drunk or elected, and as far as I'm concerned there are too many of them already. Neil Golub told me recently that nothing in the Metroplex project would do the city any harm. But, to paraphrase a great man, there is nothing more dangerous than well-intentioned stupidity. Bad planning is always harmful, if only because it uses up the opportunity to do something brilliant. And right now, Schenectady needs something brilliant. Metroplex is not brilliant … And I must warn George Robertson of Sioux Falls, S.D., and Roger Hull of New York City, and Neil M. Golub of Niskayuna, more people like me may be coming.*

Catherine's editorial turned out to be just a warning shot. She enlisted like-minded souls like Elmer Bertsch, Barbara Nathanson, and Helen Quirini (once a union organizer at General Electric) and started the Citizens for Preservation and Revitalization (CPR), which published the CPR News, a newsletter that hounded Metroplex and its supporters for years.

However, there were also editorials in favor of the downtown development plan from a number of citizens, including the editors at the *Daily Gazette*. Perhaps no testimonial was more surprising than one by County Legislator and Democrat Don Ackerman, which claimed that Metroplex may be Schenectady's last best chance: "I am of the very strong opinion that if we don't seize this opportunity to revitalize our community, we might as well hang a sign on the Thruway that says, 'Welcome to Schenectady – the Capital Region's Bedroom,' because that is all it will be good for … The Schenectady 2000 Business-Government alliance Metroplex Authority proposal is one of the most ambitious, bold and exciting concepts to hit this community in a very long time."

Schenectady City Council lukewarm in support for Metroplex plan

Daily Gazette **excerpt – March 24, 1998**
By Matthew Roy

SCHENECTADY – It could take a two-thirds majority of the County Legislature to make the proposed Metroplex a reality, County Attorney Thomas Hayner said Monday. At least nine of the 13 county legislators, rather than a simple majority of seven, could be needed to ask the State Legislature to pass a bill to enable the plan, Hayner said, citing the State Constitution. In the alternative, he said, it would take a simple majority of local lawmakers to ask for the enabling state legislation – if they were joining a request from the county's "chief executive officer."

However, County Manager Robert McEvoy is on record suggesting alternatives to a Metroplex authority. In its first extensive public discussion of the plan, the City Council on Monday took a lukewarm stance on the Metroplex, though it did arrange to be ready to formally express support for any request

from the county for state development aid … Council President Gary McCarthy has never endorsed the 1 percentage point sales tax. He said Monday he does not much care for an authority, and certainly not one with a 25-member board. "You work better with a smaller group," he said.

Emboldened by the City Council, and worried that more Democratic legislators could be swayed to follow Ackerman's example, leaders of the county board shot back. Egged on by Chairman Frank Potter, County Manager Robert McEvoy offered a lengthy rebuttal to criticism in the *Daily Gazette*, asserting that neither he nor Potter were opposed to downtown development. "This is not the case," he said. "The opposite is, in fact, true." After all, they had participated actively, programmatically, and financially in plenty of renewal projects, citing Proctor's and Broadway Center, among others, and even helped with the rehabilitation of the *Daily Gazette* building itself.

Moreover, McEvoy claimed, the County had purchased and cleared land "across the street from the County Office Building and developed and recommended to the Legislature an office, trade show and parking facility on this site that would have provided for our county and city courts … This project did not require any tax increases and could now have been under way." (In fact, this was Frank Potter's own plan – to build a new courthouse and convention center downtown.) Then, once the County had paid an architect to submit renderings, the corporate leaders of Schenectady 2000 could not only support the plan but could urge the County to submit it to Senator Hugh Farley to help fund it. However, as soon as the Metroplex idea arose, those same corporate leaders pulled their support for the County's plan and asked them to discontinue work on the project. Further affirming the County's benign nature, McEvoy wrote, "The group asked us not to pursue those contacts, and in the interest of harmony and cooperation, we did exactly as they asked and began seeking other private-sector development projects for our cleared development site."

McEvoy wasn't a rookie in the political game. Airing this betrayal wasn't his only strategy to deflect adverse public opinion. As the official responsible for implementing policies that the county legislators pass, the County Manager was obliged to protect the citizens of Schenectady County from costly mistakes like Metroplex, in his considered opinion. McEvoy revealed that, "When the proposal to create a state authority and raise the county sales tax was presented, we began the process – as required – to analyze and report the implications to the County Legislature … Our reports indicated that a very large commitment of county tax dollars would be involved."

McEvoy's assessment warned that, with assumed growth of 2% per year, Metroplex would siphon off $450 million from the county sales tax over the next twenty-five years. That would average out to eighteen million dollars a year dropped into the hands of a separate agency, one that didn't answer to the County Legislature. And to make things worse, the authority wouldn't be subject to local city, town and village zoning: that meant it had condemnation powers over citizens' private property. "These are serious matters," he concluded. "The authority concept should be fully understood by the public so that it may voice its approval or disapproval to elected bodies."

If Schenectady had not been in such desperate straits, McEvoy's punches might have landed with more force. Plus, he and Potter had decided to broadcast their grievances on Paul Vandenburgh's Talk 1300 radio show. Even though Vandenburgh didn't live or work in Schenectady, he fancied himself the sharpest shock-jock in the Capital Region, and he was perhaps the local personality that a majority of people disliked most. The *Daily Gazette*'s editors, ridiculing the County Manager's last-minute effort to offer an alternative to Metroplex, ran its own rebuttal, alongside McEvoy's opinion piece, on the same day near the end of March. The paper cautioned the county board members not to engage in "negativism" on the show. "We need an authority with the mandate and resources to get the job done," they wrote. "County government can best serve the people by allowing the State to help." It made some sense, after all, to back the horse that has the best chance of running in the money – especially when New York State might provide the seed money to get that horse up and running.

Time was getting short for political maneuvering, though, because the budget for the State had to be approved by April 9. Bob Farley had to win a majority in the County Legislature first, but the real battle would happen after that, once the plan was sent over to the State. The final day of the legislative session for the State Assembly was Friday, June 19. If Farley couldn't engineer his bill through the labyrinth of Senate and Assembly committees and deliberations and general red tape to secure a vote before then, say goodbye to all the work done and momentum achieved for this year. And worse than that, they would lose the $25 million in up-front money that Governor Pataki had promised to Metroplex if the proposal wasn't ready for a vote in 1998. The state budget would get passed, but innovative and profound relief for Schenectady may or may not be included.

Frank Potter hinted that the County vote in a special session could happen on Thursday, April 2, but then he reneged, and scheduled the vote for the following week. If he could delay the process enough, that State budget deadline might just come and go. Neil Golub went ballistic: "Rome is burning and these guys are playing games," he fumed. "The State Legislature may adopt a budget by then, too late to include any grant for the Metroplex plan." Schenectady's Mayor, Al Jurczynski, agreed: "If they wait, we're jeopardizing losing everything," he said. "April 9 is too late. This decision should have been made by now." And Bob Farley added a conciliatory but dire reminder: "I don't think all these people are that far apart but it's like a time bomb here, ticking, ticking, ticking."

There were, however, some promising signs: Even the legislators who stood by Frank Potter were hedging their bets, saying they should ask all the right questions, or suggesting they could support it if there was local control. Potter himself admitted that the Metroplex proposal "had improved through negotiations and revisions during the past several weeks." And Peter Guidarelli, who headed a coalition of five Republicans and two Conservatives, said that Metroplex could well win support from nine or more legislators.

So Farley continued his revisions, answering the board's complaints and massaging the thorny issues. He lowered the proposed number of Metroplex board members from twenty-five to fifteen, and gave the County Legislature the ability to appoint three of those members. They would also retain the control of approving eight other appointees chosen by the mayors of Schenectady and Scotia, the

Schenectady City Council, and the supervisors of the five towns in the county.

The final four members would be left to State leaders: the governor would select the chairman and co-chairman; the speaker of the Assembly and the majority leader of the state Senate would each pick one.

Right after Frank Potter put off the vote, Farley set up an emergency meeting on Wednesday, April 1, with the other Republicans on the county board and conceded that half a point from the county sales tax, rather than the full one percent, could be a workable solution. On top of that, his newest draft of the proposal created a Metroplex service district which would enable the authority to fund projects along Routes 5 and 7, in specific corridors, and exempt most of the city's neighborhoods from that service district. In other words, the authority was now set up to respect local rules, so people wouldn't have to worry that a brand of eminent domain could toss them out of their homes. Those changes seemed to appease the seven-member majority of Republicans and Conservatives, but meanwhile the Democrats were working on a compromise plan of their own.

A local rally in support of Metroplex the following day, organized by George Robertson – along with Bob Farley's concessions to some of the Republican demands – provided the tipping point for the Republicans. Frank Potter announced a special session and vote for two days later, Saturday, April 4, at 10:05 A.M. to address Resolution 55-98, which was listed as a Resolution Requesting the New York State Legislature To Introduce a Special Law Establishing the Schenectady Metroplex Authority.

When Bob Farley arrived at the legislative chamber for the special session on Saturday morning, the news cameras from all three local TV stations were already set up, and reporters from the *Daily Gazette*, The Albany *Times-Union*, and the smaller but well-read weekly, *The Jewel*, were all set to report on the proceedings. The place was packed with spectators: Neil Golub was there, of course, along with George Robertson. The *Daily Gazette* had produced another of its daily articles, so plenty of its readers had shown up to witness the outcome of the battle they had been following for weeks in the paper.

Frank Potter assured Bob they had the votes to pass his hefty, 48-page bill – the eighteenth draft of it – but he didn't trust Potter. Something told him he was about to get torpedoed. His name was the only one on the bill. The chairman had insisted there be no co-sponsors, not to give him sole credit, Bob realized, but so when it went down in flames all his detractors could say, "Okay, here's the stupid idiot who has been pushing this, and we've been forced to vote on it. In case you didn't know, look at his name right here at the top: this is all his idea."

Bob Farley introduced his proposal with this excerpt from his forty-minute explanation and endorsement:

> We have before us a very important piece of legislation, perhaps one of the most important pieces of legislation the County has ever had the opportunity to consider. I'm reminded quite frequently by our constituents on this issue that they're not going to remember what we say here, but they're going to long remember what we do here. We have before us an opportunity for Schenectady to come together, to provide a bright and promising future for ourselves. It stands on our shoulders. It stands on the shoulders of every citizen in our community. Many people have asked why this is such an important debate and why we believe in this. It's gotten a lot of press coverage, a lot of discussion in our community. The reason I think more than anything, and why this represents such an important step forward, is because our citizens have a new rebirth and new spirit. No longer are we talking like victims of what has happened to us in the past – what others have done to us – whether it be General Electric or any other company, the State of New York or anything else. We're now talking about how to fix our own future.

Farley went on to remind his colleagues that not only did the "community come out in droves," expressing their concerns and presenting legal issues, but also that a number of legislators and private citizens had been publicly attacked during the long run-up to the vote that day. "There is an old adage," he said, "that you shouldn't see laws or sausages made. It's a hard process." However, he went on to praise his foe, of all people, Frank Potter, whom he acknowledged as having made the process better, as well as the other Republicans and, finally, some Democrats and, particularly, Susan Savage for contributing tireless work on the plan during the preceding few months.

As it turned out, a surprising piece of Susan Savage's tireless work included, as she explained when she spoke next, a substitute plan. She was quick to compliment Mr. Farley for the relentless work on his own plan, but said, "It's much easier to just take what you're given and go with it … But no plan is a perfect plan. Please do the right thing for the people of Schenectady." And with that, she moved to present an alternate plan the Democrats had worked up in secret. Her motion was seconded by Democrat Christine Cioffi, who then went on to outline all the reasons their plan was better for Schenectady County. "I read six or seven of the last Authorities that have been done in our state and I realize this is a fourth branch of government that we are creating," she warned. "It removes from this Legislative Body the authority to control the purse strings, and we all know that when the money is removed to another entity, that's often where the decision-making power goes."

Truth be told, the key elements of this substitute plan, which included reducing the number of Metroplex board members from fifteen to seven, all of them to be appointed by the County Legislature, demanding that the authority submit a capital project plan to them every two years for approval, and designating that 30% of all sales taxes that came to Metroplex be handed over to the County Legislature, among other significant changes to Farley's bill, essentially underscored their fervent desire to ensure that the County would retain ultimate control. What they didn't mention was that the extra time necessary to implement facets of their alternate plan would disqualify it for introduction to the State budget for 1998, or the loss of the money promised by Governor Pataki. Plus, if no Metroplex bill won approval, then Bob Farley might be more vulnerable in the next election, and the Democrats might be able to win that seat back and assume the majority on the County Legislature.

After Christine Cioffi finished, Bob Farley and a couple of Republicans spoke against the substitute plan. Then, inevitably, Don Ackerman and a couple of Democrats listed the reasons they supported it. Seeing no further discussion on the motion, Frank Potter called for a vote, and most of the legislators saw that as an opportunity to wax eloquent or emotional before actually saying yes or no. The onlookers were growing restive.

The result of this first vote: Ayes – 5, Noes – 8. The motion was defeated – there would be no substitute Metroplex proposal – but Don Ackerman immediately introduced an amendment that specified "any public projects undertaken by this Authority would be governed by prevailing wage." Bob knew what that meant: prevailing wage would instantly hike the price of development projects by about 40%. It was a gift to the labor unions that he had been hoping to use as a bargaining chip in negotiations with the State Assembly. That would disappear if it went in the bill at that point. But he also quickly realized that everybody else was voting for it, 12-1, so he switched his vote to yes for the sake of compromise.

Finally, although it seemed a little anti-climactic after the attempted Democratic coup was put down, the moment for a vote on the amended resolution had arrived, and people leaned forward in their seats.

> *Legislator DeGeorgio: Today was the first day I probably in a long time looked at the newspaper and didn't see a cartoon of my friend, Frank Potter, our Chairman … So Frank, I mean, he took a lot of shots. We were right with you and I just want everybody else to know out there that this Chairman has done one heck of a job for us, and debate is good. So with that, Frank, I vote yes.*

> *Legislator Savage: We've tried to do our best. We've tried to change this and put those ideas forward but right now I have a proposal in front of me and I feel the choices I have to make are between doing nothing and doing something. I want to make this community better and for that reason, I will vote yes on the proposal that's before us.*

> *Legislator Cioffi: Sometimes I feel a little shut out of things. I think Susan and I and the other people who worked on this compromise bill, and there are many of you in this room, show that we have ideas, we have certain talents, we can bring about a dialogue, if not a consensus, and we would like to keep working in that vein. I vote yes.*

And so it continued – thirteen legislators, thirteen brief explanations, and thirteen votes to declare a surprising and unanimous YES for Bob Farley's Metroplex proposal.

County OKs Metroplex plan

Daily Gazette excerpt – April 5, 1998

By Matthew Roy

SCHENECTADY – Despite last-minute behind-the-scenes rifts in the GOP, county legislators voted 13-0 Saturday to ask the state to create a Metroplex authority to redevelop the city's downtown.

The plan got another boost later Saturday when Paul D. Tonko, a member of the State Assembly's Democratic majority, said he will introduce a bill to establish the authority, citing the unanimous vote. Tonko was previously uncommitted. State Senator Hugh Farley, R-Niskayuna, plans to introduce the same bill simultaneously – possibly as soon as Monday, an aide said.

In the County Legislature, Democrats offered up a rival plan Saturday morning to set up a local authority governed by a seven-member board appointed by the County Legislature ... Only five legislators backed the local-authority plan. But those legislators, all Democrats, subsequently backed the State authority plan offered by Robert T. Farley, R-Glenville – Hugh Farley's son – and supported by Schenectady 2000. Legislators first amended it to provide the projects undertaken by the authority will pay union wages. Then they voted 13-0 to send it to Albany for state approval.

"That is huge," Robert Farley said afterward of the consensus. "If we were divided, the State Legislature would say, "Geez, there's dissent in the county.'"

7

The Dance of Power

It would be wonderful if city builders were guided
purely by an enlightened calculus of utility. But
this is not how the world works. Urban spaces and
systems do not merely reflect altruistic attempts
to solve the complex problem of people living close
together, and they are more than an embodiment
of the creative tension between competing ideas.
They are shaped by struggles between competing
groups of people. They apportion the benefits
of urban life. They express who has power and
who does not. In so doing, they shape the mind
and the soul of the city.

– *Happy City: Transforming Our Lives*
Through Urban Design
Charles Montgomery

In upstate New York, family-owned newspapers like the *Daily Gazette* have less impact at the State level: members of the Senate and Assembly who represent citizens in that paper's subscription area have to answer to constituents at some point, of course – if perhaps only at the ballot box – but they often tend to be less susceptible to public opinion than local council or county board members might be. The pressure that had tightened the screws on Potter and McEvoy and the Schenectady County legislators probably wouldn't resonate at the state level, and Bob Farley was well aware of that. Other, more hidden forces turned the wheels of power in Albany. Bob would have to rely on personal relationships with power players like his boss at the Senate, Joe Bruno.

Bruno served as a Republican senator for thirty-one years, from 1977 to 2008, and when the Metroplex bill showed up for deliberation in April of 1998, he was the Senate's Majority Leader. Bruno, infamously, was one of the "three men in a room" triumvirate that controlled New York politics for decades. As each annual legislative session drew to its finish, the governor, the Senate majority leader, and the Assembly speaker would sit down behind closed doors, secluded from the rank-and-file legislators, and bargain out exactly how the session was going to end – which bills would get passed, and which would get tossed into the garbage. Needless to say, Bob Farley could never get Metroplex passed without Bruno's help.

Joe lived in Brunswick, a quickly-developing rural community that hugged the city of Troy's northern border, and he was partial to funding projects in Rensselaer County. Uncle Joe, as he was called, had almost single-handedly sparked a downtown renaissance in that city by relocating thousands of state workers to Troy's vacant downtown office spaces, and secured funding from the State for schools, firehouses, parks, high-tech developments, and countless community organizations. In 1998, he had shifted some energy to Albany County: Joe had already convinced the governor to agree to an "Albany Plan," which would tackle major renovation projects and build a state-of-the-art civic center in the capital's downtown. That meant he wasn't likely to get behind another major urban development plan for Schenectady in the same year.

At a meeting engineered by Bob Farley, his father Hugh said, "Joe, I need your help. My stupid son is trying to put something together. We need a Schenectady plan. We need Metroplex to pass, and we've got to get an office building with some state employees into our city." Bruno already knew all about this. He and Pataki were old friends. They basically liked the Metroplex plan, and both were well aware of the efforts to bring Schenectady back. They didn't need to be reminded that if you want a vibrant downtown, you've got to have people working and eating there, supporting the local restaurants, going to Proctor's Theater, and celebrating in the bars afterwards. For both of them, though, Albany came first. The governor didn't necessarily want to offend Neil Golub, but his pal, Mayor Jerry Jennings, had first dibs on development money that year. Jennings wanted the Albany Plan, so Pataki did, too, and he told Bruno as much. "We'll do Schenectady next year," he said to Bruno. "Let's do Albany this year." But, given the state of decay in the city, next year might be too late for Metroplex and Schenectady.

"This is what the governor wants," Bruno told Hugh Farley. "What do you want me to do here?"

"You're killing me with this Albany Plan, Joe. I've got to get something big this year."

Bob Farley, who was sitting there quietly, looked back and forth between his dad and his boss, dying a little more inside with each undecided moment. He knew what good friends these two were, from working together in the Senate and from each representing parts of Saratoga County, but also because both were boxers in the military. Joe had fought in Korea, and had been crowned the undefeated light heavyweight boxing champion of the 25th Infantry Division when he was stationed there. So they were simpatico, that was certain – but would that be enough?

"You're killing me," Hugh repeated. "Come on, you've turned Troy into the State of New York. You've got to help me with Schenectady."

Bruno smiled suddenly and said, "Okay, Hugh. I'll do what I can." And he did. He went back to Pataki and told him, "No Albany Plan without Schenectady's Metroplex and two State offices."

The governor didn't even hesitate. "Okay, we'll do both."

In a perfect world, that gubernatorial yes would have been enough. The County Legislature had voted to send it to the State. Hugh Farley had introduced the bill in the Senate, and now Joe Bruno had thrown his support behind it. However, temporarily absent from the field of battle, Frank Potter had been plotting some new strategies.

Is Metroplex Authority
being quietly killed in Albany?

Daily Gazette editorial excerpt
– April 26, 1998
By Gary Hughes

Something happened to the Metroplex proposal on its way from Schenectady to the
State Capital in Albany. And, at least for the
record, nobody is willing to say what went
wrong.

The Metroplex proposal forms a public
authority to redevelop downtown Schenectady, funded by a fraction of Schenectady
County sales-tax receipts and a combination
of state, federal and private dollars.

The proposed legislation is somewhere
in the hopper at the Capital. Legislation in
Albany is not like wine, it generally does
not improve with age; and supporters of the
Metroplex have reason to worry that whatever emerges from the Capital may no longer
be a viable redevelopment vehicle. How did a
plan that won a unanimous vote of approval
from the Schenectady County Legislature
and had the strong backing of Schenectady
2000, wind up in limbo at the Capital?

Gary Hughes, the editorial's author, went on in the full op-ed to enumerate the
facts about Metroplex as he understood them: that the leaders of Schenectady 2000
were responsible for its proposal, which was a controversial plan to rescue downtown Schenectady; that Bob Farley had to tinker with the plan extensively to get

buy-in and eventual endorsement from his colleagues on the county board to send it on to Albany for funding and for home-rule legislation; that, to date, the State had only agreed to kick in five million for the plan, not the twenty-five million that Metroplex backers thought had been promised to them; and, finally, that it was still up in the air about who would have the power to appoint the chair of the Metroplex board, if and when it actually did pass the Senate and Assembly before the last day of the session on June 19. But Hughes was interested in more than just those facts.

He surmised in the second half of his editorial that while all the county legislators in Schenectady may have voted for the Metroplex plan, a number of them may also have had their fingers crossed when they voted, knowing they would appear in favor of it for the public but could continue to fight about it locally – an excellent ploy to avoid bad press for themselves. Plus, their local fighting would provide questions, and ultimate cover, for politicians in Albany who might be waffling in their support. The end-of-session deadline was approaching fast, and Frank Potter was certainly aware there were multiple ways to skin a cat.

First, Frank Potter tried to enlist a powerful, Democratic Assembly member, Paul Tonko, who had a degree in Mechanical and Industrial Engineering from Clarkson University and was Chairman of the Assembly Energy Committee from 1992 until 2007. Although Tonko had initially been unconvinced about Metroplex, he was impressed enough by the County Legislature's unanimous vote of approval that he agreed to sponsor the bill to establish the Authority in the Assembly. That sponsorship didn't mean that he supported everything in Bob Farley's latest draft of the bill. As a trained engineer and a political veteran, Tonko applied a rigorous analytical approach to whatever legislation crossed his desk, and he thought a number of things in the Metroplex bill needed revamping.

"What they presented to me was a draft bill," Tonko remembered. "But there were some obvious shortcomings. They wanted to stretch dollars to those who would be investing in the area, but an agency can't do that, and it was set up as an agency. I told them, 'This is a major bill, and it's going to take time to review it. If we're going to do this, we have to do it right.' And I can recall a number of people being very energetic about getting the legislation amended, like almost a daily request. Well, if my name's going to be on something, I want it to be done correctly."

For a while, Frank Potter made sure his was one of those daily requests to Assemblyman Tonko. But he also hounded John Sweeney, who was a rising star in the Republican party. He had served as its executive director and chief counsel between 1992 and 1995, acted as Pataki's first Commissioner of the State Department of Labor until 1997, but then was chosen for the inner circle as Deputy Secretary to the Governor. With daily phone calls, Potter fed Sweeney a steady diet of half-truths: "This is just the Farleys, wanting power. It's not all of Schenectady. Don't let the governor do this."

But Bob Farley knew John Sweeney, too, and had helped him more than Frank Potter ever had. Bob had worked on John's campaign to become the party's executive director back in the early '90s. When Bob went to see him, Sweeney blurted out, "Frank Potter has called me twenty times on this. Why the hell should we have the governor sign it? Why are you putting him in this position?"

Bob wasn't surprised by the outburst. He had watched Sweeney's outbursts for years. He may have been secretary to the governor, but Bob was a senior counsel in the Senate – maybe not on equal playing fields, but Bob certainly didn't have to back down.

"John, you know first-hand that no one has the best interests of the governor in mind more than I do," Bob began. "I have known George Pataki since he first ran. I worked on his Assembly campaigns. I tried to get him to run for governor in 1990, four years before he ran. I worked on his Senate primary, despite the fact that the majority leader of the Senate didn't want him to, and I worked on his gubernatorial campaign. I would never do anything that would hurt anyone in this office, particularly George Pataki."

"Come on, Bob. Plenty of people in Schenectady County have said they don't want this, and you know that's the truth."

"Here's what I know," Bob shot back. "Frank Potter has got his head up his tookus. If anything, Metroplex will save Schenectady. The *Daily Gazette* has run an article every single day throughout the course of this bill's progress. Frank Potter is attached to this bill, and if it goes down, the newspaper will excoriate him, and they'll excoriate the governor, too. When this bill passes, what you could have is a signing ceremony where a Republican governor is absolutely heralded by very left-of-center people. He's going to look like the conquering hero because he's delivering both Metroplex and the State office buildings. What I also know is the Schenectady Plan can ensure that, next Fall, Governor Pataki will have the hugest reelection you've ever seen. Now tell me that's not the truth."

John Sweeney didn't have a comeback for all that.

As the last weeks of the State legislative session wore on, Frank Potter continued to fight behind the scenes. Whether it was his paranoid reckoning or not, he was afraid that wealthy businessmen like Neil Golub and Wally Graham might control the Metroplex board and steer lucrative projects to themselves and their friends, so he pressed for the right, as Chairman of the Legislature, to appoint its members. That way, he claimed, he could protect small business owners in the county like himself. And he badgered an undecided Paul Tonko to demand accountability in the bill – to mandate that Metroplex would only be able to fund projects that had previously been ranked as important by the County Legislature. That put Frank and the County Legislature partially back in the driver's seat. The problem was, those changes necessitated another draft of the bill by Bob Farley, this time on June 4, just two weeks before the end of the session. "We were totally blindsided by this," Farley said.

Neil Golub, along with Roger Hull and George Robertson, both of whom were firmly on board at that point, cancelled a scheduled debate on Metroplex at Union College and hurried over to Tonko's office. Assembly Speaker Sheldon Silver had been pressuring him as well, Tonko explained: "Shelly's words to me were, 'How are you going to get this done in the next two weeks if you have these problems?' I can't take this crap. I've got more to do than just this, okay. I've got to get energy reform done."

"And I've got a small grocery store to run," Golub told him.

Robertson tried to cool things down: "What do we do next, Paul?"

"There are principles here that are important. I guess we figure out between the Senate and the Assembly what we do," came the noncommittal answer.

In spite of the apparent problems, the Schenectady 2000 leaders were upbeat after the meeting. "Let's call it a marathon," Golub said, "but we're going to make it across the line." Robertson echoed that sentiment: "The message is clear. Shelly Silver wants a bill done." And after several more drafts by Bob Farley – which made seventy-two separate drafts in all – the State Assembly voted to pass the massive Metroplex bill on June 19, essentially at the last possible moment.

Metroplex bill passes;
Pataki to sign it

Daily Gazette **excerpt – June 20, 1998**
By Matthew Roy

ALBANY – The State Assembly passed the Metroplex Authority bill Friday, capping a bruising, to-the-wire political battle to redevelop downtown Schenectady with a public authority. The Senate had passed the bill unanimously, 61-0, on Wednesday.

Michael McKeon, spokesman for Governor George Pataki, said the bill had strong support from the community and would

benefit Schenectady. "The governor looks forward to signing it," he said.

The Assembly, without debate, passed Metroplex by a vote of 119-28 Friday afternoon – the final day of its regular 1998 session.

In this photo, George Pataki was signing the bill into law on Tuesday, June 30, 1998, thereby creating the Schenectady Metroplex Development Authority. To his immediate right is Senator Hugh Farley, then Mayor Al Jurczynski, and a half-hidden Neil Golub. Over Pataki's left shoulder stands a smiling and relieved Bob Farley, partially obscured behind Assemblyman Paul Tonko in a natty gray suit. Republican Assemblyman Jim Tedisco is reaching inside his coat. Susan Savage's head appears to float just above the governor's head. Frank Potter was also present at the signing, though not pictured in this photo, although perhaps plotting how he could possibly have the last laugh.

In the aftermath of the battle for Metroplex, there was no grand reconciliation inside the Republican party in Schenectady County, no *Kumbaya* moment of acceptance, forgiveness, and bonhomie. During the signing, Governor Pataki had called the authority "a work in progress – not the end but the beginning of revitalization in Schenectady," and he had stressed the importance of working together to make it successful. Apparently, the local legislators had suffered a collective bout of tinnitus during his encouraging admonitions, because they were back at each other's throats almost immediately.

With six months left before the eleven-member Metroplex board of directors would officially begin its duties on January 1, 1999, the County Legislature could take its sweet time interviewing applicants for the five board seats they controlled. Two selections would be made by Chairman Frank Potter, one by Minority Leader B. Donald Ackerman, and the legislators together would vote for and appoint the chair and vice chair of the Metroplex board. Schenectady Mayor Al Jurczynski, the Schenectady City Council, and supervisors of the towns and villages in the county would choose the remaining six.

Moreover, the last few months of 1998 gave the county board time to stir up trouble and try to wrest more control for themselves. First of all, they wanted the nine amendments they had proposed, and that were dismissed by Bob Farley because he said it was too late to submit them before the votes in the Senate and Assembly. Secondly, they also threatened to withhold approval for the half-percent sales tax hike, which would be the primary and continuous fundraising tool for Metroplex, as another contentious ploy to retain power. But the issue that actually caught the public's attention was the fight over who would chair the Metroplex board.

Although Neil Golub has said he never really wanted that position, many people seemed to support him for it. Neil said, "This was a job for a real estate or development pro. I had convinced OGS leader John Egan to agree to take the job. I was smart enough to realize what I didn't know." In spite of that, Governor Pataki called Frank Potter personally, making it clear that his friend, Neil, absolutely deserved the job. Bob Farley and a number of prominent people hammered away at Potter, in person and using their usual weapon, op-eds in the *Daily Gazette*, demanding that he choose Neil. Plenty of regular citizens, impressed by Golub's philanthropy and entrepreneurial expertise, or simply fans of their favorite local Price Chopper, submitted unsolicited endorsements to the paper.

In opposition, Catherine Wajda and the Citizens for Preservation and Revitalization hounded whoever would listen to them and distributed broadsides in their CPR Newsletter against Neil, against any other leader of Schenectady 2000 – Roger Hull, Wally Graham, George Robertson – and still, foolishly, against the whole notion of the authority itself. Eventually they filed a lawsuit which demanded that Metroplex be scrapped entirely. Former mayor Frank Duci even jumped into the fray, lamenting the fact that home rule legislation had not guaranteed the county board would have veto power over those Metroplex proposals which they felt the people of Schenectady County may not want. Meanwhile, as the war of the opinion pieces raged on, the sales tax slid quietly but legally upward, from seven to seven and a half percent, on September 1.

By November 7, the short list for Metroplex chair came down to three people who had already been selected to sit on the board: Neil Golub, president and COO of Golub Corporation and Price Chopper supermarkets; John Manning, a manager of mobile construction crews that built natural gas pipelines for Niagara Mohawk, as well as leader of a county economic advisory board; and Harry Apkarian, an engineer who had founded Mechanical Technology, Inc. and who had served as chairman of Proctor's Theater since 1988. Bob Farley and Don Ackerman and a few other legislators stood firmly behind Neil Golub, but Frank Potter worked hard to influence a majority, claiming that Golub had threatened people politically, though Golub vehemently denied that. The vote on November 10 went in favor of John Manning, and Harry Apkarian was chosen to be vice chair. Neil Golub opted to assume his seat on the Metroplex board, and still sits on that board today.

Years later, Potter explained his actions:

> *I liked Neil Golub. I never disliked the man. I thought he was smart and brilliant. I still do. Unfortunately, when I sat and talked with him, I felt like he was paying me a courtesy. Here I was, the Chairman of the Board of the County Legislature, and I felt like that, so I wondered,* What would I feel like if I was a small businessman in Schenectady County and I had to go in front of him? *And I felt like he shouldn't be representing small businesses if he talked to me like that. The appointment was up to the chairman, which was me at the time, and I didn't appoint him. It had nothing to do with the fact that he wasn't intelligent or that he couldn't handle it. He certainly could. Unfortunately, his personality, I thought, was wrong.*

*   *   *

The battle over Metroplex didn't end with its passage and Pataki's signing it in June of 1998. It simply retreated from broad public awareness. The governor did indeed earmark five million dollars to jumpstart the authority after he signed the bill, but the Metroplex board wasn't even chosen and seated until the end of that year. So Mayor Al Jurczynski and Schenectady Economic Development Corporation head George Robertson scarfed up that five million and promptly shelled out close to half a million to Hunter Interests of Annapolis, MD, along with other design sub-contractors, to provide yet another economic development plan for Schenectady. Neither one would admit if hiring an outside firm was a blatant rebuke to the whole concept of Metroplex and local, separate control – which could take major city planning out of their hands and effectively neutralize the Schenectady Economic Development Corporation – but without an initial, extensive public outreach, the process seemed to proceed in secret until well into 1999 when Hunter Interests finally sought public meetings in Schenectady for analysis and critiques of what they were proposing.

However, most insiders weren't airing any dirty laundry in public. "Today Schenectady," a special promotional supplement to the *Times Union* – or its reverse, "Schenectady Today," depending on who was talking about it – asked a number of community leaders about their position on Metroplex a couple of months after the legislation had been signed by the governor and here's how they started their answers:

> **Robert Farley:** *I am a sponsor of and helped to write much of the Metroplex legislation at the county level.*

> **Hugh Farley:** *It was my bill and my legislation. I think it's a great opportunity for Schenectady, for the down-town area and the county in general.*

> **Frank Potter:** *I hope that it all works out. It's a big undertaking. Now that the authority is in place, it is unusual in that you hope it does what it's designed to rather than become a dictatorship.*

> **Paul Tonko:** *Basically I am a strong supporter in investing in counties and, in so doing, caution that we do so with every degree of accountability and taxpayer protection.*

> **Peter Guidarelli:** *At this point, I think that it's the best position for everyone to be in favor of the Metroplex.*

> **Neil Golub:** *Roger Hull and I have literally led the fight to establish the Metroplex. It IS the future of Schenectady.*

Although Mayor Al Jurczynski wasn't one of the leaders queried, his lengthy Mayor's Message ran alongside the article, and here are the first few sentences of what he said:

> *We've made the turn! Things are looking up in Schenectady. Contrary to what I've heard in the past, people are sensing a turnaround in our city. With the fine work of Schenectady 2000 and county support for the Metroplex bill, things appear to be getting back on track. Gov. George Pataki comes by to visit from time to time, and is always positive and upbeat about our resurgence as a city. The governor's visits alone have had a tremendously positive impact on how we view ourselves.*

Given all the pervasive fear, crime, and scandal that had plagued Schenectady for several years, it was understandable that the city's movers and shakers needed a hopeful initiative to promote. Metroplex seemed like the best candidate but, behind the scenes, the fierce competition to retain control of the planning process continued as usual. While it's crucial to recognize that creating the new legislation which formed an independent, sales-tax-funded, economic development authority had been proposed, written, amended again and again, passed at the county and state levels, signed into law, and garnered nominal support in the wake of its signing – all in less than one year – constituted a remarkable accomplishment, the reality of what the volunteer members of Metroplex faced was daunting. By January 1, 1999, when the eleven-member Board of Directors had finally been selected and seated, Frank

Potter's choice of John Manning to act as Chairman of the new authority had set up an inevitable, and perhaps intentional, series of confrontations with the person Governor Pataki had wanted and Potter had snubbed, Neil Golub.

John Manning lived in Rotterdam and worked as an executive for Niagara Mohawk Power Company, a New York State utility company that was acquired by National Grid in 2000. John also served as the energy company's representative on the Chamber of Commerce, so while he was well-acquainted with Schenectady's economic problems, he had never been part of Schenectady 2000, nor had he participated in any of the planning for Metroplex. Finding the twenty-three-page statute for the authority vague and complex, Manning sent it to the Attorney General for clarification, and all his opponents pounced on him:

> *Well, anyway, we're seated. I'm the Chairman. No officers, no staff, no anything. And we've got a twenty-three-page statute, that most of us didn't participate in developing. Every time someone talked about something, they said, "That's not what we decided, when I was there, when we did this, and we did that." We ended up, actually, our attorney recommended it, Neil Levine. We sent it to the Attorney General's office and asked them to describe what it is and what our role is.*
>
> *It came back and the mayor told the Board, "I'm the mayor and you're dissing me and you're dissing the town." Neil Golub got upset, too. He didn't say anything to me, but what he thought appeared in the paper: "This guy is a know-nothing, he's a dope, he's got no track record, he doesn't understand these things." It was always about Schenectady 2000, and of course I wasn't on that board. They all thought they had the plan and Metroplex was only the funding mechanism. Neil was supposed to be the Chairman, and George Robertson would have been his guy. Frankly, those guys didn't bother me. They could say whatever they wanted. Unless you want to have a fist fight, the rest of this was sissy stuff, as far as I was concerned.*

Once Mayor Al and George Robertson had commandeered the five million from Governor Pataki and paid Hunter Interests for its massive economic plan, a blood-feud within the Metroplex board was preordained, and not even surprising. Schenectady had grown famous for its political brawling and its culture of intimidation. If demanding didn't work, yelling would often follow. Don Hunter, whose company had presented its Hunter-Sasaki Downtown Schenectady Master Plan in November of 1999, said in the public summary of his 300-page final report, "A true partnership of effort will be necessary between City and County governments, development organizations and Metroplex, and the many large and small investors, developers, and business interests that are downtown now … Regardless of the realities of the situation, a perception shared by many is that important leaders are working at cross purposes, with the general public being the loser." Privately, after the entire process was complete, he confided that, "This is one of the most dysfunctional communities I've ever seen. They take bickering to a new level."

So when you spend close to $450,000 for an economic plan, there's a ton of pressure to follow its recommendations, and half of the newly-appointed members of the Metroplex board felt like those recommendations fit with their particular vision for revitalizing the city. Neil Golub, who was the prime architect of Schenectady 2000, with Roger Hull, Wally Graham and George Robertson as key members of the team, could legitimately point to an impressive string of improvements they had initiated during the last several years. Their vision and investment, along with the successful work of hundreds of volunteers, had begun to renew pride and boost morale in Schenectady, so simple gratitude and common sense might dictate that following their ideas was the best way forward.

The Schenectady 2000 contingent, who had been meeting regularly and strategizing ways to influence what the Hunter–Sasaki plan would include, became known as the Client Group. Whether George Robertson was actually expressing the group's sentiments or not, he at one point was quoted in the paper as saying, "Metroplex is really just a sophisticated funding mechanism. That's all we've created, not having anything to do with anything other than paying the bills." Eventually, the Client Group, along with the City Engineer, Milt Mitchell, who was also a Metroplex Board member, presented the Hunter-Sasaki Master Plan to John

Manning as a fait accompli: "It's a 20-million-dollar plan, and Metroplex is going to pay for it," they announced. "We've all approved it. Everybody likes it." And they cited the projects that had been outlined in the Metroplex Board Member Handbook (developed by the Schenectady County Legislature's Subcommittee on Metroplex Appointments) at the end of August in the previous year – 1998 – when the chairmanship of the Board was still up for grabs:

- *A first-class trade show and exposition facility*

- *A luxury convention hotel*

- *A multi-tower, high-story, government and business office complex*

- *An inter-modal transportation facility to accommodate high-speed rail and buses*

- *A large, privately-owned multiplex cinema complex*

- *A multiple ice-sheet skating/hockey complex*

- *A transportation-enclosed pedestrian walkway*

- *Shovel-ready sites and industrial parks to promote economic and employment growth in the commercial corridors*

- *A 21ˢᵗ century broadcast center, and journalism and broadcasting internship program for the future home of WMHT television and WGY radio*

- *A new judicial court house and library services center*

- *New first-class business and office space for such entities as MVP and the Schenectady World Trade Center*

Quite an ambitious list. However, John Manning had his own ideas. As soon as he could, he moved the Metroplex meetings out of Union College and into offices vacated by an insurance company at the front of the City Center building on

State Street. Then he worked through several candidates to hire a salaried executive director and chose Jayme Lahut, the only non-volunteer in the organization, to help him implement his ideas. Jayme had been an assistant commissioner for a couple of years at the State Division of Housing and Community Renewal, dealing with affordable housing projects, before he accepted the job, and he remembers how difficult it was at the beginning:

> *The early board really was much more strategic in its point of view, looking to master planning as the core role of the authority. If you look at the legislation, it's got a litany of things that we can do. It talks about improvements in the Route 5 and Route 7 corridors of Schenectady. But it doesn't specify what it means by "improvement." Early on, the board focused on tactical objectives, i.e. the need for a convention center, a movie theater, a hotel. One of our first board members told me that, "The only reason you're on the board is to spend money." And there's some truth to that. We get that piece of the county sales tax, the 70% of the half a percent. When I started in 1999, it was five and half million dollars a year. And fifty million in bonding authority on top of it. Whoever can control that fifty million is going to have a huge effect on the community.*

Further conflict on the Board was caused by the legislation's vague definition of improvement, and where that improvement should occur. John Manning had no intention of simply acquiescing to the Client Group's list of projects – he had his own priorities, as well as a lot of questions – but he did respond to their agenda: Should we build a new headquarters for MVP Health Care and prevent them from leaving the city? Does erecting a new building fall under the heading of "improvement?" Do we add to the existing parking garage on Broadway and/or buy some private lots and solve the parking problem in downtown? After all, if we need to accommodate the Department of Transportation jobs that Hugh Farley negotiated for the city, or if we want to expand Proctor's, or entice a developer to place a new multiplex theater here, we better offer safe, convenient parking for all the expected visitors. How about fixing the 400 block of State Street – when do we remove the defunct canal and demolish the decaying buildings of Canal Square so we can revitalize that core area of downtown? But, of course, all of those projects are downtown. Should Schenectady's business center be the only beneficiary of the money and development expertise of Metroplex? And there were the neighborhoods and the towns in the County to consider, too, as John reminded them:

> I'd visited every single neighborhood group in Schenectady and spent time with them and said, "You can come any time you want, I'll talk to you guys about any issues you have." But half the Board didn't think we should be in the neighborhoods or talking to the neighborhoods. Stay focused on downtown, that's how they saw it. But I came to realize with these conversations and interviews, and in the towns as well and their members who were on our board or appointees, that there's something else going on here besides the downtown of Schenectady. And I said, "We need to start to consider how this connects to this town or to the neighborhoods, and how we bring them forward with everybody else." It wasn't a day or two later that the Gazette had an editorial cartoon with a train, and I'm the engineer. "He's taking the train off the track." Me. Because I suggested that the neighborhoods ought to be considered.

Ironically, though, and regardless of John Manning's propensity for inclusion and adherence to the specific legalities of the Metroplex legislation, most of the projects that received immediate attention were ones that the Client Group had proposed. Perhaps that was because there were restrictions on what the authority could do in the neighborhoods. The specter of eminent domain had dogged Metroplex from its inception, and many residents were still afraid the authority would swoop in and start grabbing up properties wherever they wanted. The realization that Metroplex had no bounds – the attorney general had informed them they could "do anything," after all – added to its controversial position in the city. And when the Hunter-Sasaki plan was unveiled on Christmas Eve in 1999, surprisingly nobody adopted it. Not the City Council. Not those on the Board who had once demanded that Metroplex would implement and fund all of its recommendations. And not even George Robertson in his role as head of the City IDA. Even George, to justify all his prior threats, wouldn't get behind it. After shelling out a small fortune to commission it, and after trying to bully John Manning into accepting it, Mayor Al and the rest of the Client Group failed to officially sponsor it and declare, "This is what we should be doing." So, for revitalization projects, it essentially came down to first-come, first-served.

MVP called John Manning first. They needed more space for their people. Some of their employees were in an inadequate building down in the Stockade district, and some were out of town at an old army depot. They wanted everybody in one facility, one large building that would meet all their needs, with adjacent parking, and they had lots of options outside Schenectady. Colonie had made them an offer, and other cities in the Capital Region that would remain unnamed. What could Schenectady do for them?

Well, John convinced the County Legislature to give him land they owned at the top of the hill where State Street crossed Nott Terrace. That was the land Frank Potter had held in reserve for a new courthouse and convention center, but this was his own choice for Metroplex Chair asking, so how could he refuse? "I have this spot, I think it's attractive, it's at the top of the hill which gives you a great view of everything, it's spectacular," John told MVP. "We'll need a parking garage, too," they said. That was a more expensive problem. With a larger plot, say, out in the suburbs, you could just level it and lay down a sea of blacktop and stripe it for parking spots. Pretty easy deal. But when you have limited space, you need to put up a building with ramps and tiers and everything else.

All in all, as outlined in the 1999 Annual Report of the Schenectady Metroplex Development Authority that was submitted to the Schenectady County Legislature in February of 2000, the MVP project was a behemoth: on the 2.2 acres of vacant land that the authority now owns, MVP wants "Construction of an eight-story building containing approximately 25,000 square feet per floor," and "Construction of a 1000-car parking structure."

It would cost twenty dollars per square foot more to build it in Schenectady

than in Colonie, and a "multi-deck urban parking facility is estimated to cost about $8000.00 more per space than a comparably-sized suburban surface facility." Metroplex would have to kick in ten million dollars for this project – about 28% of the proposed $36 million total budget. For an initial endeavor, the MVP project was certainly a big-ticket item. The economic rationale for taking it on included a much bigger amount: $47.9 million in total economic impact for the area during the construction period, with almost $15 million in additional household incomes during the same period. Annually, Schenectady County could expect $12 million a year after MVP was up and operating, and almost $5 million a year of personal income earned by residents who worked there. A $36-million project that returns $80 million was worth keeping in the city, and the Board approved the project. The Mayor and the Client Group should have been ecstatic, but who got the credit and who was in control were still the bones of contention.

The other important call came from Senator Hugh Farley. He had negotiated

the relocation of the New York State Department of Transportation from Albany to downtown Schenectady, and he didn't want to be embarrassed. DOT's needs were similar to MVP's: a 125,000 square-foot building on Broadway near State Street to house 450 employees, and two more tiers of parking, adding 467 new spaces to the existing garage across the street. $15 million for the building, and $6 million for the parking. But money wasn't the only problem. Metroplex needed to own a number of the buildings in disrepair on the 400 block of State Street if they wanted to demolish some to make room for new projects, and the City owned all the deeds that the Canal Square businesses had relinquished, as John Manning recounted:

> *So the initiative was, we'll take the properties from the City for a buck or whatever they want, and we'll put together a plan that the community's involved in, and we'll develop it. See, they didn't believe we could own property, and of course the statute said we could do anything with property. We can own it, we can build it,*

we can rent it, we can do anything we want. But you had to keep going back to that. All of that was lost on these people in the greater scheme of things. And almost every vote for the first year was six to five. My margin was one person. I was always dealing with this razor-thin margin. Getting the town guys to support a plan that they weren't participating in. It wasn't going to benefit them, but they saw that it was worthwhile doing, that kind of thing. And they took that as their responsibility to move those forward. So we're down to the vote and I don't have the votes to take the properties, so right as the meeting was starting, I ran all the way down to the parking lot to ask this new guy if he would vote with us, and he said yes. Six to five, and we got the properties. That

was our first acquisition, outside of the one the County gave me.
We had to own something to build on it, so that we could show the
rest of the community that we could actually do things of value.

After the vote, John Manning still had to justify paying for the addition to the parking garage for State employees who didn't have the same amenity where they were. Nobody in Schenectady would be quick to help out workers they already saw as privileged, and the $6 million price tag wasn't helping. But having DOT in the city was apparently important enough to Hugh Farley that he called John in the 11th hour and said, "I'll split the cost with you." John received a check in the mail for $3 million.

Metroplex was up and running, even if it was in fits and starts. While the conflicts on the Board wouldn't stop simmering for three more years, at least two major projects had been approved. With MVP staying in town and DOT coming soon, over a thousand jobs would be created. Derelict buildings in Canal Square were slated for removal, and a third major project that Metroplex supported – the expansion of Proctor's Theater – would do more in the next ten years to change the fate of Schenectady than anything since Edison had moved his machine works to town.

8

What Makes a City Livable?

A city with a skyline of memorable buildings or a commanding location is immediately appealing. But livability is more than skin deep, and a crucial factor in assessing it is the quality of one's daily experience. Ask yourself: Do I feel safe on my city's streets and in the parks? ... Does my city have a car-free area in the center of town for pedestrian use? Is housing available at different price ranges, for rent as well as for sale? Do I have ample choice in places to shop, dine, and find entertainment? Is my city supplied with and supportive of theaters, libraries, and museums? Has nature been incorporated as an essential part of the city environment in the form of parks, greenways, and sports fields? If the answer to most of these questions is "Yes," then you and your city are the fortunate beneficiaries of wise, comprehensive long-range planning.

– Toward the Livable City
Emilie Buchwald, Editor

Amid all the rancor that underscored this latest round of economic develop-ment hopes for Schenectady, a perceptible shift in local design discussions had begun, and in more informal venues than City Council meetings or County Legislature sessions. Increasingly, regular citizens were involving them-selves in the process of thinking about how to fix their city. Maybe six or seven years of Schenectady 2000 volunteer efforts were finally paying off, lifting civic morale and showing people that community action could indeed produce tangible improvements in a fraying cityscape.

Underlying the change was the sincere desire for many citizens, of course, that the much-touted and adequately-funded new Metroplex authority would actually work to restore some luster to a dormant downtown, as promised, although tangible accomplishments would clearly be at least a couple of years down the road. But more particularly, a surprising willingness to be less parochial surfaced, along with a renewed desire to seek empirical advice and effective models for growth. As just one example, the Schenectady Heritage Foundation scheduled a series of lecture/discussions with nationally-known authors and community leaders to be held at the First Unitarian Society of Schenectady between February and April of 1999.

Roberta Brandes Gratz opened the series in February by reading from her recently-published book, *Cities: Back from the Edge – New Life for Downtown*, which chronicled stories of innovative revitalizations in cities from Mansfield, Ohio to Manhattan. Julia Stokes, who founded the Saratoga Springs Preservation Foundation, appeared in March and explained how the city which boasted the oldest, still-operating thoroughbred horse racing track in America had distilled its historic charm into unique containers and reinvented itself. And James Howard Kunstler, another Saratoga Springs resident and renowned author of several influential books, including the 1993 best-seller, *The Geography of Nowhere: The Rise and Decline of America's Manmade Landscape*, as well as its sequel, *Home from Nowhere: Remaking Our Everyday World for the 21st Century*, warned his listeners in April about the dangers of continued fascination with the automobile near the end of the cheap-oil age, of exiling themselves to the suburbs, and of forfeiting the sense of legitimate place-identity that cities could offer. In one of his essays, "Cities of the Future in the Long Emergency," Kunstler wrote, "Fortunately, we have a whole nation full of towns and cities waiting to be re-inhabited –" a sentence tailor-made for turn-of-the-millennium Schenectady.

"Re-inhabited" neatly summed the problem up: between 1990 and 2000, according to The United States Decennial Census, another steep drop in Schenectady's population was recorded, from 65,566 to 61,821. That 5.7% decline meant that, in only fifty years, more than 30,000 people had left their hometown, essentially, for good. Kurt Vonnegut, who had worked at General Electric for several years in the 1950s and lived in nearby Alplaus, based his early novel, *Player Piano*, on his experiences there but didn't hang around any longer than his job lasted. John Sayles – acclaimed novelist, screenwriter, and independent filmmaker – grew up on Sumner Avenue, attended Williams College, and opted to never again live in the city of his birth. Famous NBA player and coach Pat Riley was a high-school basketball legend in the city, but followed his dreams and opportunities elsewhere. Hall-of-Fame race-car driver Shirley Muldowney, actor Mickey Rourke, Blood Sweat & Tears guitarist Steve Katz, David Kaczynski, who helped the F.B.I. find his brother, the "Unabomber," John Sykes, co-founder of MTV and head of iHeartRadio, and politician Andrew Yang, among many others – Schenectady natives all – chased their careers to other places.

Hardly unusual, right? Lots of people grow up in one city and move somewhere else. But the declining population, and the abandoned houses left behind and often removed from the tax rolls, decimated the city's budget. Schenectady's inability to replace almost one in every three residents during the second half of the 20th Century wasn't any great mystery – the primary reason, of course, was General Electric's 90% workforce reduction at its main plant between 1950 and 1999 – but apart from those unrelenting job losses, why were people reluctant to move there? Or, in a more basic way of thinking about it, what essential aspects make a city livable and why wasn't Schenectady able to offer some of those things?

There are plenty of books and websites that posit criteria for livability and rank cities according to the data, but there are a number of categories that appear on every list: public safety; employment opportunities; affordable housing; adequate health care; good schools; physical beauty – attractive buildings, functioning infrastructure, vibrant public spaces, and nice parks; aesthetic and cultural offerings; a variety of restaurants; diverse neighborhoods; accessible public transportation; and effective political leadership. Prospective residents of any city would prioritize specific elements according to their individual needs, of course – families with young children would care more about school systems than empty-nesters might, for instance – but physical security would be a basic need at the top of almost everyone's list. Who wants to live in an unsafe place, or move somewhere their lives might be in danger?

Like most American cities in their struggles to provide public safety, Schenectady has had a blemished record. Greg Kaczmarek, who was police chief from 1996 to 2003, claimed more than once during 1999, "We're on the right track," and that the city had reached its lowest recorded level of serious crimes in 1998. Murders, robberies, and auto thefts had dropped almost four percent from 1997, although he did have to admit that rapes and assaults had increased dramatically during the same time. He pointed out that there were 6,214 arrests made in Schenectady during 1998, and that was "the highest number of collars" since 1992.

However, the statistics masked the mutual distrust that existed between the police and many residents in some of the city's higher crime districts – Hamilton Hill, the Vale area, and Mont Pleasant – where the complaints of police misbehavior and brutality were unrelenting, especially from the local chapter of the National Association for the Advancement of Colored People (N.A.A.C.P.). If those neighborhoods were homogeneous, it would be tempting to cast the problem in black-and-white terms – mostly African-American citizens, for instance, suffering from over-aggressive tactics by a racist police department – but that wouldn't be accurate, for any number of reasons. To cite only one, drug dealers and gang bangers from downstate had plagued Schenectady all throughout the '90s, and their crackhead customers often preyed on the law-abiding black population as well as the descendants of immigrants from Italy and Eastern Europe who had moved to the city a hundred years earlier for jobs at General Electric. Skin color didn't matter much to those criminals: anyone who owned anything of value was fair game for users who were broke and jonesing for more drugs. Over time, Hamilton Hill residents especially had become resigned to the persistent drug-dealing, burglaries and muggings, until a sudden series of local and national incidents shattered the uneasy status quo.

On December 16, 1998, two elderly widows in their eighties, sisters-in-law Lois DiMaria and Matilda Montenaro, were putting up Christmas decorations at 564 Mumford Street in Hamilton Hill. Their next-door neighbor, a hairdresser named Pasquale Nicolella, allowed three of his junkie pals to run a ladder from his second-floor window to the womens' home across the alley, as long as they wrapped the ladder's feet with towels so no marks were left on his window.

George Johnson, Aaron Umber, and Dusty O'Connor shimmied across and dropped inside.

Umber crept downstairs and found a purse in the dining room. As he was scrounging through it, Johnson dragged Matilda Montenaro into the room. Matilda only weighed ninety-five pounds but she was struggling and screaming. "'What are you doing in my house?' That's what she was trying to say," Umber testified, "but George kind of had her in a full nelson. I punched her twice, but she kept crying. Dusty gave me a metal wand and when I hit her with that, she fell onto her back. Then I grabbed her by the leg, turned her over, and hit her one more time. She didn't move anymore."

Upstairs, O'Connor pushed Lois DiMaria up the attic stairs for the cash and jewelry she told him was in a locked box. A few minutes later, Umber found Lois dead in the attic with a key clutched in her hand, and decided he'd better destroy the whole place. He hurried downstairs and flicked on the gas in the kitchen stove. Then he swept a tablecloth and some decorations into a pile on the dining room table and lit them. Answering an automatic fire alarm, firefighters climbed through the same second-floor window and doused the fire before the gas ignited. When they discovered the two dead women, they called for the cops.

Three weeks later, with no arrests and no leads, the city announced a $1000.00 reward for information leading to an arrest. Schenectady County offered the same amount. Grief-stricken relatives, private donors, and local businesses outraged by the killings pushed the amount up to $13,750. Mayor Jurczynski, who had been born and raised on Wylie Street in Hamilton Hill, told the *Daily Gazette* that the murders had made his parents consider, for the very first time, moving out of the city. Then on Friday, January 8, at a City Hall luncheon with the Metroplex Development Authority's newly-seated board of directors, another elderly widow – eighty-one-year-old Angela Marzacano – showed up unannounced with a check for $11,250.00, bringing the total reward to $25,000. "It breaks your heart," she told them. "They had a right to life like everybody else. They'll never rest in peace while their killers are not found." The Metroplex leaders stood up and gave her a round of applause.

In a city full of retired General Electric employees, many of them senior citizens whose GE stock had soared and made them financially secure but who still lived in Hamilton Hill and Bellevue and Mont Pleasant where the demographics were shifting, these two widow-murders were more than ominous. Mayor Al knew he had to react quickly, and he revealed that eleven new police officers would be added to the department. Those new recruits would enable the city to establish a Directed Patrol, an elite street-crimes unit that would target high-crime areas and help protect vulnerable residents. However, before they could even get trained, a downstate murder made the situation far more complex and captured the attention of the entire country.

Amadou Diallo was a twenty-three-year-old African immigrant from Guinea who lived in the South Bronx and worked as a street peddler in Manhattan. In the earliest hour of February 4, 1999, he was standing on the front stoop of his apartment building when four plain-clothes cops from NYPD's street crimes unit mistook him for a rape suspect and approached him. Diallo turned, ran back into the vestibule, crouched down and reached to pull something black out of his back pocket. The officers fired forty-one bullets at him in about three seconds – nineteen of which hit his head and body – and then quickly realized he had no gun. Diallo had been reaching for his wallet. A year later, those police officers were acquitted on all charges by four black and eight white jurors in an Albany, New York courtroom, ten miles away from Schenectady. Capital Region residents could hardly avoid the Diallo story, just as they were recovering from the news about the widows in Hamilton Hill. Moreover, the acquittal sent a reassuring message to police officers that they could continue doing whatever they felt like on the job and probably wouldn't face dire consequences.

For the first half of 1999, Schenectady held its breath. In spite of Chief Kaczmarek continuing to crow about arrests being up and major crimes being down for the sixth year in a row, no one had been charged yet for killing the widows on Mumford Street. The seven-member team of police veterans who had been selected to comprise the Directed Patrol was finally in training, slated to hit the streets in May, even though for minority communities and some concerned politicians alike the Diallo shooting had created serious doubts about the wisdom of empowering street-crime units. Then the secret life of the police department got splashed across a series of front pages.

Patrolman Ronald Pederson acted out first: he arrested and handcuffed Jessica and Rebecca DiSorbo after Rebecca had rejected his advances at a local bar, and then beat and choked her at the police station – badly enough that she was rushed to Ellis Hospital – and the sisters eventually filed a civil rights lawsuit against the city. Simultaneously, the N.A.A.C.P. submitted twenty complaints to the Schenectady police department from drug dealers who claimed that beat cops routinely stole drugs and money from them. And naturally, the *Daily Gazette* broadcast the unfolding elements of the crisis as the fear of uncaught murderers and out-of-control cops was rising to a boil in the city's neighborhoods.

Then at 9:15 P.M. on July 28, officers Michael Siler and Richard Barnett made a serious mistake that they almost got away with: they spotted a young black man, David Sampson, on the porch at 816 Lincoln Avenue and suspected he was a burglar. "What did I do?" he asked them as they pushed him into the back of their patrol car. No answer. As they drove down State Street, Sampson assumed he'd end up at the police station on Liberty Street, but they didn't even slow down when they got there – flew right past it, turned onto Erie Boulevard and kept going up Freeman's Bridge Road toward Glenville, then drove mile after mile out into the dark countryside until they stopped on Rector Road. At that point, Sampson figured Siler and Barnett meant to kill him and refused to get out of the car. Barnett yanked the back door of the cruiser open and said, "Stick your feet out here." When Sampson complied, Barnett pulled off his boots and tossed them into the woods. After he hauled Sampson out and pushed him down onto the road, Barnett and Siler drove away.

This kind of "relocation" technique was fairly common practice for some Schenectady cops in the late '90s. Usually, the victims were criminals who were just happy they survived and didn't want to press their luck or call attention to themselves. But less than a month later, on August 23, Sampson did something unusual: he sued the police department and the city for abduction. Now lots of people in town, not just the folks in Hamilton Hill, started complaining about the cops. Chief Kaczmarek jumped right on it, suspending Siler and Barnett without pay for thirty days and charging them with misconduct in the line of duty. "There is a likelihood we will arrest them," he told the press, pretending to be shocked by the allegations and hiding what he already knew:

Siler and Barnett were basically rogue patrolmen, they were fool-
ing around with hookers and drugs, and all this other stuff. One of
our lieutenants, Mike Hamilton, had a relationship with the DEA,
by assignment. He had informants and was working with federal
authorities to make arrests, right? So Hamilton comes to me and
he goes, "You're going to hear about, pretty soon, some guy that
they took, that Siler and Barnett took off a porch in Hamilton
Hill, he was dealing drugs, and they dumped him in the woods on
Route 5S, punched him two or three times, threatened him, not re-
ally beating him up but still ... My informant just told me this, the
word is on the street, people are going to get wind of this."

What Kaczmarek also didn't tell reporters was that the recent abduction and the lawsuit it caused were just the tip of the iceberg: a few days earlier, District Attorney Bob Carney had obtained a search warrant for Siler and Barnett's lockers. Among other things, investigators had found marijuana, crack cocaine, heroin, and a scale for weighing drugs inside. Those cops were already in deep shit, and it would only get deeper.

Now Kaczmarek was certain he needed an independent voice to deflect criti-cism. Siler and Barnett were two of his best guys, decorated for their stellar arrest records, and the PBA was backing them all the way, even demanding that the city pay for their lawyers. They had commendations that he had bestowed, for chrissakes. If the rumors panned out – that they were the primary beat cops who had been shaking down the drug dealers for cash and product – how would that play out in the press, like he was in their corner, encouraging them to use whatever means necessary to cut crime rates in the city, right?

Before he had been appointed chief by Mayor Al in 1996, Kaczmarek had been forced to hold a press conference to dispel the rumors that he dealt cocaine himself – Sergeant Snow had been one of the nicknames that disgruntled rivals in the depart-ment had pinned on him – so he absolutely needed some outside agency to take the lead and create distance for him. He couldn't call the New York State Police. They didn't investigate city police departments. But it had to be a big, reputable agency.

In the meantime, he contacted Schenectady's PBA president and told him the two patrolmen should check out their pension rights and maybe plan to retire, fast. Then he called the FBI, but that didn't work out quite the way he had planned:

> So I took the County Attorney with me, Mike Brockbank, to FBI headquarters. I laid it all out for them, and told them where my information had come from. I said, "I need your help. I want to do this right. I can't have this shit happening. Nobody condones it. It's a civil rights violation. You guys ought to be able to deal with civil rights stuff."
>
> And the agent said, "I don't know if I can help you." I told him, "You're my FBI. This is happening in your jurisdiction." And he answered, "Well, we don't know if you're a target of this investigation or not. I can't really comment. I don't know which way this thing is going to go. I don't want to say too much."
>
> Well, the FBI just let it be known that I may be linked to this, because of those rumors of personal posse kind of thing – that maybe Siler and Barnett were actually doing my bidding – because we were doing phenomenal against crime. They were claiming that guys were working outside the lines with my knowledge, or at my direction. We were beating Compstat – Computer Statistics. We got invited to a thing in New York by Mayor Giuliani, to see what Compstat was doing, and the guy said to me, "How are you doing this without computers?"

Within a week of Siler and Barnett's suspensions, department morale tanked and arrests plummeted in Schenectady. Beat cops were afraid they'd be sued for any collar they made, legitimate or not. Lawyers piled on, filing brutality lawsuits for incidents that had occurred even months before. The suspension month flew by and, thanks to PBA support, Siler and Barnett were kept on the force with full pay for a year, though not trusted to work, while the Feds prepared the case against them. During that year, they ratted out other cops. One rookie who was never involved stepped up to do what he thought was his civic duty and also named names. A short time after that, feeling ostracized and ashamed, he went into work and blew his brains out in the locker room. Four patrolmen ended up with prison time, Siler and Barnett included. Three crackheads were eventually convicted for killing the widows, earning sentences from forty to eighty years, depending on what they had done, how fully they confessed, and who betrayed whom first. And for three years, the unrelenting news coverage sizzled, stoking fear, sparking pro and con op-ed pieces, and helping to sink Schenectady's reputation ever lower.

$$*\qquad*\qquad*$$

"Thanks, folks, you're in tune to *Herman Singh Showtime*, 93.5 on your dial. It's twenty minutes before 11 A.M. and right now we have Al Jurczynski, the mayor of Schenectady, New York, on the line with us. If you're thinking about purchasing a property, you should consider moving to Schenectady." Suddenly Al blurts out, "857-4000, area code 518. That's my number. If you want to buy a home in my town, give me a call. My incoming calls are free, so don't be shy."

Accompanying the unrelenting, negative news articles that had spawned fear and kept most people away, the repopulation challenge constantly gnawed at him. Mayor Al loved his city, including the Hamilton Hill area where he grew up, and he believed the city's good qualities overshadowed its problems. In his mind, Schenectady had more than its share of attractive areas: Central Park, with its lake and ball fields and tennis courts and magnificent rose garden; the historic Stockade district along the Mohawk River; the State Street and Albany Street shops, full of those deep-seated memories – Johnny the Greek's best penny-candy store in the country, Henry's cycle shop where they sold Schwinns, and Barrio's Needs and Necessities, that guy was a wingnut – along with all those other ethnic businesses; the GE Realty Plot where every rich-person house had been designed to look unique; all the different boulevards and parkways – Grand, Eastern, Glenwood, Erie, Marion, Lexington, Parkwood, Rosehill and so many more; even Vale Cemetery, where he rode his bike as a kid, thinking he could scare everybody, and where Charles Steinmetz, the GE electrical wizard-dwarf from Germany, was buried. So when Deryck Singh, who had started out in Schenectady as a clerk at a Stewart's convenience store on Brandywine

Avenue and had risen over the years to supervise twenty of their stores in the Capital Region, suggested he could distribute flyers promoting Schenectady's inexpensive houses to people in his old neighborhood in the Bronx and in Queens, the proverbial light bulb popped on and Mayor Al had them printed right up.

There was, after all, plenty of decent housing stock available in the city – some of the condemned dwellings screaming out to be razed, of course, to the tune of $16,000 in average demolition costs per condemned building – but there were hundreds of houses that were well-made and still sound and needing to be back on the tax rolls, as soon as Mayor Al could convince people to buy them. In City-Data's 1998 profile of Schenectady, it notes that only two permits for new-house construction were issued in that year, and just three permits were granted for the following year, 1999. Five permits for new houses during two years in a city of 60,000 people seems ludicrous, but the numbers don't lie. Either only a literal handful of folks believed enough in Schenectady to build a new house there, or the demolitions they had completed had not created desirable lots, or the empty houses that once held the long-gone, 30,000 former residents presented renovation opportunities that were irresistible compared with the price of building. Or all the above. However, one thing was obvious: Schenectady needed a lot of new residents from outside the Capital Region, people who wouldn't be scared off by news articles about crime and police corruption and a decaying downtown.

But now it was spring of 2001, just a few months into his second term as mayor, and Al thought about the city's abandoned houses all the time. He was constantly reminded of the squatters and crackheads who used and abused them. As a three-term member of the City Council before he was elected mayor in 1996, he had watched as a raging stream of criminals, gang members, and freeloaders had flooded in and degraded his city, and he was sick of the problems they brought with them and the atmosphere of fear they created for the decent residents. What he needed was a clear symbol of progress – lots of new people moving to his city, fixing up dilapidated houses, hardworking people who weren't easily scared, maybe because they lived in areas where crime was even worse than in Schenectady. Maybe the Guyanese were the ticket.

Deryck Singh had distributed the flyers touting Schenectady, and Herman Singh

– a realtor, mortgage broker, local celebrity with a weekly radio program in Queens, and no relation to Deryck – had picked one up and immediately realized the possibilities. Herman pitched the relocation idea on air and, a month after Mayor Al called in to his show, he rented a bus to ferry interested friends and neighbors up to see houses for sale in Schenectady. The resulting word of mouth about inexpensive housing and good job opportunities upstate turned curiosity into widespread desire in the downstate Guyanese community. So much interest developed, and so quickly, that Herman chartered a bus every Saturday. He also coordinated with Deryck and city officials to schedule regular job fairs for the prospective buyers while they were in Schenectady.

From 1999 to 2000, there were 140,000 or so Guyanese residents in New York City – primarily in Queens, Brooklyn, and the Bronx. The largest community by far was in Richmond Hill, Queens, but Herman's show was a must-listen for most Guyanese in New York City. It had been Al's spontaneous notion to shout his personal number out to Herman Singh's faithful Guyanese listeners that day, and it worked like gangbusters. Week after week, without fail, Mayor Al was part of the city team that met Herman's bus upon arrival. After an hourlong welcoming ceremony at City Hall, he led all the visitors back onto the bus and conducted a three-hour, rehearsed tour of the city, starting with his old Hamilton Hill neighborhood.

"This is Wylie Street," he would begin, "and this is the house where I grew up with my family. My mother was French Canadian and my father was Polish. Do you see these carved railings? My grandfather was a carpenter, and he made those railings. I had eight brothers and sisters. The Riggis lived in this house, and the Cooks lived in that one. Over there, where Route 890 runs now, used to be all woods, oaks and thick bushes and pine trees. We called it "the hollow" and all us neighborhood kids played in there. And this house on your right is where I lived with my wife until the year I was elected mayor, in 1996. Now Mayor Bloomberg down in New York City wouldn't take you on a tour and show you his house, would he? That alone should be reason enough to move up here, right? Anyway, I was thirty-nine when we moved out of this house and now we live near Central Park. That's where we'll go next, and where I'll get you the best ice cream there is. But first I've got to show you my wife's parents' garden."

Mayor Al's in-laws were an elderly Sicilian couple, smiling, standing in front of their modest white ranch house. They would dutifully shake the hand of every Guyanese visitor as each one stepped off the bus, and then would lead the group back to a vibrant vegetable plot with a footprint bigger than the house. And when they offered everyone a plastic cup of homemade wine or an Italian cookie, that clinched the deal. If George Robertson's list of mind-numbing facts at the welcoming – including Schenectady's founding 300 years ago as a Dutch trading post – hadn't captivated too many of them, or if the head of the local Chamber of Commerce assuring them what a great opportunity awaited them, not only as potential home-buyers but as new residents the city definitely needed, had failed to convince them that Schenectady was the promised land, the ornate railing and garden and wine and cookies in Hamilton Hill certainly did the trick.

Many of these Guyanese people, like Deryck Singh, had emigrated to America in the late 1980s, and no one had welcomed them as hardworking, desirable immigrants until this day, over a decade later, in this place with the hard-to-pronounce name of Schenectady. Mayor Al had handed each of them his personal business card as well, telling them that Guyanese people were the ones who could help put his beloved city back on its feet. His parents were immigrants, too, coming to America from Poland and French Canada.

Later in the tour, he announced, "Up here in Schenectady, people are nice to each other. We're upstate. We're regular people." Turning in his seat to face the passengers, he told them, "I'm like you. You're hardworking and ambitious, but you're also reserved and family-oriented. You don't come up here looking for hand-outs. You're the kind of people who made this city come alive a hundred years ago, and you can bring it back to life now. You already speak English, so you're a step ahead of where most immigrants are when they arrive. And living here in Sche-nectady will cost you half of what you pay now, or even less. Plus, I'm not like other mayors. You can come by my office and have coffee with me anytime you want. And maybe, someday, you can run for mayor, but not until I'm done. I'll let you know when I'm done." That final line always got a good laugh.

The Guyanese visitors were usually nodding as Mayor Al spoke. *This isn't what we thought a mayor would act like,* they could have been thinking. *His family **is** like* *ours, and his wife's parents grow all those beautiful vegetables just like our own parents did back home in Guyana. This could be a new start, a better one for us, away from the crowded noise of Queens. No more parking three blocks from our front door, afraid to be stabbed as we hurry back at night to our cramped apartments. We can have our own house here, too, a big house, with a porch and front yard and a fancy gate we can decorate with our country's flags – houses that can show everyone how well we work, and who we are.*

Mayor Al's offers seemed too good to be true, but they were real: the more dilapidated houses – if the buyers could show they had ample funds to restore the ones on the demolition list to city code – cost a dollar. Only one dollar for a whole house. Better houses went for anywhere from ten to fifty thousand – even the most expensive still a fraction of what buildings cost in Queens. After all, many Guyanese renters paid a thousand dollars a month, or more, for a small apartment in New York City where all their children were crammed into one bedroom. In Schenectady, twelve months of rent could translate into their very own three-story house – just as in Guyana, where people owned their homes and worked hard to build good lives. Life in Schenectady would be cheaper and easier.

Within a year, more than 2000 Guyanese had moved to Schenectady, and more were arriving every week. After only seven bus tours, Herman's Singh's mortgage company, Tropical Funding, had handled seventy-two mortgages for people who wanted to relocate, and Herman had even begun to accompany visitors to upstate in the second year. The new residents had bolstered Schenectady's job force, securing jobs as nurses' aides, construction workers, bank tellers, insurance salespeople, and retail workers, among many other occupations.

Mayor Al had also helped convince the diocese to sell Deryck Singh a church property in Mont Pleasant for only $20,000 – St. Thomas Catholic Church, which had been closed and unused for over four years – so he could convert it into a Hindu Temple and Community Center. Through donations from his boss, Susan Dake of Stewart's, and fundraising events held in the temple basement, Deryck paid off the mortgage in a matter of months, so the community had a designated, sacred space for Hindu services, weddings, festivals, and community events.

Soon, a West Indian grocery store opened, followed by another, and after that

Guyanese restaurants, bakeries, clothing stores, laundromats, computer repair shops, beauty salons, video rental stores, bars, and other businesses established primarily to cater to the growing Guyanese community began to appear. George Robertson and the SEDC helped to start a Guyanese-American Business Association, and a handful of entrepreneurial Guyanese contractors bought derelict houses and re-habbed them, one after another after another, and flipped them for profit.

The more Guyanese fences and facades decorated the neighborhoods, and the more identifiable immigrant businesses opened, and the more streets in Schenectady afforded visual reminders of Guyana, the more bus tour participants from down-state wanted to move north and become a part of it. Mayor Al's hunch had paid off: Guyanese people were the right ethnic group for Schenectady. They were streaming into the city, fixing the abandoned houses, and paying taxes on them again. That was all good news.

For the other minorities in the city, though, the red-carpet treatment afforded the newest immigrants stirred up resentment. Constantly noting the entrepreneur-ial prowess and strong work ethic of the newcomers implied that other minorities had not worked hard themselves, claimed Joseph Allen, an African-American mem-ber of the City Council, when he and his parents and grandparents and so many in his community had definitely worked hard and earned all they had. He also argued that Guyanese had been offered preferential treatment, and shown lists of houses for sale that the City Council itself, let alone most city residents, didn't even know were on the market. And to make matters worse, improving houses in neighborhoods like Hamilton Hill had increased property values, raised rental prices, and pushed many houses out of reach for minority workers who made lower wages.

Mayor Al's response was defensive and immediate: "We're not offering anybody anything that has not been around for quite a long time. Anyone can come on these tours. Anyone can buy these homes. It's just that up until now, nobody has taken advantage of such programs." Chauncey Williams, president of the Hamilton Hill Neighborhood Association, agreed with the mayor and said he had tried for years to get participants for the city's housing programs, and that had never worked well before the Guyanese arrived. "They make great neighbors," he said. "They're buying up property left and right, doing whatever it takes to make it work, sometimes working two or three jobs. They're running the crime element out. Houses that were once known as drug spots are now beautiful homes."

Celebrity vindication for Mayor Al arrived when urban analyst and futurist Richard Florida, author of *The Rise of the Creative Class*, presented a talk at General Electric Power Systems. Florida explained that the future of urban economies would depend on their ability to attract talented and creative people, and noted that the Capital Region of New York State ranked 17th out of 268 metropolitan areas in a relativity index he had devised, and was one of only two metropolitan areas with fewer than a million people to appear in his Top 20. And he went on to praise Schenectady's mayor for his efforts to bring new Guyanese residents to the city. "When we looked at what propels growth of a smaller to medium-sized metro area, what we called our melting pot index," Florida said, "immigrants play a larger and larger role."

However, twenty years later, some of the early resentments continue to fester, especially because the Guyanese population has exploded, rivalling other minority populations for influence. Counting only those foreign-born Guyanese who lived in Schenectady in 2019, the Capital Region Regional Planning Commission puts the number around 5,600 of the total 11,000 foreign-born immigrants who live in the city, but that figure doesn't include Guyanese people born in this country or the hundreds more who have moved to the city in the last year and a half during the coronavirus pandemic. The unofficial local estimate is well over 6,000 residents, or about 10% of the city's total population.

"In my twenty years in elected office, it was by far the one initiative that I'm more proud of than anything," Al Jurczynski said recently. "You might say I was lucky, but had I not seized on the opportunity, chances are it probably never would have happened." What is clear, in retrospect, is that the two initiatives – Schenectady 2000 and the Guyanese infusion – were the major catalysts that launched the city toward its future economic revitalization. Initially, Neil Golub, Roger Hull, and other philanthropic movers and shakers had organized and bankrolled and spearheaded volunteer efforts that not only beautified the urban landscape but also helped citizens regain pride in their city.

Adding to that momentum was the significant fact that a motivated ethnic group had chosen Schenectady as the best place to build a new community and life for themselves. The fact remained that every building returned to the tax rolls helped keep property taxes stable for all city residents, so putting aside the fact that some racial animus certainly accompanied the influx of a new immigrant group, it had to be heartening for many citizens that somebody wanted to move in and fix up the decaying housing stock. But the nagging questions about livability still hung in the air: would the new immigrants be safe in Schenectady? Would they be accepted and assimilated? Would they have decent jobs and comfortable houses? Would their children get an adequate education? Could the city offer them a cultural and aesthetic life that would make them want to stay?

9

Can the Arts Save Schenectady?

There are moments in our lives, there are moments in a day,
when we seem to see beyond the usual. Such are the moments
of our greatest happiness. Such are the moments of our greatest
wisdom. If one could but recall his vision by some sort of sign.
It was in this hope that the arts were invented. Sign-posts on the
way to what may be. Sign-posts toward greater knowledge.

– *The Art Spirit*
Robert Henri

How should we define urban revitalization? Does new life for a city depend primarily on thriving businesses, good job opportunities, and economic development? It goes without saying that cities, like people, can't survive without adequate financial resources, but is fiscal security the only essential criterion for measuring quality of life? What must a city offer its citizens beyond public safety, garbage collection, code enforcement, and a functioning infrastructure to convince them to build their lives there? What places and events can help increase a sense of belonging in a community, and will political leaders display the knowledge and courage to prioritize and fund aesthetic and cultural endeavors? If they can't, or won't, who will step up? And what balance of individual entrepreneurship and self-selecting community involvement can ensure a successful and lasting aesthetic life?

When Mona Golub returned to Schenectady after college in 1987, she lived in an apartment on Lafayette Street, a block from Proctor's Theater. "Downtown, for all intents and purposes, was dead," she remembered. "Storefronts filled with children's artwork was what you saw there, if the storefronts were filled with anything." At that time, she became the youngest member of the Proctor's Theater Board of Directors, and helped then executive director Dennis Madden with the efforts to get the theater back on its feet. "I volunteered at the concession stand, so I was there as many times as possible, helping out, enjoying some incredible shows but really wanting to see more happen. Most of the shows were singular one-offs, but they were like a taste of larger city life, real cultured urban life that was coming to visit Schenectady, as opposed to something that was truly planted here by the roots." And when a successful businessman led the charge to rescue and expand Proctor's, Mona and 300 volunteers were by his side: "Obviously, some people have a proclivity for economic development, but others think, 'Where is my place in this? How can I get involved?' And I'll never forget meeting with all those people from our community on the stage at Proctor's that night. Harry Apkarian chaired that committee, and it was Culture and the Arts."

Mona worked in her family's business then – Price Chopper supermarkets – as she still does now. But starting in 2000, she also served as a county legislator for one term, where she decided to commit herself to Schenectady's parks – specifically Central Park, the city's main landscape attraction – and to developing a world-class, summer concert series there called Music Haven. "I think there was recognition even back then that, beyond economic development, if you want people who live here to be happy, and you want people who don't live here to consider moving here, it's going to take more than new buildings and an accumulation of successful businesses."

Moreover, wide-ranging cultural endeavors in other cities had offered models throughout the 1990s and into the early 2000s, and outside experts were encouraging Schenectady's leaders to understand the important benefits that the arts could provide for their city. Even though, in the end, no one had stepped up to champion the expensive and extensive Hunter-Sasaki plan that appeared as Metroplex was establishing its early priorities, Don Hunter's final report did present some insightful recommendations. In his letter to Mayor Al Jurczynski and the citizens of Schenectady that accompanied his plan, he said, "We view the document as a reference manual which should be useful to guide specific actions and coordinate the numerous efforts necessary to successfully accomplish Schenectady's downtown revitalization … Counterbalancing some of the negative trends that cities have experienced nationwide, downtown Schenectady has and will continue to benefit significantly from a resurgence of cultural arts activities."

Leading every list of development strategies throughout that report was the Arts and Entertainment category: the improvement and expansion of Proctor's Theater; attracting a multiplex cinema complex to downtown; broadening the already-excellent General Electric collection at the Schenectady Museum; encouraging new musical and cultural venues; and establishing a restaurant row on the north side of State Street to serve the entertainment venues were all elements of recommended strategies that appeared again and again. While cautioning that "Demand for major attractions and entertainment is a function of the propensity of different population segments to spend discretionary income on leisure activities," Hunter's report also warned that, "The success of Schenectady's revitalization will not be realized without a major effort to attract the 550,750 people who live within fifteen miles to come into Schenectady for an array of reasons … Downtown Schenectady has not reached a level of critical mass and cachet that can induce a significant number of tourists to make a side trip to visit there."

However, the bulk of the money to support widespread arts development in the city had to come through efforts by City Hall and/or the County Legislature, and it didn't help that the new Mayor, Brian Stratton, had inherited a ten-million-dollar deficit from the Jurczynski regime when he took office in January of 2004. Providing new cultural offerings became, of necessity, a lower priority.

Arts and entertainment had been abundant in the good old days of Schenectady.

With workers for General Electric pouring into Schenectady from Europe, the city was in building mode, and its new citizens craved amusements and distractions when they weren't working their long days. In the later years of the 19th century, Buffalo Bill Cody brought his Wild West show to town several times. Union Hall, sitting where Jay met State Street, presented variety road shows with acoustics naturally enhanced by its twenty-foot-high ceilings. The Centre Street Opera House utilized moveable chairs so it could offer boxing matches and roller derbies once the players of *Tosca* or *The Barber of Seville* had packed up and moved on to another town. And the Van Curler Opera House opened in the spring of 1893 with "L'Amico Fritz" before a standing-room-only crowd of more than 1400 people. Even the midget-phenomenon Tom Thumb and his diminutive bride, travelling in a walnut-shaped coach, deigned to stop off in Schenectady once. And all that happened before GE grew exponentially and the city's population exploded in the first decade of the 20th century, just before F.F. Proctor – The Great Levantine, Equilibrist of the 1870s – brought his brand of family-friendly vaudeville to town and charted a course for the city's revitalization almost a hundred years in the future.

Frederick Freeman Proctor – shortened to F.F. Proctor after he had become a theater impresario and aged into his slight resemblance to Professor Marvel in *The Wizard of Oz* – was born in 1851 in rural Dexter, Maine, where his father was a physician. Fascinated by the itinerant circuses that visited small towns like Dexter, young Fred built a training gym with a tumbling mat and a trapeze in his basement and practiced juggling, aerial maneuvers and acrobatics. But when he was nine, his father died, leaving the family penniless. Country doctors in those days normally accepted produce or livestock from rural patients for their services, and the family had no savings.

Fred's mother moved her five children back to her ancestral homestead in Lexington, Massachusetts, and Fred got a job in a Boston dry-goods store although, if anything, his passion for becoming a performer increased in the city that billed itself as the cultural capital of the country. He fashioned a new, makeshift gym from packing boxes, barrels, and gunny sacks in the store's basement and trained there before the workday started – at least until the building superintendent came in early one day and discovered him juggling a barrel with his feet.

Historical accounts vary on what happened next. One online source claims that Fred got so good, so fast, that he trained and formed his fellow child-workers into a motley group of tumblers and was summarily fired for his efforts. A book commissioned by Proctor's second wife, Georgena, after he died, *F.F. Proctor – Vaudeville Pioneer* – and written by the creator of not only the Wonder Woman comic-book character but also the systolic blood pressure test, William Moulton Marston, holds that the superintendent was so impressed by Proctor's skills that he installed a trapeze in the basement for him. Unfortunately, the store's managers decided Fred was better at the trapeze than he was at fulfilling his job duties, and asked him to leave. But Marilyn Sassi, a local expert on Proctor the man and Proctor's Theater, contends that the dry-goods boss was the one who caught his young employee in training. Amazed at the boy's expertise, the boss sponsored an audition at Boston's premiere training facility for circus performers, the Tremont Gym. And Marilyn heard that version from Proctor's great-nephew.

Believe whichever account you like, but Proctor's professional career was launched from the Tremont Gym. He developed an act called "The Jeweled Barrels." To dazzle the audience and highlight the revolution of the barrel as he juggled it with his feet on a spotlit stage, according to Marston, Proctor "took a barrel and inlaid it with pieces of glass, some brightly colored and some with mirrors of silver or gold." Proctor's innovation was wildly popular, and his instinct for showmanship paid off: by the time he was twenty, he was well-known enough that the L.B. Lent Circus hired him. Proctor toured with them for five years throughout Europe during the late 1870s, performing marvelous stunts and billed as The Great Levantine.

During his time in Europe, he studied his art and his audiences. He noted the high quality of variety shows there, marveled at the "mystical scenery" that different kinds of music provided, pondered the psychology of crowds – what people liked and what they didn't – and compiled a deep repertoire of tricks and novelties for his own acts. But what impressed him most was the ornate architecture of the European theaters where he performed. Theaters back home couldn't compete with them, and he resolved to create grand palaces of amusement for people in America one day.

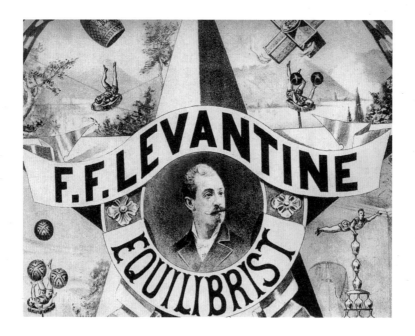

Calling himself Frederick Levantine and married to a circus performer named Mary Anne Daily, he returned to the United States for the start of the Gilded Age and settled in Albany, New York. He still worked as an acrobat, and also occasionally as an actor, but traveling and living expenses had depleted the couple's savings. Performing wasn't as glamorous as it had been in Europe, or as lucrative. Marston's book reports that after a one-night acting stand at the Little Opera House in Catskill, New York, Proctor couldn't get paid. The manager apologized profusely, offered to send a check the following week, but cited the small audience that night. The "Champion Equilibrist of Europe," Mr. Levantine, was forced to walk all the way back to Albany, along the West Shore Railroad tracks, throughout the long night. In an anniversary booklet published to celebrate the 75th Anniversary of Proctor's in Schenectady, researcher and writer Francis Poulin speculated that, "This experience may have convinced him even more to promote, not emote, theatrically."

Be that as it may, in 1884, Frederick reclaimed his birth name of Proctor, added the F.F. to the beginning, and teamed up with a veteran agent, Harry R. Jacobs. Proctor and Jacobs leased the popular Music Hall on the corner of Beaver and South Pearl Street in New York's thriving Capital, Albany, and it was an immediate success. In their seven-years partnership, they opened theaters from Albany and Troy to Syracuse, Rochester, and Buffalo, as well as in Bridgeport, Hartford and New Haven in Connecticut. At the same time, they branched out as individuals. From 1885 to 1890, Proctor opened a new theater every other year in Brooklyn. He pioneered the low-priced ticket, charging ten to twenty cents for admission to his Novelty Theater there, and advertised that "any purchaser of a 75-cent ticket will be presented with an order for a town lot 25 × 100 feet."

In his grand 23rd Street Theater in New York City, which could seat 2800 people, he ran continuous shows, from early morning to late at night, advertising on billboards, "Send your children to my theater because it will be safer for them than on the streets of New York." For another of his marketing gimmicks, he bought bright green ticket stock and mixed them in with the usual white tickets. Then he purchased 200 green parrots and had trainers teach them to speak. Every patron who was lucky enough to be given a green ticket went home with a parrot that repeated, "After breakfast go to Proctor's."

Proctor's secret was high-quality vaudeville acts to entertain the entire family at the lowest possible prices. No foul-mouthed comics and strippers that were the features of burlesque houses for his venues. Once, upon meeting a prominent judge in New York City, Proctor said, "I hope my shows are acceptable to you." The judge replied, "You don't know how acceptable you are. I've been going to your show every week now for the past two months with my wife and little girl and young niece, because you've got the kind of show that keeps families together. I'm recommending your theater for all of my future domestic troubles cases. Men don't go sneaking off alone to corrupt places of entertainment now that you have provided in your 23rd Street Theater a source of real inspiration and joy."

But Proctor wasn't interested in Schenectady at that time. The moniker for Schenectady – *The City That Lights and Hauls the World* – hadn't even been dreamed of let alone generated in the 1880s, and its population of around 13,000 was well-served by the modest venues it already had. However, twenty years can make all the difference. By 1910, with the surge in employment at GE and ALCO, Schenectady's 73,000 citizens were clamoring for newer entertainments and bigger theatrical shows. F.F. Proctor's stable of operating vaudeville houses was edging past forty by then, and included large theaters all up and down the East Coast. He was not only anxious to tap the buzzing new market that sat alongside the Mohawk River but flush enough from the profits of his other theaters to create something palatial and ornate.

Proctor tested the waters by leasing an existing building there in 1911. A successful real estate dealer named Magee had built a large theater next to the Erie Canal, between State Street and Liberty, but when his contract with a powerful theatrical syndicate in New York City failed, he abandoned the project. Proctor leapt at the chance. Spending $100,000 to complete the construction and furnish the theater would enable him to advertise a three-story stage loft, with an Orchestra, boxes, and two galleries. His newest theater would accommodate almost 1700 patrons, and would offer "flickers," movie shorts that filled in between the vaudeville acts. Proctor signed a ten-year lease for a thousand dollars a month.

While reconstruction was ongoing, Proctor, his wife, and two friends – Henry and Renee Harris – booked round-trip steamship passage to Europe. The trip wasn't unusual for Proctor: he made a habit of scouting for new vaudeville acts in Europe every couple of years, and the varied, high-quality acts he brought to America enhanced his competitive edge. Henry Harris was a well-known producer on Broadway, and he considered the trip a working vacation as well. After only a few weeks, though, Proctor's new theater manager in Schenectady wired him and said they were way ahead of schedule. If Proctor wanted to be there at the theater's opening, he would have to come home as soon as possible. Marilyn Sassi relates what happened then: "Proctor and his wife knew they wouldn't miss the opening for the world and so they cancelled their original reservations, which were on the *Titanic*. Mr. Harris drowned on that voyage and, believe it or not, his wife, Renee, was the last women to be plucked out of the sea by a lifeboat. She went on to run her husband's theatrical enterprise on Broadway."

Before Proctor's lease was finished in 1921, with GE's manufacturing facilities expanding and more workers pouring in weekly, some with extended families in tow, Schenectady's population had exceeded 93,000, and Proctor's ambitions had grown along with it. He dreamed of building the grandest theater ever there, on a piece of land he actually owned, and not paying a dime in monthly rent. He bought a lot from the city's Public Safety Commissioner, John K. Alexander, at 432 State Street, uptown in the new shopping district, and commissioned the most famous theater architect of the time, Thomas W. Lamb, to design a masterpiece. The property stretched all the way back to Smith Street, crossing above the eight-foot-diameter

pipe that carried the water of the Cow Horn Creek from up in Vale Cemetery all the way down to the Mohawk River.

The shifting areas of quicksand that surrounded that pipe didn't deter Proctor for a minute. He hired a contractor to drive 242 twelve-inch-diameter piles around the pipe – each from thirteen to thirty-six-feet long – to stabilize the foundation, erected a four-story steel framework set into place by a 100-foot crane, and bought 12,941,700 bricks from a manufacturer in Watervliet, at a cost of almost $29,000, to sheathe the building's exterior. He specified two marquees, a smaller one on the Smith Street side and a glorious, larger one for the main entrance on State

Street which held 714 red lights and 581 white ones, as well as a pulsing, vertical sign above that, soaring toward the night sky, with 1,228 lights of its own.

F.F. Proctor and his architect, Thomas Lamb, shared the theory that theaters should function as palaces for average people, where poor and rich alike could mingle and share resonant fantasies in opulent settings The era from the end of World War I to the beginning of the Great Depression – 1918 to 1932 – saw magical temples for vaudeville and movies mushroom in cities all across America and become the vibrant centers of city life. Exhausted by the horrors of trench warfare and reeling from the Spanish Flu pandemic that followed hard on the armistice, people were eager for brief respites from reality. The neo-classical or atmospheric designs of the new theaters could visually transport them, at low cost, for a few hours almost every day of the week. Factory workers and their families could escape whatever drudgery they faced in their lives, enjoy the magnificence of their surroundings, and even feel pampered by uniformed ushers. "To make our audience receptive and interested," Thomas Lamb said, "we must cut them off from the rest of city life and take them into a rich and self-contained auditorium, where their minds are freed from their usual occupations and freed from their customary thoughts."

To that end, Proctor gave Lamb *carte blanche*, and what he got in return was a fabulous interior, from the textiles – ornate carpeting, velvet drapes, embossed-fabric wall coverings – to the plumbing, with marble drinking fountains and spacious, tiled bathrooms. There were sixteen well-appointed dressing rooms for the performers, 1600 plush theater chairs for the main floor and the balcony made by the American Seating Company, state-of-the-art stage rigging that cost over $12,000 in 1926, and a $50,000 theater organ built by the Rudolph Wurlitzer Company of New York City, its 1400 pipes more than capable of fully animating the cavernous space. Sitting in silence before the talkies arrived wasn't attractive to most patrons, so piano music was added to accompany the images and suggest an emotional narrative. The great Wurlitzer organs were there to delight people before and after the variety acts and the movies.

The massive, Corinthian columns that flanked the proscenium arch, as well as the ones that ran along the walls under the boxes and the balcony, were scagliola, fashioned by Florentine craftsmen that Lamb brought to Schenectady for that project only. The hand-formed plaster columns – veined with colors and constructed, then polished with flax oil to brighten them and finally sealed with layers of wax – achieved vibrant colors and unique textures that often surpassed natural marbles. And everywhere people looked, from the domed ceiling above the brilliant chandelier to the full width of the balcony façade, was resplendent in gold leaf. "Gold epitomizes wealth, warmth, and coziness," Lamb explained, "and is pleasing and harmonious with every other conceivable color."

Proctor hated supporting columns because they interrupted sight lines, and he instructed Lamb to design a cantilevered balcony for 1000 seats without any obstructions under the mezzanine. At the back, along the sides, was fine, but nothing in front. Competitors claimed the design was dangerous, and Schenectady's building inspector, citing its unprecedented size, became reluctant to certify the building before he could determine if it was safe. So he measured the distance from the dress circle to the floor and wrote down that number. Then he enlisted Union College students to fill 1000 bags with 150 pounds of sand in each one and place a bag on every seat in the balcony. After two weeks, he had the bags removed, measured again and, when the number matched the first, he gave the balcony his stamp of approval and allowed the theater to open.

Refusing to be outdone in the fantasy department by the moguls in Hollywood and New York City, F.F. Proctor was determined to go toe-to-toe with William Fox, the Warner Brothers, Marcus Loew, and even "Roxy" Rockefeller. All of them were well aware they were selling tickets to the palaces as much as to the shows. Vaudeville was still in its heyday, though, even as the mid-1920s saw a broad increase in movie audiences, expanding from the lower classes to include a growing, middle-class population. Crowds seemed to cherish the startling assortment of variety acts, as they flocked again and again to see the famous and the bizarre: Lillian Russell and other opera stars; Carrie Nation handing out souvenir axes; ukulele virtuosos; bow-and-arrow acts; midget impersonators; table-top tap dancers; magicians who wore voluminous coats and filled the stage with the folded-up furniture they pulled from them; knife-throwers; sneeze experts; fake-Chinese yodelers; stand-up comic duos; banjo masters; animal acts, like a chimpanzee leading a donkey on a leash in circles around the stage; musical spoon experts; mayhem acrobats; street singers;

famous regurgitators who could swallow molten lead and vomit up spendable coins; giant xylophonists; plate spinners; strongmen supporting human pyramids; pet rats blowing kazoos; amazing child tumblers; all-Asian orchestras; and even playing-to-the-haircut harpists who were expected to hustle people toward the exits. If you didn't like a particular act, no need to worry – something different would always appear quickly.

The unspoken elixir of vaudeville was speed. If an act went longer than ten minutes, out came the hook. Its effect was extraordinary and counter-intuitive simultaneously: it afforded everyone a communal experience which also felt, in the very same instant, intimate for every person in the audience – those hoofers were playing only for each one of them. The theater critic John Lahr summed up the immigrant appeal of the art form: "The touching thing about vaudeville was it was like first-generation America, getting a foothold in the world of America, celebrating it, suffering it, and giving all that longing and the high times to the people, giving it back." And once the talkies showed up in 1927 with Al Jolson in "The Jazz Singer," the crowds got even bigger. Who could resist talking pictures?

On Monday, December 27, 1926, Proctor's second theater in Schenectady opened its doors, and showed the movie, "Stranded in Paris," with starlet Bebe Daniels. 7,100 people bought tickets for that first day. "Schenectady has treated me well," Proctor told the local Chamber of Commerce. "For that reason, I have constructed here the largest, handsomest, and most-costly theater that I have ever built. And it is as elaborate in its equipment and decorations as any in the big metropolitan cities." The final price tag was $1.5 million – again, in 1926.

Within two years, Proctor's son would commit suicide and his granddaughter, married to an ensign in the Navy stationed in Manila, would die along with her baby in childbirth. Proctor brought them home to be buried in the family crypt at Woodlawn Cemetery in Schenectady, but his own health would severely decline as a result.

In 1928, he began selling off his fifty-four theaters, one by one, and finally combined the best of them in a package deal to the Radio Keith Orpheum Corporation (RKO), and netted sixteen million dollars. In the months before he died, Proctor hand-wrote a 600-page will, including more than 350 beneficiaries: family, friends, employees, and favorite charities, reluctant to forget a single one. He died on

September 4th, 1929, about fifty-four days before Black Tuesday – October 29, 1929 – one day for each of the theaters he sold to ensure a substantial legacy for the people and causes he cared about. To underscore Proctor's importance to the entertainment world, John Ringling and George M. Cohan asked to serve as pall-bearers at his funeral.

Vaudeville didn't last long after Proctor was gone. By 1932, there was only one all-vaudeville theater still open in America, fittingly named The Palace, in New York City. The novelty that had characterized shows – with the repetition of all those singers and dancers and comedians, with similar acts year after year – eventually lost its cachet. Motion pictures stole vaudeville: once those acts were captured on film, the movies travelled more efficiently, and far less expensively, than the physical acts themselves. And radio was even more destructive for vaudeville, because the entertainment that radios broadcast entered listeners' homes for free, and during the Great Depression, there weren't so many dimes to spare in most of the country.

Some of the troupers were able to hang on a few more years, playing resorts in the Catskills or at State Fairs, and even serving as "coolers" between movies in the palaces they used to pack, actually giving the early projectors time to cool off. Show business had come full circle – the "flickers" had turned into the main attraction. And given the necessity of perseverance in the profession, it shouldn't seem surprising that during World War II, a number of the die-hard vaudevillians travelled overseas and entertained our troops. "What all these people had learned," John Lahr pointed out, "was how to corrupt an audience with pleasure, and there is no harder or more noble thing in the theatrical profession than to do that."

Over the next two decades, economic downturns, social upheaval, low or non-existent wages, severe climate changes, a world war that forced men into military uniforms and women into vacated jobs, and the rising, postwar availability of television all conspired to lessen the appeal of movies, and diminish the vaudeville palaces that featured them. How people viewed entertainment was shifting, and the older, ornate theaters in most cities felt like old news. For its part, Hollywood created innovations to weather the competitive storm: they encouraged drive-in theaters in suburbs all over the country to cater to the expanding car culture of America, and offered special effects that television couldn't match, like the wide-screen formats of Cinemascope, Technirama, and Vista-Vision. In indoor movie houses, they added weirder attractions like scent-o-vision, where smells were released from seats to correspond with events on the screen and heighten the sensory experience. For horror films, they installed "tingler" seats to make movie-goers jump, literally, at the scariest moments – all to lure people away from the small screens at home and to remind them that big-screen movies were the best way to appreciate motion pictures.

However, Schenectady was a lucky outlier during those two decades. General Electric was booming, sending its giant turbines all over the world, and the ALCO locomotive plant along the Mohawk was going great guns. After F.F. Proctor's grand theater opened in 1926, the Chamber of Commerce realized it needed a similarly grand hotel to accommodate visitors, so they put together the Van Curler Hotel in record time. After Lindbergh made his famous flight in "The Spirit of St. Louis" in 1927, the city fathers didn't want to be left behind in the brand new airport business so they raised the money to build a new airport in Glenville in one feverish week. And Lucky Lindbergh and Amelia Earhart each landed at that airport on promotional tours.

The Great Depression did cause some layoffs at the big manufacturers, but the orders still rolled in and their plants never closed during the 1930s. Schenectady's population remained above 90,000 through the wartime labor boom, and people continued to buy tickets, fill Proctor's Theater, and enjoy Hollywood's steady output of movies, as well as top performers like Bob Hope, Red Skelton, Louis Armstrong and Duke Ellington, at a time when many other cities were tearing their vaudeville theaters down. Also during World War II, when the Pentagon awarded prime military equipment contracts, both GE and ALCO were always among the top ten recipients. When the German tank forces commanded by the Desert Fox, General Rommel, crested a ridge in the battle of El Alamein in North Africa in 1942, they were met and stopped by the British Army with a thousand M7 medium tanks that were not only made in Schenectady but unveiled to its citizens in a parade up Erie Boulevard before they were shipped overseas. GE and ALCO needed skilled home front workers, and many local men fulfilled their wartime service by working seven days a week, twelve hours a day, joined by a major spike in women's employment right alongside them, producing the machines and armaments that helped to win the war for the Allies.

But the city couldn't avoid life-changing social and cultural changes forever, and Proctor's Theater began to decline in the early 1960s. The private owner tried a few gimmicks – afternoon Disney cartoon festivals, Blaxploitation and martial arts films, midnight matinees, and even a months-long run as a porno house – but while the unpaid utility bills and the back taxes mounted higher and higher, finally reaching over $200,000 by 1972, the unfixed holes in the roof had damaged the interior so

badly that City Hall ordered the building to be boarded up to avoid potential liability. Ignored, the theater continued to implode and, around it, State Street was turning into a ghost town. Finally, in 1977, the City seized the theater and scheduled its demolition. The days when Proctor's Theater felt crucial to the cultural life of Schenectady not only seemed distant, but the crumbling movie palace had also become an eyesore in the middle of the 400 block, ground zero for Canal Square, the urban mall that promised to rescue the city's downtown.

When Mardy Moore, Katherine Rozendaal and fellow members of the Schenectady Arts Council learned of the impending demolition, they jumped into action, determined to get the building listed on the Register of National Historic Places to save it. They had not forgotten when The Plaza – the other ornate movie palace in Schenectady – had been torn down in 1964 just to make a parking lot, and they couldn't bear to lose the only remaining theatrical landmark in the city. The leaders at City Hall weren't swayed by their conservationist arguments, but they did grant a temporary stay of execution. As Marilyn Sassi recounts it, they said, "Look, prove to us you can at least patch it up enough to put on a real show. If you can actually sell tickets and get people to come, we'll help."

However, few people had set foot in Proctor's for several years. Again, Marilyn Sassi explains:

> They came into the theater for the first time – these members of the Arts Council – and they could not believe it. The rugs were sodden, soaked through, and torn so badly that if you tripped and fell into one of the holes in that carpet, you'd never be seen again. The seats were dilapidated and horribly damaged. All the wonderful scagliola was literally falling apart because it was just plaster, of course. But the thing that really got me, when they reached right at the heart of the midsection – right there under the dome, where you look up and there was that beautiful chandelier – everything was coming apart. The plaster was coming down. And what was worse, back above the last seats in the balcony, there was a hole in the roof big enough that they could see the sky, and pigeons had gotten in and were roosting in both the box seats on either side of

the theater and flying back and forth. Now this was where they all
started to wonder how they could pull this off.

In spite of the theater's woeful condition, Moore and Rozendaal accepted the restoration challenge, but first things first: they had to incorporate Proctor's as a non-profit – which they named the Arts Center and Theater of Schenectady, Inc. (ACTS) – and then raise a pile of money. A fundraiser netted $7,000. City and federal grants provided half a million more to make the structure operationally safe again.

After that, they set in to repair the theater itself, and the City offered a thirteen-member SETA contingent, its Schenectady Employment and Training Administration workers. They were, for the most part, unskilled laborers who were subsidized by a government-sponsored program, vaguely akin to the Works Project Administration workers (WPA) who had pitched in during the Great Depression to chronicle and help rebuild the country. While volunteers refurbished the damaged seats that were too expensive to replace at that point, the SETA workers erected a maze of scaffolding so they could clean and paint. They could handle the basic restoration jobs, but a more skilled workforce had to fix the technical systems in the theater.

Joe Mangino, in charge of all the labor unions at General Electric during that time, convinced GE to donate the skills of the best members of their electrical, plumbing, audio, and engineering unions to restore Proctor's primary systems. Women from The Carl Company's drapery department used scraps from the damaged stage curtain to make burgundy booties, trimmed with lace, and sold them as Christmas decorations, raising money they gave to the theater. The Carl Co., which owned the building next door to Proctor's, donated all the material for a new velvet curtain and for the padded wall tapestries, and covered their employees' labor as well. In the end, Proctor's also sported a new roof and sprinkler system, three new boilers, and safety railings along the balcony.

Audience members had been allowed to smoke for forty years in the theater. The tar and nicotine in the cigarettes and cigars had eaten into the unique plaster work, but ACTS was able to locate a grandson of the original plaster artists from Florence. He came to Schenectady and trained local masons to refurbish the magnificent Corinthian columns, as well as the rest of the scarred scagliola. And for the all-important show, Mardy Moore was able, through a Broadway agent contact of hers, to secure the well-known illusionist, Harry M. Blackstone, Jr., whose famous magician father had played Proctor's several times in its heyday.

A capacity crowd of 2,700 people purchased tickets for the theater-saving event that was open to the public on January 3, 1979. Mayor Frank Duci, suddenly a believer, accepted one dollar from ACTS-president Rozendaal and handed her the keys to Proctor's Theater. Dennis Madden, the brand-new executive director, checked the stage supports one more time for the finale of Blackstone's act: making his trained elephant, Misty, disappear in plain sight.

However, as the curtain rose to cheers from the excited audience, the tired plumbing in the newly-burdened rest rooms in back let loose, and water began streaming down the aisles. Luckily, Dennis Madden knew where the main shut-off valve was in the basement, so the show could go on. Outside the theater, as the magic show inside dazzled the crowd, a blizzard buried the cars in the parking lot. For a bonus trick, though, Blackstone put a harness on Misty and she towed all the cars out to the plowed street. Not much had been easy reaching that night, but Proctor's had been saved.

One person alone can't make a city worth living in, of course, but F.F. Proctor made something that not only entertained generations in Schenectady but, even in its darkest era, also inspired ACTS members and many others in the community to come together and show what they valued most. Art in all its forms is crucial to a society because art is an essential ingredient in empowering our hearts. Art promotes communication, fosters optimism, and creates jobs. Art pushes us to see beyond the necessities of survival and ministers to our emotional and mental well-being. Art can connect us, deeply, and forge compassion and, as it does, becomes a barometer of cultural sophistication – a civilizing endeavor, for the makers and for those who can appreciate what has been made. And the arts bring people to the city – people who eat in restaurants before a show and talk about what they saw afterwards in bars and cafes. Arts venues are revitalizing engines.

To lose theaters that are remarkable, historic buildings, and which may well be multi-use performing arts models and cultural centers for an entire community and

region, underscores a negligence that diminishes our lives. But if a city can locate its inspirational touchstones, as Schenectady has, and continue to rescue them and renew them again and again, the shared aesthetic legacy that results may continue to inspire people and broadcast a higher quality of life in a particular place.

That's what Union College has done for the last fifty years with its renowned chamber music series: since 1971, the world's finest classical music performers have travelled upstate after playing at Carnegie Hall or Lincoln Center, so audiences in Schenectady have enjoyed their music for a fraction of New York City ticket prices. Hosting fifteen to twenty concerts by artists like Emanuel Ax, the Emerson String Quartet, Ian Bostridge and many others between October and April each year, Union's Memorial Chapel can boast an acoustic experience second to none.

That's what Margaret Cunningham did with the Hamilton Hill Arts Center: inspired by the Black Arts movements of the 1960s, she founded a cultural arts center that, to this day, promotes, preserves, and develops African/African-American art and culture for 10,000 people a year, on and off-site in the Hamilton Hill neighborhood of Schenectady.

That's what Mrs. Etta Moore did in laying the groundwork for the Schenectady Light Opera Company (SLOC): as a public school teacher in the district, she organized alumni from different schools into a company called the Bellevue Young People's Chorus in 1926 – just as Proctor's Theater was getting ready to open – and presented first concerts, then operettas, and finally full-sized Gilbert and Sullivan shows in the early 1930s. Never lacking for ideas, the SLOC has offered the community a new opera every year for the last ninety years.

That's what classical-musician and jazz-conductor Bill Meckley did with the music department at Schenectady County Community College (SCCC): when he arrived in the city in 1984, the college didn't even have an auditorium for the concerts presented by its music majors. Slowly and carefully, Meckley built a rigorous program that attracted talented musicians from inside as well as beyond the Capital Region, and eventually it became one that produced musicians who could go on to be stand-outs at prestigious music schools like the Crane School or the New England Conservatory. The college invested in a small but state-of-the-art, 400-seat auditorium, and Meckley formed a professional company – The Empire State Jazz Orchestra – that included the area's finest jazz players and called SCCC its home for many years. A burgeoning core of music aficionados, realizing the aesthetic excellence of what they were hearing, concert after concert, regularly packed the auditorium. "We had to be really patient," Meckley said. "Most schools are looking for some kind of instant elixir. It has taken us thirty years. You've got to be in it for the long haul, and you have to say, 'Well, there's going to be high standards.'"

And that's definitely what Mona Golub has done with Music Haven in Schenectady's Central Park: understanding that the arts act as a foundational cornerstone for the community, she has seen it as her obligation to present free concerts for her community since the 1980s. Mona had begun organizing acoustic shows early on, inside and outside Peggy's Restaurant in Canal Square, but also in Central Park:

What I was doing with Music Haven, which was then called the Central Park Concert Series, began to grow. And it grew to the point where we were drawing several hundred people and the shows were becoming more international and unique to the landscape. The stage itself, which was an old trailer supported by a single steel beam, was breaking down with each and every concert, to the point where we had holes in the ceiling that I thought would bring in the rain if it happened not to be perfect weather, and holes in the floor that I feared the artists would fall into. That's when I hatched the idea for a new stage, having no idea what it would cost or what it should be. And I reached out to the folks at Synthesis Architects on Jay Street. They offered to do the drawings and it went from there. Then I co-wrote a grant with an old classmate of mine at Niskayuna who was in development for the city at the time, and the state awarded us $210,000. That got things rolling.

It turned out the stage would actually cost a million dollars, so Mona submitted more grants, ran a capital campaign, held classical breakfasts inside the Central Park Pavilion, sponsored Italian-dinner, cabaret-night fundraisers, and finally raised what it would take, believing that Music Haven would be significant for more than a couple of generations to come. And it has certainly been a venue that welcomes people, is accessible to everyone, and offers musical acts few of them would ever get to hear since that new stage was christened in July of 1999: famed jazzman Nick Brignola, the Irish performers Altan and Maura O'Connell, Janis Ian, Joe Ely, Iris Dement, piano-prodigy Joey Alexander, jazz bassist Esperanza Spalding, Spain's Ojos de Brujo, and literally scores of others. And there's no way to measure how many kids from Mont Pleasant or Hamilton Hill or Bellevue were transported by one of these Music Haven concerts and promised themselves, *One day I'll be up there, doing what they're doing.*

Over the last hundred and twenty-five years, Schenectady has fluctuated from a sleepy village to a booming, mid-sized industrial hub and back again to a small city of 65,000 people. At its height, because of General Electric, it may have been able to attract leading inventors like Charles Steinmetz and other renowned scientists, but it could never compete with arts and entertainment behemoths downstate, where cultural institutions like Broadway theaters, the big museums (MOMA, the Metropolitan, Natural History Museum, the Guggenheim, etc.), and the Metropolitan Opera generate tens of thousands of jobs and pay billions in wages. Along with finance, culture is the lifeblood of New York City and establishes it as a magnet for national and international visitors, as well as for residents of the five boroughs. It goes without further illustration that Schenectady has always valued its arts, even if the audiences for those arts have remained primarily local ones. However, with two new arrivals in 2002 and 2004, that was about to change. Bill Golub's dream of making Schenectady a destination city began to look possible.

10

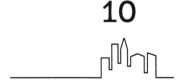

Fighting Out of the Mess

In time, places and local economies are adaptable, with the right governance and timely investment. A dead place is not a historic inevitability; it is someone's failure. A living place is someone's success. These are matters of choice and skill, not laws of physics … Before reaching the radical conclusion that American cities are beyond saving, it would be worthwhile to look again at the places that seem to be, if not saved, at least durable enough to survive the hard decades just past, and to build communities that will survive those ahead.

– *Comeback Cities: A Blueprint
for Urban Neighborhood Revival*
Paul S. Grogan and Tony Proscio

Before Philip Morris started his new job as executive director of Proctor's Theater in March of 2002, his friend Sam Teresi, the mayor of Jamestown, New York, told him, "I think you're walking into a nightmare. Politics in Schenectady are probably the worst in America. I've never seen anything worse. It's personal and it's bitter there. Good luck." Hyperbolic, maybe – but Teresi had a point. Many executives at General Electric had provided leadership, support, and stability for Schenectady's government for decades, but as the company laid off tens of thousands of its workers and shifted its attention to greener pastures, the new executives in town were reluctant to become as involved in helping to guide city politics. As tax revenues declined and problems multiplied from the mid-1970s to the early 2000s, the political factions in the city and county continued to habitually bludgeon each other. It's what they knew how to do, so they just kept doing it.

However, Philip hadn't come to Schenectady to battle his way through a political free-for-all. His arrival date was March 4th, and he took that as an imperative – march forth and get something done. He came to do what he couldn't do in Jamestown, to help revitalize the city, although it certainly wasn't for lack of trying there. With a million-dollar donation, he had transformed a decaying, 1300-seat vaudeville theater called The Palace into what is now the Reg Lenna Center for the Arts, named after the generous donor. "I did everything I could do at Jamestown," he explained. "I was saddened by the fact that after renovating a dozen properties, building housing for artists, presenting a restored theater to the city – after all those things, there was still no spark. We were the biggest property owners in the downtown, and yet there was no spark."

In Schenectady, Lionel Barthold, a Proctor's board member, offered Philip a much bigger sandbox to play in. Barthold, with six colleagues from General Electric, had left the giant company in 1969 and formed his own business, Power Technologies, Inc., which is now known as Siemens/PTI and which has offered high-tech consulting services to power companies globally for more than fifty years. When Barthold was interviewing Morris for the job, he said, "Look, do you golf?"

"I used to," Philip answered.

"Well, there's a tee in the ground, Barthold said. "And there's a flag out there someplace, but it's foggy. There's a ball ready to be placed on that tee, and we need someone to swing. If you can stand that metaphor, that's what you've got when you come here."

In the twenty-plus years between the time ACTS had assumed ownership and control of Proctor's in 1979 and Philip Morris arrived to steer the theater's course in 2002, the ball that Barthold mentioned in his metaphor had sustained quite a bit of cart-path damage, although, under Dennis Madden's leadership, Proctor's did present amazing entertainment in its first decade back. It was listed on the National

Register of Historic Places in 1980. Hal Holbrook, who had presented his renowned, one-person play, *Mark Twain Tonight!* at Proctor's several times, became the theater's patron saint during that decade, sponsoring its first challenge grant to replace the worn-out seats, and then running a public service campaign on television and radio to bolster the theater's continuing restoration efforts.

Proctor's 75th Anniversary Booklet – calling the theater Schenectady's Gem of the Arts, "just off Broadway" – boasted that "Between January, 1979 and January, 1988, nearly two million people will have passed through Proctor's doors, creating an economic impact of nearly $60 million for Schenectady and the Capital District." Big Broadway musicals were the main attraction, with shows like *A Chorus Line* and *Sugar Babies* setting all-time attendance records, but the world-class symphony concerts, big-name opera stars, and famous popular entertainers that Madden brought in had established Proctor's as a wide-reaching, regional theater for the first time.

Dennis Madden elevated the level of offerings almost immediately:

> *First I brought in Dizzy Gillespie, and the Broadway play* The Wiz, *and a show with the Celtic traditional band, Boys of the Lough, and later, James Galway. Our entire budget for the year was $100,000. Then I brought in really great acts the next year and nobody came, so we started to hemorrhage money because the Board wouldn't allow us to advertise. They just figured we would announce a show and everybody would come because they'll be excited. But nobody knew what we were doing until the area TV and radio stations began to give us free air-time. We went from having 220 people at the theater to having 2200 people on any given night. No show did poorly for a while, and after that we could devote almost half a million to advertising every year.*

Another high point was the acquisition of "Goldie," a marvelous, Wurlitzer organ with an all-gold finish that had been built in 1931 for the Paramount Theater in Aurora, Illinois. Dennis heard her at Claude Newman's mansion in Minneapolis in 1983 and decided Proctor's deserved something as grand as that organ. "Goldie" wasn't anything like a classical church organ. She was designed to replace a full pit orchestra, and featured hundreds of stops for sound effects a classical organ couldn't produce, like car horns, bird whistles, horse clops, or pounding waves, as well as an impressive array of musical mimicry – from trumpets to xylophones to various types of percussion effects – that were indistinguishable from the actual instruments. The price tag to purchase, move her to Schenectady, and install her was steep, more than $100,000, but the Golub Family and the Golub Foundation generously covered all expenses.

During the 1980s, no other venues in the Capital Region were offering the programming that Proctor's was, and Dennis Madden never missed one show. "We probably had 3000 performances during the time I was executive director, including everything we did, and I was at all of them, start to finish." Every year, he presented four major concerts, not only with respected American orchestras from Cleveland or Philadelphia but also with famous symphonies from Warsaw and Dresden and other European cities. He gave opera lovers several chances each year to hear singers like Jessye Norman and Leontyne Price and other major stars. He showcased modern dance companies from Russia and Poland and Romania, as well as national stalwarts like the Alvin Ailey Dance Theater. For plays, there was *Amadeus*, and *Cyrano de Bergerac*, and *Playboy of the Western World*, but Broadway shows, of course, buttered Proctor's bread year in and year out. Classical ballets were followed by popular singers like Kenny Rogers or Tom Jones, but unforeseen problems began to crop up.

> *And there were the crazy moments, like when we had Engelbert Humperdinck, and that ended up as one of our disasters. We sold out two shows of Humperdinck, and his requirement was that we bring in a thirty-two-piece orchestra, rehearse them, and then pay them for the two performances. So he filled the theater twice, but he never performed. It got to be time for the show to start, and we had our opening act out there, working, in front of the full house, 2700 seats filled, then all of a sudden, he said, "I'm not feeling well. I'm going over to the hospital. And he took the limousine that we provided and paid for and went to the hospital and that was it. He certainly wasn't deathly sick, but we lost a ton of money on that.*

After that, Madden booked the Shakespeare Folger Theater doing *Macbeth*, and again that sold out for three shows, but they never even came to town. Proctor's had to pay for the marketing, then pay to refund each ticket sold, with the mailing and postage costs adding insult to injury. Apart from those disasters, it wasn't like the shows weren't doing well, but you can't bring a 120-piece orchestra from Cleveland, with Victor Borge conducting and playing, and then have 2000 people in the theater. That maybe pays for the orchestra and marketing, but it doesn't contribute to the costs of having a staff of forty-two people and maintaining a big theater.

Philip Morris remembers how remarkable Dennis was, and how he tried to weather the building storm: "I probably talked to Dennis back in those days thirty times. And I give him a lot of credit for giving the first-shot impression of Proctor's as being bigger than life. There was no reason any of us thought the stuff he was doing would work in Schenectady. But he was straightforward about paying for every show from the next show's ticket sales. He would time his on-sales – sold the day you announce a show – to ensure he had the cash to pay for whatever act he had coming in that weekend. So that led to the million-dollar deficit, there's no question about it."

By 1988, less than one year after Proctor's and ACTS had celebrated their multiple anniversaries, continuing financial troubles had pushed the organization toward mortgaging the theater for a $500,000 line of credit, but the deed stipulated a restriction on taking any mortgages on the property. ACTS petitioned the City to lift the restriction, but an old nemesis, Frank Duci, who was a member of the City Council then, held up the works. Duci claimed the City should have right of first refusal to purchase the building if there was a default on the loan payments. "When we turned it over and gave ACTS the key, we wanted the place used only as a theater, but giving the bank first crack at the mortgage opens the door for it to be used for something else if there's a default," Duci said. He suggested they hold a lottery to raise money. "There isn't anybody I know who doesn't gamble."

Well, they didn't hold a lottery, and the City relented about the deed restriction. A consortium of local banks eventually contributed enough individual loans to cover operating expenses, but the huge deficit remained. Madden finally tried a Hail Mary pass: he had the novel idea to involve the community in an ingenious event to raise money – a dance marathon that involved all the high schools in the area and their students individually pledging to raise money to support Proctor's with the hope of winning a four-year college scholarship or a car – but that, too, ended in disaster when only a fraction of the students turned in what they had raised.

That was it. The new Board of Directors, under Harry Apkarian, paid Madden to sit at a desk in the back of the theater's reception area for three months while his successor – Don Schein, the recently-retired director of WMHT, the area's public television station – ignored Madden's expertise, treading water as interim ED of Proctor's until he died within the year. Dennis Madden went on to direct bigger theaters all over the country. Gloria Lamere, who had run the Albany Coliseum, held the reins for twelve years, from 1989 to 2001, migrating from Madden's risky, high-quality programming that may have been too sophisticated, too early, for the regional audience, to more standard fare that filled enough seats to keep the lights on. When Gloria died on the job as well, the Proctor's search committee pinned their hopes on Philip Morris.

What did Philip find when he arrived? "I had worked as a consultant for ur-

ban renewal projects, sometimes hired by the State and sometimes by individuals," he explained, "in cities like Auburn, Geneva, Ithaca, Corning, Watertown. I knew cities pretty well and when I came to Schenectady, I'd never seen anything like it. It was a disaster. There were few businesses, and hardly any people. The only place to eat was a little Subway shop across the street from the theater. Even the two Dollar stores had closed. When Proctor's wasn't open, there wasn't any downtown."

Philip, who had worked for many years in western New York, used to tell people the Midwest began in Jamestown because the Chadakoin River was the easternmost river that feeds the Gulf of Mexico. So as a geographically-misplaced Midwesterner, he thought of Schenectady as part of the more cultured Northeast, and couldn't quite believe that a city next to Albany, the state capital, could be that bad. But he quickly learned it was.

The center of downtown, the nine-building Canal Square, was completely dilapidated at that point, its unimaginably-ugly unibrow facades – meant to lend the urban mall a homogeneous appeal – providing a hideous reminder of all the buildings sacrificed for an idea tailor-made to fail. At least the canals had been filled in and paved over, and the dangerous load-in bridge over the canal behind Proctor's back entrance had been removed the year before Philip got to town.

Metroplex, however, having taken title to all of Canal Square in 2001, was now organized and moving ahead with a $150 million downtown revitalization project which had, at its core, the demolition of Canal Square and the development of the entire 400 block of State Street. The first three major projects Metroplex had tackled – the new, massive MVP Health Care building with attached parking garage, the regional headquarters of the State Department of Transportation a block away from Proctor's, and renovation of the luxurious but narrow, eight-story Parker Inn with developer Chris Myers – had cost more than $60 million and were either already open and functioning or almost finished.

In the 400 block, Proctor's had been spared the wrecking ball, luckily, as had The Carl Co. building next door. The County Legislature had promised to sell that adjacent building to Proctor's for $25,000, and a resolution cementing that deal finally went through at the end of 2004. But Philip Morris couldn't help but feel that he was surrounded by collapsing buildings when he first arrived.

In addition, the streetscape project which had begun with the MVP construction at the top of the State Street hill was in full swing in front of Proctor's by early summer. State Street had for years beckoned like a drag strip, big and wide and crying out for a race, to hell with the parallel parking on both sides. Even delivery trucks used to barrel along it.

City engineer Milt Mitchell had championed the makeover, acquiring federal money as well as infrastructure money from Metroplex. The design was entirely different than the existing speedway, with designated, cut-out parking areas, abundant plantings, and a water fountain in front of Center City across from Proctor's. So for two years, beginning in the spring of 2002, the street in front of Philip's new work-home was systematically torn apart.

The buildings around him were disappearing, and for any kind of meaningful theater expansion, he would need to raise a minimum of twenty million dollars ASAP. Now which part of the tee in the ground, with the ball ready to be placed on top, then driven by him, in theory, straight and far down the fairway in that metaphorical fog, was Philip Morris missing?

Specters at that time were everywhere: the specter of Broadway going dark after the tragedy of the twin towers crumbling just a year and a half before on 9/11; the specter of Schenectady's decades-long decline and decay that was visibly apparent all around the city; the specter of Proctor's past struggles to survive and its ongoing financial woes; and, perhaps most troubling of all, the specter of *Phantom of the Opera*, Andrew Lloyd Webber's 1986 blockbuster musical that everyone in the Northeast was still hankering to see on stage and – except in Her Majesty's Theatre in England's West End, the Majestic in New York City, and the Pantages Theater in Toronto, where it played from 1989 to 1999 and literally transformed that city's warehouse district – so few could.

With *Phantom*'s unbridled success, a world tour was inevitable, but unless they had very large arts centers or theaters, most American cities couldn't accommodate its monumental production needs. The sets and lighting and rigging and costumes for the show arrived inside twenty-three trucks, and the weight loads were substantial. Proctor's stage was thirty feet deep and sixty-five feet wide, but it would need

to expand considerably – to fifty feet deep and one hundred and thirty feet wide – to handle *Phantom* and the big shows that were designed in its wake, like *Cats* or *Mamma Mia* or *Wicked*.

The Proctor's Board of Directors were well aware of the problem and the opportunity that *Phantom* posed years before they brought in Philip Morris. They had hired the New York theatre design specialists Sachs Morgan Studio to prepare a stage expansion feasibility study in 1999, and its projected price tag for that expansion came in at over $16 million in Fall 2000 construction costs alone. With additional soft costs, no one was willing to vote for the project, even if it meant they would miss out on the *Phantom* craze that was spreading across the country and lose the hefty profits that larger venues were hauling in.

However, the Sachs Morgan Studio study demonstrated key conditions in its Market Issues section: it concluded that the Capital District market was sufficient to support the new level of Broadway programming, and the producers of those top-quality musicals wanted their shows to play at Proctor's. In particular, the producers were impressed that two recent shows at Schenectady's theater, *Chicago* and *Rent*, had each grossed over $700,000 for their week-long runs there. Only two touring shows listed in *Variety* for that week which ended on May 30 had grossed more – *Phantom of the Opera* in Buffalo and *Miss Saigon* in Sacramento. In simple terms, if they made it big enough, the shows and the people and the profits would probably follow.

Digesting the report and learning that there were more people living in the four cities and surrounding suburbs of the Capital Region than in Buffalo or Rochester, the Schenectady County Legislature committed a million dollars to kickstart an expansion fund in 2001. However, leaders in Albany had been reading the entertainment tea leaves, too, and had put forth their own champion in the so-called theater war – the Palace Theater – and negotiations were underway to perhaps expand the Palace, allow Proctor's to manage it, and let New York's capital city become the upstate destination for Broadway musical aficionados. Eventually, that deal was enshrined in a document that Mayor Al Jurczynski of Schenectady signed, but Mayor Jerry Jennings of Albany did not. Rumor had it that Albany planned to purchase the large lot behind the Palace and take the leap on its own.

When Philip Morris took over in 2002, the Board told him, "Figure out what's going on with this. That's your job," so Philip talked to Jayme Lahut at Metroplex and said, "Why don't we just do this ourselves," because Metroplex seemed like it wanted to be a significant part of the deal, but Jayme, poker face intact, wouldn't commit to a specific dollar amount. Then Philip talked to Mayor Jennings in Albany, but they couldn't hash out a path to move forward together either. And during that first year, he simply hadn't had enough time to build a network of donors to fund the expansion on his own. The order of the day was hurry up and wait, but keep planning.

In the meantime, Philip approached Frank Gilmore, a prominent local architect and a founding partner of the architectural firm of Stracher-Roth-Gilmore (SRG). During the 1990s, Frank had worked up a vision plan to treat the 400 block of State Street, including an expanded Proctor's, as a fertile series of buildings that might be replaced or renovated into a performing arts center. With the demolition of Canal Square, that idea had to be scrapped, but Philip encouraged Frank to rework his original vision. The new set of drawings they produced included a movie complex at one end of the block and an expanded Proctor's, of course, but also a humongous entertainment center that included a three-story IMAX theater and an observatory on top of the building – remarkably ambitious but unworkable, again, without the backing of major investors and/or big federal and state grants. The notion of trans-forming downtown into a viable entertainment complex and luring the *Phantom* to town had to sit on the back burner for a while.

While he assembled a network of contacts and donors, Philip laid the ground-work for systemic change. His mentor had been a man named Joseph Golden, who had written a book called *Olympus on Main Street:* A Process for Planning a Community Arts Facility, which became Philip's bible. Joe Golden's primary theory stipulated that arts centers and theaters have to feature democratization – they have to be of the people, by the people, and for the people. They have to function as schools, as community centers, as places of healing and making and assembling. They have to be of community. They have to mean everything and be vitally important to the places they serve or there is no reason for them to exist. And Philip Morris brought that mindset with him to Schenectady, knowing, of course, that he also had to keep a theater running and make a profit.

For example, late in 2003, with the streetscape nearing completion, Philip noticed that every day there would be a group of homeless guys, often in puffy jackets, hanging around the fountain. Inevitably, somebody would call the cops, and a patrol car would eventually roll up, its siren blasting. Same scenario, every day, for weeks, and it sustained an atmosphere of tension in the heart of downtown. Finally, Morris approached Mike Saccoccio, who ran the City Mission, and they agreed the situation had to change.

I said, "Michael, what if we did something together, something like a Union Square Park and we just had chess outside? Just to have something normal going on." And he said, "I love it. Let's do it." So we did chess at that point twice a week, all summer long, out across the street. Mike supplied the plastic chess boards. We supplied tickets for prizes, and tables and chairs. And any time we were playing chess there were no police cars.

So the following year we came up with the idea of why don't we ask our staff, volunteers only, if they would be willing to go have lunch at the fountain? Just lunch time because that was the only time when this problem was happening. And that summer, every day, somebody from one of our two organizations had lunch at the fountain. After that, Mike got a part-time social worker to go down there every mid-day and check on who was taking his meds and who wasn't. It wasn't a guy with an AR-15, right, and the police never came back. When people see police all the time, they assume there's a problem. The best downtown is no police.

At the same time, it also became obvious to Philip that the 400 block of State Street, devoid of its Canal Square eyesores, presented a clean slate. Every new property that was developed there would need utilities. So he commissioned a study which asked if it was worth considering a district energy plant, and a resounding YES came back. Proctor's needed new boiler and cooling plants anyway as elements of the continuing renovations, so the Board okayed the initiative. They separated the heating and cooling functions, funded them differently, and planned to include a nine-million-dollar, natural-gas-fueled heating and cooling system that could supply all the buildings on the block as soon as a potential expansion progressed, and they knew they would get plenty of takers. Heating lines with ethylene glycol would run under all the sidewalks on that block of State Street, as well as under Proctor's loading-in area. Who wouldn't want sidewalks you never had to shovel in winter? Art and science could combine to provide theatrical entertainment, community welfare, and outside-of-school education – those were the key aspects of the dream. All Philip needed was the money to turn his wish list into reality.

*   *   *

Metroplex wasn't working right. Neil Golub had been complaining about various issues from the outset, periodically sending letters to John Manning, the Chairman. These opening excerpts exemplify the increasingly fractious tone:

January 27, 1999

Dear John:
It is unfortunate that we have not yet had the opportunity to
clearly study and understand the varying roles of the Metroplex
Authority. Much has been said and written that confuses the
issue. One thing is for sure, we are not starting out with a clean
sheet of paper. Some work is already in progress and we will
have to respond …

Neil Golub

February 10, 1999

Dear John:
I have a growing concern that you are unilaterally carrying
out Metroplex business by excluding Board members from

*their rightful due diligence. Continued actions of this type
will only alienate Board members and put us right back into
Schenectady's adversarial history …*

Neil Golub

December 6, 1999

*TO: John Manning, Chairman, Metroplex Authority
    Metroplex Authority Board Members
    Jayme Lahut, Executive Director, Metroplex Authority*

*Based on actions of Chairman Manning, it is my belief that the
by-laws are flawed. While Chairman Manning has received a
spending privilege up to $25,000, I do not believe the Board
intended to abdicate its responsibility to provide the Chairman
with its advice and consent on contracts, consulting, and real
estate deals prior to closure …*

Neil Golub

George Robertson, who was still head of the Schenectady Economic Development Corporation, continued trying to undermine the efforts of Metroplex. As the MVP parking garage was being constructed, for instance, George told a colleague, "This isn't about making the parking garage look good. This is about driving up the cost of it and making John Manning look bad." Board votes on most of the initial projects remained close for the first few years, usually six to five in favor of the Manning contingent, even as some early accomplishments – like the MVP headquarters and the State Department of Transportation building – were touted as unqualified successes. However, by 2003, the chorus of voices in opposition to John Manning's leadership was growing. It wasn't just Neil and the Client Group complaining. Even staunch Manning advocates like Harry Apkarian were starting to vote against what he was proposing.

There was constant fighting over loans and grants that Metroplex was offering.

Giving public money away just went against the grain of some Board members: nine million to Proctor's for its future district energy plant; four and half million for infrastructure improvements on various, key blocks, with new water lines, new sewer lines, new storm drainage, new streetlights and pavement and curbs and sidewalks from Nott Terrace all the way down to Erie Boulevard; and increasing the Broadway parking garage from two floors to five, not just to provide parking for new State DOT workers but also to accommodate visitors to a multiplex movie theater that hadn't even been built yet. Everything was in anticipation of finding people to invest in Schenectady's downtown, of course, but most of the entities receiving the grants were not obligated to pay them back. Chicken or egg: which comes first, the infrastructure or the businesses, and would businesses take the risk to open in the city without the infrastructure being in place?

Metroplex Executive Director Jayme Lahut sided with John Manning. Do the work while literally nothing is going on, that was his mantra. Set an attractive table first, play the long game, and investors will realize the opportunities there. But to make things even harder for Jayme and John, many of the debilitated downtown buildings had been acquired for a song by slumlords who had been ignoring code requirements for years. Now that Metroplex had a steady stream of sales tax revenue and wanted to clean up the area, those absentee clowns were jacking up the asking price on their badly-maintained buildings. Using eminent domain to pay them a reasonable amount would definitely generate I-told-you-so recriminations in the press – *If you don't work with Metroplex, they'll just take your building away from you!* Metroplex was just getting started, and they didn't need more bad articles. So the Board, knowing they would be gouged, had to weather public criticism for paying exorbitant prices to keep moving with their revitalization plans. Readers of the *Daily Gazette* didn't care all that much about the behind-the-scenes details: *Metroplex was the big promise, so where are the immediate results?*

The final straw for the Manning regime occurred with the fourteen-plex theater they had hoped to build at the corner of State and Clinton Streets. Omni Development out of Albany was the first developer that wanted to work with Metroplex, and they had hooked up with Empire Cinema in Amsterdam for the movie deal in Schenectady. One of the first ominous signs was Empire's stated plan to install used theater seats they had stored in a barn. If that wasn't bad enough, one of the principal partners at Omni, David Swawite, had suddenly and tragically lost his son, and he was so devastated that he lost focus for the project. He was grieving, and John Manning, being compassionate, wanted to give him time for that process. "He's our guy," John told Jayme and the Board. "We're not going to abandon him." But the weeks dragged on into months, and Jayme eventually lost his patience:

> He was the decision maker and he couldn't make a decision. I was recommending we just had to move on. It's not like it was just a week, we're talking about six months later. It's like he can't decide, he's not interested. You can tell he's depressed, he wants to help, but you're talking about millions of dollars, no, tens of millions of dollars, and he's not ready to do it because he's grieving and he's in a bad place. And we hung in there with the movie guys way longer than I would have put up with, because they were afraid. They were afraid of Schenectady's crime problem – "Can you ensure that every night there are patrols in downtown Schenectady, so people can go safely from the parking lot to the movie theater?" – "No, that's what the police are for."

The deal was still unresolved when election day in November, 2003, arrived. That's when everything suddenly changed. Republican Mayor Al Jurczynski wasn't running for a third term, and Democrat Brian Stratton, son of former Schenectady mayor and long-time U.S. Senator Sam Stratton, was elected to replace him. Sharon Jordan, who had headed the Schenectady Municipal Housing Authority (SMHA) from 1987 to 2003, had acted as Brian Stratton's campaign manager, and she had pulled out all the stops. She even persuaded Hilary Clinton to come to town for a fundraiser that helped Brian win a convincing victory.

Sharon had many talents, and she knew everybody in town. She was an excellent grant writer, and during her human services tenure with SMHA, she pulled in 120 million dollars to renovate housing projects, initiate family investment services, and help low and moderate income people acquire decent homes – all while the city was falling apart around her. "When I was there," Sharon remembered, "we were the one place that money was coming into. My motto was to bring housing into the community and the community into housing."

Inevitably, her populist background led her into political activism with Don Ackerman and other devoted Democrats during the decade that Republicans were mayors and controlled the County Legislature – from 1993 to 2003 – but the stars had never fully aligned for the Democratic Party in Schenectady County until Stratton took over in January of 2004. The Schenectady City Council remained Democratic, and the County Legislature also achieved a strong Democratic majority for the very first time. *Okay, this is it,* the Democrats believed. *We're finally in charge. No more incessant fighting. Now we can straighten things out.*

However, within weeks after his election, Brian Stratton discovered what had been going on for the last couple of years:

> *I mean, they were using capital funds for day-to-day operating expenses, which you're not supposed to do. Capital funds are money that you bond and borrow for capital projects, like if you're going to build roads or bridges or a new DPW garage – large-scale, high-spending, high-ticket items. There's no way around it, you're really not supposed to do that kind of thing. Those are borrowed funds, those are capitalized funds that you sell bonds for, and day-to-day operating expenses are generally paid for from the property taxes. So the former mayor was using money that was borrowed and set aside for capital projects just to pay day-to-day bills, and that produced a deficit when I came into office of about ten million dollars. I think Schenectady's budget at that time was, I don't remember exactly, about seventy million, so that deficit was more than 10% of the budget. Yeah, a huge deficit.*

Moody's Investors Service downgraded Schenectady's bond rating from Ba1 to Ba2, making it the lowest in New York State. Brian wasn't necessarily intimidated by the dire situation, because his ten years on the City Council during the 1990s had amply illustrated the challenges his city faced. But he never imagined that level of malfeasance, and he knew he had an uphill battle on his hands. He knew he had the political chops for the job, but he also realized he lacked adequate administrative experience, so his first act was to ask Sharon Jordan to take early retirement from SMHA and serve as his chief of staff, which she reluctantly accepted. Brian's second act, also that December, and before his new administration had even moved into their offices in City Hall, was to borrow money from the County to make payroll. Schenectady's government was totally broke. There was literally not enough money to pay the city's workers.

Brian and Sharon, along with the City Council, determined there were a few immediate ways out of the mess that had been left for them: raise property taxes 25% to get money to pay back the capital funds that had been misused, which made finding a buyer for your house in Schenectady difficult at best for fed-up residents; sell the downtown parking garage to Metroplex to erase what the city still owed on that and generate some income; and liquidate the city's tax liens. A company called American Tax Financing (ATF) offered to buy the city's delinquent taxes, up front, dollar for dollar. If your city had seven million dollars in unpaid taxes, ATF would cut you a check on the spot for that seven million, then go out and collect those taxes, adding charges and fees for financing plans. That's how they made their profit, if everything went as planned. It didn't go so well for ATF in the long run, but Brian clinched that deal as fast as he could, and wiped out most of the inherited deficit in his first few months as mayor.

There were no dull moments over at the County Legislature either. 2004 is when all the significant action started, as far as Susan Savage was concerned. She was the Democratic legislator who had made life difficult for Bob Farley in the run-up to Metroplex being confirmed, and had ascended to Chair after the Democrats won the majority. She had never been happy with the County losing so much control to the independent Board of Metroplex, and now she could see an obvious way to rectify that problem. She resented the Republican mayor who had moved the plaque honoring General Electric workers from the front of City Hall because he blamed GE for the city's financial woes, and she resented the businessmen who had applied political pressure to create this entity, this public authority, in order to revitalize two blocks of downtown. "You needed the leadership for a county which had resources when a city had none," Susan explained. "You needed the county to have the political will to take taxpayer dollars and dedicate them to economic development."

The first term for all the volunteer members of the Metroplex Board was expiring, and as Chair of the County Legislature, she had the power to appoint a new leader for the Metroplex Authority. A lot of the Metroplex Board members "seemed ticked off they had to appear before the County Legislature and say why they should be reappointed," as Susan Savage remembered. "It was beneath them. They acted like we were kind of dumb, and they were the leaders. And so I recall asking John Manning, 'What do you think the role of the County Legislature should be in economic development?' He paused and he turned his head and he looked at me and he said, 'Cheerleader.' And the course of history changed in that moment."

Susan chose Ray Gillen to become the new Metroplex chair, but getting him to accept the job was hardly a slam-dunk. No Democrat had been the Chair of the County Legislature before, and sitting right before her was this huge opportunity. The Democratic legislators had not been able to be the decision makers for so many years, and this was their big chance. Unfortunately, Susan desperately wanted to hire someone who really didn't want the job. As a matter of fact, Ray had been offered the job five years before and had turned it down. He worked at the Economic Development Agency of New York State, and he loved his job, but Susan was unrelenting. "She would call me every day and say, 'You've got to take this job. This is your hometown,'" Ray remembered. "She and Brian both, they wouldn't stop, but mostly it was Susan. And it was career suicide, absolute career suicide. 'I work for the State of New York,' I told her. 'Chair of Metroplex isn't a real job.' And the State, and to this day this has never happened again, they actually countered to try and keep me. Because this is all I'm good at. The rest of it, I can't do anything."

Eventually, Susan wore Ray down. "Ray, this is your community more than it's mine," she reminded him. "You've lived here your whole life, you're raising your kids in the city of Schenectady, and I'm going to give you eight million dollars a year to make this city what it can be. I'll run the interference, I'll take the shots, and whatever problems there are, I'll do the blocking." And she engineered a novel solution: because the Metroplex position was volunteer, Susan needed to find Ray a salaried job. When Director of Planning Dave Atkins retired, he was the highest-paid employee in the county, making $120,000 a year in 2003. Susan simply changed the job title to Commissioner of Planning and Development and plugged Ray into that position. Problem solved.

When Ray walked in for his first day, he said:

> *Listen, these are the rules: we're not having any politics, I'm not going to any fundraisers, I'm not going to anything. We're going to solve the General Electric tax issue, we're going to stop suing our biggest employer, and we're going to put the GE plaque back in front of City Hall. We're going to throw out the Hunter plan and change it with a Schenectady plan. The whole place is depressed. It's the most depressed downtown in the state. We have to create momentum to break the down cycle and show people that we can have a win, and we start with a Corridor of Strength. We do one block, the Proctor's block. That's Deal One. You can't call it the 400 Block of State Street now. Anyone who does that puts a quarter in the swear jar. We're not going to burn Jack Welch in effigy downtown anymore. We're not going to scream and carry on and threaten people. That era is over. We fix the Proctor's block and we go on from there.*

The new day in Schenectady had dawned.

*   *   *

F.F. Proctor, remember, was an equilibrist – an acrobat, a balancer – and it turned out that saving the grand theater he built in Schenectady had always required various financial and physical balancing acts, as well as the creative collaboration of thousands of community volunteers, during the decades since he died. Philip Morris may have been pondering that metaphor when he announced on April 7, 2005, that he was shuttering Proctor's Theater for almost eight months.

"This is a great place," he began, "and now we're going to expand the possibilities here. When we open back up on December 1st, the square footage on our stage will nearly be tripled. From the curtain line to the back line is going to be fifty feet. Right now it's only thirty feet. We're going to have a much wider stage, too, and our height will go up ten feet as well."

The producer of *Phantom of the Opera*, Cameron Mackintosh, had stipulated that any production of *Phantom*, anywhere, had to replicate the original staging. Diminished productions would hobble his vision. That demand had turned plenty of smaller venues into sore losers. Mirror what we have created in London and New York – in other words, spend millions to expand your stages – or miss out on the theatrical wave of the future. That was the unwavering message. Take it or leave it.

"For years, Proctor's has had to say no to shows like *Phantom*," Philip continued, "or we've had to put on smaller versions of other Broadway shows. That will no longer be the case, and we're thrilled about it. Now we have no limits. Imagine, we're going to have a show like *The Producers* that's really hot in New York City right now. We're going to have that right here." Ever the showman, Philip punctuated his point by saying, "This is the biggest news to hit downtown Schenectady since

F.F. Proctor opened the theater on December 26, 1926."

Then he went on to list the first four shows he had booked for the upcoming theatrical season: *The Producers* would run from December 6th through the 11th, the usual weekly run for touring Broadway shows; *Peter Pan*, with Cathy Rigby in her last year performing in the title role, would run the week of January 10, 2006; two weeks after that, *Phantom of the Opera* would play on Proctor's new, expanded stage for almost a full month – from February 1st through the 26th; and *Doctor Dolittle the Musical*, with stage animals fashioned by the artist who had created the creatures in *The Lion King*, would appear from May 31st to June 4th.

Mayor Brian Stratton followed Philip and told the assembled crowd, "Proctor's is a fantastic, historic theater, and every new business we're getting – every expansion – is because of what's going on here. Businesses want to be a part of this. I believe the economic impact will be tremendous, and Proctor's is undeniably at the center of everything we're trying to do to promote Schenectady." It was true that some businesses were thinking of opening in Schenectady again. Angelo Mazzone, for instance, had built a wide-reaching restaurant and catering empire in the eighteen years since he watched his first restaurant burn in Canal Square. Angelo was planning to start an upscale restaurant named Aperitivo on the exact site where his original eatery, Peggy's, had been., but he was waiting until 2007, when the bulk of the expansion construction would be finished.

The most popular part of the Proctor's project was the main stage expansion to support the largest musicals, of course. Philip was well aware that musical theater had acted as a gateway drug to other kinds of plays and arts for at least eighty years – and much longer if you traced its roots back through vaudeville to minstrel shows. Musicals, as a genre that mixed drama or comedy with song, served as a common entry point, and complex spectacle-musicals like *Phantom* and some of the other announced shows would draw the largest audiences, without a doubt. People who loved musicals were happy to have their senses overwhelmed, and they would often pay through the nose for extravagant productions that could offer that euphoric sensation. Philip wasn't condescending at all – he loved musicals, too – and constructing a year of programming around them was simply common sense.

However, Philip also had broader plans. Proctor's mission statement emphasized education and public involvement: "Through arts and community leadership, be a catalyst for excellence in education, sustainable economic development, and rich civic engagement to enhance the quality of life in the greater Capital Region." That inclusive statement can really only work if you have the room to implement it, and F.F. Proctor had only conceived of the original, 1926 theater as a palace for entertainment – vaudeville and movies.

The Carl Co. building, next door to Proctor's and vacant for many years, was owned by Schenectady County, which used it as a storage facility. When a water main broke in 2004 and flooded its basement, all the Department of Social Services records were destroyed. Philip chose that moment to ask the County Legislature, "Would you get out of that building and give it to us?" Their answer was quick in coming: "Absolutely." However, "give" wasn't exactly accurate. Proctor's had to pay the County $25,000 to facilitate moving everything that was stored in the building, and it also had to cover $350,000 of the $750,000 owed in tax liens.

In any case, Philip acquired more than enough space to create a state-of-the-art civic cultural center and fulfill the mission statement. According to the Proctor's Theater Expansion Project Overview Report issued in 2002, the three floors of the Carl Co. building, made accessible from the Arcade that opened into the original theater, would allow for not only additional main stage support spaces like dressing rooms and rehearsal areas, but would feature a brand new, 450-seat black box theater on the 2nd floor with a 40 × 60-foot IMAX screen. There was also room in the former department store near the black box theater for a ticket sales area, rest rooms, and a large café. A 250-seat banquet hall was planned for the 3rd floor, although that was never installed.

Neither the main stage expansion nor The Carl Co. renovation was going to be inexpensive. The Project Report projected the cost for the stage expansion and the support spaces at almost fourteen million dollars. The black box theater would be three and a half million. The 12% project contingency came in at a little over two million. And soft costs – architectural, engineering, and theater design work; construction management; consulting and legal fees; and managing the capital campaign – would add another three million plus. The projected total cost in 2002 was $22,387,000.

By the time the work began in 2005, it cost much more. Roughly, ten million was raised through individual gifts, $750,000 of which came from the Golub family; nine and a half million was contributed by Metroplex; eleven million came from federal and state historic tax credits, as well as New Market tax credits; and the final nine million dollars in Empire State tax credits was paid off over a decade. That brought Philip's actual construction budget total to just under forty million dollars, and he didn't have forty million dollars on hand. As a matter of fact, he had to grow his budget as the stage expansion and The Carl Co. renovation projects proceeded, side by side, and at one point he almost lost an important piece of his federal funding.

Philip had hired architect Frank Gilmore once again to design both projects, and the stage expansion ran into trouble early on. Since Proctor's had been placed on the National Register of Historic Places in 1980, it was designated as a national landmark. That meant Philip could apply for federal tax credits from the Department of the Interior that amounted to 20% of his project. However, getting that money depended on the State Historic Preservation Office (SHPO), granting a recommendation for Proctor's application.

When Philip submitted his application, though, he got some serious pushback from SHPO. They weren't happy with the stylistic compatibility of the new streetscape. Frank Gilmore explained:

> *We had to do all of the backstage stuff in some sort of streetscape that had a different scale to it. But SHPO claimed that the former streetscape looked nothing like what I had designed. They said, "You have completely eliminated any reference to the original streetscape on Smith Street, and therefore we're not sure that it merits a tax credit." You're not supposed to slavishly imitate what gets torn down, but they wanted some reference to the old back end of Proctor's that they thought was historic, and they believed we wiped that out. Their ultimate ruling was, "We cannot recommend this to the Department of the Interior."*
>
> *Now if you don't get recommended to the feds, you don't get their money – and that was one of Philip's major sources. But you do have a chance to redeem your tax credit after it's been rejected at the State level by arguing your case in front of a judiciary board. So Philip and the guy who packaged the submission, along with an historian or two, huddled together and built an argument as to how my design actually was referential to the earlier streetscape that had been torn down. Then he went to Washington, D.C., talked his way through the hearing, and he damn well got it back.*

No one could ever deny that Philip Morris was willing to take substantial risks, and you couldn't help but admire his own constant and particular balancing acts. Even after the stage expansion was completed on time, and a sold-out week of *The Producers* went off without a hitch, there were plenty of naysayers who predicted the theater would never last. Richard Lovrich, who had been the Art Director at the *Times Union* in Albany and had left his job there to come and work with Philip early in January of 2006, said he was shocked to find so many doubters in Schenectady: "There were so many people who woke up every day and were proud to post on social media about how Proctor's was going to fail. I don't know why it gives certain people pleasure to dream about failure or feel empowered by fantasies of disempowering people who make grand efforts."

In spite of that perceived negativity, or perhaps to help counter it, Richard stayed at Proctor's, contributed his multiple talents, and thrived. Cathy Rigby came to town as *Peter Pan* and thrilled families from all around the region. The Phantom of the Opera lured visitors from Vermont and the Berkshires and the Hudson Valley and from all corners of the Capital Region, disappointing none of them with its spectacular effects and soaring music, and broke all of Proctor's previous box office records. Volunteers for the theater multiplied, and over the next year, the old Carl Co. building contributed its elements to the new performing arts center that Proctor's was becoming.

And in the dark of winter the following December, when *Wicked* was playing in town, Mike Saccoccio came to see Philip Morris and asked, "How can City Mission help Proctor's be more successful?" And Philip said:

> *Here's how you can help us. People are coming to downtown Schenectady again. They haven't been here for a while, and many of them don't think it's safe. It really is safe, the data shows that it is, but perception is reality. It's dark, it's cold. They park in that big garage and they run into the theater. That's not what this is supposed to be about. We want people walking around, shopping, having dinner, then coming to the theater. I just wish we had people who could go out, greet our visitors, and make them feel welcome.*

"All right, there it is," Mike said. "For the next three months, whenever there's a show at Proctor's, our most senior City Mission residents will go out and greet your guests. They can act as downtown ambassadors."

At the end of *Wicked*'s run, Metroplex commissioned a survey to see what people liked most about downtown Schenectady, and when they got the survey back, the Ambassadors were the highest-rated aspect.

"People were so delighted that they were being greeted on the sidewalks by friendly, smiling people, and that doors were being held open for them," Mike Saccoccio explained. "Then we made a capital investment: we bought umbrellas. And when it was raining, we'd run out there and put those umbrellas over people's heads. We called it a Sidewalk Concierge Service."

Metroplex offered $10,000 to jumpstart that simple initiative, and it quickly morphed into a full-fledged Ambassador Program. And after a couple of years, it evolved into $12-an-hour, part-time jobs for any motivated residents of City Mission who wanted to work as welcoming ambassadors throughout downtown, and its affiliated training program has now propelled half of the participants into full-time employment.

Philip Morris, his staff, and all of Proctor's volunteers – with their own initiatives but with the continuous support of Metroplex – had created an engine of economic revitalization in the middle of a downtown that was once given up for dead. They did it by presenting the most complex Broadway touring shows, and by making Schenectady into what Bill Golub once believed it might be – a destination city. They instilled civic pride by functioning as what Proctor's calls "the community's living room, a space where citizens of all stripes can gather." They did it by envisioning a School of the Performing Arts for high school students from 380 schools and fourteen counties, and by playing host to press conferences, private parties, political fundraisers, high-quality concerts, church and memorial services, and extensive movie series, to name just a few of the 1700 events each year that Proctor's offers. The spark of vitality that Philip couldn't find in Jamestown flared for him in Schenectady.

Now it was Metroplex's turn to dazzle.

11

The Tough Comeback

*There are two ways to go about a city's revitalization.
The first is to start with economic development, and the
second is to start with the development of services. In the
debate about where a declining city should put its resources,
economic development is often presented as the primary
concern because it is expected to create jobs and increase
city revenues. Residents' needs for services and safe and
livable communities are seen as secondary. But it is possible
to see a connection between these two sets of goals.*

*– Community Builders: A Tale of Neighborhood
Mobilization in Two Cities*
Gordana Rabrenovic

When Ray Gillen became Chairman of Metroplex in 2004, there were no less than twenty-seven disparate economic development and training organizations in the city and county of Schenectady, each with its own confusing acronym: SEDC, the Schenectady Economic Development Corporation; SETDC, the Schenectady Employment Training Development Corporation; SLDC, the Schenectady Local Development Corporation; CSIDA, the City of Schenectady Industrial Development Agency, and a pile of other, similar-sounding entities.

Add in these groups – Heritage Area, JOBS etc., the Little Italy Loan Fund, U-Start Business Incubator, Renewal Community, DSIC Façade Program, World Trade Center Schenectady, as well as nine regional programs, mostly centered in Albany – and you have an obvious recipe for chaos. George Robertson, as it turned out, was executive director and lead staff person for six of them, including the SEDC, with which he implemented a number of controversial projects.

Each of these organizations had a different idea about how to create business opportunities for the second-smallest landmass county in New York State, and most of them also battled incessantly with each other. At best, it was alphabet soup and, at worst, characterizing the situation with a crude metaphor could include six monkeys euphemistically handling a football, but no matter how you describe it, the menagerie of organizations and agencies clearly wasn't working. Ray Gillen had observed the melee from a safe distance for years before he accepted the Metroplex job: "There wasn't a single point of contact for investors, and there was no new development at any of the industrial parks. The only big deal was Super Steel, which was doing contract locomotive manufacturing for General Motors out of the Glenville Park, and I did that project when I was still with the State."

In Ray Gillen's opinion, George Robertson comprised the lion's share of the problem, and had steered John Manning, Metroplex, and the city of Schenectady in disastrous directions. But all of them had seriously mishandled their single biggest accomplishment, as Ray explained:

> The one actual project they completed was MVP, but they did it all wrong. They had no idea what they were doing. At the time, the Empire Zone would allow companies to pay full taxes and then get reimbursed 100% by the State. The full taxes on the MVP building should have been $1.8 million a year for ten years, so it was a lot of money. But because they didn't know anything, they gave them a PILOT (a payment in lieu of taxes) of $200,000 a year. They left $1.6 million on the table. It cost the taxpayers $16 million overall. So even on this one successful deal, they overpaid for the property and they didn't get the tax revenue. Really it was Dave Buicko and the Galesi Group who got that project done, and

Dave did it because he had a good tenant in MVP, a credit-worthy tenant.

The MVP project was just one example of planning decisions that ended up hurting Schenectady in the long run. Before that debacle, there was an insane notion to tear down Proctor's Theater and instead expand The Carl Co. Department Store, where Ray's mother had worked while he was growing up in the city. There was the never-used, half-million-dollar Hunter-Sasaki plan – which Ray referred to as "so-sucky" – to revitalize downtown. "When I got here in 2004," Ray said, "I looked at it. I read it, tore out one page related to Erie Boulevard, and threw it in the garbage. The plan was just a shit show."

Another one of George's crazy ideas involved locating a World Trade Center on the site where they finally put the MVP building and parking garage, at a time when the smallest city in America to have what it called a world trade center was Baltimore. That building was slated to be part of what Ray termed "The Four Posts of Arrogance:" the other "posts," supporting arbitrary corners of the city, would have included Schenectady County Community College, which sat in a Mohawk River floodplain by the Western Gateway Bridge to Scotia; Broadway Center, where the nondescript Lottery Building stood; and the final one, situated on a massive brown-field where the ALCO plant had once operated, at the far end of Erie Boulevard. They were unrelated projects, geographically incompatible, and not easily-walkable distances from each other. To make matters even worse, George made no effort to mitigate the brownfield at the main ALCO site along the river or renovate any of the forty buildings there. He brought in lowbrow tenants who wanted to use the decaying structures for medical waste, construction debris, and tire recycling. He was literally in the final stages of signing the lease with the tire recycling folks when Ray showed up, condemned the lease, and took over the property, but that ill-fated endeavor cost Schenectady another four million dollars in good money tossed after bad.

Apart from his incompetence and malfeasance, George exhibited other questionable behaviors. For instance, he and Al Jurczynski traveled to Guyana together. George, once-divorced and sworn to bachelorhood, met a Guyanese teenager in a pool hall while he was there, chatted her up for an evening, and wound up marrying her. He was fifty-six and she was eighteen, at most, as rumor had it. To be fair, she was divorced herself, and they did end up making a good life with each other. Together, they adopted a Guyanese baby who had been abandoned on a street corner, and stayed married until George died of cancer in Warsaw, Indiana in 2019. But in 2003, the serious age difference raised eyebrows in a mid-sized city like Schenectady. Perhaps in Guyana or Queens, a thirty-eight-year gap, or more, would have seemed like no big deal, but in upstate New York, people definitely gossiped about it and perhaps that simply underscored the general feelings of resentment toward him. George did have a tendency to lecture and sermonize and bully people whenever he could, plus he had engineered some deals that stuck the city squarely behind the eight ball for decades. Ray Gillen remembered that George had rubbed him the wrong way from the day they met:

> At the time, New York State was having a lot of success bringing in rail properties, and I had the top guy from Siemens come in to look at the Alco plant, just to try and get Alco back into the rail business. And George showed up way late, looking like an unmade bed. As he was about to talk to this Siemens guy, he took a call from Mayor Jurczynski, and he talked for twenty minutes in front of the client. Then he proceeded to tell him that he had married this girl from Guyana who has no money – all of her worldly possessions could fit in a suitcase – and the guy from Siemens looked at him and said, "I don't know you well enough to have this conversation." Kind of the perfect site visit, right? That was what happened in Schenectady back then.

In the sometimes cutthroat world of professional economic development, if George Robertson was considered a carnival pitchman peddling low-rent, snake-oil solutions to complex business problems by some people in Schenectady – or, more dramatically, as a criminal con-man, as some others truly believed – then Ray Gillen might be portrayed as a heavyweight boxer like one of his local sports heroes, Dave Zyglewicz of Watervliet. In his varied career, "Ziggy" not only went toe-to-toe with Smokin' Joe Frazier after Joe's epic battle with Muhammed Ali, the "Thrilla in Manila," but he also fought in an amazing comeback bout at the age of thirty-nine where he knocked out Clyde Mudgett in the second round and earned just five thousand dollars, ten years after an industrial accident came close to killing him. Well, Ray Gillen had adopted Ziggy's come-straight-at-you style, but he also understood immediately that the mindset at Metroplex had to be changed:

> *One of the problems with Metroplex when we first started was they viewed themselves as a separate government, kind of a stand-alone organization, which was a foolish concept, because all of our projects had to go through the planning commissions at the County and in the towns. Metroplex had to be a partner with these local governments, not a separate entity. When they first set it up, the Metroplex chairman was kind of seen as an official, an unelected king or something, which you can't do because we have to go and work with all of these people. We're bringing development projects, but there's still home rule. It's not one person. No one can do anything alone anymore. Check the egos at the door. It's about everyone working together.*

So Ray began with what looked like the best bet, one block – the Proctor's Block – that he started to call "The Corridor of Strength." As the expansion plan for Proctor's was confirmed and the private donations and federal grants began to come in, Ray concentrated Metroplex's attention on the rest of the block. "It was a very common sense approach," he explained. "You look at the patient, the patient's dying on the table, bleeding profusely. Jobs are leaving, everyone's leaving. What are you going to do? You've got to stabilize the patient. Start with one block."

The previous regime's plan to get Omni Development to install a multiplex a few doors up the block from Proctor's, at State and Clinton, using seats a theater owner in Amsterdam was trying to hide in a barn from his wife during their divorce negotiations, was obviously a non-starter. Ray's briefest assessment, "Wrong corner,

no parking there," was shorthand for a litany of reasons the deal was a loser, including the fact that Ray called the trek from that theater site to the Broadway parking garage late at night a potential "walk down Rape Alley."

The corner he wanted for a movie theater was at the other end of the block, directly across the street from the parking garage, where Broadway crossed State Street. Doug Sayles and his brother, John, Schenectady's favorite-son novelist and filmmaker, made the contact with Bow Tie Cinemas, a fourth-generation, family-owned company with an illustrious history. Its founder, B.S. Moss, was a contemporary of F.F. Proctor. He started out with nickelodeons in 1900 and quickly moved into running vaudeville theaters until 1930, when he switched to building and operating movie theaters for the rest of his career. The cartoon that launched Walt Disney's entertainment empire – "Steamboat Willie," featuring Mickey Mouse – was first shown in a B.S. Moss theater in New York City, as was Disney's avant-garde classic film, *Fantasia*. Honoring Moss's Theater of Tomorrow, in the "bow-tie" section of Times Square, the company rebranded as Bow Tie Cinemas and now runs more than fifty theatres from New York, New Jersey and Connecticut in the Northeast down to Maryland and Virginia and then out west to Colorado.

Doug Sayles enlisted Frank Gilmore's help and they pitched a new Schenectady site to the Bow Tie folks at their headquarters in Times Square, and they loved the idea. Frank's firm, Stracher-Roth-Gilmore Architects, designed the theater and Doug Sayles was instrumental in obtaining a liquor license for the location. Dave Buicko and the Galesi Group, bought the property and constructed the state-of-the-art multiplex. And at State and Clinton, the "wrong corner" site, a shiny new, $10 million Hampton Inn with ninety-three rooms was going up while Bow Tie's new Movieland theater was being completed.

With blockbuster Broadway shows in the middle of the block at Proctor's, a first-run movie theater at one end, a new Hampton Inn at the other end, a completely-renovated, luxurious Parker Inn on one side of Proctor's and an upscale restaurant, Aperitivo, on the other side, the entertainment-seeking public in the Capital Region

and beyond finally had some excellent reasons to travel to Schenectady.

Within Ray Gillen's first fifteen months on the job, Metroplex had transformed the entire Proctor's Block and scored their first popular wins. "We had to create a sense of momentum to break the down cycle and to create confidence," Ray explained. "Money follows money and deals generate more deals." What had felt like a slow burn for so long suddenly had exploded into a rapid recovery strategy. The "fear factor" for investors in Schenectady was fading away, and developers were lining up at Metroplex to launch new projects.

Administratively, Ray had begun to eliminate or consolidate those twenty-seven economic development organizations in the county and offer instead his unified team approach at Metroplex and, man oh man, was that approach working. Twenty new buildings had been added to the tax base by June of 2005, and sixteen other buildings had either expanded or been renovated, adding $158 million in new investments and creating 900 new jobs in the city and county. And an unusual confidence had spread through the Metroplex Board as well: Neil Golub and the other second-term mem-

bers were relieved to find they now had a steady hand at the wheel and, for the first time, the weekly Metroplex meetings didn't include heated arguments.

The Authority was purchasing parking lots, selling off buildings to help reimburse General Electric for years of overpayments on property taxes, and looking to develop the two ALCO sites on lower Nott Street and the massive, 60-acre ALCO site along Erie Boulevard and the Mohawk River. However, even Ray Gillen couldn't imagine what opportunities would be coming their way in the next few years.

*　　　*　　　*

Steve Raucci didn't give a damn about Brian Stratton's Schenectady 2020 Comprehensive Plan to "Reinvent the City of Invention." He was too busy terrorizing staff and faculty members at Schenectady High School to even notice it. However, Stratton's new plan, which claimed "The prior City of Schenectady Plan was completed in 1971," was a strategic and inclusive wonder. Alternately referred to as a Vision Plan, the voluminous report contained an exhaustive, 102-page community profile, as well as nine neighborhood plans, a downtown plan, a city-wide action plan, a new zoning ordinance, themes that emerged from community meetings, an adoption process and implementation plan, and a vision statement – lots of inspiring stuff for a still down-at-the-heels city.

Mayor Stratton and his Chief of Staff, Sharon Jordan, had forged this ambitious blueprint for success in a very savvy way during a two-year process that began in June of 2005. They wanted to "expand citizen awareness of issues and trends facing the city," so they devised a simple experiment with three basic questions to help residents, property owners, business organizations, and even elected officials to re-imagine a better future for Schenectady:

- *What things do I love about the city of Schenectady?*

- *What things would I change about it?*

- *When these things are preserved or changed, Schenectady will …*

They convened twenty-two neighborhood workshops and two in the downtown area. They hosted three "visioning sessions" in the community, and conducted dozens of interviews. Finally, they held a city-wide neighborhood planning summit. No one who chose to participate missed out on the chance to offer opinions and suggestions, and those who complained they had been left out of the process couldn't find a leg to stand on. One answer Stratton's people heard again and again was that Schenectady was a welcoming, open community with a hometown atmosphere – "small enough to make a difference, big enough to make an impact." So after all the research efforts were wrapped up – and the mountain of results transcribed, assembled, digested, analyzed, and meticulously graphed and written – they posted a set of initiatives that had been proposed by residents, City staff, City Council members, regional partners, and a team of consultants on a website that everyone could access. Inclusion and transparency – not much people could criticize about that approach.

The complete, microscopically-detailed Schenectady 2020 Comprehensive Plan assessed every aspect of life in the city, and provided hundreds of pages of information about demographics, employment, real estate as tax base, infrastructure, transportation, recreation and arts, public safety, parks and other natural resources, retail trends, commuting patterns, and education – pretty much all the elements that determine the livability of any city, anywhere. Moreover, the expansive report also outlined the results of all those community feedback and idea sessions, as well as the action plans themselves – the proposed "smart growth" initiatives –that the Stratton administration was advancing. Here is the plan's Vision Statement:

> *Schenectady is a city rich in history and heritage and the very birthplace of American technical innovation. Today, Schenectady remains a culturally diverse yet contemporary community of proud people who believe a brighter future lies within the strengths of their city's many assets, including beautiful parks, dynamic and architecturally unique neighborhoods, and the Mohawk River. Now through 2020, Schenectady will actively build upon this foundation of strength to become a highly preferred destination for Capital Region families of all cultures and faiths who seek quality homes and better schools in safe neighborhoods. They will*

be joined by businesses both large and small, both cultural and
technical, seeking to expand with the benefit of an outstanding
and educated workforce and to thrive within a city poised to con-
tinue its proud history of American achievement.

The Community Profile section of the Comprehensive Plan does honestly address a number of challenges the city faces – pervasive poverty (almost 48% of
the 8,973 students enrolled in Schenectady schools during the 2003-2004 school
year were eligible for the free lunch program); population loss (32.6 % of the city's
residents moved away between 1950 and 2004); decaying buildings and zombie
houses (there were 8,791 total substandard housing units in the city); and 32% of
its land remained tax exempt (churches, schools, libraries, hospitals, prisons, colleges, public service properties, etc.) – and concedes that, "Without adequate revenues and a stable tax base, Schenectady will be unable to accomplish what residents
demand." The report reads as clear-eyed and responsible all the way through.

However, what is missing amid the tone of jubilant boosterism that naturally
has to be present to inspire people are some really unsavory facts: the difficult-
to-explain, outrageous events that kept splashing across the front pages of Schenectady's *Daily Gazette*, Troy's *Record*, and the Albany *Times Union* – the regional
newspapers that so often influenced how people inside and outside Schenectady
perceived the city – as well as the persistent crime and corruption that often
dissuaded people from wanting to move there. The Vision Statement had clearly
targeted Capital Region families "who seek quality homes and better schools in
safe neighborhoods." Perhaps whoever wrote that was either optimistically blinded
by public relations zeal or was ignoring what was happening in plain sight with
Schenectady's schools and teenagers and police.

This is where Steve Raucci enters the picture. As Supervisor of Buildings and
Grounds for the entire school district, Raucci managed 125 custodians and maintenance workers, who referred to him as "the Doctor" or "the King" or occasionally
and simply as "God." He worked for the Schenectady School District for thirty-
six years, from 1973 to 2009, when he was arrested and charged with twenty-six

felonies, including arson, weapons possession, and terrorism. Robert Carney, Schenectady's long-serving District Attorney who prosecuted Raucci's case, summed him up this way: "In terms of a person who bullies people and studies the art of intimidation and coercion, I don't think there's anybody that compares with him."

Steve Raucci began at the bottom. He earned $3.12 an hour when he started as a laborer for the school district in 1973. As he worked his way up, past groundskeeper and through the maintenance department, he grew to understand the intricacies of the various physical systems – knowledge he would put to sinister use later to sabotage people he wanted out of his way. But first he had to get power. When the maintenance department was chaotic in the 1990s, with utility workers complaining about working conditions and demanding better pay, Raucci saw his chance. He ran for the president of their union – local 847 of the CSEA, the Civil Service Employees Association – and won. Once he was union boss, employee problems disappeared. Grievances in his department fell from an average of twenty-five a year to zero, and the higher-ups in Administration appreciated that. A couple of years after becoming president of the union, in 2003, he was promoted to Director of Buildings and Grounds. To the school board and the outside world, everything looked great. But secretly, in Raucci's fiefdom, the pranks on fellow workers which had always been his daily amusement grew more humiliating and ominous.

He would pour salt in coffee when someone wasn't looking. He'd lay his hand on a guy's thigh and leave it there for a "gay test." In department meetings, he might reveal that someone's wife was cheating on him. If a worker screwed up somehow, Raucci would force him to write, "I will not do …" every day on the office whiteboard, for weeks. He constantly harassed his secretary, Ellen Frederick: "He'd walk behind me, pretend to grab my hair, pretend to drag me into his office and bend me over his desk." Then he got her transferred after she said he wasn't her type, that she liked Matthew McConaughey. Ellen didn't want to leave her friends in the Maintenance Department, but she heard that Raucci had threatened her in a meeting with administrators, saying, "If she doesn't go quietly, she knows what's going to happen to her, her house, and her family."

With increased power came more money. His salary spiked thirty thousand dollars, from $37,500 to $67,500. However, he had to be careful. He couldn't use his rightful title, Director, because directors or managers couldn't be in a workers' union. So his designation became "Head Utility Worker," and he retained control of his local. If a member wanted to lodge a complaint, it went to Raucci. He was the boss, so he could smother it. If he threatened somebody's job, what could they do? The Administration seemed to love Raucci, so that avenue for help was cut off. Workers started calling Michelle Tabbano, co-chair of the union's grievance committee for Schenectady County, describing his belittling behavior. She offered to file grievances for them, but they couldn't remain anonymous. The calls stopped. "God" wouldn't like it if he found out.

Still, Michelle wanted him gone. "I thought we had all the evidence in the world to prove he was part of management," she remembered. "What more egregious thing can you have than a union president who's in bed with the school board, with the facilities supervisor, with the school attorneys? Are you kidding me?" So she filed official requests with the district for financial details – the guy was making way too much for even a "head utility worker" – but never received a response. Raucci ran a tight ship, and he was saving the Administration a pile of dough.

In 2004, Lou Semione wasn't meeting his goals as Energy Manager in the district. Maybe that was because Steve Raucci controlled the computer where Lou could make energy-saving changes to the heating and lighting systems, or maybe it was because Raucci would make sure that heat and lights were left on in all the buildings, including the massive array on the football field, over three-or-four-day holiday weekends. Lou's energy numbers tanked, and Raucci told the higher-ups he could do Lou's job for half his salary and take it as overtime pay without the title – again, to not threaten his position as union head. So Lou got fired, the energy numbers improved immediately under Raucci, naturally, and his overall salary jumped once more, to almost $125,000 a year.

Schenectady School District Superintendent Eric Ely received the following e-mail from Steve Raucci, his favorite, money-saving department head: "I've often told you that you and I are alike in many ways, we just have different backgrounds. We both like to win, and we do not care how we do it as long as we win. We both tell it like it is and if someone doesn't like what we say, that's too damn bad. If we do not like someone, we let them know about it and usually do something about it.

There we may differ a little. According to rumors, when I don't like someone I force them to go away or make them disappear. When you don't like someone, you have to wait until they die of old age, unless you give me their name." A couple of days before Raucci was arrested, Ely sent him an e-mail that read, "There aren't many I trust. You are one. Thank you."

The worst trouble started in 2005. Someone told Kathy Garrison, CSEA's regional president, that Raucci was running his department like a mafia boss. Raucci found out about it, of course, and blamed Debbie Gray, who was married to one of Raucci's maintenance guys, Hal Gray. Debbie denied it, but Raucci called Hal a "rat" and demoted him. Pretty soon, the Grays woke up to find the word RAT spray-painted in lurid red across three sides of their house in Burnt Hills, about ten miles from the school district. Raucci made all his workers cram into district vehicles to tour the graffiti site, and he demanded to hear their approval for his work. Even though Hal Gray had won medals for his two-tours of duty in Vietnam, he was un-nerved. If Raucci would do that, in the middle of the night, what else might he do? Gray contacted D.A. Carney, but there was no clear evidence linking Raucci to the vandalism.

However, Raucci was suspected in many other unsolved crimes, and Carney was biding his time. Gary DiNola, for instance, who was Director of Athletics, sent a complaint letter to Eric Ely about Raucci preventing access to sports facilities. The morning after he sent the letter, he found his car tires punctured and a large explosive lodged under his windshield wiper. And in 2001, a family in Rotterdam found their metal front door damaged by a bomb and a note under a rock nearby that read, "Just wanted to let you know we don't like you and your grievances." Eventual evidence pointed to Raucci, who finally admitted he had the wrong address on that one. At his trial, an explosives expert identified the bombs Raucci used as M-1000s, nicknamed "quarter-sticks." Essentially, they were improvised explosive devices. IEDs.

It turned out that Steve Raucci knew some excellent role models: his brother had committed suicide in prison to avoid testifying against associates in organized crime, and his father, who was convicted of killing Raucci's half-brother and step-mother, had also died in the joint. A co-worker remembers Raucci telling him, "If the cops come to my door, I have my pistol and I'll blow my head off before I do a day in jail."

That was one of the few promises that Raucci didn't make good on, but getting him into a jail would take some doing. An undercover investigator had trailed him to the Blue Ribbon Diner and pocketed a fork he had used to obtain a DNA sample they could match to notes or bomb parts, so they had that at least. But there were literally scores of incidents and victim complaints, and Carney wanted Raucci for as many crimes as he could pin on him.

Peter Minahan, a detective with the Special Investigations Unit of the New York State Police, knew that a disgraced Glenville cop who had become a heroin addict, Keith McKenna, had been one of Raucci's buddies in the old days. It was a risk worth taking, but it could easily have blown up in his face. Not only was McKenna still using, but he had betrayed law enforcement before. He had promised to be a snitch a decade earlier, secretly recorded a friend for the investigation, but had then tipped off the suspect. Warily, Minahan asked McKenna how well he knew Raucci. "I know him better than anyone in the world," McKenna answered. He admitted what Minahan already knew about him, and vowed it wouldn't happen again. He wanted to make up for all the bad shit he had done in his life. Of course he did, but he was still an addict. Soon after, he was caught selling expensive pills that blocked cravings to a fellow junkie, and knew he was trapped. He agreed to wear a wire and reconnect with his old pal, Steve Raucci.

The two met at Peter Pause Restaurant for breakfast, and McKenna begged Raucci for a job; said he was down and out. Raucci told him to call in a week. They met in Raucci's office, where Raucci felt safe bragging about his exploits. "Still don't like punks. I don't like wise guys, and I still think people should get what they deserve," Raucci said to McKenna. He talked about spray-painting the Grays' house, and told him, "Probably one of the worst things that somebody could think of is not feeling safe in your own house. But I guess where I'm going with this, Keith, is that some of the things I do, like I never want to physically hurt anyone. Property damage, you can do a lot with that, but they have to know it was you that did it to them. Otherwise, it's just vandalism."

McKenna met him several times in his office, always wearing the wire. Raucci would often gesture to the photograph of Marlon Brando in *The Godfather* that hung on his wall and say, "The reason I keep that picture behind the door, that was given to me by the people up there in the administration office. They're not going to file a grievance against me. Not if they want to last or live. One or the other. Because that's the way they see me – Don Raucci – and I never even seen that whole series. I'm everybody's hero, and they know it. I always tell them, Eric Ely or the school board, 'You guys are fucking lucky you've got a Steve. When it falls on me, I don't have a Steve to go to. I've got to fix it myself.' When I die, I'll be a legend here in their eyes." Then he tossed Keith a "quarter-stick" he had been hiding behind a fake plant on top of his filing cabinet.

Well, the legend was arrested in his office on Friday, February 20, 2009. The following Monday, Superintendent Eric Ely convened a news conference and claimed he was shocked to find out that Steve was a thug. Raucci was indicted on May 6, and went to trial for twenty-two felony counts almost a year later, on March 5, 2010. District Attorney Robert Carney called sixty-two witnesses to testify against Raucci,

and the defense could only muster two. He was convicted on eighteen counts and acquitted on four. He was sixty-one years old when he was sentenced to 23-years-to-life in prison at the infamous Clinton Correctional Facility in Dannemora, New York on June 8, 2010. Eric Ely's last day on the job as superintendent was Tuesday, June 30, 2010. When reporters asked Ely why he didn't do anything to stop Raucci, that many people testified that he had just looked the other

way, Ely yelled at them, "Well, yeah, they lie. People are just lying. I won't be the scapegoat for somebody else." And three years after that, on May 3, 2013, a court ruled that pension payments of almost $79,000 a year could not be withheld from Shelley Raucci, the convicted arsonist's wife, by the New York State Office of Victim Services. Another four years of negative news stories about Schenectady.

Raucci's terrorism lasted for thirty-six years, and was willfully hidden by administrators and school board members for about thirty-five of those. They even refused Freedom of Information Law (FOIL) requests for their reluctantly-compiled, whitewashed report from the *Daily Gazette* and the *Times Union*. When they were finally compelled to comply, they offered the news organizations heavily-redacted versions of key documents. The two newspapers then sued to obtain the hidden information, but a judge who had presided at Raucci's third and final wedding, Barry Kramer, dismissed the lawsuit on the grounds that release of the report "would cause serious pain and embarrassment" to school employees who were quoted there.

The Raucci saga embodies an educational tragedy on several levels. Schenectady School District staff and faculty members were directly bullied, shamed, and terrorized on a daily basis for years by this creep, with the tacit approval of a corrupt school administration and school board. Many people were forced to work, teach, and live in a constant state of fear. That's more than shameful. Behavior that abets criminal activities should face criminal charges as well. Ample evidence would suggest that a number of willing accomplices, including Eric Ely, fell into that category but ultimately dodged a bullet themselves.

Indirectly, students were caught in an emotional crossfire of distraction prompted by fear and gossip. Most staff and teachers in the school district worked hard and provided the best education they could deliver for their students, but for a number of them it happened under unrelenting duress while Raucci conducted his increasingly-destructive reign of terror. They shouldn't all be tarred with the same brush. Moreover, despite the efforts of responsible citizens who voted out school board members that were complicit and created pressure that eventually forced the resignation of the school board president in league with Raucci – Jeff Janiszewski – not much truly changed for a while. The people entrusted with not only ensuring the adequate education and safe-guarding of our children, but also with aiding the economic development of Schenectady by maintaining good schools and attracting families with children to the city, continued to make secretive decisions to maintain their power and salaries. And then there were the suicides.

In the three months before Raucci was arrested, three African-American students, all girls, tried to hang themselves. One of them succeeded; two were rescued.

All during that time, Eric Ely and the school board had kept the dreadful incidents under wraps. Only after another girl killed herself and one more was saved on March 1, 2009 – just ten days after Raucci was nabbed – did Ely issue a statement: "We're trying to get the information out there to get these kids help," he said. "It's a scary proposition. You don't want to publicize these things because they can and do lead to copycats and clusters. In a school district neighboring my own in my past, I've seen eight successful suicides in one year. I've seen large clusters." And he added that the school at first had tried to prevent other suicide attempts by offering grief counselors after the first girl died on November 25, 2008.

However, a disingenuous response was the standard operating procedure. Ely and key members of his staff had known many of their students were in serious danger for a long time, but they were reluctant to get involved in mitigating dangerous behaviors that happened outside of school, so they hushed the hangings up. They believed and communicated that what happened in the community wasn't necessarily their problem. But they were well aware a powder keg had definitely been lit, and it simply took a few months of neglect and one suicide to touch off a rolling series of explosions they might have helped to prevent.

Kuanna, a freshman, had begun to party more and more with members of the Four Block Gang in Hamilton Hill when school was out during the summer of 2008. It was risky fun to hang with gang bangers, and she invited some friends and classmates to join her – Jalissa, Mary, Cherelle – and the boys in the gang convinced the girls they needed what they were offering: booze, weed, coke, crack, smack, and plenty of sex. Inevitably, trouble followed almost immediately. Jealous fights. STDs. Beatings. Pregnancy. Bullying – actual beat-downs as well as cyberbullying – from the guys inside, of course, and from girls outside the Four Block circle. Cherelle suffered two broken ribs and a concussion but she wouldn't tell her mother who did it. Kuanna posted a threat on her MySpace page: "If you fuck with me or my peoples, you're going DOWN." That worked for a little while, but only until Kuanna killed herself on November 25, right before Thanksgiving. Then all of it resumed. One of her friends in the group appealed to her after she was gone: "Kuanna omg plsz jusz help meh through this."

Jalissa followed Kuanna three months later, on February 23, 2009, amid a steady stream of suicidal warnings accompanied by photographs on MySpace. She posted a message to Kuanna about smoking and drinking to ease her pain, but that wasn't working. "I'll see u soon," she wrote at the end. Lynn Rafalik, who supervised the school district's social workers, said it wasn't really up to her to identify suicide risks on the site: "I do not review MySpace. I feel that would be the role of the parent."

Mary was the pregnant one, three months into her term, and she was considering an abortion. Her mother told her that was "un-Christian." Her "boyfriend's" mother called her a slut and demanded she abort her son's baby. One night, Mary's mother heard her talking on the phone to the threatening mom, repeating tearfully, "I am a child of God and I leave it in God's hands." Two days later, on March 1, Mary ended both lives. For Superintendent Ely, Mary's death was the catalyst he couldn't ignore, and he finally revealed publicly what had been happening.

Fourteen-year-old Cherelle was the only one of the group left. Without her friends to protect her, she was constantly bullied, on the bus and at school. She began attending small-group counseling sessions provided by the school district, but they couldn't make the bullying stop. The school never told Cherelle's mother about either the bullying or the counseling sessions, and Cherelle hanged herself on April 3 at 10:30 P.M. in her bedroom. "Why didn't they tell me?" her mom wanted to know. "I understand about confidentiality, but if you see my daughter's face at these suicide groups a few times, you know she's having some issues. You need to make a phone call."

After Cherelle died, prevention efforts intensified. Lynn Rafalik begged parents of students to "talk, talk, talk" about these painful subjects with their children. Community agencies and churches joined with the school district to develop a long-overdue, suicide-prevention strategy. A leading pediatrician in the city issued a cautionary statement: "Most of the girls are talking about meeting friends in the afterlife. We need to make it clear: that just does not happen." However, none of the better-late-than-never efforts saved Schenectady High School from the educational scarlet letter: New York State's Department of Education labeled the high school a "persistently dangerous school" in 2009.

Eventually, District Attorney Robert Carney's investigation, which had begun right after the first suicide, led to a federal indictment of forty-four gang members two years later, in late May of 2011. "We hope this has dealt a crippling blow to the Four Block Gang," Carney said, "and to the extent that some of these individuals may have been involved with these emotionally-fragile young girls and contributed to their belief that their lives were not worth living, perhaps today there is some measure of justice for them."

Ebony Belmar was a social worker in the school district all through the debilitating suicide cluster, and each of the girls who killed herself had crossed her path at one time or another. "I went to three of the funerals," she remembered, "and then decided I couldn't do that anymore." After those deaths, Ebony and some of her colleagues became much more involved in the community:

> I think these suicides were very powerful. The school couldn't stay the same. It just couldn't, because how do you not deal with this kind of big responsibility? The school couldn't simply be about educating these kids and sending them home anymore. It became painfully apparent that we couldn't be just an educational system. I'm not passing judgment, but once you get to know these children and they become part of your life, how can you forget about them when you know they're in crisis?

Brian Stratton didn't ignore any of the tragedies and scandals that had happened on his watch. But he didn't dwell on them either, and he certainly didn't mention any of them when he announced his resignation, three years into his second term. Governor Andrew Cuomo had appointed Stratton to be the next director of the State Canal Corporation, and Brian was excited to accept it. The position came with a $28,000 raise over his current salary of $96,906 as mayor, and some political hacks and cynics swore he was skipping town for the extra money, that he had been distracted and disengaged in the most recent budget deliberations, that he was too sensitive a type for a hardscrabble town like Schenectady. So who knows, maybe the lure of a prestigious, statewide position and a substantial bump in pay actually were the reasons he was quitting. Brian didn't elaborate. "I've achieved the things I wanted to achieve," he said.

He wasn't wrong about that. He had certainly inherited plenty of problems, including a consistently wayward police department. Gary McCarthy, president of the City Council and chair of its public safety committee, summed up the general feelings of frustration in 2009: "I'd like to go one week where we don't have a negative newspaper article about the department. It's just baffling that it keeps happening. It's human nature that people are going to make mistakes, but this just seems so institutionalized."

Brian dealt with that persistent problem by hiring Wayne Bennett to be the public safety commissioner and together, confronting the powerful police union, they created a brand new disciplinary process that actually allowed them to fire the officers who screwed up. They forced out nine rogue officers, guys who had assaulted suspects, driven drunk, slept on the job or conducted affairs when they should have been on patrol, stolen evidence, dealt drugs, and hindered investigations – just like in the bad old days of the 1990s – and, in the process, they rebuilt confidence in the Schenectady Police Department, something few people would have thought possible. And for an unexpected bonus, they got to witness Greg Kaczmarek, the former police chief from 1996 to 2002, along with his wife, get indicted on six counts of conspiracy and drug possession – crimes many people had been accusing Kaczmarek of for years. Both of them were convicted and sent to jail in early 2009.

Brian also accomplished some things no other mayor had been able to do.

He pulled the city out of bankruptcy, turning a ten-million-dollar deficit into a ten-million-dollar surplus during his first term, and in doing so dramatically improved the city's bond rating. With his Schenectady 2020 Comprehensive Plan, Brian had engineered the formidable task of providing a strategic blueprint for economic revitalization for the next thirteen years, just at the time when Metroplex had a new leader who looked like he could make substantive change happen for the first time in decades. The mayor made sure to include workable action plans for all the neighborhoods in the city, even the most problematic ones where many citizens justifiably felt they had been left out of the equation for progress by other administrations. Presenting a plan for the city that might be followed and could actually work was a novel concept, and he had paid for all of it with Community Development Block Grant funding to boot. Brian believed he had restored sound financial management to Schenectady by getting back to basics and truly doing the things that should have been done all along, and the results bore that out.

Chris Gardner, the respected attorney for Schenectady County since January, 2004, wrote the following excerpts in an op-ed piece that captured a sense of the severe problems that Brian's administration had faced when he was elected, and gave an example of the difference he had made during his seven years in office:

> The City and County were at war with the largest employer, General Electric. The City received $48 million in federal Renewal Community Tax Credits, but Jurczynski lost these credits when he did not use them. That $48 million is six years of Metroplex funding down the drain.
>
> Due to George Robertson's incompetent structuring of PILOTs, the County, City, and city school district were deprived of over $23 million in revenue because Robertson did not utilize Empire Zone credit for projects. That $23 million is three years of Metroplex funding.
>
> The new Democratic majority on the County Legislature ushered in a new era of competent and aggressive economic development under Ray Gillen and hit the ground running … The new Democratic County Legislature and Mayor Stratton also

repaired the relationship with GE, which brought 2,000 new GE jobs to our county. Stratton even brought back the GE plaque to City Hall – the plaque that Mayor Jurczynski removed.

Three weeks before he announced his resignation, Mayor Stratton gave President Obama a tour of General Electric, which had quietly been spending hundreds of millions of dollars refurbishing buildings and improving their main campus. After that, he rode with the president on a helicopter flight to Air Force One, lobbying him all the way on behalf of his city, even though he knew he was moving on to another position. Not too shabby for a swan song.

*   *   *

Brian Stratton and Wayne Bennett weren't the only ones battling Schenectady's troubled police department. The versatile actor Bradley Cooper, playing an ambitious rookie cop named Avery Cross in *The Place Beyond the Pines*, tangles with fictional veteran officers in a story inspired by actual police antics in the Electric City. Coerced into joining a cadre of bad cops who want to grab stolen bank funds for themselves, Avery kills one of the robbers – Luke Glanton, played by heartthrob Ryan Gosling – and then tries to redeem himself by returning the recovered money. No dice. The wily, crooked police chief, wary of being identified as an accomplice, won't accept it. Avery ends up secretly taping illegal activities in his own department, and thereby leveraging his way into a job as assistant district attorney. And that complex plot-line transpires in just one panel of this movie's triptych structure.

Schenectady means "the place beyond the pines" in the Iroquois language, and two of the film's screenwriters – Ben Coccio and director Derek Cianfrance – wanted to use real locations they remembered from growing up in the area, for verisimilitude if not for nostalgia: Trustco Bank on State Street; Vale Cemetery; the majestic Nott Memorial on the Union College campus; Schenectady High School; City Hall; the towering St. John the Evangelist Church on Union Street; the current Schenectady Police Department headquarters; and the Altamont Fairgrounds, where Ryan Gosling gets to perform his wall-of-death motorcycle show, among other spots.

The entire movie was shot during the summer of 2011, and frequent celebrity sightings were featured in the local section of the newspaper or flashed constantly across social media. Angelo Mazzone's thriving, upscale replacement for Peggy's Canalside Restaurant, Aperitivo, was one of the film crew's preferred after-shooting hangouts. Director Cianfrance, his production team, and all the main actors would commandeer the back room for raucous late meals and occasionally come out into the bar area to pose for photos with star-struck fans and local pols, including Schenectady's new mayor, Gary McCarthy, who had taken over just three months before, in April of 2011.

The movie's depiction of a seriously-corrupt police department was certainly credible for Gary. Right up to the day he had replaced Brian Stratton in City Hall, he had worked for thirty years as an investigator in the district attorney's office, so he had been neck-deep in the Siler & Barnett, Kaczmarek, and Raucci cases, among scores of others. Nobody knew the details of Schenectady crime any better than Gary McCarthy.

However, he was no political novice either. After some discouraging political defeats when he was in his twenties, he bounced back and pushed even harder. By the time he turned thirty, in 1986, he was Chairman of the Democratic Committee for Schenectady County, at a challenging time for their party. The 1980s and '90s were Republican eras in upstate New York: their conservative voters outnumbered Democrats in Schenectady 2 to 1, and even 3 to 1 or worse in the more rural areas of the county. But that changed slowly over ten years when Gary ran the show.

His secrets were organization, selection, and participation. "We were one of the first groups to be computerized," he remembered. "And we became more sophisticated in direct mail." He also chose candidates who had principles, people who didn't run for local notoriety or minor power but to actually get things done and make a difference. Sometimes he would prepare them for years before launching their first campaigns and, once they got elected, he would encourage them to get out there and greet people at every event they could find. Under his tutelage, not one Democrat lost a countywide race, and the party took all the marbles in 2004.

Gary became a Schenectady City Council member in 1996, ran against Al Jurczynski for mayor in 1999 and lost, was appointed to the Metroplex board in 2003, and returned to serve on the City Council again from 2005 to 2011, when he was catapulted suddenly into the city's top job. He was ready enough, though. He knew all the players, had written a good portion of the political playbook, and was no pushover. He had been on the board when Ray Gillen took the reins at Metroplex, and soon after that when Dave Buicko and the Galesi Group finally decided Schenectady was a place where they could make some money. MVP had been a reasonable hit, but Bow Tie Cinema's Movieland, with Siemens going in above it, was clearly a home run, and sparked further development on that pivotal block of State Street. In Gary's opinion, Gillen and Buicko were the engines he was betting on to power Schenectady's revitalization.

Metroplex was really on a roll in 2011. Center City – the ill-fated complex that had once housed a hockey rink where the ice kept melting – had been completely refurbished to the tune of $30 million and had opened with all new tenants, including a relocated and expanded YMCA, and with Metroplex's own offices on the building's top floor. In its first year at the new location, the Y's membership would jump from 1,000 to 6,000.

An attractive eleven-million-dollar student housing complex was underway at Schenectady County Community College, as was a state-of-the-art music building to showcase the school's amazing music department, under the stewardship of Dean Bill Meckley. Re4orm Architecture's J.T. Pollard had designed a soaring addition to the main branch of the Schenectady County Public Library, specifically to house a spacious children's area, and that was in the works. A $5 million headquarters for Transfinder Corporation, which had pioneered logistics software for transportation management for school systems and municipalities all across America, was planned to go in beside the Hampton Inn on State Street. Plus, the Authority had twelve tmillion dollars in hand to construct the new Amtrak train station on Erie Boulevard. And there were plenty of other smaller projects either starting, partway finished, or ready to open.

All in all, over $130 million had been invested in Schenectady's revitalization in 2011 alone, substantially increasing the city's property tax base, boosting sales tax revenue, and creating more than 600 new jobs. That brought the total economic investment to $620 million in Schenectady County since 2004, and included more than 5,500 jobs added during those seven years. "We've been on a tear," Ray Gillen said. "We haven't taken a day off. But many of our projects have been small wins, just fixing one building after another after another." What beckoned on the city's horizon, however, could hardly be called a small win. It was a major league, hybrid development that not only mixed a tourist destination with commercial and residential opportunities but also reconnected Schenectady with its waterfront, the Mohawk River.

12

Success

Active waterfronts are as much a hallmark of American cities today as busy sidewalks and skyscrapers were in the past. Not since waterfronts served as commercial ports and transportation hubs have they figured so prominently in city planning ... Waterfronts today, whether along a deep-water harbor, a lake, or a river, represent some of the most desirable urban real estate – not only for parks, but also for museums, tourist attractions, recreational facilities, and commercial and residential developments.

– Makeshift Metropolis: Ideas About Cities
Witold Rybczynski

"We own the MVP building," Dave Buicko explained. "Bow Tie's Movieland building is ours, too. We own the entire side of State Street across from Proctor's, which includes Center City, and the Golub headquarters building on Nott Street. In for a dollar, in for a hundred. We've had some failures, though. Anybody that bats a thousand isn't taking any risks. We take risks."

The "We" Dave is talking about is the Galesi Group, a real estate company which owns or manages eleven million square feet of commercial, industrial, retail, and residential properties. In 1969, Francesco and Vincent Galesi had the foresight to transform the decommissioned Voorheesville Army Depot's thirty buildings and thirty-one miles of railroad track into the Northeastern Industrial Park, and right after that to buy the Schenectady General Depot and convert that into the Rotterdam Corporate Park. Although Vincent died that same year, Francesco pushed relentlessly on and built a diversified empire.

Galesi's "group" refers to ventures, not owners, and those ventures include other industrial parks in Glenville, New York, and in the Bronx, dozens of apartment complexes in seven states, and the E&B Natural Resources Management Corporation, which produces natural gas and oil in Louisiana, Texas, Kansas, Wyoming, and California. E&B also owns and operates over twenty active fields that yield 11,000 barrels a day. However, the Galesi Group has focused much of its energy on the Capital Region, and has always had its headquarters here. By 2019, it owned 116 buildings in the upstate area, valued at almost $694 million and containing 213 tenants with 9,600 employees. It paid twelve and a half million a year in taxes on those properties. With that kind of deep investment in the region, it's no wonder Ray Gillen and Gary McCarthy have trusted Galesi to deliver on major projects in Schenectady.

By the mid-1980s, Francesco Galesi was more than wealthy – he was listed among the richest people in America – but he wasn't too interested in talking about it. Notoriously private, he hired a hotshot accountant in 1982, Dave Buicko, to monitor transactions and deal with the public. Dave rose quickly in the ranks to become Chief Operating Officer and has managed the company's day-to-day business since 1986, connecting with local CEOs to foster synergistic projects. One of Galesi's bigger projects in Schenectady began when the Golub Corporation outgrew its traditional headquarters in Rotterdam. Dave was good friends with Neil Golub, and he was also one of the few business people who could get along with Gene Weiss, who owned a defunct plaza anchored by a Big N department store that sat on one of the old ALCO train-manufacturing sites on Nott Street. As Dave remembered him:

Gene was a tough son of a bitch. He had been a prisoner of war in Auschwitz, numbers on his arm to prove it. His brother, father, and three other siblings all got gassed. He didn't, because he spoke three languages and was off in another barrack, teaching, and came back to find everybody gone to the gas chamber. And that was the brother he had saved on a death march. You fell, they shot you on those marches. His brother fell, Gene picked him up and carried him to the end so the guards wouldn't kill him. Shows you the type of guy he was.

Dave convinced Gene to partner with him in a redevelopment deal, but all three of the ALCO sites were brownfields, jam-packed with hydrocarbon compounds like diesel oil and other petroleum products, the polychlorinated biphenyls (PCBs) in transfer fluids, paints and lubricants, and various other toxic pollutants. The United

States Environmental Protection Agency (EPA), along with New York's Department of Environmental Conservation (DEC), had scared off many developers who became wary of sites where 19th century manufacturing had taken place, worried they could be held liable for past, rule-free contamination: what would they find under the surface, what might have leached onto adjoining sites, how much would an extensive clean-up add to the cost of their project, and how many bureaucratic hurdles and lawsuits would they have to weather?

However, in October of 2003, Governor Pataki had signed into law the New York State Brownfield Reform Act and, seven or eight years later, by the time Dave Buicko was needing a financial incentive to tackle the ALCO sites, plenty of money was available. A developer could be awarded 18-22% of the mitigation costs for an approved brownfield site, depending on the amount of remediation necessary. "You get a percentage of clean-up, but you also get a percentage of capital investment," Dave revealed. "It's more than clean-up, but it's capped. Or, rather, NOW it's capped. People used to take it, they'd do a million-dollars-worth of clean-up and get $20 million in tax credits. That was before they closed the loophole, and that loophole was closed before we did the Golub headquarters."

While that Golub building was a terrific project and met Neil Golub's expectations for a spacious, new base of operations, it sat across Erie Boulevard, east of the Mohawk River, on lower Nott Street. The sixty-acre section of the old ALCO manufacturing site that included a mile of river frontage – the most desirable one – presented a couple of additional challenges: first, George Robertson, when he ran the Schenectady Economic Development Corporation, had sold one of the largest buildings on the site to STS Steel, which ran a large steel fabrication facility there, for $350,000. The price wasn't the problem. The problem was the forty-year lease, at one hundred dollars a year, that George had given them for the property under the building. That meant whoever developed the entire site would have a truly ugly structure, as well as stacks of rusting steel beams outside it, lying right there at the entrance to whatever new buildings they constructed – an eyesore that sat close to Erie Boulevard and would establish any visitor's first impression of the area – for another thirty years.

The second challenge could have easily been the deal-breaker. Preferred

Development out of Philadelphia already owned the property. Fortunately for the Galesi Group, Preferred couldn't handle it. "We lucked out," Dave Buicko said. "Preferred wasn't paying their taxes. They were behind on their water bills. It was a complicated situation. You had to deal with every state agency – Department of Transportation, Empire State Development, the Canal Corporation – and nationally, DOH, Army Corps of Engineers, plus then every city division in Schenectady."

Preferred wanted out, and Dave wanted in. He was used to working with all those different agencies. He wasn't entirely sure what he'd do with the site and all those rusting behemoths either, but sixty acres on the river was something he figured they could eventually use. On the deed to the property, the sales date was April 1, 2010 – April Fool's Day – which, as it finally turned out, was ironic. The place became a gold mine.

Ray Gillen had been thinking about that prime river site for quite a while. Before the Galesi Group bought it, Metroplex had a meeting with Dimension Fabricators, which was interested in buying just a portion of the property, so that discussion didn't go too far. But when Dave Buicko became the developer for the entire plot, minus the STS Steel portion, of course, Ray jumped in with both feet. Metroplex conducted a thorough investigation of the site and produced a 1000-page environmental impact statement, focusing on potential re-uses. That helped convince the New York State Historic Preservation Office – the same SHPO that had tried to derail the Proctor's Theater expansion – to allow demolition of the forty-or-so decaying buildings there, provided Metroplex hired a professional photographer to capture and chronicle what had existed there.

As the ALCO buildings came down, the price of steel remained high, so sale of the salvaged steel offset a small portion of the massive clean-up costs. Then the

pollutants had to be trucked away and replaced with clean fill that New York State's Department of Transportation was hauling away from its Rexford Bridge replacement site. Bad dirt out, good dirt in. In the middle of that process, Hurricane Irene barged into town and inundated the ALCO site. The deep pools left in its wake gave Dave a good idea: he could build a harbor, use the dredged soil to help raise the entire sixty acres above flood-plain height, and construct a drainage system that would simply direct storm water down and into the new harbor. The Mohawk River was part of the canal system, after all, so why not provide a harbor that could attract boaters?

What else should a waterfront development offer? "Location, location, location," Dave said. "We're right there at one of your main entrances to the city. Think about it, coming over Freeman's Bridge, first thing you drive by will be our complex on the river." Since Proctor's Theater was booming, the established restaurants like Riccitello's, Ferrari's, and Aperitivo were thriving on the before-and-after-show crowds, and new restaurants were popping up every month. "We knew we were short of hotels," Dave explained. "The Hampton Inn, downtown, which was probably one of the highest-performing Hampton Inns, was full all the time. Our friends at BBL had a relationship with the Marriott franchise, and they said, 'The one thing we know, we can locate a hotel here, we think there's need for office space, and we know that people like to live on the water.' So we decided we'd go with apartments, maybe condos or town houses, and then for commercial space, an office building, parking garage underneath, and some restaurants. With the harbor, that would fill up half the land, thirty acres of it, and we'd figure out what else we could do later on."

For Hollywood, films like *Ironweed*, *The Age of Innocence*, *Scent of a Woman*, and *The Place Beyond the Pines* – all shot fully or partially in the Capital Region – had stuck a red pin on the map where upstate New York sat, and a company called Pacifica Ventures approached Dave about putting in a movie production studio on Galesi's Mohawk Harbor site. That seemed like a promising idea, but Governor Cuomo's people were pushing to do it in Syracuse and the governor wasn't offering tax credits to Schenectady. The other thirty acres stayed empty. Then lightning struck.

In May of 2013, Cuomo proposed awarding gambling licenses to seven non-Indian, live-table casinos in New York State. The State Senate majority GOP modified the proposal to specify that three of those licenses would be awarded during 2014, and one of them would go to a winning site in the Capital Region. After some more tinkering by the Assembly, the bill was approved for a statewide referendum on Election Day in November. The arguing started almost immediately.

Church leaders weighed in quickly on the moral challenges. Chambers of commerce, mayors, economic development agencies, city councils, county legislatures, and business folks all over promised pie-in-the-sky property tax reductions and spin-off spending that would boost sales tax collections and balance sagging budgets. A month before the vote, Cuomo's Department of Budget estimated that New York State could receive $430 million in additional revenue, every year, if the referendum passed.

Philip Morris led a successful charge that added protective language to the bill that was finally approved by the Legislature, calling for "a fair and reasonable partnership with live entertainment venues," and the head of the New York State Gaming Commission had agreed with the inclusion. But Philip was still worried that casinos, with their hefty profits, could easily outbid theaters and other arts venues for talent, perhaps because six months earlier in the process, the governor's office had told him, "This is the free enterprise system. You guys compete with each other. Why can't you compete with casinos?" Philip had heard more than his share of legislative double-speak over the years.

Proctor's Theater was joined locally by Albany's Palace Theater, the Saratoga Performing Arts Center (SPAC), and the Times Union Center in a coalition of arts providers – "Upstate Theaters for a Fair Game" – sounding the alarm a few weeks before the public would vote on the casino act, and by then the governor's people had ostensibly changed its tune. "We're concerned about the casinos," Philip Morris said. "We've been talking about this for six months, and we feel it's important information for any voter. People should vote the way they feel, but we're not saying, 'Our problem is done. Victory.' What's important is that our problem is understood and the process is committed to solving it."

The referendum passed, although a majority in Schenectady County did not vote for it, and that meant casinos outside of Native American reservations were now definitely coming to New York State – one of them destined for a site in the Capital Region – and there would be a fierce competition to win that spot. The city of Rensselaer wanted it, and so did a group in Albany called E-23, shorthand for its proposed site off Exit 23 of the New York State Thruway, and they were aligned with the regional Off-Track Betting Corporation, the powerful OTB. Saratoga, naturally, with the oldest thoroughbred race track in the country and its Saratoga Racino and harness track, wanted to win, although there was plenty of opposition to it inside that city. Howe Caverns in Schoharie County, a system of spectacular caves that is the second-most visited tourist site in New York State after Niagara Falls, also threw its hat in the ring. And finally, there was Dave Buicko and his thirty open acres along the river.

None of them were a shoe-in, and the New York State Gaming Commission's 80-page RFA – or Request for Applications, the set of criteria for submitting an application – promised the process would be arduous and expensive. The ante to apply was a cool, non-refundable million bucks and, if chosen, the licensing fees could run as high as $70 million more. Say good-bye to the casual players. Prospective applicants would also need to obtain the support of local legislative bodies, so citizens wouldn't feel a potentially unwelcome activity had been slipped past them. 70% of the Gaming Commission's decision would be based on economic impact, 20% on the degree of local support outside the municipal government for a casino in a specific community, and 10% on the assurance the casino would hire locally.

Serious applicants went to work selling the casino idea to their communities. Dave Buicko put together a graphics-rich video presentation that showcased his plans for Mohawk Harbor – a hotel with adjoining retail stores; unique, architect-designed condos with balconies that overlooked the long, oval harbor with its protected boat slips; new, chi-chi restaurants with spacious patios; and a big white box with the word CASINO inside as a placeholder – and he presented it on one of the big screens at Bow Tie's Movieland. All of it looked good to the mayor: "At this point, I'm supporting the application for a casino," Gary McCarthy announced.

However, Dave already knew he could count on Gary and Ray Gillen and Neil Golub and the other economic movers and shakers in Schenectady. They weren't the ones he was worried about. He had to convince the City Council to back his move, and there were some wild cards on there – Vince Riggi, John Mooteveren,

Marion Porterfield, Carl Erikson – and he knew how easily they could be swayed by sustained vocal opposition at a Council meeting. Dave absolutely needed that "resolution passed by the local legislative body of its host municipality supporting the application." Without that, a casino in Schenectady was dead in the water. It was a crap shoot, and it still felt pretty amorphous. Hell, he didn't even have a casino to partner with yet.

County Attorney Chris Gardner was a Pittsburgh Pirates fan, and he had gone to Pittsburgh with his pal, Ed Graves, to watch the team in the playoffs a month before the casino referendum, in October of 2013. They were staying at PNC Park, half a mile away from the Rivers Casino there. Ed was the legislative representative and lobbyist for Neil Bluhm, co-founder of Rush Street Gaming, parent company of Rivers Casino. Chris joked with Ed that he knew somebody who might be interested in trying to get a casino. Chris remembers the subsequent meeting he had with Dave, Ray Gillen, and some of the Metroplex folks back in Schenectady:

> *Make a long story short, there was some discussion on our side as to who to pick. And Dave liked the Rivers Casino, but others were thinking about the Hard Rock. And Ray liked the Rivers Casino, too, but he was having some second thoughts. But if you look at the political dynamics of the situation, the guy who owns Rivers Casino was this fellow named Neil Bluhm. And he was one of Barack Obama's top campaign finance fundraisers in 2008 and 2012. And I said, "In my view, when Governor Cuomo's looking at who he wants to make happy or unhappy, that might actually have an impact on him." Dave developed a very good relationship with those guys.*

"We had no idea about casinos and one of the lobbyists brought in some guys from Rush Street," Dave explained. They came in a couple of weeks before Christmas and Neil Bluhm was with them. He was from Chicago, and was actually Deputy Finance Chairman for Obama's campaigns. He was going to Obama's Christmas Party in a private plane and he stopped here with his entourage. Snow was deep then, but we drove through it in my truck and looked at the other sites – Rensselaer, East Greenbush, Albany – and we sold him on ours. His PR person, Judy Gold, used the word "kismet." Meant to be. After that meeting, we just hit it off. I flew out to Chicago, visited their casino out there, and we shook hands on a deal."

At the City Council meeting to vote on supporting the Galesi Group's casino application or not on June 9, 2014, eighty people signed up to speak during privilege of the floor. The seats in the City Hall chamber were all filled, and a line of people snaked out the door. Many in the crowd waved NO or YES signs, and the opposing sides began yelling at each other, growing more frantic as they worked to drown the other side out. As the first speaker finished, her supporters broke into loud, long applause. Peggy King was president of the City Council then, and she said, "Folks, if you're going to do that after every speaker, we're going to be here for a very long time. I probably have eighty or more people signed up to give their opinions, so I'm going to ask, number one, that you not applaud and, number two, that you stick to your three minutes. If somebody ahead of you has said what you want to say, maybe you could just agree with them and be done with it."

In the three-hour session that followed, people trotted out all the usual pros and cons about casino gambling:

- *The city will have to face the dangers of gambling addiction.*

- *A large number of people in the community want it. People have problems with alcoholism, too – do you not let anyone drink?*

- *The city could get a projected $5.7 million in annual revenue.*

- *The casino will spawn burglaries, panhandling, more assaults, and more prostitution.*

- *Rush Street Gaming pays $20 an hour for the average hourly worker, more for supervisors and management,* *plus benefits, and predicts they'll be creating 1,100 jobs. These are living wages.*

- *The city can't trust that the revenue earned will be used to lower taxes.*

- *The City Council promised that its share of the revenue would be entirely used to reduce property taxes.*

- *The State gambling market is nearly saturated.*

- *It will be good for the city. It will bring in more people and more jobs.*

- *Its impact can't be anything but negative for a fragile, small community.*

- *A casino would fit in nicely with the casino employee training program developed by Schenectady County Community College.*

- *People will get hooked, lose their rent money, neglect their families, hock their valuables, and commit crimes to feed their gambling addiction.*

- *Remember the unemployed! Think about the neighbor-hoods – Hamilton Hill, Mont Pleasant, Vale! People need jobs. I hope the State chooses Schenectady.*

And so on, for three hours. Luckily, some people got tired and left early. In the end, the vote was five to two in favor of the application, with Riggi and Porterfield opposed. One day later, after only fifteen minutes of public comments, the Schenectady County Legislature voted unanimously to support the casino application as well. Legislator Gary Hughes said, "I honestly am not a great fan of gambling, and I sympathize with the folks who just have a philosophical problem with this, but here in New York State, that train left the station almost thirty years ago."

With the city endorsement in hand, Rush Street doubled down on its commitment to Schenectady. They liked the name, of course – their casinos were named Rivers, and the Mohawk Harbor site stretched alongside a river. They liked the proximity to a highway system, and they were encouraged that everybody wanted them – the city, the county, the business community. "We really rolled out the red carpet," Dave Buicko remembered, "and they were comfortable with who we were:"

> *In all honesty, they could relate to us. We're a large real estate developer and so are they. They're JNB Realty, and Rush Street is their gaming entity. As JNB, they did Faneuil Hall, Quincy Market, Chicago Mercantile Exchange, Century City in Los Angeles, Four Seasons in Milan, shopping centers, a lot of big deals. They were a great partner, and the deal was fun. It was playing a multi-dimensional chess game. Our presentation was excellent – we had local, we tied up with a community college, we partnered with Mallozzi's for food management, dotted every "I" and crossed every "T." Even the head of the Gaming Commission*

complimented us. He said ours wasn't just about a casino, it was
an economic development project.

Dave Buicko was on crutches when the award was announced on Monday, December 21, 2015. He had torn his Achilles tendon. "I felt like Tiny Tim," he said, "but it was like New Year's Eve in Schenectady when it got announced. The Gaming Commission had granted a license to Rush Street Gaming, who pledged to spend $330 million to build Rivers Casino at Mohawk Harbor. With Galesi spending $150 million on its own, the entire project would eventually reach almost five hundred million dollars, and become a planned community that included two hotels – a Courtyard by Marriott plus a luxurious Landing Hotel attached to the casino – fifty condominiums, fifteen townhouses, 206 apartments, seventy-five thousand square feet of office

space, 100,000 square feet of retail and restaurant space, and a landscaped waterfront and harbor accessible for walking, kayaking, and biking. It was a tourist destination, of course, with a thriving casino complex and a three-acre harbor with fifty docks, but it was also, like Proctor's Theater, something

that citizens of Schenectady could feel proud about. It didn't just reconnect the city with its river – it restored some long-lost bragging rights.

What the Galesi Group, Metroplex, and all the other builders, philanthropists, foundations, and grants-providers accomplished with Mohawk Harbor and throughout downtown Schenectady amounted to a form of alchemy – the fanciful chemistry and philosophy that claimed it could transform base metals into gold that was practiced in the Middle Ages – but in this case, the end products turned out to be real, and literally glittering. In the half-decade between 2015 and 2020, the economic progress in the city seemed unstoppable, part of Newton's first law of motion: if a body is moving at a constant speed in a straight line, it will keep moving in a straight line at a constant speed unless it is acted upon by a force.

Metroplex's straight-line momentum and Ray Gillen's unified economic development team approach had produced amazing results year after year. During the Authority's first twenty years, the one-half percent of sales tax revenue in Schenectady County that had been given to Metroplex totaled almost $140 million, and had enabled it to engineer close to one and a half BILLION dollars in private-and-public-sector investments in more than 700 projects. Moreover, in that time, Metroplex had also been awarded over one hundred million dollars in state and federal grants, and had been responsible for creating about 8,000 new jobs in Schenectady County.

Deals generated deals and money followed money, as Ray had predicted, and the steady drumbeat of announced accomplishments – usually over a hundred each year between 2015 and 2020 – underscored the cumulative, profound changes that were occurring in the city: the $480 million, and growing, private investment in Mohawk Harbor, where 350 events and conference meetings were held in its very first year of

operation; founding of the New York Biz Lab; a second life for the Armory, reconfigured into a viable sports and entertainment venue; Clarkson University establishing its Capital Region Campus in the former Union Graduate building; new Schenectady County Public Library branches in Hamilton Hill and in Mont Pleasant; the completely-renovated Annie Schaffer Senior Center on Nott Terrace; hundreds of PILOTs during those five years that delivered an average of fifteen million dollars a year in taxes where those properties had contributed zero before; a $50 million commitment to the Albany Street corridor in Hamilton Hill, creating affordable housing in the Joseph Allen and Hillside View apartment complexes, as well as spending ten million dollars to renovate Summit Towers; completion of the $23 million Amtrak Station; plus scores of infrastructure upgrades, façade enhancements, demolitions of zombie houses and condemned properties to make way for new-construction replacements, and hundreds of new apartments in new projects by developers Jeff Buell, John Roth, J.T. Pollard, and many others. Just the before-and-after photos that Metroplex generated would fill, literally, hundreds of pages.

Good things just kept happening for Schenectady. On April 12, 2014, for instance, the Union College Division I hockey team did the unimaginable: they defeated perennial powerhouse Minnesota, 7-4, to win their first-ever NCAA championship. A small, private, liberal arts college with about 2,200 undergraduates had toppled the five-time-title-winning Golden Gophers, a team which could draw from over 31,000 undergraduates on its Twin Cities campus.

"I think Union's sports teams, especially hockey, became Schenectady's teams," Stephen Ainlay said, "and we saw that really clearly at the parade that Mayor McCarthy so kindly sponsored after we won the national championship. Somebody said – maybe it was in the *New York Times* – but someone remarked that Minnesota has more students than Union has living alumni." Ainlay was president of Union College for thirteen years, starting in 2006, but he saw a sea change after Union beat Minnesota. "I would travel around the country and when people learned where I was, they made the connection, not just with the national championship in hockey, but with the city. It wasn't only Union. It was Union and Schenectady. If they saw me with Union gear on, they'd ask me about the city. The impact of that win was really something."

Ainlay also pointed out that the media was only interested in the David and Goliath angle of the story. They didn't care about the fact that Union offers no athletic scholarships to hockey players. "The combined GPA of the five seniors on that team was extraordinary, and they were engineering and economics majors. That's college athletics the way it was intended to be played. And I think that what Union has been able to accomplish by way of reputation as a really excellent liberal arts college has been an important part of the way in which people perceive the city."

Even the troubled Schenectady School District made some important changes after Eric Ely left, and it was definitely headed in a healthier and more honest direction. The school board brought in an interim superintendent, John Yagelski, and he steadied the ship for two years as the board searched for a more permanent leader. In June of 2012, Laurence Spring was hired. He had served as Superintendent of the Cortland Enlarged School District for the previous six years, but he had been actively looking to work in a bigger, more urban district. A friend said to him, "You like to do stuff. You like to reform. You're going to struggle if you go to a big district that's performing well. They'll get tired of you real quick because they may not necessarily want to change. You should look at Schenectady."

What Larry saw almost right away was the district's lack of resources for its students. "There was this intense need that the kids had," he remembered. "I was struck by the level and the intensity of the mental health situation:"

> And that prompted me to do some research and I discovered a batch of studies around how poverty can actually act like trauma on kids. So we started talking about chronic trauma as opposed to acute trauma, and asking ourselves, "How do we get services for these kids?" And then realizing how underfunded we were and, because the district has been so underfunded, the tax rate had gone up quite a bit and it kind of created this economic doom loop. The more underfunded the district was, the more that the local tax base had to support it. So the higher that tax rate went, the more depressed the property values became, because people don't want to buy and invest in a place with a high tax rate. And so it was like this doom loop.

Larry knew all too well about underfunding. He had battled New York State on this issue for the six years he worked in Cortland. "What the State was doing was discriminating against poor kids by not giving them the foundation aid they were supposed to," he explained. "All the poor districts in the state tended to get a lower percentage, and Schenectady is one of those districts. We're only getting 55% of what we're owed. That means we get shorted $62 million a year. There are thirty-seven other districts like us, school systems with non-white majorities, who are treated the same way. Institutionalized racism. Power and influence always follow wealth."

So Larry approached the School Board. "Let's get the kids in Schenectady what they're owed." The members were nervous at first. They knew how vindictive Governor Cuomo could be. But one finally said, "How much worse can it get? He's already keeping $62 million from us every year. What more could he do?" In the end, they voted to file a civil rights complaint against the State of New York, The Governor of New York, the New York State Legislature, the State Comptroller, Tom Di Napoli, the State Education Department, and the Board of Regents, arguing that the funding structure implemented by New York State results in discrimination against school districts with predominantly non-white student populations, English Language learner students, and students with disabilities. The Office of Civil Rights (OCR), and the Department of Education took the complaint, reviewed it, and subsequently determined it was worth an investigation, saying it was the first time that OCR would be considering this kind of complaint from a school district.

Larry Spring was thrilled they would investigate but, in the meantime, he also had a district full of kids chronically traumatized by poverty and other sources to deal with. He brought in a neurologist from New York University to describe the depth of their problem to his administrators: "Your concentration of childhood poverty is higher than Chicago's," she told them:

> Kids who experience four or more adverse childhood experiences
> (ACEs), before they're five years old have some pretty significant
> changes that happen to their body – some biological differences,
> actual neurological differences – not just social-emotional ones.
> There can be cellular malformation based on chronic stress.
> And it manifests itself in a number of diseases, not necessarily
> just risky behaviors, so asthma, diabetes, and certain kinds of
> cancers. When kids see terrible things, their brains flood with
> cortisol, so in that moment of heightened anxiety they're not able
> to make rational decisions. And when these repeat, the brains

become accustomed to it and the anxiety states become normal-
ized, and they're unable to process decisions in ways we want
them to. They're constantly in flight, fight, or freeze situations.
You can't expect them to act like non-traumatized children.

Larry used that information to spark meaningful changes. He and his fellow administrators started to think differently about many of the kids they were serving, and about their families, and to try and understand where they were coming from. They had to shift from "What's wrong with you?" to "What's happened to you?" 80% of Larry's staff was white, and he explained what their new attitudes would have to encompass:

As people who work in public education in an urban setting, you
don't get to be neutral. If you're not going to be an advocate, if
you're going to try and play it down the middle of the road on
issues of race and equity, really what you're doing is furthering
unworkable, past practices. And if you're going to work here,
you'll have to work to mitigate them. You have to be aware of
that connection between things like redlining and these neighbor-
hoods. You have to be aware of what kinds of experiences kids of
color carry with them when they walk into school. You don't get to
be ignorant of that. You don't get to be color blind and say, "Don't
be disrespectful to me. I was respectful to you when you walk in
the door, these are the rules of the school." You don't get to do
that. You're not walking in that kid's shoes, you don't know what
he's walking in from, you need to seek to understand him first.

Larry got some pushback, inside and outside the school district, but it was an assiduous attempt to right past wrongs and create a more inclusive and compassionate school community, and a huge, positive change from past school administrations. Plus, it mirrored what other leaders in the business community were beginning to understand: that a truly successful economic revitalization must at some point include everyone. "The casino was a great tax revenue generator for the community, a lot of jobs, 1,100 jobs," Ray Gillen said. "It was really tough at the beginning, and we had to start somewhere so we focused on downtown. We had to, and you see how that worked. But we're moving into the neighborhoods right now. We have almost $100 million in work underway in Hamilton Hill, and we're working our way up Eastern Avenue. One of the mistakes that was made when Metroplex was formed was the statute that said we couldn't touch any one-or-two-family home anywhere in the city, so we've had to use other tools, like the Land Bank, but we still have a tremendous amount of work to do in the neighborhoods."

Dave Buicko was on board as well, advocating for continued investment in the neediest neighborhoods. "We're building moderately-priced housing that's attractive and affordable in Hamilton Hill, and I don't think those projects are getting enough accolades. We can't forget our neighborhoods and we can't forget our kids. We have to continue to address our school system, reduce property taxes, and keep working collaboratively. There's no silver bullet at this point. Like Ray says, it's small ball. It's just all a bunch of singles and doubles. That's how you win the game."

Gary McCarthy sounded similar notes in these excerpts from his State of the City address delivered on January 6, 2020:

> *Working together we have produced five straight years of tax cuts for property owners in the City of Schenectady. We have seen a steady increase in the value of property in our city. Our HOMES Program – Home Ownership Made Easy in Schenectady – has helped create ownership opportunity and show people the value of real estate in our community.*
>
> *Tourist spending in Schenectady County increased 10.5% to $309 million in 2018. Rivers Casino, which hosted almost 200 meetings, conferences, and events last year, and along with Mohawk Harbor, are becoming the number one tourist destination in the Capital Region.*
>
> *I want to thank Metroplex Chair Ray Gillen and original board member Neil Golub for their work. Last year we had over fifty businesses in the City of Schenectady open, expand, or otherwise make some type of investment. It seems I see Mark Eagan from the Capital Region Chamber at ribbon cuttings*

more than I see my wife. In November, Schenectady was awarded $10 million as part of Governor Cuomo's Downtown Revitalization Initiative (DRI).

We are continuing to revitalize our neighborhoods. Neighborhood development projects are continuing along Albany Street, Craig Street, Van Vranken Avenue, and Eastern Avenue, where the new Renaissance Square is currently under construction. The Craig Street streetscape project, part of the Craig-Main connection initiative, will move forward this year. This will complement the Electric City Barn, the ongoing development of Hillside Phase 2, and the recent transferred properties to the Miracle on Craig Street. At the other end of the Craig-Main Connection, we have the new County Library.

The new Boys & Girls Club will officially open on the 13th. It is a great facility that is going to create opportunity for kids in so many ways. If you haven't been there yet please try and get a tour. I want to thank Mark & Terri Little, who are with us tonight, for chairing the fundraising committee and their personal support which made this project possible.

The Thriving Neighborhoods Challenge will have committed $500,000 to fund approximately 20 neighborhood initiated improvement projects by the end of this year.

The downward trend in crime continued in 2019. Since I've been mayor, Part 1 Crime measured by the highest charge is down just over 36%. That reduction is happening because of data driven policing and the strong leadership of Commissioner Eidens and Chief Clifford.

The Fire Department does a great job every day. About 70% of the calls for service are for Emergency Medical Services. We saw a slight uptick last year in our calls requiring Advanced Life Support – these are the most serious calls. Calls for Basic Life Support remained about the same.

We continue to work with the Land Bank to demolish the worst of the blighted and distressed properties – over 200 since 2014. More than 5,200 permit applications were processed in 2019 representing over $72 million in investment in our city.

We held four open houses with National Grid and our partner vendors to help people better understand the options and potential of our Smart City Project. What is a Smart City? Smart Cities use data and technology to solve public problems and manage the delivery of services at a pace, scale, and level of effectiveness not even imaginable a few years ago. The goal is to enhance public safety, improve transportation and mobility, environmental sustainability, and connectivity with public Wi-Fi. Last year we were showing about 6,000 unique visitors each day. We are now over 11,000 each day, or a 90% increase in public use. On the secured side of this network we are seeing greater utilization by police, fire, codes and other city employees.

Everyone in this room has helped in some way with the progress and revitalization that is happening in our community. You all count. Crime is down. Taxes are down. The value of homes is up. Investment in our city continues. The State of our City is very good. I thank you for your support and look forward to working with you this year.

Echoing the mayor's upbeat assessment, an earlier, comprehensive report by the Brookings Institute, which had studied seventy counties across America that used to function as major manufacturing centers, had concluded that the economy in Schenectady County was in better shape than its industrial peers nationwide. Based on its performance during the first two decades of the 21st century, Schenectady was designated as an "emerging area" because jobs there had grown 3.2 percent while other industrial counties had posted losses in employment that averaged 1.4 percent.

Everyone, it seemed, was in agreement: create more projects and jobs, remove blighted properties, keep the forward momentum going downtown, and start to focus even more on the neighborhoods. Under Ray Gillen, Metroplex, and the unified team approach, Schenectady's body had certainly been moving in a straight line at a constant speed, to quote Newton again. The future of the city looked more than bright. What force could be fierce enough to knock it off course?

13

Who Thought This Would Happen?

Here are voices from a community in crisis: dramatic monologues based on interviews with some of the people who worked to care for Schenectady's citizens during the initial eight months of the Covid-19 pandemic and to preserve important elements of the hard-won comeback of the last decade here.

Ebony Belmar

Social Worker at Mont Pleasant Middle School

Life even before the pandemic was challenging. Our kids live in Mont Pleasant and in Hamilton Hill, and so you've got more families dealing with unemployment or low employment, being under-employed, with food insecurities, and more likely to hear gunshots, you know, more likely to have interactions with the police, more likely to have a parent with mental health issues or drug and alcohol issues. Our kids academically tend to struggle. It seems to be the most challenging population.

Mont Pleasant has always been in a different situation than the other two middle schools in Schenectady. We are different by location and, as a matter of fact, in the opening training that was done this year, one of the things they spoke about was redlining. And the pattern that we always thought was there, they discussed, which is that certain students were always sent to Oneida Middle School, another type sent to Central Park, and another type sent to Mont Pleasant. It's based on race. With everything that's happened, that's still our reality. And Mont Pleasant has always been the school that had the kids with the most stressors.

We deal with more fights – not that the other two middle schools do not – but there was a year when the police were called here so much that it made the news all the time. The police arrived almost on a daily basis. We had students fighting each other, and we had parents fighting with parents. Staff was hurt a couple of times. In the schools, they were overwhelmingly fistfights. Parents and family members would try to get into the school to protect their kids, or to rescue their kids, and I think the concern has consistently been that others would get involved in the fights. When they were in the communities, oftentimes adults did get involved, to protect their children from family members of other kids. Sometimes it started with issues that had moved to us from New York City or from Puerto Rico, ongoing family feuds. Those tended to be more after school, but things happen over the weekend, on Facebook and everywhere else, and those problems come into the schools afterwards, of course.

I was called a lot because I've been here a long time, eighteen years. I know the families – just from having been here longer. So I think I ended up communicating with them a lot more than your average person in the building. There are always new faces, but mine was familiar, or I had more relationships with folks from the community, so I was called to just see if I knew someone, if I could reason with someone, and maybe de-escalate a situation. I believe in prayer, so those meetings usually went well. I have never had a parent verbally or physically in any way abuse or threaten or intimidate me. I've been blessed that way. I'm not saying they were always thrilled with me, but they were relatively respectful of the situation and they could be reasoned with. But the fights did mean more needing to find clothing for kids, or more needing to maybe drive someone home because he or she was suspended more frequently. More needing to reach out because their attendance was not as good. More phone calls that someone is hungry, or that someone is about to lose an apartment. Just more of the pieces that come with lack of money, lack of support, lack of information.

Now when the pandemic hit, we just didn't see anyone.

There were kids I didn't see at all, online or otherwise. The home visits didn't produce much. I'm a people person, so when this all started I would try to be on the buses, delivering food, delivering lunches, just so I could see students and connect and see that they were okay. After the schools were closed, we continued to provide lunches. We had specific stops, and families would come out of their houses and apartments to pick up their food. First it was every day, and then we moved to three times a week. We made phone calls and put it up on the website so families knew where we would be and when we would be there. And that lasted up until the end of the school year.

The food was provided by the School District, as well as Chromebooks for every student. Thousands were purchased, and different staff members found lots of creative ways of getting those into the hands of students and families. When we were delivering Chromebooks, I was more than willing to take the drive to go to the homes to deliver them. At the beginning, it was more people driving their own cars, especially if you knew the person and had a relationship with them. People who knew you would call up and say they didn't have one. When we moved to the buses, maybe in June, they would make different stops at different locations so people could go there and pick up a Chromebook.

For the kids with limited internet access, we also delivered Hotspots. You buy them, they're in a box, and it's just like delivering wi-fi. At one point, we were working with Spectrum to make sure that as many families as possible had service. An issue came up when I had a couple of families who weren't able to pay their bills, so Spectrum either would not turn it on or what they were putting the family through to turn it on wasn't worth it. It was just more than the families that I was dealing with could go through. So for those people, we delivered Hotspots. The school district paid for those, too.

Our success with getting students online varied. It was not easy to call who was going to make the transition over to virtual. Some kids who were really doing well with in-person learning struggled when everything switched over to virtual. I heard stories of kids who started doing much better with virtual, and who knows if they were less intimidated, you know, or whether they were more computer-tech-savvy. You heard varying stories. For some of our kids, it was the best thing that could happen, and for others, we never saw them. They never logged in. They never even checked into a classroom.

Most of my social work sessions were done virtually. Initially, we started out with Zoom, and that didn't work so well, so the District went to Google Meet. I would either call a kid or text a kid or try to e-mail them, or speak to them if they were in class, and try to set up a time when we could meet. And they could go to Google Meet on their Chromebooks and we could see each other, or we could hide our faces and have a session. And still, there were kids I didn't see, but there were others who were online constantly. At 2 or 3 A.M., they were on there. For some kids, their sleep patterns became really irregular. I wouldn't necessarily answer at those times, but after a while I also learned to turn off my phone and not be so worried that everything would get me wondering. Again, it varied. There were kids who you still could not connect with, and then there were others that you just couldn't get away from.

It varied. Some of them were lonelier kids who didn't have friends who they could be texting, so you became that person for them. Some were truly in crisis and didn't have anyone that they could turn to and share what was going on. It was a little bit of both. For example, there was one family where the Child Protective Services would figure out how to meet that family's needs, and I worked together with them. Sometimes it was just talking to the family to help them think through or talk through whatever the crisis was. If it was maybe a kid who was depressed or possibly suicidal, you would have to assess just how unsafe they felt and, if necessary, they would have to go to the hospital to be evaluated. We also have a crisis team in the District, so if there was a situation that was actually that frightening, we would try to access them also, and also contact Ellis Hospital, and get everybody to help guide the parents through the situation. Often I lost sleep over some crisis or other, but I'm a poor sleeper anyway. You can't help but worry, especially when you're in the habit of seeing these faces and knowing which ones were going to be in really difficult situations. I don't think there was anyone who didn't lose some sleep. We all did. It was hard.

And now with Governor Cuomo threatening 20% aid cuts, we have suffered all these layoffs. Teachers and paraprofessionals – you name it – hall monitors, classroom assistants, office assistants, secretaries, a lot of social workers. I forget the number. Something like 200, and 100 teachers. So many of our young people were let go – the new people, the people of color, the black and brown people – who were connecting so well with our kids. You saw our kids thriving with them. It's a tough hit, you know. The paraprofessionals were the people our kids knew. They knew them on a more real level than they know teachers. Oftentimes, they were people from the community, or people who had similar experiences. And they're gone, and the kids are gone, too, because they're virtual now. The paraprofessionals were overwhelmingly people of color, and the new teachers also. This is from my personal experience, not looking at the data. I'm not sure if the District shared that data. But I know a lot of the people who were fired. I met them, and they were people of color. I have read the explanation given for the layoffs, but it doesn't really sit well with why it was done. And why, if we say we want to be more equitable, why wasn't there more thought to being creative in dealing with the situation? If we're saying that we're aware of the trauma that our kids suffer. I don't understand how things work at that level, but with hearing that, I still don't fully understand why we moved so quickly. It does leave a pretty sour taste.

I think the consequences of all this are dire. I think more kids are going to check out. I don't know how you regain the last six months, which were pretty much lost for a lot of our kids. I think we're going to have to be very creative to get our kids to believe that education is still important. A lot of kids had questions about it anyway. It's like, "Well, I didn't go to school for three months. I'm all right." I think what's going to happen is that the gap between rich and poor is going to get bigger, because if you have money and you have all those resources, chances are your parents have gotten you a tutor. So there you go. You're further ahead of the game. And then, if you didn't have the tutor or the proper technology, the education gap is just going to widen.

I think people who run the District need to have more conversations. I don't think it's because they have necessarily lost personnel who can give direction. Maybe they aren't as organized as they think. I guess that's the reality of this crisis, that peoples' eyes have been opened and what you thought you had under control isn't so much under control. I just hope people who run this District are strong enough to learn "and not feel like they have the answers. They need to understand that they're part of the community, and to connect more with the community, and listen to the community because it knows its children and its strengths and its weaknesses better. And I do think we were going in that direction. The community is the expert. That's where the expertise lies, and to find ways to make those conversations go both ways. I don't think our parents are listened to as much as they should be, with the type of ears that need to be listening to them. Somebody might say thirty things and twenty-five of them might not add up, but that other five – if you can learn how to listen – those five things they say might make a huge difference.

Karen Bradley

Director of the Schenectady County Public Library

T he county manager, Rory Fluman, called me on Friday, March 13th, and said, "Karen, I'm locking you down. You're going to be done." And I said, "What? You mean like right now, Rory?" And he said, "Well, I'll give you tomorrow so people can come in and get stuff." I let the staff know, then we came "in and worked on Saturday.

Right away, we realized, "Hey, we have a lot of projects we can get done without the public in here," and so everybody started in on those. But then as the week went on, the governor started his cascading thing of how many people you can have at work, and we dropped from 50% to 25%, but by Friday the 20th, that had changed again. At noon that day, the Governor came on and said, "We're in 100% lockdown." So the county manager commanded, "Everybody home," but he did call me that same night and said, "Karen, we're ramping up an operation at Public Health. I need you to get me as many library people as you can to report up there tomorrow morning." And I said, "Well, what time?"

"9 o'clock."

Fortunately, most of my library staff numbers are in my phone, so I just started calling them that night. And people asked me, "Well, what would I be doing?" And I told them, "I'm not really sure. He didn't really say what we're going to do." But

I did get five or six people who were willing to come anyway.

They had these little Walmart Track Phones for us, and they had stacks of printouts of people who were in quarantine, people who were COVID-19 positive, organized by zip code. And they wanted us to check on every resident, so we were supposed to drive to each house number and then, on the little track phone, make a call inside and they were supposed to wave out the window at you, or maybe come to the door. If they were home, you would ask, "Have you taken your temperature today?" Most often, if they even answered, they would say, "I can't take my temperature. I don't have a thermometer." Then we'd have to make a note that they needed a thermometer, and write down their symptoms and everything. Or you might call these houses and nobody would be there. Pretty quickly, they realized the amount of time it took to drive around the county and, by day three, we were no longer doing that.

Then on the 27th – another Friday, seems like Rory Fluman called me every Friday for a while – he called and said, "Karen, can you get in your car and go up to the Boys and Girls Club, right now? We're setting up an emergency-response-coalition call center up there, and you'll be in charge of it." And I said, "Call center? What is that?" He explained it was for food and supply distribution. Well, within a day, we had this call center set up there, with the same cheap phones that were a real nuisance. But we did have a computer and my assistant, Devon, started a database for all the people who might be calling for help – their addresses, their phone numbers, and all that. We needed contact information to run the delivery system, right? Now on the second day, Shane Bargy, the Club's executive director, asked me for our library van, because they had no way to deliver the food and supplies, and we haven't seen that van since then.

I always had six people, and we worked in shifts. That new Boys and Girls Club is modern, and perfect. We had this huge space on the second floor – our own bubble up there – and the tables were probably ten feet apart, and we just wiped down everything before we started working every morning. We had a DSS social worker, Tanya, and we got a woman from City Mission, Isabelle, who speaks Spanish, and boy, were we glad to have them. The minute you would come in each day, you could see the phones lighting up, buzzing. People started calling at 6:00 in the morning, calling for everything. They were having trouble with their rent, and they didn't know what to do, and Tonya would do the call back. Or she got people who had never been on food stamps before, and she would get them all set up. She'd mail them all the paperwork they needed to get into the system. Everyone wanted masks, of course, but initially we didn't even have masks. People needed everything and, within a week, once they advertised the call center, we were flooded with calls. And mind you, we never once had any cleaning products to give out to people.

We even had some medical providers who called us. One was a nurse, he said he was directly caring for COVID-19 patients. He told us he stripped off his contaminated gear and left it in his car before going into his house, but he was still afraid he'd make his family sick. He needed cleaning products. That's all he wanted. And we had nothing. But I knew we had a big box of cleaning products at the library, so we dropped some things off on the steps of his house. And then one of the doctors from Ellis was quarantined at a motel to be away from her family because she had children. She had very specific, high-protein food needs and we had nothing like that. So I called her and I made a grocery list and I actually called my husband, Dave, and asked him to go to the grocery store for her. She was putting her life on the line, separated from her family for all that time, and it was the least we could do. We met a lot of out-of-pocket demands like that.

There was no Ensure for weeks, so Dave and I bought Ensure. There were no diapers, or Depends, and there was an elderly woman up in Glenville whose husband was on dialysis and she was terrified to leave and go anywhere and bring Covid-19 back to her husband who was so compromised. So I put it out on my Facebook page, and then somebody from the Methodist Church right up the street got in touch with me and said, "We've got tons of diapers in our storeroom." So we arranged to go pick them up, and we got 1500 pounds of diapers from them. There was a variety of desperate situations like that. One woman, along with her husband and her mother were all in Ellis Hospital, in the ICU, and she called me from there. She had left three children at her home and they needed food. So it was constantly sobering for us, seeing the pandemic's real impact on peoples' lives.

The last month we were there, we started getting these calls from Queens and Brooklyn. I guess they really thought we could deliver diapers and food downstate. And then after that, we started getting calls from around the whole country – from Florida, the Midwest, even got a call from California – it was really unbelievable. We told them, "We're located in upstate New York. It's just an operation to serve the residents of our county." I told everybody, "We need a map with little pins." They didn't know where we were. Nowadays, phone numbers can be from everywhere.

We worked there until May 22nd. And then we got another very abrupt call from the county manager's assistant. "Yep, you guys are done," she said. And I wanted to know what would happen next. "Well, we've got this schedule, so who's going to be doing this? I mean, all these people are calling," I told her, and finally she agreed to give us three more days, but then we would be finished. They had the Schenectady Foundation come in and then they tried to get volunteers to take our place until they could transition down. They shut down near the end of June, when the food pantries reopened and staged mass food distributions, because the Boys and Girls Club had modified summer programs to run. Serving that immediate need, it felt so rewarding, and we kind of went through withdrawal when we came back to the library. We've not been given permission to have any patrons in here yet, and we can't do it until the county says we can, so for now we're just offering curbside pickup. For the poor parents with children, though, and for the homeless people who spend their days with us, we're a refuge. So it's kind of heartbreaking for us that we can't be there when people really need us.

Libraries are the educational, recreational, and information centers, the hubs of communities. No matter how small you are or how big you are. And I certainly think during times of national tragedies – I mean, if you go back to Katrina, Sandy, you go to Ferguson –whenever there have been these national tragedies, the libraries have always been the force in the community, the gathering place for people. It's like equity, like fair, equal treatment, providing factual information for everyone who comes in. But everything, not just libraries, may now be on the chopping block due to this pandemic.

The county sees the tremendous benefits we provide. That's why they built two brand new libraries in the two neediest parts of the city. The new Bornt branch, in Hamilton Hill, has been a smashing success – we took in almost $23,000 of revenue in 2019 at that one location – from faxes, copiers, all the photocopies – it's absolutely like the small business center for that neighborhood, and now what are the people in that neighborhood doing? It was part of what our board called the "corridor of hope," and the county wanted to extend that corridor and replicate that success in Mont Pleasant, but we've had one obstacle after another there. Most retired people in that neighborhood were afraid to go to the old library because of the drug dealers who worked out of Chubby's, the pizza joint next to it, so once that was purchased and torn down, we could go forward with replacing the old library there. We thought we could

be a beacon of hope, a safe haven with a big new parking lot with handicap spaces and program rooms for seniors during the day.

And then when the pandemic came, the vandalism began. When the weather improved around mid-April, young people started coming out of their houses, spray-painting graffiti and knocking holes in our walls. We could see it all on our video feed, middle of the night, the parking lot full of cars and tons of people, but we couldn't identify any one particular person and hold him responsible. Plus, people in that area are afraid to say anything. And now, we had the shooting last Sunday night – a young mother who lived in the green house across from the library was killed – and I think that will spark a huge setback for the revival of this neighborhood. What's going to happen now with education in this community? We were on such a great track before.

Robert Carreau

Executive Director of the Schenectady Foundation

We had grand plans in 2020. Actually, it was a two-year plan to go deeper, to make bigger investments in neighborhoods, with really listening to the voice of the people who live there and to get them more engaged, not directly in our governance, but by informing our governance. Sometimes you do things, and they're good things, but then you find something and you say, "Wow, we have to stick with that." For us, that was essentially getting down to a neighborhood level, through our Neighborhood Challenge but also through other things. We were still primarily working through organizations and nonprofits and had them as our partners, but we were much closer to the ground. We knew the people in the neighborhoods better. We could hear more directly from them as to what their view of the city was, or their view of their own neighborhood, and be responsive to that, because sometimes if you have too many intermediaries, what are you actually seeing? And how accurate are their ideas versus the view of the folks living in those particular neighborhoods?

The other thing we had decided, which in its way was perfect timing for the pandemic that was bearing down on us, was to really take on the issue of food security. We could see that there needed to be more coordination and cooperation between food pantries. We could see why there hadn't been, because they tend to be small, volunteer-driven, and coming out of congregations or little neighborhood groups. We entered 2020 with that also, that we were going to spend the year really just trying to understand the food system in Schenectady County and to create relationships with all of those grassroots folks, to get them on board and to gain their trust. After that, we thought we might try to identify some bigger investments for 2021.

So those were the two largest areas that we really wanted to focus on as our priorities. When COVID-19 hit, okay, we couldn't work like we were working before, of course, because everything became virtual all at once. Everyone had to get out of the office and go home. First order of business: get a Zoom account like everyone else and then, how do I use this? Okay, got that. Now can we start creating webinars? We found some of those things came pretty naturally, while others are still in process. But in terms of being able to work directly down in neighborhoods, that wasn't about to happen because you have to be there, personally, and you can't now. Even a number of the projects we had signed off on for Neighborhood Challenge, they won't happen this year, either. Maybe a handful of them might make some progress, but we're pretty much figuring this pandemic will be with us for quite a while.

This is unlike anything else we have faced. This isn't like the Mohawk River flooding – that flood comes in, washes someone's porch away or badly affects someone's livelihood and then it's gone, and you can go in to help them rebuild their property and their lives. But we didn't know where this virus was going, and we didn't know what the repercussions would be. There were all these questions about everything: Can I get a test? Where do I get a test? How will I get groceries? Do I trust the guy who just delivered groceries to me? What do I do with my kids at home? How can they keep learning? We were all in the crisis ourselves, inside that stress while we were trying to help other people, trying to get answers and stay safe and still do the work we needed to do.

In mid-March, I contacted directors of some other non-profits in the city – the YWCA, City Mission, Schenectady Community Action Program – and they all came on board immediately to form a leadership team. Our initial focus was on providing food and shelter, and making sure those shelters were locked down. The Boys and Girls Club in Mont Pleasant became our base of operations. Karen Bradley ran the call center there, and we used the gymnasium as a warehouse distribution center for food. Normally, the Regional Food Bank would have helped us distribute their food, but they were backed up with orders for the whole Capital Region and then they started losing their employees to Covid. Luckily, Schenectady County jumped right in. They said, "We've got our DPW guys and trucks, they aren't out doing roadwork yet, we'll send them over to pick it up."

So twice a week, we sent tractor trailers over to the Food Bank and then they unloaded all the food they got into the gym. The County even engaged a company to deliver a refrigerator truck so we could keep produce and dairy and meat over there. Most of the deliveries then were being done in the first four weeks by DPW employees, and it was interesting how they embraced that mission, probably because they don't get too much appreciation from the public for their regular jobs. There was so much fear and desperation, as well as the dread of the unknown, but here was this *one* certainty: here they came, the DPW, bringing groceries to people's front doors, and people just wanted to hug them.

Mid-to-late April saw the highest demand. I kept charts, and graphed the whole thing. On average, we got maybe 700 calls every day, and made over 400 deliveries. But right at the height, near the end of that month, the DPW guys had to go back to

fixing roads, so I made a call and asked the National Guard to come in. And they became enthralled with the mission, too, because up to that point they had been deployed as glorified traffic directors at testing sites.

By the time June rolled around, our call volume had dropped to maybe 200 calls a day, and about 150 deliveries. We were all volunteers at that point, and we had cobbled together a new fleet of organizations to maintain a decent level of deliveries. Karen Bradley's team had to go back and initiate a curbside pick-up service at the main library, and the National Guard had been deployed somewhere else. The County pulled the rest of its people out, too, and they took their forklift with them, so we had no way to unload the pallets of food from the trucks. I called the County Manager, and never received a call back. Then I called the County Legislature, and they, for whatever reason, couldn't pry it loose for us either. Finally, Chuck Thorne, who had retired as City Clerk, made some calls and persuaded someone that it was almost impossible to operate without it, so at least we had that forklift back until the end of June, when the Boys and Girls Club took over their facility again. All in all, we received 29,000 phone calls, and made 16,500 deliveries. We helped a lot of people when they needed it most.

I do think there's something that was tricky through this whole thing, though. What is government's responsibility versus what is a non-profit sector's responsibility? And there's always this gray area. I think a lot of us felt that while the county stepped up big time at the start, the follow-through wasn't there. The coordination that we had asked them for in terms of – "Well, don't just tell us that tomorrow you're out. Let's figure out the hand-off. We want it to be a good hand-off –" well, that didn't exactly happen. Our leadership team had a Zoom call with the County Manager and his closest people, which we had asked for. It was about coordination and the hand-off. So we figured that was going to happen. "Let's talk about it now and together we can put together a whole thing," I said to them. "This is what we're asking for. This is our hope for how this will happen." And they said, "Oh, yeah. We can do that. Yeah. That's good." One week later, I got a phone call from the assistant to the County Manager. "We're pulling out next week," he announced. "What?" Mike Saccoccio yelled. "What does government do? What is their role?" To put it in a grander sense, I wonder, *What are the obligations that Schenectady County and the*

City of Schenectady have to their people? Aren't they supposed to take care of us?

However, our government here in this county – I think it may be different else-where – has never really seen any role in providing a coordinating structure. You'd think with all of the funding that comes through, whether it's coming from the state through the county to services or it's coming from federal government through the city, that there would be some interest in that. Why don't they say, "It's not just about handing the money out. How do we leverage this by getting organizations or programs to connect?" It just seems like they've never wanted to step fully into that.

Although here's a silver lining: this is still conceptual, but it's kind of coming together. I think Schenectady has always been ahead of the region when it comes to collaboration and partnerships, so we already had that as part of our DNA here, but the pandemic forced the issue further because there was no option. As non-profits, we couldn't just sit in our own spaces and run our programs. We had to be connected. This isn't necessarily a program – it's more like a cultural thing. What's emerging is this concept of one Schenectady when it comes to serving people. So we will be launching a phone number where, if you need help, you call that number and there will be a menu. It'll be limited at first. We don't want to be overwhelming. But if you're needing access to food, press one. Bam. You'll get directed to the Food Pantries of the Capital Region. They'll be able to set up a delivery, because we're keeping a very modest delivery system going. Habitat for Humanity will take over for regular deliveries, and City Mission would do deliveries for the priority people or the elderly in quarantine. Or if you're in a domestic violence situation, press 2 and bam, you'd be patched directly to the YWCA. Those are examples of what we're thinking about.

Covid-19 has pointed up the gaps in the existing system very clearly – the people who were not being served, and those who could have been served – whether it was Meals on Wheels or something else. For one reason or another, they didn't qualify or they were on a waiting list. You always knew they were out there, but now you could actually see very specific examples of who was not getting help, and realize there was something you could do about it. The question is, "Who's going to pay for it?" And are our local governments going to have the stomach to say, "Well, yes, we ought to take care of them, too."

Eric Clifford

Chief of the Schenectady Police Department

In February of this year, before the pandemic hit, we were riding pretty high. We were feeling really good about ourselves. All our hard work was being reflected in positive statistics. People were starting to feel safe in this city. We were doing so good that, from a strategic perspective, we were looking at really fine-tuning things. Crime was down. Now we're always looking to go from good to great, so what little tweaks can we make here now to get it even better? Schenectady has always had such a bad reputation for crime that my goal has been to have Schenectady be perceived the way Saratoga Springs is. I'm not saying that Saratoga is necessarily safe, but it's perceived to be safe. And that's what my goal is – to have Schenectady perceived as a safe place to live.

I understand our city is different than theirs. I mean, there's a reason why but look, a lot of crime that we have, the really bad crimes, are not reflective of city residents. There are some, sure, but not all. A lot of the really horrific stuff, like the shooting near the Mont Pleasant library that just happened over the weekend, there's somebody from out of town involved in that, somebody from Middletown. You look back at the last forty homicides in this city, you might be surprised to learn that with three-quarters of them, they're perpetrators from out of the area – from the boroughs of New York City or near there. So the question becomes, why do people from out of the area come to Schenectady or Albany or Troy to commit these crimes, when they don't usually come to Saratoga Springs or suburbs like Niskayuna? My best guess is that it's who they're coming to visit, or many people who may come from outside the area to move up here might end up in Schenectady because our housing costs might be lower. They're probably not going to Saratoga because they can't afford it. People leave the New York City area to have cheaper housing, that's a fact.

It's not only here, you know. All up and down the Thruway, Route 87, along the Hudson, there are a lot of stops – Newburgh, Poughkeepsie, Kingston, Albany, Troy – and these perpetrators might have girlfriends in every place with apartments they can work out of. We're talking about traveling salesmen. But it's not just from New York City. I think it's coming from the Canadian border through Vermont, the Burlington area, then down through Glens Falls. And it follows the Thruway again, the Route 90 part, all the way past Schenectady, Utica, Syracuse, Rochester, and on to Buffalo. There are a lot of similar crimes happening in those cities, too, and in the adjacent towns.

Now the pandemic has made all of that worse. When it first hit, we became all about safety. We had to modify what we were doing to ensure the safety of our officers. We went from having some two-man cars to one-officer cars, so we had officers work alone more often. And I think that what we saw was that when an officer is working alone, they may be less inclined to stop somebody or interdict with somebody unless they had back up. It's hard to see somebody who is doing something that normally might grab your attention and say, "Send me a car. I'm going to stop this person," when the department is spread so thin. So I think that we saw a slowdown there.

With COVID, nobody wanted to be around other people, and so we just saw less policing. And quite frankly, I told my officers, "I don't want you to put yourself at risk right now. I want you to stay safe, I need you to be here, I don't want you going out there being proactive, getting sick. Clearly, if something happens in front of you, you have to address it, but don't go turning over stones if you don't have to." Of course, we considered whether that would be endangering the community, but what we actually saw was there wasn't anybody out there to be stopping anyway. At the start of the pandemic, the community actually didn't need to be policed as much.

There were only a couple of statistics that were going up, like domestics, clearly, and assaults. Everything else was going down. Burglaries were almost non-existent, probably because people weren't leaving their houses, so there was less opportunity there. We were doing really good for a while, but once that curve got flattened and things started opening back up, it was like a dam broke – right around the time of George Floyd's murder.

When the protests after George Floyd's death started, we got really concerned the night Albany was burning, and we just knew they were coming to Schenectady next. So we got our plan in place, we had our building surrounded, and they were claiming that they were going to burn down our police department. We have cameras in front of our police department so we watched the protest unfold on those, and we pulled up Facebook Live – they were broadcasting it so we were able to listen in addition to watching. We didn't go out there, I talked to the mayor about going out and speaking to them and we decided no, it wasn't a good move. We weren't invited, we weren't asked. If they had said, ahead of time, "Come on out," then I may have.

After they marched down to City Hall and did their thing, a smaller group walked back to Veterans Park, and then headed down Nott Terrace, middle of the street, turned onto Liberty and came back to the front of the police station. At that point we started watching them. They banged on the front doors, and then they all moved around to the side, chanting and yelling. My lieutenant came out and said to me, "One of the organizers says he wants to talk to a boss." A boss. That's the term he used. I said, "All right. Tell him to come on in. Invite him into the police station."

So he went and got him, and he brought him in, and when he came in, I knew who it was. It was Damonni Farley. My prior dealings with Damonni, on a community level, had all been good. He wasn't necessarily a friend, but he was certainly an acquaintance. We had each other's phone number in our phones. So as soon as he came in, I'm like, "Hey, what's up, Damonni?" He was kind of pumped up, and he said, "If you come out, the crowd has a few questions for you. If you come out and answer them, I promise you this will end peacefully." And my response was, "That's it? They just want to talk? Yeah, let's do this."

Well, nobody could hear my answers, because they didn't have a microphone. I had my officers pull a police car up and we used the PA system. So we did a question and answer session, and it went good. I mean, there were a few people in the crowd who just weren't letting go. They weren't happy with my answers. But for the most part, people seemed pleased with what I said. And then one of them said to me, "Take a knee with us." And I looked around in the crowd, and I went, "What, we're going to say a prayer now?" And he said, "No, no, no. Just take a knee with us." So I said, "All right." All I was thinking was, *Here's a group of people who are emotional and they're hurting, and they're asking me to take a knee with them, so why wouldn't I say yes, if that's going to make them feel better.* Then he said, "I want all your people to take a knee with me, too." "No," I said, "I can't make them take a knee. I'll take a knee with you, but I can't make them." Well, once we all started taking a knee, my officers just kind of fell in line with me. I didn't have to tell them to or ask them to, they just did it. And the crowd started clapping. You could almost sense the relief at that point.

Right then, a different person came up to me and said, "Come on, march with us." I said, "March with you?" He was like, "Yeah, march with us." I told him, "My officers are on post, so all of them can't march with you, but I'll march with you." And then one of my detectives who was working that day, he said, "Chief, I'll march with you." So he literally went ahead of me and grabbed some person's hand and just started marching with them. When I began marching, someone handed me a sign that read, **Black Lives Matter**. All right. I had a hand on one side and the person I was

marching with had a hand on the other, and so we did it together. We walked around the block, ended up at the front of the police station, stopped, and talked a while longer. We made promises that we would get in touch with each other and we would talk more, start doing things together, and then it was over. In the week after that, I made attempts to get a hold of the people who were there, but nobody would return my calls.

I had my lieutenant try to reach them, too. I reached out to the president of the City Council. I called up the cousin of one of the protesters, a former police officer who works in this community now. I asked her to have her cousin call me, and I never heard from her. Not a word from any of them. As the weeks went by and the protests continued, it became apparent to me that they weren't necessarily interested in talking anymore. Then finally they submitted their thirteen demands at one of the protests that followed. No discussion – they just wanted them implemented.

I think they want power. I think they want to be in control. And my response to that is, "Take the police exam, go to college like I did, and get your master's degree. Then work for, in my case, fourteen years to get to where I am, to become the Chief of Police, to have the ability to change policy. Do all that, and then you can be able to sit in my chair. But don't just show up at my doorstep and demand things from me without ever doing what I've done in my career to get here." People are screaming, "Defund the police." But if you don't have police, who's going to defend everybody? They don't want the police to have military gear. Without them, who are you going to call? The actual military? You do that and then you'll see some real military gear. It's just a mess now and again, not to be too political, but you kind of wish that we would have some leadership at the national level. We're not seeing it from the President, and we're not seeing it from the Majority Leader, or the Speaker of the House. I don't know if we're at a civil war level in this country yet, but you might start seeing small militias form and go at each other during these protests. That's my real concern.

Ray Gillen
Chairman of the Schenectady Metroplex Development Authority

D uring the 2008 recession, it was tough, but we kept going. These last few months have hit all of us hard, but we'll keep going through this, too. Let's go back to early March of this year: we had more people working than ever before in any given time in the history of Schenectady County. We had reached an employment high, and downtown was bustling. Our unemployment was in the 3% range. You had many underemployed people getting better-paying jobs, and you had a lot of people re-entering the workforce. The employment numbers were just spectacular. We had engineered one of the biggest investments in upstate, the $550 million Mohawk Harbor project, where our casino was rocking and rolling, and where we had created a large number of tech jobs in the office building there. Lower State Street was really taking off with the Mill Artisan Project. And, on top of all that, we had just won $10 million from the state for the Downtown Revitalization Initiative. Things had really jumped.

But this Covid-19 pandemic has delivered a tough blow. The casino is not open. Proctor's Theater is not open. Bow Tie Cinemas is not open. Unemployment has reached 11%-plus countywide. I never thought I'd see that again, anything close to that number. It's had a huge impact on the colleges. We don't think of ourselves as a college town, but we are: with Union College, with SUNY Schenectady, with Clarkson growing, even some of our trade schools like Paul Mitchell, and Modern Welding, and the SEED Center downtown. We have a lot of employment-in-training folks who can't do their jobs because of Covid-19 now. So it's been a tough blow.

Now, that being said, we're luckier than a lot of other communities. A lot of our employers kept working through the shutdown: General Electric kept working – main plant as well as the R&D Center in Niskayuna. GE Gas Power has a major presence here in downtown and, of course, around the world. It's a global business. But I think a lot of orders in the power industry were delayed because of the Covid crisis, and I think the company has to take actions depending on their order book. There was a sometimes fractious relationship between the company and the community, but we have had a much closer and more cooperative relationship since 2004 because we understand that it's an order-driven business. And with their plant here, the company has invested over $700 million in the downtown plant during the last fifteen years. It's a modern tech campus now.

In addition, Bel Gioioso Cheese finished their new $30 million plant in Glenville. Adirondack Beverages has a million square feet of space out there, too, and they continued to operate. We were very fortunate that so many companies here were deemed essential employers and could continue to keep their people working during the shutdown. But still, we've got 11%-plus unemployment.

Now, for Metroplex, sales tax in the county has gone down, and that's what funds us. Again, first quarter in 2019, we had a record sales tax. Even this year, January and February of 2020, sales tax numbers were terrific. Then in April, May, and June, the numbers weren't as bad as we thought they might be. So we're cautiously optimistic that they'll continue to recover. Sales tax is a good indicator of the local economy. While the pandemic has certainly had an impact, we didn't stop. We haven't missed a day. We're continuing to work on projects. And we're hopeful the local economy will surge back.

When we took over downtown in 2004, it was arguably the most distressed downtown in New York State. I'm critical of the people that came before us, because we're still cleaning up their messes. We had a room full of plans from fancy organizations that were poorly done and very expensive that we just tossed in the garbage can – starting with Arthur Cotton Moore and including the Hunter Plan and a bunch of others that were established by the prior regimes. We came up with a strategy of "From Schenectady *for* Schenectady" for our first phase. Very basic. A child of five could understand it. We needed to make a recovery, and the obvious answer was to build out the area around Proctor's Theater. So we beautified and improved the area from Broadway down to the Proctor's block, and down Jay Street to the new Golub headquarters.

And then we realized the second phase was ending the contentious relationship with GE, ending the ludicrous court challenges over assessments, and inviting GE to invest in Schenectady again. Well, they did that – again, putting almost $700 million into the main campus. Plus, we wanted to revitalize Erie Boulevard by taking over the failed ALCO plant, which had been criminally mismanaged by the previous economic development people. That site had lain fallow for fifty years – my entire adult life – from the day that ALCO closed in 1969. We kept hearing a cry of "Can't" from previous mayors and failed economic developers who said, "You can't do ALCO." We were laughed at.

Well, with Dave Buicko and The Galesi Group, we turned that site into a $550 million waterfront attraction, building that gorgeous, "green" building on a former brownfield. In the process, we gave Schenectady back a waterfront it had never really utilized. We never had a place to congregate or do anything on the Mohawk River. Now people are down there canoeing, kayaking, walking, living in beautiful condos, working, going to the hotels and restaurants there. Again, it was from Schenectady for Schenectady. So that was the second phase of redevelopment.

The last and final stage is Lower State Street, where we have development going on – with the new Gateway Park, and we fixed up the old YMCA, got behind the Mill Artisan Project, which is $40 million. We continue to follow that plan. We're known for our work downtown, but we have projects in all the towns as well. We've got to finish up our work on Lower State Street and continue to create linkages, as we're doing with the DRI between downtown and the harbor – to join those two together with trails and connector roads and other potentials – and then, of course, take the work out to the neighborhoods, which we've been doing. We have, in fact, more development now going on in the neighborhoods than we have going on downtown, on Albany Street, on Eastern Avenue, in targeted areas, like phase two of the $70 million renovation of Yates Village. Remember, we took over a city that was in an extremely distressed condition in 2004, and then we went through the worst financial crisis in history in 2008, and now we're going through the worst health crisis in America's history. We're sticking to the original plan: start downtown first, create a tax base with new jobs and economic activity, and we've done all that. People always mention the neighborhoods. We have major developments going on in all the neighborhoods right now. Again, look at the pictures of downtown in 2004. People forget about that. Downtown looked as bad then as some of the neighborhoods do now. So we've got to continue our work. We have a plan for all of this.

We work with city governments and the county government. We're an instrument of county government, and we're a state-chartered Authority. But it's more than us, it's the whole team. Everybody does try to do the right thing, and people are in government for the right reasons. They're there to try to make things better. And no, it's not a perfect situation. But we've got major opportunities to continue to expand the revitalization into other quarters and try to make a difference.

Right now, homes are selling in Schenectady. Our housing market offers amazing value, and people are moving here to work at the tech companies at Mohawk Harbor, to work at GE, to work in government. They're coming from all over. I meet with local realtors all the time, and there's a lot of activity in the real estate sector, even despite Covid-19. They say they've had some of their top two months in home sales recently. And the residential units we've built downtown are leasing up really fast. The Mill Artisan district, still under construction – out of the 70 units in the building, 54 units are leased already, and the commercial space in the building is fully rented. The brand new Electric City Apartments are almost fully leased. The Mohawk Harbor Apartments have a waiting list. All the apartments that Redburn has built, they have a huge waiting list. The newly-converted YMCA downtown, with its phenomenal units for seniors are, again, priced affordably and filling up fast. News flash: loads of people want to live downtown. This might be something that those of us who are older don't always understand, that people don't see the single-family home as the dream scenario anymore.

Outside of downtown, with our neighborhood projects, we're also creating quality, residential units for people that are also affordable: going up Albany Street, the Joe Allen apartments; Summit Towers has been remodeled; the new apartments we're doing at the old St. Mary's School on Eastern Avenue, with more new units that went into the two old schools on Craig Street. I never thought I'd see some of those properties come back. These are beautiful apartments. You'd be proud to live in these units – central air, all the amenities. But again, we're creating higher-quality housing in these neighborhoods that people are proud to live in, and removing older, energy-inefficient homes that have mold problems, that are not safe, that are fire risks.

There's talk about how people are trying to get out of the cities now and come to smaller cities like Schenectady. I don't know that we're necessarily going to see a big outmigration from larger metropolitan areas and an influx here, but I know that Schenectady has always bounced back from difficulties – from a fur-trading village to a canal town to a locomotive center to the home of General Electric, one of the most inventive and prosperous corporations in history. Here you have a fairly small city in upstate New York that has had such a transformational impact on the world. This area's centrally located among the Northeastern markets, and has benefited from good location from day one. Our area's economy is one of the strongest in the upstate region, and people follow jobs. That's one of the main reasons people want to move from where they are and live here. Schenectady has always been resilient, and we're in the process of reinventing ourselves once again.

Neil Golub
Chairman of Price Chopper and Market 32

The pandemic created fear in the minds of all Americans: if everything is to be locked down, will there be enough groceries available to meet our needs? First instincts were to stock up on the basics. In a matter of days, store shelves had been stripped of paper products, disinfectants and hand sanitizers. Less visible were many other categories such as baking products, soups and canned vegetables.

Over the years, customers have come to expect full shelves with very few stock outs. We created a replenishment system that allowed us to order product, deliver it to our stores, and stock overnight so each morning the shelves were prepared for the day's business. What happened is something that we had never seen before – many items were wiped out overnight. Normal replenishment cycles for the entire industry were shattered. Every manufacturer and producer of consumer products was being overwhelmed with orders that they could not fill. Empty shelves became a serious problem.

Manufacturers were forced to make tactical decisions to reduce package sizes, and this contributed to shelves out of stocks as well. For a short time, we left the holes, expecting the items would soon be available, but that did not happen. For the producers and manufacturers, their normal flow of product was completely interrupted – the cadence of most manufacturer production was in turmoil. Everyone was scrambling to get supplies. Distressing to our company was that some large producers were providing the bigger retailers preferred service at our expense. We found this most disturbing as we energetically defended our turf. During that period, we searched out dozens of alternative sources, which helped fill the gaps.

When President Trump suggested that people should consider consuming disinfectants and bleach to avoid Covid-19, we gasped in horror for obvious reasons. This advice was flat out stupid and completely out of order. Many gullible people were injured by this advice. Adapting to the severity of the coronavirus was an amazing experience for my colleagues and teammates. The safety and security of our customers and employees suddenly presented an enormous and scary responsibility. Our Safety Executive is an all-American performer. Sanitation and safety is a daily discussion throughout our system. Keeping people safe is a company mantra. Following the leadership of our governor, we put a defense strategy into operation immediately. During the first sixty days, masks and disinfectants became a minute-to-minute struggle. We tapped all known resources and then again had to go to places we had never used before to find and maintain supplies.

In response to their courageous efforts, we awarded all teammates an additional $2 per hour as recognition. Our teammates performed miracles overnight. Plexiglass dividers at all check stands, masks, six-foot rules, one-way aisles, disinfectant-disbursing stations, and shopping-cart sanitation appeared within hours. I am convinced that due to the ultra-high level of safety and sanitation, we were able to meet the established requirements very quickly. Hats off to all of our teammates. They have provided both customers and colleagues with a high level of safety. It is amazing to me that, with all the people moving through our stores, the number of positive Covid-19 cases was close to zero. And that was generally true throughout the supermarket industry.

My career in the company started in the stores. One day, traveling with my Dad when I was about eight, we visited a store. While I was waiting for him to finish his business, I noticed some boxes of shoe polish sitting on the floor in front of the shelf. I asked if I could put them on the shelf. "Yes," was the answer. I got a price stamper and did the job. As we left, the Store Manager gave me sixty-five cents for my work. "That's pretty good," I said. So at an early age, I was exposed to most parts of the business. I came to respect all of the people I met: warehouse workers, truck drivers, store clerks, cashiers. We all had the same job – to insure our customers received our best. That is a message I have never forgotten.

Over the past few decades, more and more, people had been eating out at all kinds of eateries, from the franchises like McDonalds to high-priced, elaborate restaurants and, of course, at numerous mid-range establishments. In recent years, food eaten away from home has approached 50% of American consumption. The pandemic swept away this 50% like a Category 5 hurricane. Except for the small percentage who found a way to create a take-out business, the doors of most restaurants closed. Meanwhile, the supermarket industry became a willing home-delivery partner. After years of starts and stops, the home delivery system finally caught on, although it was only a small percentage of our business. Customers learned their local supermarkets were there to serve them. Armed with new rules – masks, social distancing, one-way aisles, early morning shopping for seniors – supermarkets provided a safe place for people to shop. Whatever the stores had done to protect customers was working, and working well. Even with limited inventory and empty paper aisles, sales were brisk but at a heavy price for retailers, particularly back-stage expense. Price Chopper's old saying when they opened twenty-four hours – "We are always here when you need us" – took on added meaning.

In the past six months, unfortunately, we got jammed up. It was like a basketball player trying to drive to the basket and a 7-footer steps in his way and bashes him. That's really what's happened to our community. Everybody's been stalled. Restaurants closed. Businesses closed. Institutions closed. In Schenectady, with our new attraction, Rivers Casino and Mohawk Harbor, Schenectady had all of a sudden become a destination location. People were coming from everywhere. More than a dozen new restaurants had opened and people were coming to Schenectady from a lot of different places, and from all over the Capital Region, for those restaurants, and for shows at Proctor's and for the casino. Now in many ways, but not all, we're in a holding pattern. We do still have all kinds of economic development going on.

Twenty-five years ago, local leadership at General Electric was changing and its interest in Schenectady was waning. Once known as the Electric City, Schenectady was being abandoned as GE moved most of its assets to other areas of the country. By 2000, the handwriting was clear: Schenectady needed its own re-development program. In 1998, Governor Pataki signed the Schenectady Metroplex Development Authority into existence, and in 1999, the Authority Board was put in place. Progress from 1999 to 2003 was slow at best, but things changed rapidly when Ray Gillen was appointed the Chief Development Executive for Schenectady County and Chairman of Metroplex in 2004. From that year on, Schenectady has been shedding its reputation as a tired, run-down community. And what has occurred in Schenectady during the past sixteen years under Ray Gillen's leadership has been astonishing.

Right under our noses, Schenectady has become a medical hub. With Roswell Park Oncology Center coming to join Ellis Hospital, and the planned merger with St. Peters Health Partners, Schenectady is on the verge of creating its own state-of-the-art Medical Center. Bellevue Women's, part of Ellis Medicine, is the premier OB/GYN hospital in the Capital Region, and Sunnyview Rehabilitation Center possesses a regional reputation. Situating all this medical expertise in one place will create a stunning new level of health services for our community and, given our concerns during this pandemic, that's deeply reassuring.

One of our other strengths is in education: we are lucky to have Union College, Clarkson University, and Schenectady County Community College. Over the past decade, Union College has imagined and created an enormous presence for STEAM: Science, Technology, Engineering, Arts & Math. The college's $100 million investment in on-campus learning facilities is truly amazing. With the relatively recent entry of Clarkson University to Schenectady, we have now earned an enhanced reputation for STEAM education. Clarkson School of Education is dedicated to producing future teachers who will excel in experiential education, and that happens to be a strength of our own Museum of Innovation & Science (MiSci) programming. In the future, MiSci and Clarkson will explore developing an experiential graduate degree program and working together.

Five new hotels have opened here just in the last couple of years, and most of downtown has been remodeled. Frog Alley, one of the newest development projects on lower State Street, will provide a combination of living, entertainment, and business, and even operates its own brewery. However, for me, the most significant statistic is that over 2000 new living units have been built during the last five years here, and most of those 2000 units are rented or owned already. That tells me people want to leave where they are and live in Schenectady now. They see all the positive changes that are happening, and they want to be a part of this city's bright future.

Gary McCarthy
Mayor of the City of Schenectady

T he state of the city at the beginning of 2020 was classified as very good. We were firing on all cylinders. Downtown was good. Proctor's was good. Rivers Casino at Mohawk Harbor had established its base, and was putting a growth model forward. Our finances were good. We'd done five years of tax cuts. We were controlling our expenses, and our revenues were coming in. The expected sales tax was up at the beginning of the year. We had a number of projects going on in the city at Eastern Avenue, on Albany Street, on Craig Street. We were optimistic about the future – it looked bright.

So we had all these positive things going on when I first became aware of the virus near the end of January, I think. A few people were talking about it, but I was just peripherally aware of it back then. I heard how China was shutting down some cities and taking some fairly aggressive actions, but then I paid closer attention to some of the information coming here. By the time it got to mid-March, we all realized that we were going to have to deal with a far more serious situation. By virtue of the standing-order protocols that are in place, we have procedures to handle crises, whether it's a fire or a flood or whatever disaster may come up. Ray Senecal, our Fire Chief, is the Incident Commander, and he assumed that role, so we scheduled meetings in our conference room every day. Finally, on March 13th, I issued the order to close City Hall, to minimize people's potential for contamination. I was the first one to do it. The Governor's order to lock down New York State came a couple of days after that.

And there was some controversy about my decision. People said, "Why are you doing that? You're overreacting." A lot of second guessing, except by the staff at City Hall. They were relieved. Almost immediately, we looked at police and fire protocols, which reflect their high levels of interaction with the public. How do you make sure they have the right personal protection equipment, adequate PPE? We had some of that in stock, and we were able to work deals to get some product quicker and faster than other communities so that our frontline workers had it, even though we weren't completely sure in the early days what the proper protocol was. There was a ton of conflicting information being put out there. Some people were stressing, "You should have a face mask," and some others were telling us, "Well, the face mask really doesn't help. It's still washing your hands, practicing social distancing, and checking if you have any symptoms."

City life here simply came to a standstill. The virus shut down Proctor's, shut down the casino, shut down Bowtie Cinemas. The schools all closed. Bars and restaurants were shuttered for indoor dining by the Governor's order, too, but they were allowed to offer take-out. So we went from firing on all cylinders to coasting a little bit, and then we really ran out of gas. It was a major jolt for the community although now, hopefully, we're starting to bounce back from that, but in a manner where our path is still not quite clear.

Again, we were meeting every day with department heads in March and April, reviewing what information we had, what protocols we could still put in place to provide essential services for the city: picking up garbage, maintaining the streets, ensuring police and fire could respond to calls. Our police and fire calls actually dropped initially and that helped with the delivery of services. When you have less calls coming in, you can balance things better than when you have a high call volume. In our meetings, we initially gathered everybody in the conference room – preparation counsel, fire chief, police chief, school district representatives, people from the County health and dispatch centers, and myself – but we pretty quickly shrank the numbers to maintain social distancing. We had cameras set up already in there, so we established remote access with Webex so we could protect individuals. We were also participating in national meetings with the Bloomberg Foundation, the U.S. Conference of Mayors, and in other venues to exchange information. What was happening in other places? Even though New York State was the epicenter at that time, we wanted to learn what people were doing all over the country.

Early on, New York City hospitals which had reached capacity were shipping patients upstate in special medical buses and on helicopters. Our caseload here at Ellis Hospital wasn't as bad, so we set up a primary landing zone in the high school parking lot, sent over the appropriate apparatus to light the zone, and stationed paramedics there with an ambulance to transport those patients to our hospital. We weren't the only city upstate to help out, but we were glad we could. We still review

the updates from Ellis daily – the number of cases in Schenectady County, people that are in quarantine, the procedures that we are using in the city – and we also issue constant recommendations for our businesses and venues to, again, minimize the potential downside of the health threat and the economic slowdown still present from this pandemic.

However, another dynamic that's in play, on top of the coronavirus, is some of the social unrest in the racial tensions dealing with policing. Where we initially saw a reduction in our calls, we're now seeing those go back up. The level of local violence is dramatically increasing, so that we have a lot more shots fired, more shooting victims, and more homicides. Many social developments seem to be intertwined right now, so it's hard to pinpoint one thing. I think there are people who may be taking advantage of some of the social unrest in issues that are being raised about the appropriate role of police and their responses in some situations. We're seeing traffic again from outside our community coming in here, individuals who are just making poor choices and engaging in acts of violence while they're in our community. People just selling drugs is one thing, but it's the surge in violence and the use of guns that are at a much higher level than they were in the 1990s. It's clear there are some elements which are not random – there's some level of organization. But what's happening also requires a longer investigative process to put together more complicated fact patterns with the inter-relationships of some of these individuals who are perpetrating these acts. And providing services for these kinds of expensive, violent events when we're under strained financial conditions in the city is really taxing. Luckily, we have been able to maintain adequate staffing in the police department, although we've had to hold up the hiring of new officers. We're taking it one day at a time, trying to stay ahead of the curve of criminal activity.

It's also a shocking period for our school system right now. There are two aspects of it: one is the distance learning because we're keeping kids out of the schools, which I think is fairly appropriate, and then you have the financial impact of the school district having to institute the recent layoffs. First of all, they had to withdraw job offers to people they were going to hire, they had to let many of their paraprofessionals go, and a number of teachers have been laid off as well. So you have our kids who have high needs to begin with, and now they're not getting what they need. I believe it's crucial to have that social interaction in school. It's the collective engagement of the classroom that produces the educational environment where you get the strongest learning and the greatest potential. It really is a long-term challenge because the implications for this will replicate and reverberate for years to come. But I also assume with this whole thing that there will be people who'll look back at this time and say, "There are components of distance learning that we should have done a long time ago."

So we're in this period where we're shutting down schools, and these kids don't have a lot of options. The current situation will manifest itself in higher crime rates, more teenage pregnancies, and greater drug use, but we're working with the school district to match up the kids who have the highest needs so we can continue to provide free lunch and other things, as well as trying to secure internet access for the kids through our Wi-Fi network. I'm a proponent of our big Smart City deployment although, unfortunately, the City Council this year didn't move on a capital budget for it. The school district was originally paid $37 a month per student for an access point that they were giving to kids and I think they were initially deploying 4000 of them. I had two million dollars in the budget this year that the Council did not advance. Not only could we have built more of the network out to support the school district, but we also wanted to improve Wi-Fi capacity for people who are now working at home. And it's too late now – to get a bond in place, that doesn't happen overnight. You've got to get the money, you've got to spec out where you're going to go, and so we've lost a really critical year.

Everybody can see what a difficult time this is, but it's in the difficult times that you see real leadership. I see that leadership as some of our department heads step up, and in so many employees who are doing it. With city and public safety employees, Schenectady has done relatively well. In our police department, in our fire department, and with all city employees, we have not had one COVID-19 case that has been contracted as a result of their employment. It's been family ancillary engagement, or for some people, where they have traveled. So our protocols here that we put in place under Chief Senecal have paid off.

Now, having said that, we're still in the middle of this whole crisis, and many of our citizens have been hurt during this time: the people who've been laid off from the restaurant industry, for example. Many retail places, and other venues, are still struggling to survive. The pandemic has had a very significant impact for many people in our community. It was initially mitigated because of the Federal Assistance for the Enhanced Unemployment Benefits, but that help is gone now. I don't think we know the full impact in some of these neighborhoods or in many of the families that have been affected by it. The kids aren't going to school, the parents aren't working, and it's very hard for them to pay their bills. The ramifications and the full details of that are still being felt out and found.

But that aspect of the coronavirus crisis has kind of lit the match to some underlying issues that have dealt with policing throughout the country. So now we're trying to respond to what I would call a vocal minority – so how can we shift those protests into policy? You go back two decades, and Schenectady was just a terrible place in terms of some of the things that were happening within the police department. We want police to be respected, we want them to be community leaders, we want them to provide that stability which is such a great thing within this country. How can we achieve that in a manner where, again, they're respected but where we don't have any of the negatives? We spend a lot of money on police, and we need to ensure that they deliver those services for our community at a high level, with procedural justice that justifies the amount of money we're spending.

The Governor has issued an Executive Order which directs the mayor and the police chief in every community in the state to set up a process that involves community leaders and residents to address some of the systemic issues of racism in policing. We have already made some initial changes, and we're now in the process of what will be a multi-month engagement. We've brought a Steering Committee together. We've done an outreach to community groups – unions, neighborhood associations, the business community, not-for-profits, the School District, the Housing Authority, other major players – and we have asked them to put forth two representatives who will come together in a community-wide forum to assess the things that we're doing well, and to look at those things that we should improve on, all with an eye toward affecting police reform. How do we make Schenectady again a better place to live, work and raise a family? That's what we're trying to do. I want the message broadcast uniformly across the city, that police are there to serve you, to work well, to partner with our neighbors. And there should not be those artificial barriers that may be perceived as racism or any level of bigotry.

So much has shifted so quickly. Some long-standing grievances have risen to the top, and I think people are waiting and watching. They want to see if Schenectady can bounce back. Do we have the leaders here that can make a difference and position the community for long-term, sustainable growth? We still need some financial assistance to stabilize both the city school district, the city government, and county government over the next eighteen to twenty-four months, and I hope the federal government will step up and help to provide that assistance. We're still in that downside where a large number of people are unemployed. We've taken a big hit to the economy, and it's taking people a while to adjust. Some things in Schenectady have slowed down a little bit, but we're still seeing people moving here, and there are still projects in the pipeline that are moving forward in an appropriate fashion. People see this as a community of opportunity, and I remain generally optimistic that we'll continue to move forward.

Philip Morris
Proctor's Theater and Proctors Collaborative CEO

My son-in-law, Nate, is an anthropologist with a specialty in urban health. He had been linked to all kinds of virology stuff for many months, and right after Christmas last year, he started sending me things to say, "Look, this is serious." By early March, I was reading his virology reports and I thought, *Okay, somebody has his head in the sand, this is really bad.* When the day came that the Governor said, "We have to make a change," I talked to my Board and to my staff while I was in quarantine. I did not get COVID-19, but I had been in contact with a woman at Union College who had tested positive and I was traced to have had lunch with her, so I had to be home in quarantine.

I made the decision to lay off 130 people and that just shut the whole Proctors Collaborative down. Had to do it from my house on a conference call. I couldn't look at people. I haven't fully grieved it yet, to be honest. It was awful. We had a conference call telling those 130 people we were making permanent lay-offs. We wouldn't even call them furloughs because that didn't make sense. The sooner they were on the ACA, the better. The sooner they got on unemployment, the better. It didn't make sense to, what I called at the time, make rolling errors. You have to understand that this was a place people didn't leave. We couldn't necessarily pay them that well, but they didn't leave. And we have always worked with our neighbors – our housekeeping staff, our maintenance staff – probably 20% of the people we laid off walked to work, and had once lived in the City Mission. A lot of them came from the Ambassadors Program. They were good, and they were loyal. People like coming to work here. This building looked like Schenectady's workforce – not its leadership – its workforce.

In 2019, we hosted over 3000 events: 1200 or so were ticketed events like live theater or movies; 800 were meetings or rentals of some kind; about 500 involved classroom work; 470 repertory, and maybe 200 at Universal Preservation Hall, so again, over 3000 events. But to cover those, you're running buildings eighteen hours a day, seven days a week, and that's why we had a staff of 150 to 160 people.

Some of what we do – what the governor called "essential businesses" – fit into that category. Our power plant, because we generate utility, was an essential business. Our ticket service, because we provide ticketing for eleven or twelve other facilities, was deemed essential. And Open Stage Media, because it's communications, media. So those three essential businesses we kept open, and we reduced staff but kept them staffed. We closed everything else. So March 17th, we closed food service, we closed theaters, we closed the projection rooms. We closed Capital Repertory, which was ten days into a forty-day run. So that went dark. Universal Preservation Hall in Saratoga? Closed its doors ten days after it opened. We just shut everything down, and went from a business that generated thirty million dollars a year to a business that won't even make two million a year, if you project forward from March 17th through the end of 2020. Radical, radical change.

We're not rich. We never had $100 million endowment going on, number one. Number two, my sense early on was this pandemic was going be a long-term thing. That it was not, "Yeah, we'll close for a few weeks and then hit the button again." When I laid people off, my staff thought maybe I was being a little too aggressive, because there were certainly folks thinking we'll shut for a month or so, and that'll be that. But I didn't think that. So I kept thirty-four people, the ones who I thought were the most flexible and jack-of-all-trades sorts, people who could restart. Now we think we could make it through September of 2021, if we had to do it, with just these thirty-four. But that's not paying our old bills. We've warned all our creditors we can't pay those bills. We tried to pay the small ones and the really individual ones. We're trying to pay a little bit, but some businesses are not getting paid from us, and no one has screamed yet. We've communicated with them all.

Look, performing arts is a team sport. It's the opposite of social distancing. Singers need to be twenty feet apart from one another to be socially distanced safely, because of the deep breathing, the exhaling, the deep breathing, the exhaling. And they're a risk to others because, in fact, they throw far. Plus, it would be hard to imagine watching actors with masks on. Hard to imagine actors backstage with thirty or forty stage fans. These facilities weren't built for social distancing. In my musical training, I was taught to sing to the last row, right? Well, when you think like that, you spread like that. In essence, the core of what we do just has to make us among the last to return.

Now I think we're a pretty resilient institution, and resilience has defined a lot of the discussions with the employees who are left. How can we best use this property for the community, if we can't do events? Well, within the first month after lockdown, we opened the Safe Studio on the main stage – that's a 4500-square-foot space which we transformed into a recording studio. At first we would only allow two, three people at a time, but now we allow up to ten because that meets all the guidelines and everyone's far away from each other. By virtue of doing that, we were able to record Kids Arts Festival rather than do it live, and build kits of supplies and distribute them to poor kids through the Albany and Schenectady Housing Authority for a weekend of activities that was broadcast on Open Stage Media. We've opened the Arcade and Key Hall, because we were able to make it safe for two different blood drives, and for a back-to-work clothing distribution by City Mission, when 175 people came here and got fresh clothes to go back to work.

There are not many spaces like ours in the community that are this big and where you can line people up at one end and let them exit at the other end and have lots of air. In that regard, we studied our air-handling systems before the governor even was telling people what to do at the malls. We were exceeding it. We put in MERV 13 air filtration. And now we're about to put in ultraviolet light in every property that the Collaborative is part of. We'll get our buildings safe, but all those upgrades are very expensive. Again, even if people are just here for a blood draw, I want the place to be as clean and safe as possible.

Will we lose what we have built? No. We won't lose this. We will lose half a generation. We're going to lose young people who don't have a chance to be on the stage. We'll lose young people who won't learn how to do the trade. School participation, with all kinds of stuff, will be far less. But we're not going to lose the arts. For now, I'm relieved that we can turn to virtual art, but personally I can't watch it – it's just not good enough – and I have great sound, but virtual isn't the same as live. What gets lost, truly, is what we do best, which is bring people in the room together, in the same physical spaces with actors and magicians, singers and musicians, or watching great movies. I think people want to be with people, largely, and people will want to be with other people again, and when they can do that safely, we will be here.

An Open Letter Published on April 17, 2020

We love you. We miss you. We will be back.

Everything has changed.

*We must isolate and focus all civic energy and economy on saving
lives and supporting our medical system.
It makes total sense. It is necessary.*

*And our country will need the arts to restart our communities,
our economies and our democracy.*

*The arts are where we convene across skills, customs and differences.
The arts are how we collaborate.*

*Proctor's, UPH and the REP, among many others, will be where the
citizens of the Capital Region will heal when this is over.*

And over it will be. We just do not know when.

Certainly, we will not start as quickly as we stopped.

We will begin to convene cautiously at first.

*But along the way, simply maintaining our $75 million of historic
properties will take millions.*

*It is difficult to focus on this cultural need when we still are desperate
for masks and ventilators, yet some of us must.*

The Proctors Collaborative — that is Proctor's in Schenectady,

Capital Repertory Theater in Albany and the new Universal Preservation Hall in Saratoga Springs — just did an absolute shutdown, along with all of our peers.

It included laying off 80% of our staff; putting millions of dollars of high-tech sound, lighting and systems safely to bed; and building a new method for the remaining staff to communicate with one another, plan for an unknowable future, inform thousands of patrons, protect beloved historic properties and try to imagine when and how to begin to restart.

Make no mistake that Gov. Andrew Cuomo's leadership has made clear what had to happen and why. Also make no mistake that we do not sit by idly, even with our own internal crisis of $22 million a year of revenue dissolving immediately to zero.

Now we work to support the local sewing community's effort to make and distribute 35,000 masks.

We imagine web-based educational programming for our many students while at home. We build a film program of art for our patrons and broadcast the best of past productions from the REP.

We weren't prepared for this disruption, yet we are all fully involved in it. But we must be prepared for the needed restoration.

When our communities are opened again, the need for what we do will be unprecedented in our lifetimes.

I ask that private philanthropy, in addition to supporting the medical emergency we are in, consider supporting the maintenance needs of cultural organizations with beloved properties so that they remain functional.

I ask donors and patrons to speed up their gifts if they are able.

I ask ticket-holders to be patient as all of us try to figure out an unknowable future schedule.

I ask government to be aware of our cultural institutions' needs, in addition to the primary need to support our health care systems.

If we allow our cultural resources to collapse, we will have repeated the mistake we made in not being prepared for COVID-19. The writing is on the wall.

It will take us all to survive this pandemic — and it will take us all to return to the human necessity of being together.

Stay home. Stay healthy.

– Philip Morris, Proctors Collaborative CEO

Will Rivas

Founder and Director of Save Our Streets,
Executive Director of C.O.C.O.A. House

I think it really started when the word came out about the coronavirus. We were running our after-school mentorship program, C.O.C.O.A. House on Stanley Street, and nobody really knew what the pandemic would mean. But I remember it was the day we found out the schools would be closed, and we had to tell our kids that the program was over. I remember the look on their faces. What was even harder, though, was that there was no certainty about what would happen next for those kids.

You have to realize we're dealing with a school system that doesn't fairly give our kids the tools that kids in other communities get, and I was afraid of what would happen to these youths with a lost educational year. So being part of the Schenectady County COVID Coalition with Bob Carreau and the other providers, I came up with an e-mentorship program to offer some help, some educational assistance. I'm an adult who has come from the community, so I understand the problems in the community. I understand the domestic violence in the homes, and the gang violence. I knew all that would be magnified by our kids just being home every day. A lot of people don't understand that, for many of them, school means an escape from home and from the trauma of the things that they're dealing with there.

When people look at our youths in school and their test scores and behaviors and all these other things, the thing they never take into consideration is that school is not just an escape, it's also the one meal a day that they're getting. To have that taken away from them, I really feared what was going to happen, which is why I started delivering pizzas. I delivered 1800 pizzas throughout the entire COVID experience to families, to kids. We delivered school supplies. We delivered art supplies. We just made sure to engage with these kids as much as possible because I look at it through an historical lens: what will these young people remember about how they felt during this time?

I was very upset with the City of Schenectady to begin with because there was a very slow response. Nothing was said, really, and there was a lot of backlash about that here. They would not give a word – not to the media, not to other people. What you need to know about me is that I walk in my truth, so I don't care because, again, I take into consideration the people from the community. What I was getting from families was pure fear. People didn't know how they were going to eat, and they didn't know how they were going to pay their bills. *What will life look like for us now?* That's what they were worried about.

Unfortunately, I believe what's been happening during this pandemic is that the face of social oppression has been exposed. Now, I don't believe everybody who has a position, an elected position, is part of an unjust system, or that they choose to be part of an unjust system. I'm not saying that. I believe a lot of people get into government because they really do want to create change. The problem is that there's an overarching mechanism that really controls what you can and can't change. When you have a political structure such as the Schenectady Democrats, who have been in place and in power for so long, when they really haven't had to answer to anybody, why would they answer now? In the beginning, I didn't get that. A couple of years ago, I was friends with all the politicians and I was in the pipeline to become a part of the Schenectady Dems and do all these things, until I realized what it meant to do that – to sacrifice a piece of myself and my personal integrity to become part of a structure that really isn't looking out for all the people.

So throughout this pandemic, what you're seeing is all the flaws in the system have been exposed. The City can say, "Well, we care about people of color," but our experience is showing us how much it really doesn't. I don't want to say, or believe, that's intentional. But I will say it does look intentional. Because again, for quite a while, nothing was said. Unfortunately, it's obvious they've made the decision that some people are not a concern for them. I hate to say it like that, as blatantly and plain as that, but in everything I've seen, certain communities have been left out of everything. I still am upset with the City of Schenectady.

In a way, though, I blame this on us. I blame the lack of response on my community because we've never held the city accountable. Community accountability is key to creating change. In other communities, where people own businesses and people own homes, and there's a more in-depth understanding of political structure and economics, people get stuff done faster because they understand how to. In my community, we are so distracted by the fact that we don't have food, or we lack true educational resources, and lack enough good employment opportunities. We are so constrained with dealing with the day-to-day that it's hard for us to worry about accountability for the City. "Man, I don't worry about no political accountability, I've got to feed my kids." That's what I hear all the time. This is how they have maintained control for so long.

I will say this, I thoroughly respected Schenectady County's response. Again, I can speak to the word from the County because I was a part of the County's coalition. So I know the meetings we were having every day. I know the resources they poured into the community – the food, the volunteers, the clothing, everything – because I was a part of it. And it was beautiful to see because while it wasn't an immediate response, it was very well-timed. It came rather quickly, actually. Bob Carreau and the people from the County – Jason and Keith and all those guys – they were phenomenal. They basically lived in that Boys and Girls Club, and the work that they poured out into the community was monumental.

However, the good thing about it is, throughout this time, people from the community started to believe in themselves, because it was the community assisting the community. Now the beauty in that is we're starting to create this community structure. We understand that we have the tools, we have the resources, we have the people in place to make our own change, to make our own demands. And this is kind of what you're seeing in the marching, in the protests, and things of that nature. If you starve people, you can't expect to invite them after that to come back and sit at your table. "No, we wanted to sit at your table when we were starving. You wouldn't let us sit at your table, so now we're creating our own."

Part of what the community needs, they need control. What I mean by that is, I'm not just talking about giving people jobs to make more money, because people coming out of poverty don't understand the nature of finance. They don't understand how to save because they've always come from a place of lack. You get a stimulus check and you go buy a TV that's too big for your house. Or you go buy 400, 500-dollar sneakers because you don't understand priorities. Don't just give people money, teach them how to utilize the money. We need a total overhaul of education, total overhaul of employment opportunities, and a total overhaul of investment opportunities. That way, people in our community could be investing not only in themselves, but in their community. Their vested interest then would become a part of their society. The problem with people and all this violence and stuff in our communities, people have nothing to hold on to. It's incredibly frustrating. You wake up every day, your entire family has lived in poverty and also on welfare. Everybody's been incarcerated. You see nothing and no options. What is a good option when all the options you have are bad?

What we do to revitalize our own community is we stop begging people to help us. In researching what has been done in Downtown Schenectady and in inner cities across America, I've come to understand the BID process – Business Improvement Districts. What they did with the Downtown Schenectady Improvement Corporation, the DISC, was beautiful because a lot of people really don't understand that Downtown Schenectady was actually the worst part of the city for a very long time. And when they had the opportunity to sit down and look and plan, because they understood very clearly what they wanted to do, what they did from a business standpoint was marvelous. We've seen the revitalization of downtown, and yet very important organizations in Hamilton Hill have been closing, So there's this disparity.

So what I propose to people of color in Schenectady, to our own business owners, is we start our own BID. There are more than enough business owners of color in our area. Keep the community dollar in the community. Purchase from local shops, support local artists, invest in local businesses. We've been socially conditioned to try to find a way to get the oppressor to help the oppressed. And the thing is, they're never going to do that. Their mechanism, their structure, is not built to do that. It's got to be more than one person. It can't be, "Well, here's William Rivas coming down here to complain about stuff again." We don't have to beg the developers. We can become the developers. As a collective voice, as a collective mechanism, controlled and structured, now we become a force because we're following their rules. We're not playing their game, but see, we're understanding the rules of war.

And all that is why I have to give credit where credit is due: a lot of people continue to say, "Well, the system is broken." No, no it's not broken at all. It's working perfectly fine for those it's supposed to work for. When you're up here, at the top of this mechanism, the top of this machine, and below you all these things are breaking down or hazardous, you're not really concerned with what's going on at the bottom because to you, it's not affecting you up here. You think, *From where I sit, the view is just great.*

Mike Saccoccio

Executive Director – City Mission of Schenectady

Sometimes adversity causes us to think more creatively about partnership. I do see this as a daunting time, but as I said to Bob Carreau the other day, "Aren't we blessed at this point in our careers to have to face this big a challenge?" Because, you know what? I've been working at City Mission for thirty-one years, and the one thing I never would have wanted was to coast it out, right? And here I am, facing my biggest challenge ever. Oh, that's such a gift for somebody at my age. What a privilege this is. Let's go for it. Even though, like anyone, I wish the virus would end, and I don't want to see people harmed. But from a leadership perspective, this is what you train for.

Before the pandemic, one of the programs we were building was what we call the Cornerstone Project. There is a verse in the Bible that says, "The rejected stone has become the cornerstone." So our belief is that a lot of folks who come to us have been rejected stones, but our passion is that God is calling you to be a cornerstone for your family, and for your community. You should never just settle for survival, because there's greatness in you. I sincerely believe in that and, if you want to be about that, too, then we want to go on your journey with you – realizing at all times that our goal is for you to exceed us.

And so back before March of this year, we had developed new ideas and courses that were meant to help with that goal. It was exciting, because we were seeing really good practice with it. We watched as people emerged as leaders – I mean, true leaders – realizing that their life experiences, although on the surface they might appear problematic or seem full of struggle, were actually a tremendous resource that they had. Our folks here at City Mission have a wonderful expression, they say, "My mess has become my message." That's probably accurate for many of us, right? So you don't have to live in fear that you were incarcerated, for example. You don't have to live your life feeling like, "What if people find out?" Not that you necessarily want to broadcast your challenges everywhere you go, of course.

But this is where I think being a faith-based organization really matters. We say, "God is redemptive." God wants us to use our struggles. He might bring someone to you who just came out of prison and doesn't feel there's a path forward, and that's where you get to say, "Well, I need to share something with you. I've been there." As the folks here also like to say, "Walked up that driveway. I've knocked on that door. I know what you're feeling. But let me tell you what can happen." So you can broadcast a message that is priceless because you have lived at that ground level.

Increasingly, getting our residents to trust in those messages was essential for that program. So we started what we called the Cornerstone University with a mix of in-house programming, but we also brought in professional trainers and paid them to give our people classes in sales and business development. We identified four blocks of our cornerstone. The first one was discipleship, and that involved acquiring a real faith. Then the second included life skills and work skills – so workforce development. The third block was supportive housing. We now have twenty-four apartments, and we're hoping to build twenty more next year, okay? It's crucial to understand that people can't make that redemptive journey if they're not living in a decent place that they can afford. And then the fourth block encompassed health and wellness. So again, what are we doing through nutrition? How are we teaching these things? How do we go deeper with smoking cessation? Health and wellness is the plan, but getting people to embrace the fact that health is not episodic, it's a lifestyle. To help with that part, we opened up an expanded medical clinic with Ellis Medicine, where they've been bringing doctors down here every Tuesday. Plus, we just started a mental health center. And we had an exercise program that got put on hold, with this pandemic, but we'll get that going again when the governor allows fitness centers to open. So all four of those things, those cornerstone blocks, were in place last February. We had good momentum, and we had just opened up eight brand-new apartments. It was a million-dollar project, and we cashed it out. Then we completed two more – so we had ten apartments in three months, all cashed out, ready for our people.

For me, I think the transition week was somewhere around March 15th. The schools had just closed, and I went to a party. It was my brother's 60th birthday, and we were still gathering at that point. I remember, nobody was even wearing a mask then. Now we were all in the same room together, multiple generations, and my sister, who is a teacher, said to me, "I don't think we're going back to school," and I found that hard to believe. It just sounded too severe to me, but she's a smart lady, and I said, "Really?" Then over that weekend, I think Monday is when the NCAA canceled the basketball tournament and, all of a sudden, the governor announced the pause that same week. So we were all hit in the face with this. The police told us

we had to keep our shelters open, and we were declared an essential business. We wanted to stay open, of course, but we certainly didn't want to risk the lives of our volunteers, and that ended up costing us 700 hours a week of labor.

We have 100 people on staff, and we decided we were keeping everybody, though we did have to close our thrift store. Now keep in mind, we never close. We're like a hospital, right? We're open seven days a week, twenty-four hours a day. People were working multiple shifts and all that. So we gathered with our residents, as well as with our graduates who are on staff. And we said, "Okay, we're up against it now and we're turning to you. City Mission can't look anywhere else. We're asking you to stand in the gap and get us through this." A favorite quote of mine is, "Crisis reveals." We learn a lot about ourselves and other people in a crisis – things we may never see in normal conditions. Some people dropped away, and I understood why, but many stepped up and stayed in that gap. What I began to hear, more and more, was, "It's my turn. You know what? Other people have helped me, this is my turn to be the one, to be the problem solver, to be the one who keeps faith." And then I started hearing people saying they had found a purpose in the pandemic, inside that crisis. "This feels good, this matters," they said to me. "I don't want to lose this." It became a crucible for putting our theories to a dramatic test in a short-term season. Our residents were so good that after three months, we decided to hire five of them to come on staff, and they're still working for us.

I think this pandemic has created a crossroads for Schenectady. Intense times cause us to do one of two things: to withdraw and surround ourselves with people who think like us, look like us, talk like us, and in whom we can find security because the times don't feel secure at all. Familiarity becomes our silo. Or the crisis shows us a different way, where we might say, "If we're going to make the future better than the past, we have to reach out more. We have to go outside of that silo, we've got to extend ourselves, and build something that's broader than it was before." I don't think you can ever say where you might go when you reach a crossroads, but I believe it begins with at least recognizing the crossroads moment. I'll paraphrase Lincoln here, "We're not enemies, but friends. We must not be enemies. The chords of memory will swell again when touched by the better angels of our nature."

If all we do is transfer one bad situation for another, where maybe the hierarchy's been flipped, I don't see how things will get better. One of the things that has helped us most at City Mission is sitting with our folks who are chronically under-resourced and saying, "There's a lot of people who *are* resourced, but who may not be your adversaries. In fact, they can become your best allies, and you can become their best ally."

For all our flaws here, and our flaws are legion, one thing we do very well is we recognize that the essence of community is not uniformity. It is celebration of not only the diversity, but also of the mutual benefit. There are a number of wealthy people who have formed friendships with City Mission residents, who will then say, "They gave me what I needed in my life." Likewise, the City Mission people, the ones who make it, often form really good relationships and friendships with people who are very successful. We all have to embrace that. At the end of the day, you don't want to replace one wall with another.

We had a graduation, where we did caps and gowns with masks, everybody spread out, but I got to say this to our graduates: "You kept faith in a pandemic, at a time when many successful people ran for cover. You kept faith." Then I told them, "You'll never have to wonder what's in you now. You will never have to ask that question. You've got it, there's greatness in you. And *we know* it's in you now. The next question you have to ask yourself is, 'Will I live and listen?'"

This has been a great challenge, hasn't it? And it will continue to be one for some indefinite time. But for all the struggles of this time, it has given us a groundswell. It has offered an emphatic boost to a theory that we have been developing slowly over a period of time, and we have acknowledged a quantum moment: we realize now we are never looking back – our people can do this.

Jim Salengo

*Executive Director – Downtown Schenectady
Improvement Corporation*

A t the end of February, beginning of March, we launched into our annual restaurant week promotion, which is always a big thing. That ended on March 7th, so we were able to get that in and provide a nice infusion of business for our restaurants. Actually, 2020 was set to be a dramatic change year for the Downtown Schenectady Improvement District, in a very positive way, because for the first time in our organization's history, on January 1st, we expanded our service footprint. We had worked all last year with our Board and with the City Council on expanding into three different areas. Our original footprint was one square mile, more or less – everywhere from Union College all the way down into the Stockade, from SUNY Schenectady Community College up Erie Boulevard to Union Avenue, up behind Proctor's and then up Nott Terrace. Essentially, that was the footprint.

So with all the new development that has been happening, we got approval to expand up to the circle in front of Mohawk Harbor and the casino, and then we also included the little Italy section of North Jay Street, and straight down Broadway from Clinton Street to Exit 5 of Route 890. Following the economic development patterns, we feel these are pieces it was important to connect because we want continuity of services and visuals and promotions to really position downtown as a bigger, more vibrant area with plenty of options. We're simply trying to tie it all together. I've been here at DSIC over twelve years and, I mean, there was just a lot of new, different energy and change before the pandemic hit. But I'll bet that most people in Schenectady felt the same way before this crisis. So at the beginning, we had to look at our organization and ask ourselves, "How can we keep doing what we're doing and address the major challenge of so many things closing down? How do we best use our resources and our mission to continue positive work in the face of really unprecedented circumstances? Where do we fall and how can we pivot like everybody else is doing?"

Looking at Governor Cuomo's guidelines, it became pretty clear that our outside program, which included cleaning and maintenance and garbage pick-up and a pile of other initiatives, was considered an essential service. For instance, any high-touch surfaces out there – like push-buttons to help you cross the street, or public benches – we had to keep those clean and safe. We used social media to let people know, "Hey, we've got your back. There's someone here, a group that's dedicated to downtown, and we're still working out there for you."

I put guidelines in place to keep our people safe before New York State even required them. I told everybody, "This is what you guys have got to make sure you're doing: wear a mask; stay far apart; disinfect whichever vehicles you're using; wipe down anything you touch; work independently, if you can; and try to take your lunch breaks at different times." It actually became a little point of pride that we could continue to provide a service even though downtown had kind of hit the brakes and there was nowhere near as much traffic. The fact that we could have guys out there, keeping an eye on the store, if you will, made us feel kind of important. Some people were still coming downtown, after all. There were properties we needed to maintain.

To tell you the truth, though, we had quite a few employees who opted to leave us at that time, and I wasn't going to make anybody do anything they thought might endanger them, of course. But then I also had some people who said to me, "Well, we've got to do our part, we've got to double down." So for a period, we had to regroup with the outside program and we did everything we could to just continue. We got a PPP loan because we're a non-profit. We usually rely on grants. And fortunately for us, last fall, Mary Moore Wallinger, who's a local landscape architect, along with Walter Simpkins, who runs Community Fathers, told me about a young man named Kenneth Brooks. He lives up the hill from downtown, and he was launching his own landscaping business called, I believe, *Ground Up*, that he was starting with kids from his neighborhood.

I got in touch with Kenneth and we brought on Kenneth and five kids from his group in early June. These kids are amazing. They listen. They ask questions. They work hard, they show up, they've just been a godsend. So far, I've been able to cover them through our regular budget, but also the PPP funds have helped. It's a win-win situation, and the fact that we were able to follow through from that original conversation last fall into this summer to actually bolster our program, it's just been amazing. Kenneth is learning some business practices, as someone who oversees the team, his kids are learning valuable skills, and we're helping the community, all at the same time.

A lot of people don't understand what we do. The primary job of business improvement districts is to make a place clean, safe, and attractive. First impressions are everything. When people come into your city, they want to get an idea of what the place is like. So if you have beautiful baskets of flowers hanging from light-poles and colorful banners, the initial message visitors get is, "Hey, this is a community that cares about itself." And if you're an employee in downtown, or a business owner, or an investor, you want to be in a place that feels vibrant, where you might think, *I can envision my business in this place.*

Residents want to be proud of where they live, and we try to help with that desire. One of the best things we do is our Hometown Heroes banner program. Usually, we hold an event in the Armory every June where we bring hundreds of people together, often with older veterans, and I can't risk putting all those people together in one room at this time. But it's important for us to keep that program going because it's so personal and because it means so much to the community. So what we did instead is we took out a full-page ad in the *Daily Gazette*, featuring all the heroes. Plus, we have a whole page on our website, and we've got bios up from the people who supply them, and of course we hang the banners all over downtown. We just couldn't do it how we normally do it, but it's really important to celebrate these Hometown Heroes, and this program does double duty – honoring the individuals, of course, but also building community pride and making our citizens feel more connected. It's beyond beautification. There's nothing we do on an annual basis that duplicates that.

The resiliency of the business community in Schenectady is very heartening to see. I've been so proud of these businesses that looked at the dire situation and said, "How do I make lemonade out of these lemons?" They found ways to offer their products and did drive-through service and offered family meals and just found creative ways to meet the needs of people in our city. I don't even know how to say it, but some of the extreme concerns that occurred in some other downtown communities didn't happen in downtown Schenectady because it seems like it was much more of an organic process here. Our mayor said, "We want to encourage people to be outside. We'll get rid of the fees. If you want to expand your outside, write up a little plan. We'll look at it and make it as easy as possible." I'm listening to some of the other county managers saying that their offices are being flooded with complaints and calls. How come this? How come that?

I don't have a crystal ball, but if things don't change dramatically, I just think we have to look at the overall mix of how we get funding for the DSIC. I see the outside mission as ongoing because the downtown environment needs to be maintained, but I do believe we will have to be as creative as possible with events that shine the spotlight on our business community. We have to be willing to pivot quickly, and give things up that may not seem to make sense anymore. Apart from a vaccine, which hopefully will work and which we'll have within a few months, people are not going to stay locked down forever, they just can't. Whether we all have to wear masks all the time or gloves, we will do that and continue to go out. This is the hand we've been dealt, and we'll continue to make the best of it.

Marcy Steiner
Vice President/Executive Director –
The Foundation for Ellis Medicine

A t Ellis Hospital, we had been looking at how we needed to reconfigure ourselves as a health system to address all the recent developments: the movement toward telemedicine; the changes in procedures; patients not staying
in the hospital as long and things really shifting more to outpatient care. All of those
and many others had accelerated over the last couple of years, and we were assessing
our responses. What did we need to do and what did we not need to do? And that's
where we were in February of 2020.

Then, through the New York State Department of Health and the governor's
office, we started getting the early coronavirus reports. We're fortunate at Ellis that
our Chief Medical Officer, Dr. David Liebers, is a specialist in infectious diseases.
He started his career with the AIDS epidemic, and became known as the primary
AIDS doctor in our region. With AIDS, Swine Flu, SARS, and Ebola, he has been
at the forefront of studying infectious diseases, and he knows a lot. Very scholarly,
extraordinarily well-read, he had been closely following stories and trends in the
medical journals, and he had us all watching the epidemic ramp up in Washington
State. The hospital there in Seattle put out an incredible white paper on their initial
response to the coronavirus, and some of the things they did around no visiting,
masking, all that stuff, we instituted pretty quickly here because Dr. Liebers jumped
on that. By the middle of March, of course, it became apparent to everyone there was
a pandemic.

After that, a lot of things happened very quickly. We'd read all the information, and we were trying to put systems in place that would be effective. Doing COVID testing – what does that look like? Okay, find the COVID test; get the re-agents for the test; partner with the health department in the community; set up testing in the parking lot; deal with multiple iterations of the COVID tests; establish protocols for all the different things. Everything was new, and everything kept changing.

It seemed like we were switching up our process every couple of days, because we would discover a little glitch here or we'd read this other report there, or the Health Department would shift its messaging, so we were always adjusting, always adjusting, always adjusting. Hospitals and healthcare facilities were required on a daily basis to send in very specific reports, detailing how many COVID-positive patients they were treating; how many COVID tests they had on hand; how many respirators were available and functional; how much Personal Protective Equipment we had; all of those items. We had to do that every single day, and it's where Governor Cuomo got all his great material. Then his office came out and said they wanted what they called the Surge Plan, because at that point, they were doing all this modeling about what would happen if there was a surge. And so we had to flex up, 100% to 150% in terms of ICU beds or Critical Care beds. So we developed an incredibly comprehensive plan to turn our pre and post-op areas into ICUs.

The culture in an acute-care hospital like Ellis is Emergency-Department-focused. You see a problem, you take care of it, all hands on deck, and you coalesce around that. If you've got a problem, you're going to fix it. People in pain come into the ED, okay, you're doing real-time assessments, and you're trying to come up with the best ways to solve their problems. That's very much the way a newsroom works. Early in my career, I worked for a Gannett paper in Niagara Falls. There was always a buzz in there because you were on deadline. You were always in a hurry. You had to push it, to get it right. You needed to locate three sources. You had to do all that or else they would kill your story, right? Well, an acute-care hospital comes really close to that culture. The tempo of an organization is predicated on the department that works the fastest, and when you work in an ED, that can be the most rapid-fire environment in a hospital. That atmosphere of necessity permeates the organization, and it's a different vibe than if you walked into a skilled nursing facility, for instance. Very different kinds of deadlines, right?

At our peak, we were treating an average population of around forty Covid-19 patients, although individual patients came and went all the time. We were constantly focused on safety, on keeping our patients and staff safe, of course. Now I can say that, but it's a complex issue. How, exactly, do you ensure safety in each and every instance? In terms of staff, we really encouraged working remotely, so that helped a lot for those who could operate that way. But for doctors and nurses and other staff who had to be hands-on with patients, working remotely wasn't an option, so how do we ensure safety for all of them?

For example, we had a staff member visit his parents in Chicago a few weeks ago, when Illinois was still on the permitted-states-to-visit list, and he had subsequently been back home for ten days when Illinois was suddenly added to the no-visit list. When he presented for screening at work the following morning, they asked him, "Have you visited a prohibited state?" He said, "Yes." Well, boom, the lights went off and people ran over: "You have to go back to your car. You can't even come into the building. You have to call the employee COVID line and you have to tell them what happened." Once he explained the situation, and they determined he had been home for ten days already and still showed no symptoms, he was allowed back into work. Our safety protocols had to cover everyone, and as new information came out, we had to adjust to it. You had to turn on a dime.

Our staff was really good. People felt protected. There were some times we ran low on PPE, and we were really scrambling, but the community was wonderful to us. Construction sites and Habitat for Humanity donated N95 masks. Local companies with 3D printers made face shields for us. We had one manufacturer in town who said, "I've had to lay off my crew, anything you need, we can help repair beds or whatever." Now when you intubate or extubate a patient, that can be dangerous because there's often respiratory spray, and with a virus spread by aerosols like Covid-19, it's a serious problem. One of our ED doctors saw online these intubation boxes that you could put over the patient, with a place for your hands, which could offer protection from that deadly spray. So we asked the manufacturing company, which typically fabricates with steel, "What do you think? Can you make us some?" We tested a prototype, they ordered what they needed, and they made us thirty-six custom intubation boxes. You can't ask for more than that, right?

One of the things that was very difficult on the staff was seeing the suffering of the patients. We have this one nurse who, with her friends, made patients care baskets with puzzles and things they could do because they couldn't have family visiting. Remember, it wasn't just Covid-19, a lot of patients were passing away from other diseases, too, and family members couldn't be there with them at the end. The chaplains were really extra busy because all of our volunteer chaplains had to leave. But we never let anyone die alone. There was always somebody there. And we would either set up a phone call with the family or provide an iPad so patients could FaceTime with them. Even with that, this time has been extraordinarily hard for not only the people who work at Ellis, but for everyone.

Our mission here is helping people, and providing life-saving care for the residents of Schenectady County and the Capital Region. And we're a big employer here in the city, so our economic impact is significant. We have about 2,800 full-time employees, probably the second-most in the city after General Electric, although the school system employs quite a few, and there are plenty of New York State employees as well. That doesn't count the physicians who come in and work at the hospital but who are not our employees. We generate between 400 and 415 million dollars annually as a business, normally, but not this year, not in 2020. Medically and financially, this has been a challenging time for us. In March, April, and May, we performed no elective surgeries, and we took really big hits. Revenue for all our hospitals – and that includes the McClellan Street Health Center, Bellevue Women's Center, the clinic at City Mission, the Breast Care Center, and the new Ellis urgent care facility at Mohawk Harbor – are 35 million dollars below budget. But we have a great new initiative coming soon, and we're more than positive about the future of Ellis Hospital and Schenectady.

I tend to be very optimistic. I believe that positive change can emerge from chaos, and that people won't change unless there's a compelling reason to do that. This year, we've seen some compelling reasons, that's for sure. I think that, by and large, people in this community are people of extraordinary good will, and they want to do the right thing. I think that we have to appeal to that goodness in people, and we have to all come together to drive the change.

Our generation is being challenged by these events. Have we gotten too comfortable in our own little world, and have we failed to see the other? However, I think it's very much the way atoms collide – when they crash together, there's energy released. So what I feel right now, although many people might feel anxiety, what I'm feeling is a ton of released energy. How we use that energy to make our community better will tell us if we have learned the important lessons of this time, and of what we have already accomplished in phase one of our local revitalization. That's what I see.

Ellis, Roswell Park Team Up

BY JOHN CROPLEY
Business Editor

August 12, 2020

Ellis Medicine will debut a significant expansion of its cancer care services in 2021 as it creates a new treatment facility in partnership with Roswell Park Comprehensive Cancer Center. Ells and Roswell announced the collaboration Tuesday.

A first-floor space at the main Ellis Hospital building on Nott Street will house a medical oncology/chemotherapy/infusion center when renovations are complete, and will provide access to advanced clinical trials of new treatments.

Founded in Buffalo in 1898, Roswell is the only comprehensive cancer center in the state north of New York City, as designated by the National Cancer Institute. Its affiliation with Ellis is part of a growing number of such relationships Roswell has established with local hospitals across New York State – the Roswell Park Care Network – to increase its reach and effectiveness. Its doctors will work with Ellis doctors and nurses to provide care in Schenectady.

Ellis Medicine CEO Paul Milton said the hospital must sometimes send patients as far as New York City or Boston if their needs can't be met with Ellis' current range of treatment options. "It's limited, which is why we're doing this, to bring in a partner with the reputation of Roswell Park," he said.

The partnership will greatly expand cancer treatment options at Ellis, Milton said, and eventually will lead to an increase in staffing. Ellis expects to invest up to $4 million building the suite, which will include twelve infusion chairs and six exam rooms. The new facility should be able to host its first patients in the summer of 2021.

Aneesa Waheed

Executive Chef and Owner of Tara Kitchen

Okay, I was working in New York City, not in cooking or anything like that. I was in publishing. After I met and married my husband, we wanted to start a business, but neither one of us were business people. We just knew that we didn't want to work anymore in a corporate setting. So we began selling imports from India, Pakistan and Morocco. It was easy for us to source, it was easy to open a boutique, and we decided to do it in Schenectady rather than in New York City, purely for cost. It was just cheaper to try here.

Our retail store opened in 2008, and while we were doing that, we had the idea to do food, too, so we started cooking food at The Greenmarket. Then that grew into a few different markets, the few different markets grew into a catering business, the catering business grew into our first location on Liberty Street in 2012, and from there, we expanded into selling our sauces. Pretty quickly, we dropped out of all of the markets because we really wanted to focus on the brick and mortar, plus we had two small kids. Most recently, 2017 is when our Troy restaurant opened, and last year is when we first started planning a new one in Guilderland. We've had good success, and we were actually gearing up for a pretty spectacular year.

The pandemic has slowed the progress of everything down, of course. Prior to COVID, we did maybe about 5% in takeout business at Tara, because it was never really a focus of ours. We've always been more of a dine-in, sit down, enjoy the food and the atmosphere – that kind of concept. And then it all went away. 100% of it went away. It was numbing. First, there was the shock of, *Does this mean we could lose the business? Does this mean that this virus could bankrupt us? We could lose a year. We could lose all our customers.* Those were our first thoughts. In terms of our finances, we have always planned for the worst, so it wasn't necessarily like, "How are we going to make rent next month?" It wasn't a fear of the immediate consequence, but more the long-term effects, and that fear was definitely real. We kept asking ourselves, "What if this continues three or six or eight months or a year and nobody wants to go out and eat and we have to shut everything down?" That idea was extremely frightening.

On March 15, the Governor said to close anything that wasn't an essential service, but that restaurants could be open for take-out. That was on a Sunday. Many people in the restaurant industry said, "We're just going to shut down until we can figure this out." So the decision I made was that I would take Monday – that one day – and determine how to stay open on Tuesday, instead of saying, "I need time to work this out." Yeah, I mean, the immediate thoughts obviously were, *We've got to save the business, because that's how we live. There's no other way to live other than to make income from here.* And then we also had to think about, *What if we get sick?* I think that was huge for us, because while everyone else was closed, we were one of the very few places open – even in the whole Capital Region, for that matter. Even now, look, people are wondering about restaurants, "Are they open or are they not? Are they dining-in or not?" We gained a lot of new customers because we just stayed open for take-out the whole time, and it helped us not lose a beat with our regular client base.

Of course, at the beginning, everyone was in panic mode. Nobody knew whether they should go out of the house, whether they should wear gloves, or if they should have a mask. Now, aside from that, for me the idea was if there was no mandate to shut down completely, 100%, we were not going to do it. That was it. We were not about to voluntarily lie down and say, "We can't do this." That was not an option. And so we didn't have a single day where we were closed. We pivoted the business immediately on that Monday, after we checked in with the staff, the crew – "Who's willing? Who's not willing? Who's able or not able? What do we need to do?"

At first, we didn't apply for any loans. Eventually we did. We applied for the Personal Paycheck Protection, the PPP. That first day, though, there was zero thought about any of that stuff. The thought was, *You have to stay open, and you have to follow every single guide.* And I also was very confident in knowing that just, as a restaurant, we've always been very cautious about how we operate and what we do because, obviously, any disease can start here. So right away we had to rearrange all of our setups. To do takeout is actually maybe a hundred times more work than it is to do dine-in. That created an extremely interesting challenge for us to figure out in our small kitchen. Where do you keep all the takeout containers? Where do you put all the food that's been prepared? Because normally, you cook the food, it goes to the table and you're done. But now you have to cook the food, you have to pack the food, you have to bag the food, you have to put on the seal, you have to shelve the food until the customer picks it up. All of that and, apparently, everybody wants to eat only at 5:30 P.M. So there were challenges with that, and there were a lot of other steps in this process that we were not used to.

Now our sauce business took off like crazy, because I guess everybody was cooking and eating at home. We saw a massive increase in sales there, but the restaurant and sauce businesses are separate, so one doesn't necessarily offset the other. We don't commingle any of that cash flow or debt. Either way. We've kept every building, every business, every entity, very, very separate and independent of each other. So at the end of the year, it may balance out. We'll have to see. However, the goal for me as a business person has always been to make every one of my entities operate as an individual. So if one gets cancerous for some reason, you cut it out without affecting anything else.

Closing the restaurants was never even a thought. The sauce business is a chunk of our ultimate bottom line, but it's not our bread and butter, and it isn't the bread and butter for our twenty employees. So even if, in my mind, even if we had to hit pause on that business, we knew we would just solely focus on keeping the restaurants. That being said, every statistic you will read will tell you every restaurant is maybe two days away from a close or shut down, simply because of how restaurants operate and how thin the margins are and how delicate and precarious the finances for a restaurant are. And just look, within the past five months, what's happened, solely in our area, forget even this country or state. We've had a tremendous number of restaurants already shut down. They're permanently closed, for various reasons.

Again, going back to the point that most restaurants are very precarious to begin with, if you're already at the edge, something like a pandemic will push you over. If you're already struggling to manage and maintain your restaurant, even two weeks or a month of no income could be catastrophic for you. So that's point one. Second, the uncertainty of a pandemic is very different from the uncertainty of anything else during regular times. Not knowing when it might end – whether it's going to last three, four, six, eight, ten, twelve, eighteen months – that makes it very difficult for people. When will our customers come back? When will Proctor's reopen? When is GE starting up again? What about City Hall being closed? How can you get your head around all that uncertainty? I mean, that's what the woman who runs Puzzles Bakery said: "There's nobody downtown. My entire business is lunch, with people working in downtown. It's been five months, and I can't do this anymore." Rather than dragging the process along, it's easier to just shut it down because at least then you're not incurring more debt. And now she's gone.

From day one for us, March 16th, it had to be all hands on deck, all the time, to make sure that we never even got to that point. That was our constant focus. Failure was not an option. Shutting a location down was never an option for us, either. Many people were afraid to pivot, and maybe some people believed the pandemic would be short-term. Many restaurant owners thought, *Okay, you know, my business really doesn't do takeout, we don't want do takeout, and it's scary out there right now. Since I don't know what to do, I'll just hide under this blanket and it'll probably be gone in a couple of weeks. By April, mid-April, we'll be back to normal and then we can ride it out.* Once you've lost the time, the surge, and the momentum, it's very hard to come back from that. And I heard what the administration was telling us, but I lived through 9/11. I know not to trust the government.

So many businesses here have already closed. Puzzles, Crossroads Wellness. Daley's is still not open. Their entire staff was laid off and I don't know what's going on with them. I think the lack of public coming downtown to work or eat or shop, not seeing people walking around, that's been huge for us. Then slowly starting to see these really small, very precarious businesses start to shut down, that's hard because Schenectady did so much work to try and revitalize the city. Metroplex, and the city, and small business owners – so many people spent so much time, money, and energy to try and bring Schenectady from the brink of extinction back in the early to mid-2000s. Are we returning to that bad time now, with fancier buildings? Who knows?

I predicted back in March that the effects of this pandemic will probably last about five years. That's my personal prediction. Again, I went through 9/11, and I went through the 2008 financial meltdown in New York City, and that's what my gut tells me about this. A few different and significant things have happened because of COVID-19: how we work, how we interact, how we socialize. What is important to us has changed because of this, and I think that will impact how people move forward even after the masks come off, even when the social distancing restrictions are done. This will have a life-long impact on people and I think that's why the changes will be pretty dramatic. You are going to see a slow-down in the economy because people have realized, *I survived five months doing X, Y, Z, and I found new activities or new ways to live and do what I need to do.*

Another impact is a lot of people might not even go back to work in office settings anymore because they've seen that they can make this work-from-home routine viable. But I also think those effects will be short-term, because everyone's on a high right now, thinking, *Oh, this is great.* And then in a couple of years, they're going to change to, *No, this sucks.* Because people are already realizing that not seeing people, and not going anywhere, and never getting a break from their kids, essentially sucks. There's a reason why we have a system in place which has worked for hundreds of years. But even in that short-term, people not going back to the office will have a massive impact.

This is huge, this is grand scale, this is nothing like we've ever seen, but this stuff has happened before in history. We've had plagues, we've had pandemics, we've had all the wars with their devastating effects on people. What I'm saying is that at every point in history, there's always been something that humans have had to overcome. Now something that's really hard is happening to us, here in the United States, and it will change us in ways we probably can't predict. Change is guaranteed, but I don't think that this is where we'll be for a long period of time. We will overcome this. I do know that the future will be survival of the fittest, just like the past has been. Everything is about survival of the fittest.

14

What's Next?

Over the past two decades, cities have grown as never before. Urban space has flourished across the globe as humanity rushes into an urban era. More than ever, cities are human magnets. Why? It seems that in the collective frenzy of the network, the death-of-distance theorists forgot something crucial to human experience: the importance of physical interaction between people and with the environment.

— The City of Tomorrow: Sensors, Networks, Hackers, and the Future of Urban Life

Carlo Ratti & Matthew Claudel

"Oh, there goes Chief Clifford, the man who shut down everything about community involvement in the task force. Good to see you, buddy. Fuck you," the woman shouted.

Police Chief Eric Clifford, Mayor Gary McCarthy, and the new superintendent of the Schenectady School District, Anibal Soler, Jr., were standing in the parking lot of the Trustco Bank on State Street on Thursday evening, August 26, 2021. Schenectady police officers, firefighters, and code enforcement employees, as well as representatives of the County Sheriff's Department, MVP Health Care, and Trustco Bank, were standing at tables, handing out free supplies and informational brochures to families. The loud woman led a handful of African-American compatriots – the majority of them angry women – along the tented displays, all of them capturing themselves and their abusive behavior on their outstretched cell phones.

"Look at all the police officers giving out stuff to black kids. Oh yeah, I'm the one you guys locked up for the chalk a couple of weeks ago. Who do I go to, to file a complaint? Aw, are we interrupting your happy event where you hand out free shit to black kids? As if you actually give a fuck," the leader of the pack ranted.

She had been part of a Black Lives Matter protest earlier in the year and had been arrested for scrawling obscenities on the walls of the police station in what she kept describing as washable chalk, identifying herself with that action: "Yeah, I'm the chalk bitch," she chanted again and again. Although Gary McCarthy had been standing next to Chief Clifford for several minutes, it took someone in the protest group quite a while to recognize him. Then the chalk bitch got really excited.

"Oh, not Mayor McCarthy. Oh, my god. With the police chief. Not Bozo #1 and Bozo #2. Yeah, me and McCarthy know each other. What happened with the community task force review board that I was on, when you guys said that we had no power in this space? I recorded that, you know." The mayor stood there, hands clasped low in front of him, looking at her as she babbled, not responding. Chief Clifford turned and moved away.

"Those things weren't made public. You literally told us that there was no space, no power for these people, including myself, and you let Chief Clifford, with such a loose rein on how to treat people, incarcerate me overnight for washable chalk and kill Andrew Kearse, but the thirteen demands were way too much for you. You don't have enough money for that. But the Schenectady Police Department has more and more money every single time I find out about it. There's money for this – to give hand sanitizer to black kids – but they didn't have money for the "Be a Youth Group" event that just ended at Jerry Burrell Park."

Andrew Kearse was an African-American man who died of a heart attack after being arrested in May, 2017, and the officer who drove him to the police station was investigated by a grand jury but not brought up on charges. The thirteen demands, reflecting the 13th Amendment which banned slavery, were made by the Schenecta-dy-based activist group, All of Us, and included its final demand, *Demilitarize law enforcement and defunding of law enforcement agencies with the funds reallocat-ed to Community Based Restorative Groups for conflict resolution and restorative practices and other community based services and solutions* – in other words, eighty-six the police department.

One of the group pointed out Liz Joy – a white, Republican woman who ran against Paul Tonko for Congress in the last election cycle, unsuccessfully – and the loud woman got re-invigorated, saying, "It must be disgusting to be you. You must go home at night and cry, bro," and then telling her friends, "She was just literally about to say the "N" word. She literally lost. What a fucking loser." Chief Clifford, clearly exasperated, told a reporter on the scene that he had no comment, but Gary McCarthy indicated the group's obnoxious behavior spoke for itself. "We're out here in a professional manner, trying to have a dialogue with the community," he said, and the protesters drowned him out.

The loud woman took a final shot: "They're trying to interface with the community, right? You want to know what was supposed to be interfacing with the community? That was the community task force review board that I was a member of and got mis-gendered and got told that I had no power here. It's funny, but is it funny that Andrew Kearse is fucking dead because of these fucking pigs? Fuck you. I hope you lose your fucking jobs. But let's not get uncomfortable. You're not going to lose your fucking jobs, because you're

white. God forbid. Actually, I hope you keep your fucking job in the middle of a pandemic." Finally, she raised her middle finger into the frame so her cell phone could overlay it on the people she despised.

Apparently, for extreme social justice advocates in Schenectady, it doesn't matter that Chief Eric Clifford took a knee with them to honor George Floyd, or that he marched with the protesters and held up a **Black Lives Matter** sign on Sunday, May 31, 2020, and announced publicly, "People in my profession need to truly empathize with how our communities feel about the police and police brutality. I want to lead by example." And when Governor Cuomo signed Executive Order 203, titled New York State Police Reform and Reinvention Collaborative two weeks later, on June 12, 2020, requiring every local government in the state that has a police agency "to conduct a comprehensive review of its department's force deployments, strategies, policies, procedures and practices," that served as just another catalyst: All of Us leaders issued their thirteen demands the same day, before Chief Clifford and Schenectady Mayor Gary McCarthy even had a chance to establish a community task force review board. By July 9, the City had already implemented policy changes in the department. "These reforms are just the beginning and, as community conversations continue," Mayor McCarthy said, "additional reforms and changes will be made and immediately communicated to the public." For the protesters, good faith gestures, police department policy reforms, and the opportunity for ongoing dialogue don't seem to mean much. For them, it's meet the thirteen demands, or else. This racial showdown has been coming for a long time and, regardless of what we may believe, policing in America will be put squarely under the microscope for the foreseeable future. Any assessment of a city's future must take social unrest into account again.

However, Schenectady has a right to be proud of its transformation. To go from a basically bankrupt city wracked by scandals to a tourist destination in just fifteen years is a remarkable achievement. Few cities of any size can match the speed of that recovery. A world-class theater that was left for dead more than once – Proctor's – has morphed into a wide-ranging entertainment collaborative spread across the Capital Region and includes a respected tech-component that builds Broadway roadshows, although a return to completely packed houses may not come for a while. Philip Morris has been able to hire about thirty employees recently, and *Come From Away, Dear Evan Hanson*, and *Cats* are among the shows scheduled for the upcoming season, if people actually attend. The drop rate for Capital Repertory's first show of its season, *Ethel Waters: His Eye is on the Sparrow*, was 38%. That means people bought tickets but didn't show up, even though Proctors Collaborative now requires masks and proof of vaccination to enter all its venues. Still, having a full theatrical season ahead is a vast improvement over the last year and a half.

A half-billion-dollar riverfront complex with two hotels, a casino, marina, and luxury dwellings – Mohawk Harbor – glistens where a sixty-acre brownfield once off-gassed, and helps to reduce the city's tax burden. A unique museum of innovation and science – miSci – is now talking about partnering with GE to showcase its current, futuristic marvels and designing its own travelling exhibits. A one-of-a-kind economic development authority – Metroplex – has taken a ghost town that was down to its last dollar store and created a glittering urban core whose success continues to spread in every direction. The city has been nurtured: trees planted; boulevard medians cared for; streets and sidewalks constantly repaired; bridge-trestles sculpturally high-lighted; hero-banners hung; hanging planters maintained; and walkability enhanced with street-corner embellishments. Businesses and responsible developers have provided thousands of new jobs and thousands of modern apartments that millennial professionals and senior empty-nesters are filling up in this city. A changing perception of the city is finally in the air. What is there not to admire in the rags-to-riches revitalization of Schenectady?

However, a city isn't just its shiny new face, and not all boats are raised equally by a rising recovery tide. Attention has to be paid at some point to all its residents, right? The pandemic has also changed our expectations now, in Schenectady and everywhere. The Delta variant has sparked a surge in Covid-19 cases across the country and, although Schenectady County can boast that almost 80% of its population has received at least one vaccine shot, positivity rates are climbing here again as well. The Trump era emboldened and encouraged monsters inside so many people that coarse discourse and violent confrontations have become the norm. Derek Chauvin murdered George Floyd in plain sight, and that event, after so many other heinous crimes against people of color committed by police officers, became the profound turning point that has sparked Black Lives Matter protests and reframed race discussions.

Who could have conceived that a bloodthirsty mob of insurrectionists would storm the Capitol on January 6, hunting for Mike Pence and Nancy Pelosi and other members of Congress, then brag about doing all of it on Facebook and other social media platforms? Partisan courts, day after day, are revoking constitutional rights that were legally secured fifty or sixty years ago, and are supporting new voter suppression laws to rig elections. And millions and millions of people refuse to be vaccinated to protect themselves and their neighbors from contracting a deadly virus that has already killed more than 700,000 people in this country, in spite of new mandates issued by President Biden early in September, 2021.

That number – 700,000 dead, and climbing daily – might seem abstract until we realize this pandemic has claimed more than 233 times the number of people who lost their lives in the terrorist attacks on the World Trade Center on 9/11. That profound tragedy cost us just under 3,000 lives, with desperate people jumping and so many crushed in the collapse of the buildings. However, the despair that follows slow-motion tragedies like a pandemic can be just as deep as the shock from a sudden event, and a general satisfaction with what we do and where we live can certainly be affected by that. A city remaking itself has to weather all these storms as well.

Hope has to be an integral part of city planning. Remember, on that terrible day in New York City, no one who was injured was triaged according to race, religion, political persuasion, gender, or body type: first responders and fellow citizens helped anyone and everyone who needed help. We are trying to survive perhaps an even greater time of crisis now, where our mortality is threatened and our social fabric is being shredded, and that earlier, unifying spirit of altruism could serve as a guiding principle.

People usually have a choice about what they do: they can act as agents of creation or destruction. They can choose to build something beneficial that supports human civilization or they can mindlessly tear something down. In Schenectady, luckily, the destroyers are a foul-mouthed few and the vast majority who work and try to help people are relatively quiet builders. Because of those builders, and in spite of the existential burden of a persistent pandemic, Schenectady seems in many ways to be thriving. That may be hard to believe, given the events of the last year and a half, but by many significant indications, it's what has been happening.

Jamel Muhammad, for example, works the same neighborhood streets as the angry protesters, but he has run one of the community-based services that are referred to in the activists' 13th demand for the last several years, with the cooperation of Police Chief Eric Clifford and others. In 2014, Jamel founded the Youth L.I.F.E. Support Network's "One Life to Live," a program focused on preventing violence before it occurs, as a part of the Schenectady Bridges Project started by Bob Carreau at the Schenectady Foundation. While "One Life to Live" is based in Schenectady, it also has to contend with outside influences, as Jamel explains: "Some of the violence and some of the things we're dealing with – gun violence, knife, domestic, or whatever – they transfer across county lines. If you have an issue going on with a group in Albany, once they start getting the heat on them, they can spread out to Schenectady County fast."

However, no matter where it originates, gun violence is a continuing problem in Schenectady, as it is in cities everywhere. When Jamel spoke at Mont Pleasant Middle School to a group of eleven-and-twelve-year-old boys who usually participated in Boys Day Out Youth Enrichment Services – a community program run by Assistant Director Dennis Green of Washington Irving Educational Center and Ebony Belmar, a social worker at Mont Pleasant – he asked them a series of questions.

"How many of you know someone that has been injured by gunfire?" Ten boys – nine hands went up.

"How many of you have a family member or someone close to you who has been lost to gunfire?" Ten boys – nine hands went up.

"How many of you, when you leave home and go to school in the morning, fear that you may not make it back home safe at the end of the day?" Ten boys – seven hands went up.

These are the children Jamel is trying to save, the boys who will be pressured to join gangs, the young men who might succumb to the lure of violence and end up dead, and whose younger brothers will have to remember, and raise their hands about, for some questioner in the future.

It isn't the same in suburbs like Niskayuna or Guilderland or Clifton Park. For kids in Schenectady, it's about trauma and survival, Jamel explains:

> This is where, when you talk about economic revitalization and neighborhoods, you have to take these things into consider-

ation. How are you going to deal with the trauma of a community? You can bring and build beautiful buildings all day. You can build all you want. But if you don't build people, those people will destroy the buildings that you spend money building. And this is why we do our part. Working with the young people and the older.

I know, and we know – my team, coming out of the same elements as me – know that unfortunately in the black community, prison is a rite of passage. If you went there, then you the man. You did it. You got the respect, you got the honor, you got everything. The only manhood that they could identify with. We knew that if we tried to just go at the young people and leave the older ones to their devices and to their attitudes, then we would be working against the grain.

Kids are looking at these guys that have the street honor and reputation, but we're saying, "No, you don't need to listen to that. Come over here, do the right thing. And we got you." So we wanted to go in and work with them, get them connected and reconnected with services, employment, education, housing. Work with their needs. And it wasn't just the individual. We identified the family needs that were there.

To reduce the cycle of homicides and retaliations in the city, and with tips about simmering blood feuds and potential hot spots supplied by the Schenectady Police Department and the Schenectady County Sheriff's Department, Jamel sends his outreach workers and violence interrupters into clubs and bars and onto the streets at night. He compares his staff to firefighters who will run into explosive situations that other people would run away from: tipped off that trouble was brewing, his colleagues "would go in and get the sense of what's going on, where it's coming from, why it's happening, and try to put that fire out, if you will."

Jamel and his people aren't the moral police. They want to mediate, not punish. "We know who the gun carriers are," Jamel says. "We know who the trigger men are. We know who was shot last night. We know who's responsible for the homicide, and we know why the homicide happened. And these are all things that we have in confidence with our clientele that is never shared with law enforcement or prosecutors.

We're not trying to crime fight and drug claim. That's law enforcement's job. Our job is to reduce the likelihood of injury and harm." And just to pick one year, Jamel remembers his people mediating in seventy-two separate conflicts in 2017 – situations that could have gone in any direction. But that's one of his biggest challenges in justifying his work: "How do you document what didn't happen? How do you tell a story about something that didn't occur so you can take credit for it?" At least many people in law enforcement in the city do notice and give Jamel credit. When it's relatively quiet, D.A. Bob Carney knows whom to thank, and Chief Clifford acknowledges, "That program has been great. We continuously try to get more funding for it, and the idea behind it makes so much sense."

The change in downtown Schenectady over the last ten years is so striking, and so visible, that smaller, grassroots concerns and projects that try to improve the quality of life for people who live in the city's neighborhoods often go unrecognized, but they all contribute to a city's happiness quotient. Camille Sasinowski, who heads the Goose Hill Neighborhood Association and holds monthly meetings the last Thursday of each month, lobbies the police chief, the mayor, and the City Council all the time: fix our sidewalks; improve business facades; maintain code enforcement; quiet partying, disrespectful neighbors; and devote a regular patrol car to our area to cut down on the drug dealing in Steinmetz Park and to arrest the shoplifters who steal food from the local Rite-Aid by hiding it in baby carriages. These are things that will never matter to tourists dropping in to play the slots at Rivers Casino but which can make a real difference in the daily lives of Goose Hill residents. Camille doesn't have to do what she does, but her neighbors' lives are definitely better for her efforts.

Pat Smith is president of the Mont Pleasant Neighborhood Association, and nobody would call her by her high school nickname anymore – Pat Pure Heart – because she's turned into a professional thorn in the city's side. When General Electric maintained a large work force in Schenectady, Mont Pleasant was one of its richest neighborhoods, full of employed, well-compensated factory workers in two-family homes. During the decades of layoffs, family after family moved out, renters moved in, and absentee landlords let many of the properties slip into disrepair.

Currently, about 60% of the properties in the neighborhood are sub-standard, and 87% of them are rental properties, but Pat has enlisted plenty of fire power to combat the problem. She urged David Hogenkamp of Metroplex to use Land Bank funds to demolish zombie houses. She corralled then-director James Flacke from Better Neighborhoods Incorporated (BNI), and Madelyn Thorne from Habitat for Humanity, and even tapped Mayor McCarthy's HOMES (Home Ownership Made Easy) program to enable qualified, motivated applicants to become first-time homeowners who will care properly for their houses and improve her community.

Remove the boarded-up eyesores, replace the rented wrecks with owner-occupied, well-maintained new houses, call the cops on the drug dealers constantly, and Mont Pleasant will lower its crime rate and live up to its name again, if Pat Smith has anything to say about it. "I get very passionate," she says. "I want to get up in the middle of Crane Street and shout, 'You idiots, listen up, this is what you can be but you've got to do it together, in numbers. You are entitled to a better life. Yes, it can happen. But life is not an entitlement program. If you want it, you've got to work for it.'"

Rosa Rivera initially founded the 501c3 Miracle on Craig Street in 2015 to renovate the defunct, 20,000-square-foot Carver Community Center in Hamilton Hill and to create a positive change in her hometown. However, since then, the non-profit organization has also grown into a collaboration of neighborhood residents "that is focused on health and wellness through physical activity, food and farming, and personal development and healing." Rosa's emphasis is on providing opportunities and resources that will raise the socio-economic status of African-Americans in her part of the city, and a newly-functioning Carver Community Center would help immensely. First opened in 1969 and inspired by the civil rights movement of the 1960s, the original Carver Center spawned several important and still-running community organizations like the Schenectady Community Action Program (SCAP), New Choices Recovery, which offers comprehensive addiction treatment services, and primary-care-provider Hometown Health Services.

"I know that people here are feeling like some of the developments that have happened are not taking into account the people who are actually in the neighborhood," Rosa explains. "They're worried that gentrification will kick them out." Hamilton Hill residents might acknowledge major investments like the Joseph Allen Apartments, for example, but they may not feel that kind of investment is intended specifically for them. They ask, "Who are those new, expensive apartments for?" while they point out trash piled in city-owned lots, root-cracked sidewalks, and pot-holed streets without adequate lighting. Rosa wants to give them something that's clearly for them. Miracle on Craig Street took ownership of the Carver Center in December of 2019, and it has been designated as a federal historic building. Rosa and her organization have raised $345,000 since then, enlisted more than one hundred volunteers, and renovations have begun.

The list of the from-the-bottom-up, unsung builders who are crafting a better future for Schenectady is a long one, and it includes people like Will Rivas, who directs the Altamont Program that works with ex-cons and runs the after-school C.O.C.O.A. House for kids, among other programs. Will also distributes presents to needy kids at Christmas: "To be able to go through the city on Christmas Eve and give gifts to 750 families every year," he says, "and to actually shut down traffic, I never thought I'd do that. Wow. When I was a kid, I used to get chased by police. Now they're on the bus, escorting me all over town."

There is also Will's mentor, Walter Simpkins, who started Community Fathers in 2000 when it was first named Father Time, and who literally saved Will's life after Will got out of county jail and was determined to commit suicide. Community Fathers grew out of the realization that fatherless-ness was a significant problem in the lower socio-economic community and that many men were showing up with problems that couldn't be resolved inside a support group. Family court issues, custody battles, and child support demands couldn't be simply talked away. So Walter incorporated Community Fathers in 2009, and it has evolved into a comprehensive fatherhood program that coordinates a range of solutions to drug dependence, domestic violence accountability concerns, and other real-world dilemmas. Bob Carreau of the Schenectady Foundation included Walter's organization in a city transformation grant to City Mission, and Community Fathers enrolled all of its members in Mike Saccoccio's Bridges Out of Poverty training so they could start to stack credentials. "You need credentials to be able to do things," Walter explains. "You might not have a higher degree, but that doesn't mean you've not been trained and certified to do things." Providing hope, a way forward, and a glimpse of a better future – that's what neighborhoods need as much as they need new economic developments.

Now Schenectady's schools will get a fresh start in a number of ways as well, and major improvements can't come soon enough to enhance Schenectady's appeal as a family-friendly city. The school district's reputation, inside and outside the city, has needed an overhaul for twenty-five years. In the fall of 2021, students and teachers will be attending classes in person again for the first time in a year and a half, and with a new superintendent.

On Wednesday, March 25, 2020, during the second week of school closures due to the pandemic, then Superintendent Larry Spring abruptly quit. Neighborhood leaders like Will Rivas were shocked: "I am having some trouble with the fact he did this now," Rivas said. "We have a world in crisis, now is the most important time to stick together and show people exactly what our communities are made of." Neither Spring nor the School Board would say why he resigned, claiming it was a personnel matter and all parties were constrained from using any "disparaging language." What was that code for? Seven weeks later, the Albany Times Union reported that, "An internal investigation prompted by a sexual harassment complaint" was the reason Spring left. For years, the Eric Ely craziness, and then this.

However, Spring did a lot of good, and his achievements are likely to be buried by whatever misdeeds ended his tenure. He initiated a lawsuit to obtain Schenectady's fair share of New York State Foundation Aid, and he worked hard to oppose prejudice and change entrenched attitudes in the district, broadening understanding of the chronic trauma that many minority students struggled with daily. Although a number of parents, teachers, and staff members blamed him for creating a chaotic atmosphere and an unsafe environment through enforced compassion or lax discipline for trouble-makers, his eight-year reign couldn't compare to the horrors of the Ely-Raucci era. As a matter of fact, certain parts of his legacy are impressive.

Just a year after Spring resigned, money poured into the district. A federal stimulus package, earmarking $38 million for Schenectady in March of 2021, was for Covid-19 relief and may not have been directly Spring's doing. But three weeks after that, on Tuesday, April 7, state lawmakers agreed to fully fund foundation aid for New York State's school districts, and that was a direct result of Spring's tireless efforts and the lawsuit he started. Schenectady's school aid would jump from $104 million to more than $147 million annually for the next three years. That extra

$43 million could reverse many of the Covid-layoffs and solve myriad problems, if we could actually rely on what was reported in the news. "The foundation aid is not fully funded, although that's the belief," the new superintendent explains. "It's being phased in."

An interim superintendent, Aaron Bochniak, held down the fort for over a year while a search dragged on. The school board finally hired a more permanent replacement in July of 2021, Anibal Soler, Jr., who seems especially qualified to lead Schenectady schools. Anibal left his job as superintendent of the high-needs Batavia City School District to come to Schenectady, but he has also worked as an associate superintendent for Buffalo City Schools, and as a principal and teacher in the Rochester City School District. Anibal was named by President Obama as a White House Champion of Change: Latino Educator in 2014 for improving academic outcomes in Rochester's East High School, which was designated as "persistently dangerous," just like Schenectady High School had been.

"Foundation aid is supposed to be fully funded," Anibal continues, "but now we have a new governor, so we'll have to wait and see. Remember, Cuomo didn't really do that last year – he just increased our funding, so he didn't get us back to full foundation aid. That's the hope, over the next three years, but there's nothing in writing. The legislature approved it, but there's no statute that says they have to fully fund it. Nothing is holding them legally obligated to do it. And obviously the federal money does help, but you know it's a one-time, non-reoccurring allocation – $38 million spread out over four years, so almost ten million a year – and we have to think strategically about how to use it. We want more staff, more teachers, more counselors, more social workers, of course, but those are reoccurring expenses and that makes it a little more difficult."

Being the first person of color to serve as superintendent in Schenectady, Anibal Soler, Jr. got an earful when he hit town, and now he has a whole lot piled on his plate. He understands that a number of helpful programs have been set in motion, and he's grateful that Larry Spring started equity work in the district. But an early challenge will be measuring the impact with students who have been away from the school for the last eighteen months. Are outcomes actually looking better for students of color? Are teachers feeling any more comfortable with some of those issues around equity and diversity and inclusion? Is it true that many administrators sat there in professional development about equity and didn't really engage with the information being presented? Did they just sit there because they were required to sit there? There's a fine line between mandating behavioral modification for employees and relying on intrinsic motivation and buy-in. Anibal knows he'll need to do some resetting to counter the culture of mistrust that Larry Spring left in his wake when he high-tailed it out of town.

Luckily, this is not Anibal's first education rodeo. He has wrangled teachers and administrators for years, and he came up through tough Rochester schools himself. "I didn't view myself as poor or having trauma, but I had all the same indicators on the trauma assessments that many of the kids in Schenectady do," he remembers. "I just looked for caring adults to help me through the system and advocate for me. And I'm someone who very rarely had teachers of color in my career. I did well because

I had teachers who cared about me."

Anibal certainly wants more teachers of color in a district where currently 80% of the teachers and only 20% of the students are white, but he isn't about to minimize those white teachers either: "As long as they're strong and they have great relationships and they know how to connect with kids, then you can still get good outcomes. We have to focus on quality teaching and learning, regardless of who is delivering it. It would be great to have more diversity, and we'll recruit for it, but we just really need excellent teachers who are trauma-informed and who know the different challenges our kids bring with them."

Restoring hope and trust in the district won't be easy. After twenty-five years of scandals and mismanagement, hidden crimes and tragedies – all of them generating bad press that scared families away from the city – there is widespread frustration and distrust. A lot of hurt emotions. A lot of people who didn't return and went on to teach and work in other districts. "We've got to reestablish a culture where people enjoy working in the Schenectady City School District," Anibal says, "and just try to become a district in good standing by 2025, where none of our schools are labeled or cited. I want to bring in new initiatives – after-school programming, potential clinics, food pantries, clothing closets, things of that nature – and make our schools the hubs of the community."

The future will unfold one basic layer at a time. For now, the plan, as simplistic as it may sound, is to bring the majority of students in Schenectady back to school. To actually fill the empty schools up again is the first step. During a Board of Education meeting on Wednesday, September 8 – one day before schools in Schenectady reopen for this school year – Anibal says, "Our mantra has been Schenectady rising, and that's what we're going to hope to do. We're going to rise up. It's a big challenge for us. It's a big day. There probably won't be a lot of teaching going on. There'll be a lot of, 'Hey, I miss you. I haven't seen you.'

So public safety in Schenectady, even with substantive policy reforms in place and a concerted effort to expand community outreach, will probably face unrelenting scrutiny and knee-jerk opposition for the next few years. The school district, with new leadership and more financial resources, has an excellent chance to serve its students more effectively and to shape a better educational image for the city. And in spite of inspiring, individual efforts to make life better in the neighborhoods, poverty, crime, and resentment in Mont Pleasant, Bellevue, the Vale area, and in Hamilton Hill could continue to present serious roadblocks to progress there.

Even before the pandemic, global polls to determine key emotional states for city residents in different countries have indicated that the number of people who are significantly angrier than they have ever been has reached record highs, close to 25%, and that people who feel they "face a lot of worry" make up an even greater number of respondents – close to 40% of those polled. The world is in a sorry state. However, many people also told researchers that "social support" – the knowledge that someone will care about them in times of crisis – ranks near the top of the pile as a source of happiness. In Schenectady, much of that social support is provided by four compassionate and involved foundations: the Golub Foundation; the Little Family Foundation; the Schenectady Foundation; and the Wright Family Foundation.

Price Chopper's Golub Foundation, which is the charitable segment of the Golub Corporation, has been awarding grants to 501c3 non-profits since 1981. But in addition to that, with a separate series of sustaining donations, Neil and Jane Golub have been considered two of the region's most prominent philanthropists for many years, active in supporting Ellis Medicine, Bellevue Woman's Center, the United Jewish Federation, miSci, Proctor's Theater, the Muscular Dystrophy Association, the Double H Ranch, the Schenectady Jewish Community Center, the Special Olympics, Union College, A World of Difference (an anti-bias educational program), the Breast Cancer Research Foundation, and many other important organizations.

Mark Little was an executive with General Electric for thirty-seven years, acting as GE's Chief Technology Officer and Director of Global Research during his last decade with the company. His wife, Terri, has served on the board of the Schenectady Foundation and has been involved with many local charities. Together, they run the Little Family Foundation, and their combined expertise qualifies them to support and help to implement a number of activities that range from Mayor McCarthy's Smart Cities initiative to a unique educational program they created called Rise High.

The Little Family Foundation started their Rise High program by recruiting a cohort of twenty-two local sixth graders and offering them a Science, Technology, Engineering and Math (STEM) curriculum outside of school, using Schenectady school teachers who are connected with Clarkson Graduate School and undergraduate "engineering ambassadors" from Rensselaer Polytechnic Institute. "The idea is we're going to eventually have grades six through twelve," Mark Little explains.

"We'll add a new cohort each year, build the program up slowly. The sixth grad-ers will go up to seventh, then we'll add another sixth grade class, and we'll keep going until we get to twelve. If the kids all stick with it, they'll go all the way through twelfth grade together."

Chad Kilbourne, along with four of his cousins, manages the Wright Fam-ily Foundation, which was founded in 1997 to provide funding for neighborhood revitalization, jobs and career support, education and social needs. Begun with a twenty-million-dollar endowment from Schenectady International, the founda-tion has provided more than 500 grants in the last twenty-four years, giving away about one and a quarter million each year, and is focused entirely on Schenectady at this point. That's where the greatest need is. "The poverty indicators in Schenecta-dy are worse in every way that poverty indicators can be worse," Chad says. "The population in the city is getting poorer and poorer. 20% of the kids in the school district move every year, for reasons having to do with poverty. Fathers aren't around, mothers lose jobs, families leave apartments because they can't afford the rent, and the kids end up in Troy the next school year."

Chad earned his financial and political stripes working for a large consulting firm, first in Manhattan and then heading the firm's office in Washington, D.C. for twelve years. After that, he spent seven years in the New York State governor's office, so he understands money and politics and what it takes to get projects done. And he believes a consortium of foundations will work better together than individu-ally. "We have to be adroit about playing our cards to leverage in resources in order to be able to do things that are big enough to move the needle in the right direction," Chad explains. "The thumb print of that thinking is really evident in the newest neighborhood library, for example, the branch in Mont Pleasant on Crane Street, which we all worked on with Carmel and Sharon."

Sharon Jordan, Mayor Brian Stratton's chief of staff, is a member of the Schenectady County Public Library's (SCPL) Board of Trustees, and Carmel Patrick was president of that board from 2015 through 2019. "All four of those foundations participated in helping us with the money that we needed to build the Mont Pleasant branch of the SCPL," Carmel explains. "With the Mont Pleasant branch, that was a perfect example of a public/private partnership. The fact that the four foundations

came together, along with the funding that the library system already had in place from the County and the State, was amazing. I think that's the way a lot of things should be happening more and more as we move forward."

Angelo Santabarbara, a New York State Democratic Assemblyman who shows up to serve meals at every Italian and Greek festival, or races from one ribbon-cutting event to another to honor important accomplishments, spoke at the opening: "I grew up here. This was my home for a very long time. My parents were immigrants and we all lived in one house with my grandmother and my aunt. I was the only one that learned to speak English. I credit my teachers, and I also credit the library where I learned to read. I learned to do things that enabled me to chase dreams and be able to be successful in life. So I can tell you, libraries make a difference."

Bob Carreau, Executive Director of the Schenectady Foundation, couldn't agree more, and all his efforts go toward making dreams possible for as many people as he can. In the foundation's early days, most of its money came through someone's will or estate plan, but now other foundations like Golub contribute to it as well. The beauty of those sources is their unrestricted nature – many foundations are hamstrung by donor-directed funds – so Bob is able to earmark his foundation's money to gain ground against what he sees as some of the more significant social issues in the community, and he prefers to do that collaboratively whenever he can.

"I think 2011 was the turning point for us,' Bob remembers, "when Hurricane Irene slammed into this area." The small, impoverished village of Rotterdam Junction, right next to General Electric's main campus, was inundated in that storm, and residents asked the Schenectady Foundation for help when the Red Cross and the Salvation Army pulled out after just a few days. "We changed from being a foundation up in its ivory tower, analyzing things and making decisions from above, to one that was on the ground, wading through flood-water, talking to people in the community, finding out what the real story was and doing what we could to help them. That really substantially changed us."

The Schenectady Foundation has supported Working Group on Girls, which sponsors Girls Day Out at the Glen Sanders Mansion in Scotia for middle-school girls and strives to help them grow up to be strong and healthy. The foundation has given operating money to Walter Simpkins' Community Fathers and provided managerial consultation to that organization. It has donated funds to Mona Golub's Music Haven series in Central Park, which brings free concerts of unique acts from all over the world throughout each summer, as well as to many other organizations that offer educational and aesthetic benefits to community members. Life for many people would have been diminished without Bob Carreau's concern and the foundation's aid.

Fast-forward to now, as the Schenectady Foundation, with substantial aid from the City of Schenectady, has recently awarded the first round of its Thriving Neighborhoods Challenge grants, four months after asking local residents to submit their ideas for improving their neighborhoods. "People want to change the appearance and environment of their neighborhoods," Bob says. Awards ranged from $800 for Canvas Murals in Vacant Homes to $55,000 for a Spray Pad Cooling Area in Woodlawn. All in all, the first round of grants totaled $250,000. "It's about creating pride and bringing citizens together to address their needs."

For many people who already live in Schenectady, especially the needy residents of the neighborhoods who may not trust that economic developments in the city are working to help them, Jamel Muhammad, Pat Smith, Bob Carreau, Rosa Rivera, Angelo Santabarbara, Camille Sasinowski, David Hogenkamp, Madelyn Thorne, Will Rivas, Carmel Patrick, Walter Simpkins, Sharon Jordan, and Mike Saccoccio, with the invaluable backing of foundation leaders, are some of the change agents who refute that notion. Often working in conjunction with Metroplex and the City, they represent the boots on the ground who prevent violence and get libraries built, the ones who save community centers and distribute gifts, the ones who demolish blighted properties and build new, affordable houses, the ones who rescue the homeless and train people for new jobs, and the ones who work consistently to forge bonds of relationship and trust. If the neighborhoods are improving, and they are, the people who live in them have all these stakeholders to thank for that.

More than at any time in the past, Schenectady's leaders now seem committed to giving residents the inclusive city they deserve. The pandemic has clearly illustrated that our health, our safety, our economy, and our fortunes are inextricably linked. At a time when many American cities are becoming more effectively segregated – by wealth or ethnicity, zip code or opportunity – Schenectady is diversifying its economic development efforts across a broader spectrum of communities and neighborhoods.

However, it's also crucial to remember what halted the city's skid almost twenty years ago and turned its prospects around. The central component of the Schenectady Metroplex Development Authority – that half percent of county-wide sales tax which ensures a continuous funding stream for economic development in Schenectady and in its surrounding towns – was a stroke of genius conjured by Bob Farley. In its first twenty years, building on the efforts of Schenectady 2000, there is no doubt that Metroplex and its development partners have systematically transformed a dying company town into a model of urban resurgence for Rust-Belt cities. Any pivot to rebuilding the city's neighborhoods at this point has been made possible by the successful revitalization of Schenectady's downtown.

The decision by Ray Gillen and Metroplex to focus on the Proctor's Block, one project at a time, is what sparked what has now become a remarkable economic comeback for the city. Proctor's stage expansion brought the biggest Broadway shows to town, from *Phantom of the Opera* to *Hamilton*, and theater lovers from all over the region flocked to Schenectady to experience them. New restaurants and bars sprang up to serve the influx of visitors, and older establishments were packed, first on show nights and then almost every night. Developers recognized real investment opportunities when they saw them and, within a few years, the city had a multiplex movie theater, an impressive array of new businesses, hotels, and apartment complexes, plus Mohawk Harbor, the planned community that combines luxury, harborside condominiums, townhouses, and apartments with two new hotels, restaurants, retail shops, office space, a fifty-slip marina, and Rivers Casino and Resort – one of the first licensed gaming spots in New York State outside of Native American reservations. And while the Covid-19 pandemic slowed progress down for a year and a half, Schenectady is once again roaring back to life.

Perhaps the most surprising development of all is the bumper crop of money headed Schenectady's way. The city won a $10 million Downtown Revitalization Initiative grant (DRI), in 2019, and Ray Gillen estimated that will allow Metroplex to leverage more than fifty million dollars in total investments. The city was also awarded $52.9 million over two years in the Biden Administration's American Rescue Plan, and half of that already flowed into Schenectady's coffers early in August, 2021. There is also the possibility of more federal money – between half a million and two and a half million – that would be specifically earmarked for broadband development.

That targeted award would mesh perfectly with Mayor McCarthy's Smart Cities Initiative. He describes the Smart Cities Concept as a program that will use new technology to gather data that can offer the potential for future innovation, with the ultimate goal of making Schenectady safer and more efficient. "What we're looking to do here is take and replace all the street lights with LED lights," the mayor explains. "That's a no-brainer, and it will save us a lot of money. But when we do it, we're going to simultaneously put optical sensors and environmental sensors on the light posts, forming a communications platform. With the sensors, that's how you get the data back to City Hall or to the police station to be able to use it, but it will also allow us to provide a Wi-Fi network for the community." Although there are Covid-related supply-chain issues right now, the city has been working with National Grid, who is laying cable and putting up more access points as they build out the network. The mayor thinks it will be operational in the next few months, and believes the Wi-Fi alone will be a game-changer for the neighborhoods.

In April of 2021, a survey by Realtor.com that was posted on CNBC named

Schenectady as one of the ten best cities for first-time home buyers, and the only city designated as such in the Northeast. With a median listing price of $210,000 in March, Schenectady ranked #3 in affordability, and it had the highest active listings percentage at 17.6 per 1,000 households. Coincidence or not, Schenectady's housing market heated up right after that.

The City Council manages the city's HOMES program to flip city-owned properties. Currently, the city owns 464 properties – the majority are vacant lots, but 183 have buildings on them. So far this year, the Council has sold 74 of them, for a total gain of $2.8 million. Councilperson Karen Zalewski-Wildzunas, an accomplished local realtor, has been in charge of managing the city properties for sale and acknowledges that bidding wars have been developing for a number of the parcels recently, and multiple offers above the asking price are common.

"People used to give zombie properties away for a dollar, or they would auction them off," Mayor Gary McCarthy explains. "One of my things here has been that we don't do that. We do negotiated sales, and we're getting 20, 30, 40, 80,000 dollars for some of these properties. People still have to put 25, 50, 100,000 in them so they meet code and get them up to what people expect in terms of living accommodations today." Even then, those refurbished houses will be well below the median price that won Schenectady its spot on the Realtor.com best-places list.

Young people have recently discovered Schenectady. Jeff Buell, who had worked as Economic Development Coordinator for the City of Troy, founded Sequence Development and merged his company with Redburn Development a few years ago. He predicts that people under the age of forty will soon become the largest demographic in cities: "Millennials, Generation Z, they don't want to live in a cul-de-sac, and they don't need two cars and two and a half pets and three kids. They got sold the bill of goods on the American Dream and it doesn't actually exist in the way they heard it would."

Redburn is a new breed of developer that doesn't consider ROI, return on investment, as the only important criterion for investment. The company believes in community partnerships, environmental sustainability, historical preservation and adaptive re-use whenever possible, and socially-responsible development that provides affordable and vibrant living accommodations. And that brand of business conscience seems to be working. Both Sequence and Redburn were doing about $20 million a year before their merger and the adoption of a shared, mission-driven aesthetic, and by 2019 the company was making well over $120 million. With 141 new apartments already finished in Schenectady, and 94 currently under construction, plus over 100,000 square feet of commercial space planned or already developed in mixed-use buildings, Redburn is one of the largest and most ethical landlords in Schenectady, and their apartments aren't the only ones that are fully rented.

Architect J.T. Pollard's most recent project, Mill Lane Artisan District, is a brilliant, adaptive re-use of the old Breslaw's department store building that included the replacement of several adjacent buildings in the 100 block of State Street just east of SUNY Schenectady Community College. The hybrid project tripled in cost from its original estimate and landed finally at $43.5 million.

Mill Lane contains a wood-fired pizzeria, a Bountiful Bread restaurant and bakery, a brewery named Frog Alley which can produce and bottle the beer from up to 14,000 barrels each year, office space on its top floor for a local tech company, and seventy-four apartments that rent for $1,250 to $2,500 a month. As in most of the Redburn buildings, all the apartments are rented. Farther east on State Street,

John Roth's spacious, new Electric City apartment complex is almost filled up as well. So are the condos, townhouses, and apartments down at Mohawk Harbor on Erie Boulevard.

Although Schenectady's population doesn't seem to be rising, according to the disputed 2020 census, over 2,000 new living spaces have been added to the city over the last ten years, and people continue to fill them up. Whether it's a result of the pandemic-inspired out-migration from large metropolitan areas to smaller metros like the Capital Region, or the simultaneous shift of businesses allowing their employees to work remotely, all indications are that Schenectady's demographics are changing once again, and a larger population would certainly work for Mayor McCarthy: "Schenectady is on the rebound, and we have the capacity. We're at about 67,000 people now, but we once had a population here of 100,000, so we have the water, the sewer, and some of the other infrastructure that can handle that level of rebound. And we have all those new apartments."

Vic Abate, Chief Technology Officer at General Electric's Global Research Center, sees all the new development as positive for the area: "We're bringing in probably 200 fresh-out-of-school Master's Degrees and Ph.D.s into our Edison Program, and they tend to communicate with each other. Ideas will just spread and flow in there. In Schenectady, you've got Proctor's, you've got entertainment with the casino, you've got the riverfront, and all of that would be attractive to our kids. How many of them will choose to live here? How do we get this city to be the destination spot?"

Improvements are happening throughout Schenectady, money is flowing into the city and the school district, and people seem to be energized again. So far, so good. But what about Schenectady's future? In the second half of 2021, the Delta variant has ensured that no discussion of the future anywhere on the planet can ignore the threat of Covid-19 and its relentless mutations. The people of the world either find a way to get fully vaccinated – or at least protected enough to establish an effective herd immunity, and soon – or we could all be overwhelmed by some variety of this quickly-adapting virus. The definition of public safety has to expand now to include not just police and fire protection but also health care. If we get seriously ill, will our cities provide adequate hospital care that can save our lives?

Ellis Medicine, of course, exists to provide that life-saving care for Schenectady. But in terms of health care advancements, an expansive branch of the Roswell Park Comprehensive Cancer Center in Buffalo, New York opened its doors at Ellis in the summer of 2021. Cancer patients in the Capital Region will now have local access to the expertise and innovation of a nationally-designated cancer institute, and can benefit from top-flight, life-saving oncology services without having to endure a long, debilitating trip to New York City or Buffalo.

As simplistic as it may sound, communities that can find ways of working together can produce significant changes in their cities if they identify worthwhile, inclusive goals. During its eventful history, the citizens of Schenectady have done just that: uniting to secure the nascent manufacturing powerhouse, General Electric, as its signature company; volunteering to save and maintain Proctor's Theater; beautifying the city and lifting morale with Schenectady 2000; using Metroplex in inspired ways to fashion a dramatic economic comeback and, most recently, shifting their focus to enhance and develop all of the city's neighborhoods, among many other endeavors. That instinct toward collaboration has renewed this city again and again in the past, and if Schenectady's residents can move beyond their differences, a better future is theirs to construct.

It turns out that a more global future has already arrived here, although most of Schenectady's citizens don't realize it. Perhaps that's because the city has learned by necessity to neglect the company that put it on the map over a hundred years ago, or maybe it's that some people still harbor old resentments about the period of layoffs that decimated the population and led to Schenectady's decades-long decline. Regardless of the reason, it may be time for the city to reconsider General Electric.

GE Power has always been based in the city, but since 2005, so has GE Renewables. The GE Research and Development Center in Niskayuna (R&D), is now called the Global Research Center (GRC). Engineers and scientists at GRC are working with government agencies, multi-national corporations, and research universities to tackle massive challenges and design real-world products that will literally alter key aspects of our current reality and possibly save millions of lives. And without much fanfare, GE has sunk seven hundred million dollars into its main plant in Schenectady over the last thirty years, making that campus vastly more attractive to a new generation of employees, many of whom have chosen to settle in the city.

General Electric is working on projects, right here, that could literally change the world. Vic Abate has run GRC since 2015, and one of the current initiatives there is carbon capture and sequestration, as he explains:

> When you think of carbon, CO_2, there's a constant carbon exchange between land and air, and the ocean and air, several hundred gigatons a year. Mother Nature wants the atmosphere somewhere around 250 parts per million, and what's happened is, with the use of fossil fuels and the industrialization of the world, carbon that was captured over millions of years is being released now in hundreds of years. That time constant is the problem, and the concentration in the atmosphere is now in the 400s and it's probably on its way to 600. That affects the thermal balance. So the first question is, how do you decarbonize the emissions?

In simplistic terms, you use sorbents, chemical sponges that absorb carbon when air flows through them. That's the capture part. Then you apply heat and desorb it, empty that carbon back into a salt mine or some deep cavern where it returns to where it started – that's the sequestration part. Because of GE's additive manufacturing and 3D printing capabilities, the company is able to create the contact, or filter, that holds the sorbent. After all the recent, devastating fires, the more powerful hurricanes, and the record rainfalls and attendant floods that have all resulted from climate change, any chance that GE can capture carbon dioxide at scale and get it out of the atmosphere is something worth supporting. And they've figured that potential solution out right here in Schenectady County.

There's far more to what GE is currently tackling, including working with Verizon to apply 5G technology to tele-health, shifting the point of care to the patient, or with the Navy to use that same 5G technology to revolutionize how inventory in giant warehouses is tallied – reducing a cumbersome process that now takes a year to an improved one that can do the same job in just a few minutes. The applications are endless, and the visionary ideas and products coming out of GRC are the stuff of science fiction. Could this be the best time to dismiss the past grudges and work together to make Schenectady's present era better? What will happen if the city embraces the healing future that General Electric is working toward?

"That 45,000 to 5,000 shift, all those lost jobs, that sucked," Vic Abate admits. "But it's ancient history. So now, let's play forward."

Bibliography

Alexievich, Svetlana. *Voices from Chernobyl: The Oral History of a Nuclear Disaster*. Picador, 2006.

Algren, Nelson. *Chicago: City on the Make*. University of Chicago Press, 2011.

Anderson, Sam. *Boomtown: The Fantastical Saga of Oklahoma City, Its Chaotic Founding, Its Apocalyptic Weather, Its Purloined Basketball Team, and the Dream of Becoming a World-Class Metropolis*. Crown, 2019.

Antonelli, Henry and Quirini, Helen. *The Story of Local 301, IUE-AFL-CIO: Reflections*. Local 301, 1987.

Bissinger, Buzz. *A Prayer for the City*. Vintage, 1998.

Blackwelder, Julia Kirk. *Electric City: General Electric in Schenectady*. Texas A&M Press, 2014.

de Botton, Alain. *The Architecture of Happiness*. Vintage, 2008.

Buchwald, Emilie (ed.). *Toward the Livable City*. Milkweed Editions, 2003.

Buell, Bill. *George Lunn: The 1912 Socialist Victory in Schenectady*. Troy Book Makers, 2019.

Buell, Bill. *Historic Schenectady County: A Bicentennial History*. Historical Publishing Network, 2009.

Caro, Robert A. *The Power Broker: Robert Moses and the Fall of New York*. Vintage, 1975.

Caro, Robert A. *Working: Researching, Interviewing, Writing*. Knopf, 2019.

Chakrabarti, Vishaan. *A Country of Cities: A Manifesto for an Urban America*. Metropolis Books; 2013.

Churella, Albert J. *Success That Didn't Last: The Decline and Fall of the American Locomotive Company in the Diesel Locomotive Industry*. Schenectady Heritage Area, 2001.

Cornett, Mick. *The Next American City: The Big Promise of Our Midsize Metros*. Putnam, 2018.

Desmond, Matthew. *Evicted: Poverty and Profit in the American City*. Crown, 2017.

DeVol, Philip E. and Krebs, Eugene K. *Bridges Across Every Divide: Policy and Practices to Reduce Poverty and Build Communities*. Aha! Process, 2018.

Dyja, Thomas. *New York, New York, New York: Four Decades of Success, Excess, and Transformation*. Simon & Schuster, 2021.

Eaton, Susan. *The Children in Room E4: American Education on Trial*. Algonquin, 2009.

Florida, Richard. *The New Urban Crisis: How Our Cities Are Increasing Inequality, Deepening Segregation, and Failing the Middle Class and What We Can Do About It*. Basic Books, 2017.

Florida, Richard. *The Rise of the Creative Class*. Basic Books, 2002.

Florida, Richard. *Who's Your City? How the Creative Economy Is Making Where to Live the Most Important Decision of Your Life*. Basic Books; 2009.

Ford, Kristina. *The Trouble with City Planning: What New Orleans Can Teach Us*. Yale University Press, 2010.

Frank, Thomas. *Rendezvous with Oblivion: Reports from a Sinking Society*. Metropolitan Books, 2018.

Frieden, Bernard J. and Sagalyn, Lynne B. *Downtown, Inc.: How America Rebuilds Cities*. MIT Press; 1991.

Friedman, Benjamin M. *The Moral Consequences of Economic Growth*. Knopf, 2005.

Garreau, Joel. *Edge City: Life on the New Frontier*. Anchor Books, 1992.

Garvin, Alexander. *The American City: What Works, What Doesn't*. McGraw-Hill, 2013.

Glaeser, Edward L. *Triumph of the City: How Our Greatest Invention Makes Us Richer, Smarter, Greener, Healthier, and Happier*. Penguin, 2012.

Goetz, Edward G. *Clearing the Way: Deconcentrating the Poor in Urban America*. Rowman & Littlefield, 2003.

Goldhagen, Sarah Williams. *Welcome to Your World: How the Built Environment Shapes Our Lives*. Harper, 2017.

Goldstein, Amy. *Janesville: An American Story*. Simon & Schuster, 2017.

Graham, Wade. *Dream Cities: Seven Urban Ideas That Shape the World*. Harper, 2017.

Gratz, Roberta Brandes. T*he Living City: How America's Cities Are Being Revitalized by Thinking Big in a Small Way*. Wiley, 1995.

Gratz, Roberta Brandes, with Mintz, Norman. *Cities Back from the Edge: New Life for Downtown*. Wiley, 2008.

Green, Hardy. *The Company Town: The Industrial Edens and Satanic Mills that Shaped the American Economy*. Basic Books, 2010.

Greenberg, Ken. *Walking Home: The Life and Lessons of a City Builder*. Random House Canada, 2011.

Grogan, Paul and Proscio, Tony. *Comeback Cities: A Blueprint for Urban Neighborhood Revival*. Basic Books, 2001.

Gryta, Thomas and Mann, Ted. *Lights Out: Pride, Delusion, and the Fall of General Electric*. Mariner Books, 2020.

Halberstam, David. *The Fifties*. Open Road Media, 2012.

Hammond, John Winthrop. *Men and Volts*. J.B. Lippencott, 1941.

Hareven, Tamara K. and Langenbach, Randolph. *Amoskeag: Life and Work in an American Factory City*. Pantheon, 1978.

Hart, Larry. *Schenectady: Changing with the Times*. Donning Co., 1988.

Hart, Larry. *Tales of Old Schenectady*. Old Dorp Books, 1976.

Hayden, Dolores. *Redesigning the American Dream*. W.W. Norton, 1986.

Hedges, Chris. *America: The Farewell Tour*. Simon & Schuster, 2018.

Henri, Robert. *The Art Spirit*. Silver Street Media, 2011.

Hicks, Granville. *Small Town*. Macmillan, 1947.

Jacobs, Jane. *The Death and Life of Great American Cities*. Modern Library, 2011. *Citizen Jane: Battle for the City*. Documentary, 2017.

Katz, Bruce and Nowak, Jeremy. *The New Localism: How Cities Can Thrive in the Age of Populism*. Brookings Institution Press, 2018.

Kotlowitz, Alex. *The Other Side of the River*. Anchor, 1999.

Krieger, Alex. *City on a Hill: Urban Idealism in America from the Puritans to the Present*. Belknap Press, 2019.

Kunstler, James Howard. *The City in Mind: Notes on the Urban Condition*. Free Press, 2003.

Kunstler, James Howard. *The Geography of Nowhere: The Rise and Decline of America's Man-Made Landscape*. Free Press, 1994.

Kunstler, James Howard. *Home from Nowhere: Remaking Our Everyday World for the 21ˢᵗ Century*. Touchstone Press, 1998.

Kuykendall, Mary. *Rebuilding the GE House Jack Blew Down*. CreateSpace, 2015.

Landry, Charles. *The Art of City Making*. Routledge, 2006.

Lessard, Suzannah. *The Absent Hand: Reimagining Our American Landscape*. Counterpoint, 2019.

Lesy, Michael. *Wisconsin Death Trip*. Pantheon Books, 1973.

Levinson, Marc. *The Great A&P and the Struggle for Small Business in America*. Marc Levinson, 2019.

Lovrich, Richard and Eck, Michael. *Encore: Proctor's at 90*. North Country Books, 2016.

Marston, William Moulton. *F.F. Proctor – Vaudeville Pioneer*. Read Books, 2016.

Mayer, Martin. *The Builders: Houses, People, Neighborhoods, Governments, Money*. W.W. Norton & Co., 1978.

Medoff, Peter and Sklar, Holly. *Streets of Hope: The Fall and Rise of an Urban Neighborhood*. South End Press, 1999.

Mitchell, Lawrence E. *Stacked Deck: A Story of Selfishness in America*. Temple University Press, 1998.

Moe, Richard and Wilkie, Carter. *Changing Places: Rebuilding Community in the Age of Sprawl*. Henry Holt & Co., 1997.

Montgomery, Charles. *Happy City: Transforming Our Lives Through Urban Design*. Farrar, Straus and Giroux, 2014.

Moore, Arthur Cotton. *The Powers of Preservation*. McGraw-Hill, 1998.

Morris, Edmund. *Edison*. Random House, 2019.

Moskowitz, Peter. *How to Kill a City: Gentrification, Inequality, and the Fight for the Neighborhood*. Bold Type Books, 2018.

Moss, Jeremiah. *Vanishing New York: How a Great City Lost Its Soul*. Dey Street Books, 2018.

Mumford, Lewis. *Art and Technics*. Columbia University Press, 2000.

Mumford, Lewis. *The City in History*. Mariner Books, 1968.

Norquist, John O. *The Wealth of Cities: Revitalizing the Centers of American Life*. Basic Books, 1998.

O'Boyle, Thomas F. *At Any Cost: Jack Welch, General Electric, and the Pursuit of Profit.* Knopf, 1998.

Pollak, Marcus and Rutkowski, Ed. *The Urban Transition Zone: A Place Worth a Fight.* Patterson Park Community Development Corp., 1998.

Putnam, Robert D. *Bowling Alone: The Collapse and Revival of American Community.* Simon & Schuster, 2000.

Quirini, Helen. *Helen Quirini and General Electric: A Personal Memoir of World War II.* 1987.

Rabrenovic, Gordana. *Community Builders: A Tale of Neighborhood Mobilization in Two Cities.* Temple University Press, 1996.

Rae, Douglas W. *City: Urbanism and Its End.* Yale University Press, 2005.

Ratti, Carlo and Claudei, Matthew. *The City of Tomorrow: Sensors, Networks, and the Future of Urban Life.* Yale University Press, 2016.

Reding, Nick. *Methland: The Death and Life of an American Small Town.* Bloomsbury, 2010.

Reynolds, Jackie, Ott, Jim, et al. *From Vision to Action: Best Practices to Reduce the Impact of Poverty in Communities, Education, Healthcare, and More.* Peer Reviewed Articles and Interviews. Aha! Process, 2012.

Roach, Craig R. *Simply Electrifying: The Technology That Transformed the World, from Benjamin Franklin to Elon Musk.* BenBella Books, 2017.

Robb, Walt. *Taking Risks: Getting Ahead in Business and Life.* Meadow Brook Farm Publishing, 2014.

Rogers, Richard. *Cities for a Small Planet.* Basic Books, 1998.

Rose, Jonathan F. P. *The Well-Tempered City: What Modern Science, Ancient Civilizations, and Human Nature Teach Us About the Future of Urban Life.* Harper Wave, 2016.

Rosner, Elizabeth. *Electric City.* Counterpoint, 2014.

Rudofsky, Bernard. *Streets Are for People: A Primer for Americans.* Doubleday, 1969.

Rybczynski, Witold. *City Life: Urban Expectations in a New World.* Scribner, 1996.

Rybczynski, Witold. *Makeshift Metropolis: Ideas about Cities.* Scribner, 2011.

Schuyler, David. *A City Transformed: Redevelopment, Race, and Suburbanization in Lancaster, Pennsylvania, 1940-1980.* Penn State Univ. Press, 2002.

Sennett, Richard. *Building and Dwelling: Ethics for the City.* Farrar, Straus and Giroux, 2019.

Slater, Robert. *Jack Welch and the GE Way.* McGraw-Hill, 1998.

Smith, Monica L. *Cities: The First 6,000 Years.* Penguin Books, 2019.

Speck, Jeff. *Walkable City: How Downtown Can Save America, One Step at a Time.* North Point Press, 2013.

Spencer, Chris. *Shovel Ready: Razing Hopes, History, and a Sense of Place.* (Master's thesis; MIT, 2011) Schenectady Digital History Archive, 2015.

Steinbrenner, Richard T. *The American Locomotive Company: A Centennial Remembrance.* On Track Publishers, 2003.

Stross, Randall. *The Wizard of Menlo Park: How Thomas Alva Edison Invented the Modern World*. Crown, 2008.

Townsend, Anthony M. *Big Data, Smart Cities, and the Quest for a New Utopia*. W.W. Norton & Co., 2013.

Welch, Jack. *Jack: Straight from the Gut*. Grand Central Publishing, 2003.

Welch, Jack. *Winning*. HarperCollins e-books, 2009.

Whitehead, Colson. *The Colossus of New York: A City in Thirteen Parts*. Knopf Doubleday, 2004.

Wilson, Ben. *Metropolis: A History of the City, Humankind's Greatest Invention*. Doubleday, 2020.

Young, Gordon. *Teardown: Memoir of a Vanishing City*. University of California Press; 2013.

Acknowledgments

The only simple aspect of this book, for me, is its origin. Almost four years ago, Mona Golub asked me if I would write a book for her father, Neil, to celebrate an important birthday. Her idea envisioned some kind of memoir, perhaps including his insights about running a successful supermarket corporation but – big surprise – Neil wanted to do something else. "There's only one thing I care about," Neil said when we met at his office. "That's the economic revitalization of Schenectady." This was back near the end of 2018, before the pandemic changed so much about the world, when Schenectady's revival was hitting on all cylinders.

"That's a village-of-the-happy-people book," I said to Neil. "Everybody wants to live in that story, but not many people want to read it." I told him my specialty wasn't necessarily happy books, and suggested that if he wanted me to chronicle the roller-coaster ride of Schenectady's last thirty years, with some broad background exposition about General Electric and Proctor's Theater and other key elements of the city's history woven in – a much larger undertaking – then I'd be interested. To my astonishment, Neil agreed, and then the actual work of finding the compelling narrative thread in this urban business book began.

Storytelling has always been a communal process, and I knew from the outset that I wanted to include a lot of different voices in the book. That's why there are ample quotes, as well as separate blocks of monologue throughout the chapters. While I didn't want to do an exclusive oral history a la Studs Terkel or Svetlana Alexievich, I was thrilled to devote the longest chapter to a series of dramatic monologues that effectively captured a sense of what Schenectady went through during the initial eight months of the coronavirus pandemic. This is a story about a community, and I hoped the reader would feel closer to Schenectady through hearing the voices of so many community members. As I learned, it took a lot of people to save this city.

With that in mind, telling the story of Schenectady's economic revitalization could never have happened without the generosity of the people in this community who agreed to share with me their individual experiences and their recollections of events in the city's history. At the top of that list, of course, sit Neil and Mona Golub. Neil's focused belief that the tale of Schenectady's comeback could serve as a valuable model for other struggling cities, along with his advice and patronage, made this multi-year project possible. Without the Golubs, I would have never tackled this task.

Next in line for my gratitude are the 107 people who agreed to be interviewed, some of them – like Vic Abate, Stephen Ainlay, Ebony Belmar, Bob Carreau, Eric Clifford, Jim Duggan, Bob Farley, Ray Gillen, Frank Gilmore, Neil Golub, Chris Hunter, Al Jurczynski,

Jayme Lahut, Angelo Mazzone, Gary McCarthy, Philip Morris, Will Rivas, Mike Saccoccio, Jim Salengo, Marilyn Sassi, and Marcy Steiner – two or even three times. And I would not have been able to secure interviews with many people without the introductions made by Bob Carreau, Neil Golub, Jayme Lahut, Gary McCarthy, Nicole Parisi and Angelo Santabarbara, Everyone I interviewed not only told me plenty of things I didn't know, and probably would not have learned from other kinds of reporting and research, but they also helped me along the confusing path of finding the elusive story. People spoke to me honestly and usually at length: the transcriptions of the more than 130 total interviews ran to over 7,000 pages.

There are almost 100 illustrations and photographs in *Metrofix*, and the following people and organizations more than generously provided photographs and steered me toward images I may not have found on my own:

- Ray Gillen, Jayme Lahut and Jennifer Medler at Metroplex
- Richard Lovrich and Philip Morris at Proctor's
- Dave Buicko at the Galesi Group
- Le Grande Serras for his classic shot of him with President Reagan
- Chris Leonard at the Efner Center
- The staff of the Schenectady County Historical Society
- Chris Hunter at miSci
- Debbie DeLuke and Kim Perone from Schenectady 2000
- Most of all, John DeAugustine and Miles Reed at the *Daily Gazette* gave me permission to use as many of their wonderful photographs and articles as I needed to help tell this story, plus Jeff Wilkin and Bill Buell combed through the *Gazette* photo archives and tracked some down for me. I honor all of them for their generosity here.

Apart from the interviews I conducted, my other major sources of information were news articles, organization reports, city plans, legislative records, diaries, dissertations, city budgets and, of course, all the books in my Bibliography, although there aren't too many nonfiction books on Schenectady's history except the ones written by Bill Buell, Larry Hart, Chris Leonard, and the various authors who chronicled General Electric's long story. I want to thank Don Ackerman for voluminous documents and clippings from Karen Johnson's records as mayor and Metroplex board member; the City of Schenectady for its trove of urban plans; Jim Duggan and Le Grande Serras for Canal Square planning charts, brochures, maps, and news clippings; Roger Hull for excellent close reading and suggestions; Chris Hunter for invaluable General Electric information; Al Jurczynski for materials on the Guyanese influx; Jayme Lahut for Metrofix transcripts and videos; Cathy Lewis for the Schenectady School

District's "Changing in Schenectady" reports; Brian Merriam for a video-cassette-tour of mid-1980s downtown Schenectady; Philip Morris for all of Proctor's Expansion Project studies and for "Combative;" Steve Strichman for early Schenectady 2000 booklets; and Chuck Thorne for thirty-three years of city budgets.

Finally, this book wouldn't exist without the production and marketing team of Lisa Comstock, Mona Golub, Jennifer Kenneally, Phil Pascuzzo, Carmel Patrick, Susan Petrie, Jonathan Pierce, and Nick Yetto – all of them creative powerhouses. And it wouldn't be half as good without the careful readings of, and the excellent suggestions by, Bill and Terri Roller, Michael White, and Carmel Patrick – my first readers – although Carmel may claim I don't make most of the changes she thinks I should.

Contributors

VICTOR ABATE was President and CEO of General Electric Renewable Energy from 2005 to 2013 in Schenectady, and is currently Senior Vice President and Chief Technology Officer at GE's Global Research Center in Niskayuna, New York.

B. DONALD ACKERMAN had a thirty-year career teaching Social Studies to middle-schoolers and has had an almost sixty-year involvement with politics. His political history involves running and being elected to office, helping others to get elected, and holding a number of political party positions. Don was Minority Leader of the Schenectady County Legislature when Schenectady's Metroplex was created and adopted.

STEPHEN CHARLES AINLAY, Ph.D., President Emeritus, Union College served as Union College's 18th President. He began his service in 2006 and stepped down after twelve years in 2018. Before joining Union, he had served for twenty-three years at the College of the Holy Cross in Worcester, MA. where he was Vice President for Academic Affairs and Dean of the College. A sociologist of knowledge, Ainlay has published in the areas of aging, religion, and disabilities.

GEORGE A. AMEDORE JR. represented the 105th District in the New York State Assembly from 2007 to 2013 and, until 2020, represented the 46th District in the New York State Senate. He is currently a businessman and homebuilder in Rotterdam, New York.

EBONY BELMAR is a social worker at Mont Pleasant Middle School in the Schenectady City School District, has been awarded the "Roots and Wings" award as one of the founding mothers of Working Group on Girls, and serves as vice president of Boys Day Out.

KAREN BRADLEY, earning her M.L.S. from SUNY Albany in 1981, worked as a rural hospital services librarian for Albany Medical College for five years and as a reference librarian for Schenectady County Public Library (SCPL) from 2000 until 2012. Karen was appointed by the Schenectady County Legislature to serve as Library Director of the SCPL in October of 2012, and she has been excelling in that position for the last nine years.

JAMES A. BRADSHAW became a Schenectady police officer in 1980 and worked on the force for twenty-six years, most of them in Hamilton Hill. He is currently a judge on the Justice Court in Rotterdam, New York.

STEVE BRANSFIELD was in charge of operations and responsible for union activities for General Electric's power business in Schenectady between 1993 and 2005. He represented GE on the committee of local executives and attorneys who worked with Schenectady 2000 throughout the 1990s.

DENISE BRUCKER served on the Schenectady City Council the first time from 1998 to 2005. She then returned to it in 2006, chaired the Council in 2012, and retired from it in 2014.

BILL BUELL is a Schenectady County native who spent forty-one years as a journalist at the *Daily*

Gazette. He has won numerous writing awards, including a 2018 New York Press Association award for his contribution to a *Gazette* series on the history of the General Electric Company. He has written books on Schenectady and Albany County, as well as *"George Lunn: The 1912 Socialist Victory in Schenectady."*

JEFF BUELL founded Sequence Development in 2013 after spearheading economic development efforts for Troy, New York. In 2016, Jeff was named the Entrepreneur of the Year by the Capital Region Chamber of Commerce. He is currently a principal with Redburn Development Partners.

DAVID BUICKO was appointed Chief Operating Officer of the Galesi Group in 1986 and elected as President and Chief Executive Officer in 2016. He is responsible for the day to day operations of all the company's divisions, including commercial real estate, industrial parks, distribution, and logistics.

ROBERT M. CARNEY has been the Schenectady County District Attorney since January of 1990, having been first elected in November of 1989. He is now in his 29th year of continuous service in that position, having been re-elected seven times. Mr. Carney is also a hands-on prosecutor who has personally tried dozens of cases, including the notorious case of Steven Raucci, who terrorized his enemies with explosives and repeated acts of vandalism and was featured on the National Public Radio show, "This American Life."

ROBERT CARREAU, formerly President of United Way of Schenectady County, has been the Executive Director of the Schenectady Foundation for almost twenty years. In addition, he has volunteered for the Arts Center of the Capital Region, Rotary, Empire State Youth Orchestra, and the Community AIDS Partnership of the Capital Region.

ERIC CLIFFORD, the current chief of the Schenectady Police Department, joined the force in 2002. He is a graduate of Schenectady County Community College (A.S. in Business Administration), Union College (B.A. in Economics), and Marist College (Master of Public Administration). He is also a graduate of the Federal Bureau of Investigation National Academy, Session #274. Beginning as a patrolman, Chief Clifford worked his way up through sergeant, community police officer, and lieutenant to detective lieutenant in 2011 before being promoted to chief in 2016.

BECKY DANIELS is now Director of Community Engagement for CAP COM Federal Credit Union. A native of Schenectady, she graduated from Schenectady High School in 2003, left for college, and returned to act as Digital Marketing Leader for General Electric Renewable Energy. Becky is also the former Executive Director of Discover Schenectady, the tourism promotion agency for Schenectady County.

JOHN DE AUGUSTINE has had a long and varied career in the newspaper business. He served as Corporate Vice President of Circulation in Connecticut for the Hearst Corporation, was Director of Sales and Marketing for the *Pittsburgh Tribune Review,* and worked as Audience Development Director for the Albany *Times Union.* He is currently the publisher of *The Daily Gazette.*

FRANCA DI CRESCENZO runs Armida Rose Realty Group, a concierge service with a diverse and specialized network of consultants, in Schenectady, New York.

MICHAEL DELLA ROCCA spent thirty-seven years in the Schenectady Fire Department – serving as Assistant Chief from 2001 to 2011, and as Chief from 2011 to 2014 – and was a member during the Canal Square fire in 1987.

DEBBIE DELUKE was instrumental in planning and running the galas at Union College for Schenectady 2000.

KRISTIN DIOTTE is the Director of Planning, Zoning and Community Development for the City of Schenectady. With a background in Architecture, her professional focus has been on urban redevelopment in upstate New York. She serves on the Board of Directors for the Capital Region Land Bank, Homeless Services Planning Board and Capital District Transportation Planning Committee. Her passion is in community-based, sustainable design and urban resiliency.

FRANK DUCI served four terms as Republican mayor of Schenectady – 1971 to 1983 and 1991 to 1995 – and was a member of the Schenectady City Council during many of the off years. After his retirement, he moved to Florida and died there, at 97 years old, in 2019.

JAMES E. DUGGAN is a native of Schenectady who graduated from RPI in 1957 and then worked in facilities planning in support of innovative research projects for the United States Air Force. Jim is a registered architect who designed the conversion of a former warehouse into WMHT studios, among other projects, and who served as Executive Director and Planner for FOCUS Redevelopment Corporation, which advocated for adaptive re-use of urban properties.

MARK EAGAN serves as president and CEO of The Chamber of Schenectady County and the Capital Region Chamber. Eagan has served four chambers in three different states over his more than thirty-year chamber career. He is past chair of the Association of Chamber of Commerce Executives, which represents more than 9,000 chamber professionals in the U.S. and Canada.

ROBERT T. FARLEY served as a Senior Counsel with the New York State Senate before his retirement in 2020. Prior to joining the Senate, Bob served as Deputy Attorney General for New York State. He is currently also an adjunct professor of law at the University at Albany. As a five-time elected county legislator in Schenectady, from 1993 to 2011, Bob served as both Minority Leader and Chairman of the Legislature. He is also the author of the Schenectady Metroplex Development Authority Law.

HUGH FARLEY is a professor and attorney who was first elected to the New York State Senate in 1976 and became a respected, powerful senator. He sponsored legislation establishing the Schenectady Metroplex Development Authority in 1999, and served until 2016.

RICHARD FERRO worked in Insulating Materials for most of his seventeen-year career at General Electric, and has been a Commercial Division Realtor for the last twenty-nine years with Berkshire Hathaway in Niskayuna, New York.

SARA FOSS was an excellent news columnist at *The Daily Gazette* for twenty years, from 2001 to 2021, and her many columns brought sharp-eyed perspective and unique angles to the important events happening in Schenectady.

CHRIS GARDNER, after attending West Point and Cornell, earned his degree from Albany Law School and has been a practicing attorney for thirty-nine years. He has served as Schenectady County Attorney since January 1, 2004.

RON GARDNER has been Schenectady's full-time affirmative action officer since 2017, focusing on diversifying the city's workforce, reducing barriers for minority-owned businesses seeking city contracts, and increasing communication about those opportunities.

RAY GILLEN is a Schenectady native who worked on economic development policies in Congress right after college. In 1982, he began a twenty-two-year stint with the New York State Department of Economic Development, but left there in 2004 to become Chairman of Schenectady Metroplex Development Authority.

FRANK F. GILMORE, R. A. worked as an Urban Designer for the Mayor's Office of Lower Manhattan Development, and earned a Masters of Urban Design from CUNY. After that, Frank joined an international team in Iran to help design Shahestan Pahlavi for the Shah and Shahbanu, and then worked in London for two years. He joined an architectural firm back in New York with work in the Capital District, relocated to Schenectady, and joined SRG Architects, where he has worked on projects like the Albany International Airport, the Rensselaer Train Station, Schenectady's Bow Tie Cinema, the Siemens Headquarters Building, and the redevelopment of Proctor's Theater, as well as high-end homes throughout the region.

MARY D'ALESSANDRO-GILMORE is a licensed real estate broker with Berkshire Hathaway who is also Chair of the Mayoral Task Force Committee for the Real Estate Community in Schenectady, President of the Historic Stockade Foundation, board member of Schenectady's Zoning Board of Appeals, and a former board chair at Better Neighborhoods, Inc.

MONA GOLUB is Vice President of Public Relations and Consumer Services for Price Chopper/Market 32. She is also the Founder and Artistic Producing Director for Music Haven, Schenectady's award-winning free concert series presented in Central Park each summer. Mona was presented with the Patroon Award, the city's highest honor, in 2014, and she sits on the boards of The Schenectady Foundation and Proctors Collaborative, among others.

NEIL GOLUB has been awarded the Liberty Medal by the New York State Senate and the Citizen Laureate Award by SUNY Albany, among many other honors, for his tireless philanthropic efforts. Neil has served as president of the Golub Corporation, a director at Food Marketing Institute and, currently, is CEO and Chairman of Price Chopper/Market 32.

WALLACE GRAHAM joined SI Group, Inc. in 1991 and became Chairman of the Board and CEO in 1995. During his almost thirty-year tenure there, the company expanded to twenty-two manufacturing sites in thirteen countries and exceeded $1.3 billion in annual revenues.

DENNIS GREEN is Assistant Director at the Washington Irving Adult and Continuing Education Center in the Schenectady City School District. He is also a co-founder of Boys Day Out, a program where at-risk students acquire skills to become active and successful members of the community.

DAVID HOGENKAMP has been Project Director at Schenectady Metroplex Development Authority since July of 2013, and has also served as Executive Director of the Capital Region Land Bank, an organization dedicated to removing blight and helping to revitalize neighborhoods, for the last five years.

JIM HORTON was a BCI Senior Investigator with the New York State Police, and took charge of the Major Crimes Unit during the 1990s. As such, and in conjunction with the Schenectady Police Department, Jim investigated and successfully closed numerous homicide cases during the 1980s and 90s.

ROGER HULL is a lawyer who started his career on Wall Street. Roger acted as legal counsel to the Governor of Virginia, served on the National Security Council's Law of the Sea task force, and was a college president for twenty-four years at Beloit and Union (fifteen of which were at Union). Roger is the founder and president of the Help Yourself Foundation, which seeks to change the lives of at-risk kids through the creation of after-school programs on college campuses beginning in third grade. He is also the founder and president of the Schenectady-WIN Foundation, which takes unemployed, non-high school graduates and gives them a high school degree, life skills, construction training, and a guaranteed job at the end of the roughly year-long process.

CHRIS HUNTER is Vice President of Collections and Exhibits at the Museum of Innovation and Science, miSci, in Schenectady. Chris oversees exhibition development at the museum and is a leading authority on the history of electrical and electronic technologies.

KAREN JOHNSON was a community activist who became the first woman elected to the Schenectady City Council in 1975, as well as its first woman mayor. Karen served two terms, from 1983 to 1991, and remains the only woman to serve as Schenectady's mayor. She died in June of 2019.

SHARON JORDAN was the Executive Director of the Schenectady Municipal Housing Authority for sixteen years before she served as Chief of Staff for Mayor Brian Stratton between 2004 and 2011. She has also been a Board Member of Metroplex since 2004, serving as Secretary and Treasurer, and is a Trustee on the Schenectady County Public Library Board.

AL JURCZYNSKI was elected Mayor of Schenectady in 1996 and served for two terms. His initiative that brought thousands of Guyanese to the city and resulted in the renovation of hundreds of houses was one of his signature accomplishments.

GREG KACZMAREK went from being an Air-Vac Medic to a Registered Nurse before he joined the Schenectady Police Department in the mid-1970s. He worked his way up through the ranks to be the Chief between 1996 and 2002. In 2008, he was convicted of a drug felony and spent two years in prison.

JOHN KELLY grew up in a General Electric family, went to Union College, and spent his career as an executive with IBM. He is currently Chairman of the Board at Union College.

CHARLES E. KILBOURNE has worked in several capacities on housing and urban policy for the State of New York. Mr. Kilbourne is a Member of the Board of Directors of the Federal Home Loan Bank of New York, and also serves on the Board of Trustees of the Wright Family Foundation in Schenectady.

DR. MARGARET (PEGGY) KING retired from SUNY Schenectady County Community College as the Associate Dean for Student Development in 2010. She was on the Schenectady City Council from1996-2002, and again from 2006-2015, serving as Council President from 2008-2010 and again from 2013 through 2015. Peggy was appointed to the Schenectady County Legislature in March 2019 to serve the unexpired term of the late Karen Johnson.

JAYME LAHUT has been the Executive Director of the Schenectady Metroplex Development Authority from its inception and organization in 1999 to the present. He also currently serves as Board Chairman of the Capital District Transportation Authority.

BILL LEADER joined General Electric's Financial Management Program in 1969, held a series of managerial assignments across GE businesses in Schenectady, within the power industry, and became Manager of General Accounting, keeping the books for all of the energy business field.

RAY LEGERE'S father worked at the American Locomotive Company when Ray was growing up in Rotterdam, so it's fitting that Ray's company – Legere Restorations – occupies a portion of the old ALCO site. Ray also owns the 1936-era Armory on Washington Avenue in Schenectady, a location most recently for the filming of the second season of "Modern Love."

CHRIS LEONARD has served as City Historian in Schenectady since February of 2018, and is the author of *Schenectady's General Electric Realty Plot*.

BRAD LEWIS has been a Professor of Economics at Union College since 1979, and serves as Vice Chairman of the Schenectady Metroplex Development Authority.

CATHY LEWIS retired from General Electric Company as a Senior Tax Manager, and is in her eleventh year as a member of the Schenectady City School Board. She served as President from 2010 – 2017 and is currently the Vice-President.

MARK LITTLE worked at General Electric for thirty-seven years. As GE's CTO and Senior Vice President and Director of the GE Global Research Center in Niskayuna from 2005 until 2013, Mark developed fundamental technologies to help GE compete and grow in every one of its businesses. Mark and his wife, Terri, founded and operate the Little Family Foundation.

RICHARD LOVRICH is a photographer, scenic designer, former art director at the Albany Times Union and creative director at Proctors Collaborative, among other things, and the author of *Have a Very Bad Day*, a collection of short stories that turns dark humor into a very good day for us readers.

DENNIS MADDEN was the Executive Director of Proctor's Theater from 1979 through 1988, and was instrumental in not only saving it but also in getting it listed on the National Register of Historic Places. He also served as the Mayor of Scotia, New York, and managed theaters all over the country after he left Proctor's.

JOHN MANNING worked as an executive with Niagara Mohawk Corporation and served as the first volunteer Chairman of the Schenectady Metroplex Development Authority from 1998 to 2004. John is also a veteran of the United States Marine Corps.

JOHAN MATTHEWS serves as Principal of Mutual Design, a strategic design collaborative that aims to create shared social change at the intersection of self-determination, social innovation and sustainability, and collaborates with local leaders, designers and investors to facilitate equitable change in its emerging communities.

ANGELO MAZZONE has been the CEO of Mazzone Hospitality, LLC for the last forty-one years. He started at his grandfather's pizzeria at the age of eleven and became the youngest Director of Food Services at Union College. Through operating Peggy's Canal Side Restaurant in the 1980s, launching a successful catering business, renovating, expanding, and managing the Glen Sanders Mansion, and founding 677 Prime in Albany, among many other endeavors, Angelo has built a first-class catering company that serves the entire Capital Region.

WILLIAM MECKLEY is Dean Emeritus of the SUNY Schenectady School of Music and founder/ former Music Director of the Empire Jazz Orchestra. He earned a PhD at the Eastman School of Music. In addition to his work as an educator, Dr. Meckley is an active professional musician who has performed with Aretha Franklin, Johnny Mathis, The Temptations, and many others. As Director of the EJO, he conducted concerts featuring Benny Golson, Jimmy Heath, Dave Holland, and many other major jazz artists.

BRIAN MERRIAM has worked as President of the Merriam Insurance Agency in Schenectady for the last thirty-eight years, and has traveled to Haiti many times in the last fifteen years as an emissary of the Schenectady Rotary's Haiti Water Project, which donates systems that provide clean water to needy towns and villages there.

MELVIN MINTZ owned Time Center Jewelers in downtown Schenectady for 25 years.

JUSTIN MOORE was the Assistant General Manager of Rivers Casino in Mohawk Harbor.

PHILIP MORRIS is celebrating his 19th year as CEO of Proctor's Theater and has been a leader in considering the arts from a regional perspective. He arrived in Schenectady in early 2002, after twenty-five years as executive director of the Chautauqua County Arts Council in western New York. Under Morris's leadership, Proctor's has spent $42 million on expansion and renovation during his tenure, turning the theater into a landmark destination.

MARSHA MORTIMORE, an author and expert in Schenectady's African American history, has championed programs for disadvantaged people with government agencies, private industry, organized labor, and nonprofit organizations for many years. In 2018, Marsha was named a NYS Assembly Woman of Distinction by Assemblyman Angelo Santabarbara.

JAMEL MUHAMMAD is the President and CEO of Youth L.I.F.E. Support Network's "One Life to Live," a program whose mission is to provide community outreach, violence intervention, education support and recreation throughout the Capital Region, with a focus on public safety and a commitment to working with high-risk youth and their families.

CHRIS MYERS, owner of Concord Development Co., has built more than 400 homes and condominiums in the Capital Region, including the Lofts at Union Square in Schenectady. Chris formerly refurbished and owned The Parker Inn in downtown Schenectady.

CARMEL PATRICK has served on the Schenectady County Public Library Board of Trustees since 2014. During her tenure as Board President, the Phyllis Bornt Branch Library and Literacy Center opened in Hamilton Hill, and a new branch library was constructed in Mont Pleasant. In January 2020, Carmel was sworn in as a member of the Schenectady City Council.

KIM PERONE is currently a Success, Bereavement & Resilience Coach. As owner of The Center for Clarity, Compassion & Contentment, and through her coaching practice, Kim aspires to support individual growth for her clients. Kim served as the Program Director for Schenectady 2000 for six years, starting in April, 1994.

J.T. POLLARD is an architect who serves as Principal for Re4orm Architecture and Development. His unique design style and vision can be seen in much of the built environment in Schenectady, including the Mohawk Harbor Riverfront Apartments, Bowtie Cinemas, Center City, 151 Lafayette St, the Schenectady County Public Library, and a variety of other projects. J.T. is also President and Founder of Frog Alley Brewing.

MARION PORTERFIELD is the first African-American woman elected to the Schenectady City Council.

FRANK POTTER served as Chair of the Schenectady County Legislature in the late 1990s, and is the organizer of the annual Harley Rendezvous Classic in Mariaville, New York.

LEW RICCITELLO began working at his parents' restaurant when he was in high school in the 1960s. He has owned and operated John Riccitello's on Foster Avenue – one of the best Italian restaurants in Schenectady – since 1969, and he can be found behind the bar, mixing drinks, every night they're open.

VINCE RIGGI was born, raised, and educated in Schenectady, and has lived in the city his entire life. As a blue collar worker, a member of the public, and as a speaker for twenty years, Vince attended Schenectady City Council meetings on a bi-weekly basis. He was elected to the City Council in 2012 and served for two terms.

WILLIAM RIVAS is Executive Director of the C.O.C.O.A House and the Altamont Program. In 2015, William and his family started their own movement called Save Our Streets, which has grown from an event to an afterschool program to a 501(c) 3 non-profit organization. William has dedicated his life to change through his work, and he is committed to the process of rebuilding communities in crisis.

ROSA E. RIVERA is an urban farmer, doula, avid reader and writer, teacher, and director of Miracle on Craig St. Rosa has a strong feminine energy, and her purpose on this earth is to be and to facilitate love, care, and intentionality.

WALTER L. ROBB, after getting his PhD in Chemical Engineering at PSU and Illinois, joined GE in 1951 at KAPL and then the Research Lab. He rose through GE to become General Manager of the Medical Systems business in Milwaukee, and then returned to Schenectady to become Director of the GE Global Research Center. Retiring in 1993, he spent twenty-six years helping start-up companies, both as a director and an investor, and succumbed to Covid-19 in 2020.

GEORGE ROBERTSON arrived in Schenectady in the mid-1980s and served as President of the Schenectady Economic Development Corporation (SEDC). During the 1990s, he worked with Neil Golub and Roger Hull to provide administrative functions for Schenectady 2000. Robertson died in Warsaw, Indiana, in 2019 after a prolonged struggle with cancer.

RICH RUZZO is the Founder and COO of Shepherd Communication and Security, with a demonstrated history of working with advanced and legacy technology in the electronic security, structured wiring, and carriers' services telecom industries. Rich is also Chairman of the Board of Directors of the Land Reutilization Corporation of the Capital Region – the Land Bank.

MIKE SACCOCCIO has been the Executive Director of the City Mission of Schenectady since 1996. City Mission, a faith-based organization founded to aid the homeless, started with a single building on Hamilton Street in 1906, but it currently occupies a whole city block and includes a men's shelter, a nine-apartment women's and children's shelter, a fitness center, health clinic, and an administration building, plus twenty-three additional apartments on nearby Lafayette Street.

JIM SALENGO has served as Executive Director of the Downtown Schenectady Improvement Corporation (DSIC) since 2008. Jim leads a diverse and dedicated team that enhances the visual appeal of the area through daily sidewalk maintenance, seasonal plantings & decorations, and other special projects. He also manages comprehensive print, online, and e-mail programs to increase public awareness and patronage of the heart of Schenectady.

ANGELO SANTABARBARA is a first-generation Italian-American and lifelong resident of Schenectady County, but is also a Democratic member of the New York State Assembly, representing the 111th New York State Assembly District, which comprises all of Montgomery County and parts of Schenectady and Albany Counties.

CAMILLE SASINOWSKI was educated in the Schenectady School System, at the Art Institute of Boston, at Schenectady County Community College, and at the University of Minnesota in Minneapolis-St. Paul. She was a Teen Program Developer for the Girls Club of America, and also served for fifteen years as Director of "Total Estate Care by Camille." Currently retired, she is very active as president of the Goose Hill Neighborhood Association.

MARILYN SASSI is a museum curator, an expert in regional antiques, an adjunct professor at Hudson Valley Community College and SUNY Schenectady Community College, and a treasure trove of information about Proctor's Theater and its founder.

SUSAN SAVAGE was Chair of the Schenectady County Legislature from 2004 until 2011, when she resigned to become Assistant Deputy Commissioner at the Office of Real Property Tax Services in the administration of Governor Andrew Cuomo.

DOUG SAYLES is an accountant, financial consultant, and the President and Owner of Cornerstone Advisors. Along with J.T. Pollard and local developers, he is responsible for brainstorming many successful projects in downtown Schenectady. In addition, Doug is a member of the team of Schenectady Film Commissioners.

LE GRANDE SERRAS is a well-known restaurant owner, raconteur, philanthropist, and auctioneer who has raised more than twenty-two million dollars for charitable organizations in the Capital Region. He owned Peggy's Canal Side Restaurant, served as President of the 400 Block Corporation that built Canal Square, and for many years owned and operated Reel Seafood Co. in Colonie, New York.

WALTER SIMPKINS holds a B.A. from the City College of New York, an M.A. from SUNY Albany in Africana Studies, and is the Executive Director of Community Fathers Incorporated. He is also a certified Fatherhood & Healthy Relationship practitioner, as well as a Bridges Out of Poverty facilitator.

DERYCK SINGH moved to Niskayuna, New York, bought land and built a house there in 1987. He worked as a store manager and supervisor for Stewart's for over thirty years, and is responsible for planting the idea of broad Guyanese immigration to Schenectady in Mayor Al Jurczynski's ear.

JAN SMITH worked as a Human Resources manager for General Electric, and became Communications Director for GE in Schenectady.

PAT SMITH has worked as a property manager for many years, and has served as President of the Mont Pleasant Neighborhood Association since 2015.

ANIBAL SOLER, JR. became the new Superintendent of the Schenectady City School District in July of 2021.

LAURENCE SPRING served as Superintendent of the Schenectady City School District between 2012 and 2020.

MARCY STEINER, with more than twenty-five years of experience in public relations, marketing, and print media, has worked for The Schenectady Museum, Seton Health in Troy, New York, SUNY Schenectady Community College, and is currently Vice President and Executive Director for Ellis Medicine in Schenectady.

BRIAN STRATTON was Mayor of Schenectady between 2004 and 2011, and currently serves as the Director of the New York State Canal Corporation.

STEVE STRICHMAN worked for two different administrations, and for seventeen years, as Director of Planning and Economic Development in Schenectady and was an integral part of launching the city's revitalization efforts. Steve became Commissioner of Planning and Community Development in Troy in 2016.

CARL STROCK worked for the *Schenectady Gazette* – later *Daily Gazette* – from 1981 through 2012, as a reporter, an editor, and eventually a columnist, writing "The View From Here" three times a week.

BILL SWEET has spent 30+ years in the real estate and development business, both as a principal and a consultant. Projects have ranged from grocery store construction to development of auto dealerships, to the development and construction of multi-story office buildings. Bill continues to represent a number of high profile clients in their real estate and development efforts.

CHUCK THORNE served as Schenectady City Clerk from 2012 until his retirement in 2019.

MADELYN THORNE has lived in Schenectady for over fifty years. She and her husband, Chuck, share three children and five grandchildren. Currently, Madelyn is Executive Director of Habitat for Humanity of Schenectady County, a Board President of the Friends of the Schenectady County Public Library, a Board Member of Schenectady Housing Development Fund Corporation, and a Board Member of New Choices Recovery. Madelyn volunteers for a wide array of organizations and causes.

PAUL TONKO represented the 105th District in the New York State Assembly from 1983 to 2007, and was instrumental in helping to pass the Metroplex bill. He is a Democrat and the U.S. Representative for New York's 29th Congressional District, which includes Albany, Troy, and Schenectady. Currently, Paul serves as Chair of the House Energy and Commerce Committee's Subcommittee on the Environment and Climate Change.

ANEESA WAHEED and her husband, Muntasim, opened the first Tara Kitchen in downtown Schenectady in January of 2012, serving their version of Moroccan cuisine and garnering rave reviews. They now own and operate a catering service and opened two other Moroccan restaurants, in Troy and Guilderland, in 2017 and 2020. Today, Aneesa oversees the management of her restaurants, as well as the production and distribution of an award-winning line of Moroccan Cooking Sauces under the name Tara Kitchen.

MARY MOORE WALLINGER has over fifteen years of experience in landscape architecture and urban design. She is the founding Principal of LAndArt Studio, and a staunch advocate of smart growth, low impact development, and celebrating the landscape in ways that shape the human experience.

THOMAS C. WILSON is a life-long builder who worked with Bovis Lend Lease, a large international construction management firm, in Ithaca, New York City, Los Angeles, and San Francisco. In 2002, he founded TW&A Construction Management, a full-service construction management firm, and Tom is proud of the role he has played in helping to rebuild downtown Schenectady.

BERNARD WITKOWSKI worked as an electrician for General Electric for thirty-six and a half years, with a two year break while serving in the US Army, including fourteen months in Vietnam. Bernard is currently retired and does volunteer work for Habitat for Humanity in Schenectady County.

KAREN ZALEWSKI-WILDZUNAS is a member of the Schenectady City Council, and a licensed real estate broker with Berkshire Hathaway.

Many of these biographical entries were supplied by the contributors themselves, and only edited to maintain format, length, and consistency.

Image Credits

CHAPTER 13: WHO THOUGHT THIS WOULD HAPPEN?

CHAPTER 14: WHAT'S NEXT?